Repeated Games with Incomplete Information

T0312062

Repeated Games with Incomplete Information

Robert J. Aumann
and
Michael B. Maschler

with the collaboration of
Richard E. Stearns

The MIT Press
Cambridge, Massachusetts
London, England

Library of Congress Cataloging-in-Publication Data

Aumann, Robert J.
    Repeated games with incomplete information / Robert J. Aumann and Michael B. Maschler with the collaboration of Richard B. Stearns.
        p.   cm.
    Includes bibliographical references and index.
    ISBN 978-0-262-01147-1 (hc. alk. paper) — 978-0-262-52626-5 (pb.)
1. Arms control—Simulation methods. 2. Disarmament—Simulation methods. 3. Game theory. I. Maschler, Michael, 1927–   . II. Stearns, Richard E. III. Title.
JX1974.A845   1995
327.1'74'01593—dc20   94–33653
                                                                      CIP

To the memory of Oskar Morgenstern

Contents

Preface

Most game situations have an ongoing element. When people interact, they have usually interacted in the past, and expect to do so again in the future. It is this ongoing element that is studied by the theory of repeated games. Inter alia, the theory "predicts" phenomena such as cooperation, altruism, secrecy, trust, punishment, and revenge, and deals with the specific forms that these phenomena may take.

This book is devoted to one aspect of the theory of repeated games: the informational aspect. The basic point is that vital information may be revealed *implicitly* by a player's actions, and that dually, a player may wish to refrain from certain actions in order to avoid such revelation. Some of the flavor of the considerations is captured by the well-known story about Lord Rothschild, who, upon being privately informed of the outcome of the battle of Waterloo, sent an agent in his employ to the London stock exchange with instructions discreetly to *sell*. Shortly thereafter, he sent several different persons, not usually in his employ, with instructions to *buy* as much as they could without significantly driving the market up. As Rothschild had anticipated, his agent was recognized; the fact that he was selling—all the more so as he was trying to act discreetly—caused the market to surmise that Wellington had been defeated. As a result, prices plunged, and Rothschild made a killing.

The moral of the story, of course, is that one's information is normally revealed by one's actions. Rothschild recognized this, and was able to turn it to his advantage.

This story typifies the competitive, "zero-sum" side of the theory, treated in Chapters One through Four. There is another side, which concerns "cooperative" phenomena, where one player may want to signal information to another. Surprisingly, this is sometimes impossible; there are situations where the uninformed player cannot "believe" the signal, even when it would be to the mutual benefit of both players if he would. These matters are treated in Chapter Five.

The book had its genesis in the period 1966–68. This was the height of the cold war; the United States and the now defunct Soviet Union were engaged in an intensive arms race, involving nuclear explosives and the systems needed to deliver them—missiles, aircraft, submarines, even railroad cars. Both sides wanted to slow down—perhaps reverse—the alarming increase in these dangerous, expensive weapons systems, but neither could afford to do so without being reasonably sure that the other also would.

It was in this atmosphere that the two superpowers agreed to a series of conferences designed to craft an agreement or agreements to achieve such a slowdown or reversal. The American side of these negotiations was the responsibility of the United States Arms Control and Disarmament Agency (ACDA), a government agency that, while nominally independent, was close to the State Department and, indeed, was housed in the same building. In the mid-sixties, the ACDA became convinced that it had something to learn from decision theoretic disciplines such as game theory and utility theory. Mathematica, Inc., a Princeton-based consulting outfit in which Oskar Morgenstern and Harold Kuhn played leading roles, was retained to gather a group of specialists whose mission was to study the decision theoretic aspects of the arms control and disarmament enterprise and report to the agency on its findings.

The group was active during the three years 1966–68; among those affiliated with it during part or all of that period were Gerard Debreu, John Harsanyi, Harold Kuhn, Jim Mayberry, Herbert Scarf, Reinhard Selten, and the contributors to this book (Robert Aumann, Michael Maschler and Richard Stearns). Tom Saaty, who at that time worked for the ACDA, provided scientific liaison. The group would meet every few months in or near Washington, D.C., to report to the agency on its findings, to get input from the agency on its problems, and to enable interaction between the members of the group (who were geographically dispersed from Jerusalem to Berkeley). With their odd mix of highly theoretical and extremely practical discussions, these meetings had an extraordinary intellectual intensity.

The work of the group was summed up in Technical Reports, ranging over a number of decision and game theoretic topics related to arms control. Among these reports were the five on which this book is based: Aumann and Maschler [1966, 1967], Stearns [1967], Aumann and Maschler [1968], and Aumann, Maschler and Stearns [1968], corresponding to Chapters One through Five respectively. All five were inspired by a single concern: that the negotiating strategy used by the Americans in a series of arms control conferences might implicitly send signals to the Russians about the nature of the US arsenal, or about what the US knew about the Soviet arsenal—signals that the US might or might not wish to send. At that time, little or nothing was known about the theoretical underpinnings of this phenomenon; we set ourselves the task of developing the theory.

Scientifically, the time was ripe for such a development. During the fifties, several models of ongoing game situations had been investigated, prominent among which were the stochastic games of Shapley [1953]. Repeated games were mentioned already in the influential book of Luce and Raiffa [1957]; the relation between repetition and cooperation had been studied by Aumann [1959, 1960, 1961]. At the end of the decade, the fundamental "folk theorem" for repeated games (see Chapter Five) was already known to the cognoscenti, though not yet by that name.

By the early sixties, then, the beginnings of a theory of repeated games were in place. All this, however, concerned games of complete information, i.e., games in which the payoff is commonly known.[1] Games of incomplete information—where the payoffs are not commonly known—offered grave difficulties of formulation, both for the fundamental case of one-shot games, and for applications to repeated games.

Then in the mid-sixties came the path-breaking work of John Harsanyi [1967-8], which for the first time enabled a coherent formulation of games of incomplete information. Harsanyi discussed his ideas at the Jerusalem Game Theory workshop in 1965, which was also attended by Aumann, Maschler, and Stearns. Thus, when the ACDA group was organized in the following year, the fundamental tools needed to study the informational aspects of gradual disarmament were available: the beginnings of a theory

---

[1] Though the phrase "common knowledge" was coined only later (by Lewis [1969]), and until then, the concept behind the phrase was only dimly perceived.

of repeated games, and a theory of games of incomplete information. These two theories were combined to create a theory of repeated games of incomplete information: that is, of games in which some game is repeated, but the players have incomplete—and different—information on which game it is. This was the approach taken to attack the gradual disarmament problem; the idea was that, in the repeated disarmament negotiations, neither player really knew what his own payoff would be for any given agreement, because of uncertainty about the other side's arsenal and weapons production technology.

Harsanyi's work has two basic elements. First, he overcame the fundamental problem of formulation to which we alluded above, by developing a formal model of games of incomplete information, which he called "I-games". Second, for every I-game he constructed an extensive game of complete information, called the associated "C-game". This game starts with a chance move, about which the players in general get different information; after they get this information, the position is essentially identical to that at the start of the original I-game. Harsanyi showed that an I-game and its associated C-game have the same equilibria, which suggests that an I-game can be studied by studying the corresponding C-game.

We are thus led to the following basic model, which is the one studied throughout this book: Chance chooses which of a number of possible games will be played in the future; the probabilities of the choices are common knowledge. Once chosen, the same game is repeated again and again; the successive repetitions are called *stages*. Immediately after the game to be repeated is chosen, each player is told something about which game it is. In general, the two players get different information; for example, one player may be told exactly which game is being played, while the other is told nothing. While the players are not necessarily told their payoffs after each stage, each observes what the other does at each stage, or at least gets some information on this; and of course, he knows what he himself does.

The upshot is that, to the extent that a player is ignorant about the game being played, he must learn what he can about this from the actions of the other. This is the heart of the phenomenon treated in this book.

Though disarmament is clearly not a zero-sum game, we investigated the conceptually simpler zero-sum case first, to allow us to build the foundations of the theory with a minimum of complications. This research strategy turned out successful: The non-zero-sum theory eventually constructed (Chapter Five) depends heavily on the fundamental ideas discovered in the zero-sum investigation. Looking back, it is clear that it would have been impossible to do the non-zero-sum case without doing the zero-sum case first.

Thus the first four chapters of the book deal with zero-sum games. Chapter One treats the case in which the incomplete information is "one-sided"; that is, one player is fully informed of the game being played, whereas the other is told nothing (beyond the commonly known original probability distribution). Moreover, the information that the players get at the end of each stage is "standard"; that is, each player is informed of the strategy that the other used during that stage (and of course, remembers his own). Chapter Two treats several topics. First, the material of Chapter One is reviewed and formulated precisely; the presentation in Chapter One was relatively informal. Next, we analyze the case of "two-sided" incomplete information, where each of the two players gets different information about the true game being played. Last, non-standard stage information about the actions of the players is introduced and analyzed. Chapter Three provides a formal definition of "amount of information", and uses it to analyze the case of two-sided incomplete information introduced in Chapter Two. Chapter Four is devoted to an in-depth treatment of the case of non-standard stage information; this is especially important when the game being repeated is extensive, so that the strategy used by a player would in general not become known to the other player. Finally, Chapter Five treats the non-zero sum case. The five chapters correspond to the five ACDA reports mentioned above.

In reproducing the ACDA reports here, we took care to maintain the text essentially as originally written. Some of the original material has been omitted, the literary style has been polished, notation has been unified, misprints and arithmetical errors have been corrected; but there have been no substantive additions or changes to the text. To distinguish footnotes in the original reports from those added now, we have marked the latter by an asterisk (*).

The reports were aimed at a varied audience, ranging from ACDA officials with little or no mathematical background, to sophisticated mathematicians and decision theorists. The level is thus quite uneven. On the one hand, there are detailed examples and verbal explanations, and, on the other hand, some of the proofs are comparatively abstruse and difficult. It may well be that a given reader may find some of the material too easy, or some of it too hard, or both. Also, since the five reports were presented to the ACDA over a three-year time span, there is some overlap between them, with a conscious attempt in the later reports to review material presented earlier.

Over the years, these reports have spawned a large literature. Many—though by no means all—of the problems left open in the original reports have been solved, and new problems and issues have arisen. To each chapter (except Chapter Three), we have appended a set of postscripts, describing some of the developments since the reports were written. These postscripts are confined to issues directly related to the material in the body of the text, and even there the coverage is far from complete. New issues and problems that have arisen in this literature over the last two decades are not treated in the postscripts. For an overview of this literature, the reader may consult various excellent survey articles, including Mertens [1987, 1990], Forges [1992], and Zamir [1992]. Also, a comprehensive advanced book, which we highly recommend, is being written by Mertens, Sorin, and Zamir; a preliminary version is available (Mertens, Sorin, and Zamir [1994p]).

The bibliography at the end of the book includes all items to which we refer in the main text, in the postscripts, and in this introduction. It also includes a sort of "citation index": That is, a compilation of published papers and books that refer to the original reports. Though we made this compilation as complete as we could, we have, needless to say, probably missed many items. No attempt has been made to list citations of the "second order"— works citing works that cite the reports—or of higher order.

The general index at the end of the book is preceded by a symbol index, which usually lists only the page(s) on which a symbol is defined.

We are very grateful to Richard Stearns for allowing us to use material of which he was author or co-author. Chapter Three is by Stearns, and Chapter Five by Aumann, Maschler, and Stearns; without this material, the book would have been sadly incomplete. The other chapters are by Aumann and Maschler, as are all the postscripts.

The preparation of this book for publication—including all the typesetting and drawing of the figures, and much of the word processing equipment—was funded by the Oskar Morgenstern Foundation at the Hebrew University, established with the aid of a generous gift from Professor Martin Shubik of Yale University. Nitai Bergman read the proof sheets and made many helpful suggestions. The typesetting itself was done by Florence Da-Costa, using $\mathcal{A}_{\mathcal{M}}\mathcal{S}$-TEX; she cheerfully dealt with countless revisions and corrections. Peter Grosmann prepared the figures. Michael Spivak, the creator of $\mathcal{A}_{\mathcal{M}}\mathcal{S}$-TEX, helped us with his index package. Teresa Ehling at MIT Press provided invaluable liaison. Our gratitude is extended to all these individuals.

Jerusalem, Israel, Nissan 5754 (March 1994).

CHAPTER ONE

GAME THEORETIC ASPECTS OF GRADUAL DISARMAMENT

1. Introduction

The task that was assigned to this group concerns the application of utility theory to disarmament, and the study here described is addressed to that task. However, the implications of this study range far beyond the area of disarmament and touch on all areas of negotiations and international relations in general.

Before starting, let us express at once what we think can be a role of mathematical studies and mathematical model building in the realm of international politics. Undoubtedly, many questions of international politics are too ramified to be directly amenable to exact mathematical treatment. No mathematical treatment can possibly take account of all the implications involved in a political decision. One therefore builds a simplified mathematical model, which is an abstraction that treats in highly simplified form just one or a few of the aspects of a complex situation. The analysis of such a highly simplified abstraction can very seldom lead to any specific recommendations in a specific situation. But it can lead to insights of a general nature. These insights can then be used by policy makers in making specific decisions or in formulating general policies.

Thus, for example, an analysis of a simplified model may direct attention to a new procedure not previously discovered because of the complexity of the actual problem. It is this kind of use of mathematical models that concerns us here.

Needless to mention, the relation between the mathematical model and the real situation works in both directions: It is the real situation which provides hints as to how the model should be constructed; it is the mathematical analysis of the model which directs attention to new procedures which can be used by the policy makers; and it is the attempt to consider the implications of these procedures in reality which leads to a new and more sophisticated model for a further study.

In any bargaining situation, it is of the utmost importance for each side to know how the other side evaluates the situation. Consider, for example, the following famous problem: Two brothers, Tom and Dick, must share a pie in a "fair" manner between them. A reasonable procedure would be that one of them should divide the pie into two parts and let the other one choose one of the parts. Clearly, if the divider cuts the pie into two parts that seem to him to be of equal size, then each brother is satisfied at the end that he has received at least half the pie, which is fair enough.

Consider now a pie with a cherry. Suppose Tom is indifferent to cherries; namely, does not care whether there is a cherry in his part or not; and suppose that Tom knows that Dick likes cake but also knows that Dick loves cherries. Using the above procedure he would then divide the cake into unequal portions, leaving the cherry in the smaller part, knowing that his brother would pick up this part—leaving himself with a greater portion of the cake. How small the portion with the cherry should be depends, of course, on Tom's knowledge of the amount of cake that Dick would be willing to sacrifice for the cherry.

Clearly, it is advantageous for Dick to hide his preference for cherries, or at least to give the impression that the preference is small.

Consider now a case in which Tom is indifferent to cherries (and Dick knows this) and Dick loves cherries but Tom does not know this, although he may suspect it. (Dick knows that Tom does not know his preferences.) Suppose, however, that both brothers also know that they will have to divide a cake every day during many days. It stands to reason that Tom should test his brother's preferences by cutting the cake into different sizes during some of the days and check which part has been chosen. If Dick would always pick up that part which he really prefers, he will reveal in a few days his trading price; and henceforth Tom would be able to take full advantage of the knowledge thus acquired.

Should Dick act this way? Should he act as if he does not love cherries? Should he choose the smallest portion in a random way, according to a fixed probability? Or should he act in still another way?

These questions are not frivolous: the kind of considerations they typify are basic for disarmament negotiations. Suppose, for example, that a gradual disarmament procedure is proposed, under which both the United States and the Soviet Union propose gradually to destroy a given collection of weapons. One way of doing so is to let each country divide its own remaining collection each year into, say, ten parts and let the other country choose which part should be destroyed. Clearly, a "naïve" way of choosing may reveal secret military preferences and advantage can be taken of this when the remainder is to be divided, not to mention other political and military advantages that may accrue. How, then, should one choose in an optimal way?

Our object in this chapter is to study some very simple examples —examples that can be solved explicitly—and point out several interesting features of the solutions. We shall also describe a general result concerning the solution of a class of such games.[1]

2. A Case When a Player Cannot Benefit in the Long Run from His Information

Consider the following two games:

	Player 2	
	L	R
L	1	0
R	0	0

G_A

	Player 2	
	L	R
L	0	0
R	0	1

G_B

In each game, Player 1 has two strategies, L and R, and Player 2 has two strategies, L and R. The numbers in the boxes represent the amount that Player 2 must pay Player 1 after the strategies have been chosen (each player makes his choice without knowing the other player's choice). Clearly, the values w_A and w_B of G_A

---

[1]This chapter should be regarded as a heuristic introduction to the subject. Precise definitions and statements may be found in subsequent chapters.(*)

and G_B are zero; i.e., Player 1 can guarantee himself 0 in each game and Player 2 can guarantee not to pay more than 0.

Suppose now that one of these two games is played, but that Player 2 is not informed which one, although he does know that he is playing one of these games. Furthermore, suppose Player 2 believes that the probability that he is playing G_A is 1/2. Player 1, however, knows exactly which game he is playing. Can he use this knowledge to his advantage?

In his theory of games with incomplete information, J. Harsanyi [1967-8] recommends and justifies the following procedure for both players:

Consider the 2-person constant-sum game Γ_1 described by[2] Figure 1. (The left branch of this tree represents G_A, and the right branch represents G_B). It is quite easy to see that the only optimal strategy for Player 1 in Γ_1 is: *Choose "left" if you are at A*, and *choose "right" if you are at B*. For Player 2, any pure or mixed strategy is optimal. The value of the game Γ_1 is 1/2.

So much for Γ_1; but how should one play in the original game, which is G_A or G_B? Harsanyi recommends that Player 2 should

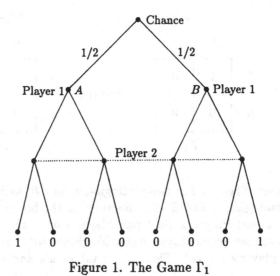

Figure 1. The Game Γ_1

[2]We use the convention that information sets are indicated by dotted lines.

play in the original game the same optimal strategy as in Γ_1—in this particular case any pure or mixed strategy he wishes. For Player 1 in the original game he recommends that if G_A is being played (which Player 1 knows), Player 1 should play his optimal strategy for Γ_1 ass...ming that he has already reached the vertex A in the figure; namely—"left". Similarly, if G_B is being played— Player 1 should choose "right".

In order to shorten our description, let us refer to Player 1 when G_A is being played as *type* A of Player 1, or simply Player 1_A. Similarly, type B of Player 1, or simply 1_B, is Player 1 playing the original game when G_B is being played. The term "Player 1" will be reserved for Player 1 playing Γ_1 only. No distinction will be made for Player 2 since he does not know whether G_A or G_B is the true game, and so must play the same way in both cases. With these notations we can summarize the outcome as follows:

    i. Player 1 can assure himself $1/2$.

    ii. The payoffs to 1_A and 1_B depend on the strategy of Player 2. If Player 2 chooses left with probability λ, where $0 \leq \lambda \leq 1$, then 1_A's expected payoff is $v_A^1 = \lambda$ and 1_B's expected payoff is $v_B^1 = 1 - \lambda$.

Note that $v_A^1 \geq w_A$, $v_B^1 \geq w_B$, and at least one of these inequalities is sharp. Thus, either 1_A or 1_B, and usually both types, are able to take advantage of Player 2's ignorance.

The situation becomes much more complicated if, after the choice of chance, G_A or G_B is played infinitely many times. In other words—if the same game, say G_A, is repeated. Player 1_A knows that G_A is being played but Player 2 does not. His a priori subjective belief is $1/2$ for G_A and $1/2$ for G_B. Let us call a single play of, say, G_A a *stage* in this grand game. At the end of each stage both players are informed of the choices made by their opponents at that stage. Also, at the end of each stage— the appropriate payoff is put aside to the player's credit (debit—if the payoff is negative), but the players are not informed of the amounts.[3] Of course, 1_A can calculate his own payoff since he

---

[3] Playing a game without knowing the exact payoff is the usual case in international relations. If, say, there is an agreement under which the Soviet Union destroys 100 I.C.B.M.'s, then if these are all the I.C.B.M.'s they have, the payoff to the United States caused by the destruction is high (from the

knows the strategies and the game. Both players want to maximize their *average* expected payoff; i.e., their expected payoff per game.

Harsanyi's model for this game—call it Γ_∞—is an infinite tree whose first two stages are given in Figure 2. Here the appropriate payoffs are written at the end of each stage. Player 1 wants to maximize the average payoff and Player 2 wants to minimize this average. Player 2 has four information sets at the second stage, each containing four vertices.

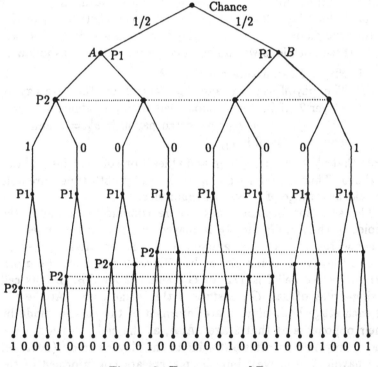

Figure 2. Two stages of Γ_∞

military point of view); but if the Russians have 1000 I.C.B.M.'s, then the the payoff is negligible. Intelligence information may yield some information, but it may be wrong. At best, one can assign subjective probabilities to the various possibilities.

How should Player 1 play Γ_∞? Clearly it is not advisable to play each stage in the same fashion as in Γ_1 (left on the A-part, right on the B-part). If this were the optimal way of playing, then Player 2 would know it. He would then infer from the choices at the first stage what chance's choice was. From the second stage on he would then be able to force w_A or w_B, i.e., zero payoff for each stage, which would make the average expected payoff for Player 1 tend to zero as the number of stages tends to infinity.

But Player 1 can assure himself more than zero in Γ_∞. For example, one way for him to do so is to act as if he himself does not know the choice made by chance. In other words, one option for Player 1 is to regard himself as playing an infinite game Δ_∞ whose first two stages are drawn in Figure 3.

It turns out that playing Δ_∞ is equivalent to playing the 1-stage game Δ_1 of Figure 4 infinitely many times.[4] Game Δ_1 in normal form is represented by the matrix

Player 2

		L	R
	L	1/2	0
Player 1	R	0	1/2

and optimal strategies for it are for each player to choose left with probability 1/2 and right with the same probability. This yields the value $u_1 = 1/4$.

As indicated in the last footnote, a value for the game Δ_1 repeated several times or infinitely often exists and it, too, is $u = 1/4$. Moreover, optimal strategies for each player are to play each stage as a 1-stage game; namely, to choose left with probability 1/2 and right with the same probability.

Suppose now that Player 1 plays this very same strategy in Γ_∞ instead of in Δ_∞; then he would still assure himself a payoff of 1/4. Indeed, all he does in playing Γ_∞ is to ignore his information

---

[4]Clearly, an optimal strategy for each player in Δ_∞ is to play a Δ_1-optimal strategy at each stage.

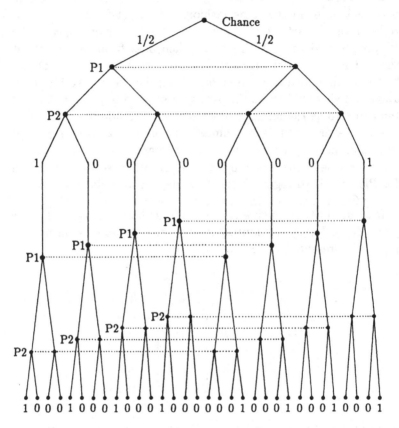

Figure 3. Two stages of Δ_∞

on chance's choice, so that his way of playing does not reveal any information on the choice of chance.

We have seen that ignoring his information while playing Γ_∞ assures Player 1 of 1/4. We have also seen that using that information for a 1-stage game yields the value 1/2; but repeating the same optimal strategy at each stage of Γ_∞ is bad. Could Player 1 play better in Γ_∞ by using his information on the choice of chance to guarantee himself an average expected payoff higher than 1/4 (of course less than 1/2)?

The surprising answer is that he cannot—*the value v_∞ of Γ_∞ is exactly 1/4.* The proof of this statement is relatively complicated;

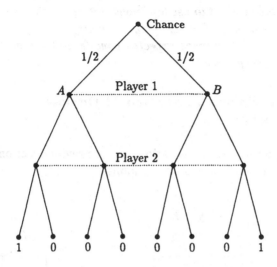

Figure 4. The game Δ_1

it will be given in Section 5. Thus, in this particular case Player 1 cannot benefit in the infinite game from knowing the choice of chance. His optimal strategy is to ignore his knowledge, i.e., play as if he were playing optimally in Δ_∞. We shall see later that any strategy of Player 1 which takes into account his knowledge of the choice of chance will not be optimal.

Let us say at once that Player 2's optimal strategy is quite complicated (it will be discussed in Section 6). His strategy for the game Δ_∞ is simple: "Play left at each stage with probability 1/2." This is certainly *not* an optimal strategy for Γ_∞, because it can be answered by Player 1 going left if chance chooses left and right if chance chooses right. Such a strategy assures Player 1 an expected payoff of 1/2 at each stage, which is greater than the value of Γ_∞.

Let us now look more closely at optimal play in the game Δ_1— this time from the point of view of players 1_A and 1_B in Δ_1 (see Figure 4). Clearly, the expected payoff for Player 1_A is $u_A = 1/4$ and the expected payoff for Player 1_B is $u_B = 1/4$. (These are also the expected average payoffs if Δ_∞ is being played optimally by both players.) Note that $u_A > w_A = 0$ and $u_B > w_B = 0$. We may summarize these remarks by saying that *if Player 1 commits* *himself in advance not to use his knowledge of the choice of chance, and if both players, 1 and 2, play optimally (in Δ_∞), then both 1_A and 1_B receive average expected payoffs that are greater than w_A and w_B, respectively.*

3. A Case When a Player Should Disclose His Information

In this section we use the notations of the previous section, except that here G_A and G_B denote the games

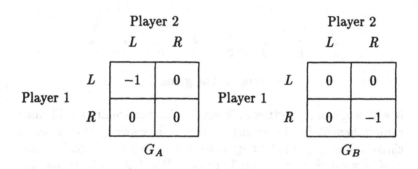

Here, again, $w_A = w_B = 0$.

In the last section it behooved Player 1 to act as though he did not know the choice of chance. Such an action is obviously wrong in this game. For in this case, Δ_1 is the game

		Player 2	
		L	*R*
Player 1	*L*	$-1/2$	0
	R	0	$-1/2$

whose value is $u_1 = -1/4$, and so equals the value of Δ_∞; whereas Player 1 can assure himself a higher expected average payoff in Γ_∞, namely 0, by playing always right if chance chooses left, and playing always left if chance chooses right. This way of playing is optimal for Player 1 because the entries in G_A and in G_B are nonpositive, so Player 1 assures himself the maximum amount by playing this way. Of course, if Player 1 plays optimally as above and Player 2 knows this, he will conclude, immediately after the first stage, what the choice of chance was, by observing Player 1's choice in the first stage. Thus, any way of playing while keeping this knowledge secret will not help Player 1.

Unlike in the previous section, here there is a simple optimal strategy for Player 2. It is: "play anything you wish." Any strategy chosen by Player 2 guarantees that he will not pay more than 0 to Player 1; and since Player 1 can guarantee 0, such a strategy is optimal.

Note that this means that in the original game Γ_∞, Player 1_A gets an average expected payoff $v_A = 0$, and similarly $v_B = 0$; hence $v_A = w_A, v_B = w_B$.

The absurdity of Player 1 playing in Γ_∞ as if he were playing optimally in Δ_∞ is also seen by comparing the values u_A and u_B with w_A and w_B. Indeed, if Players 1 and 2 play Δ_1 [or Δ_∞] optimally, then Player 1_A receives an expected [average] payoff of $-1/4$, and so does Player 1_B. Summarizing, we find that *if Player 1 commits himself in advance* not to use his knowledge of the choice of chance, and *if both Player 1 and Player 2 play optimally under this commitment (i.e., in Δ_∞), then both Player 1_A and Player 1_B receive expected payoffs that are less than w_A and w_B, respectively.* This commitment is silly because both Player 1_A and Player 1_B can assure themselves a zero payoff at each stage by making use of their knowledge of the choice of chance; indeed, they can even allow Player 2 to deduce this.

4. A Case When a Player Should Partially Disclose His Information

In one of the previous examples we found that $u_A \geq w_A$ and $u_B \geq w_B$, and Player 1 could play optimally by not making any use of his knowledge of the choice of chance.[5]

---

[5] It will turn out that this is not always an optimal procedure even if $u_A \geq w_A$ and $u_B \geq w_B$.

In another example we found that $u_A < w_A$ and $u_B < w_B$, whence such behavior is certainly not optimal. In that case we found, however, that Player 1 should play as if he knew the choice of chance and, in fact, reveal the choice of chance immediately.

But these cases do not exhaust all the possibilities. It may happen that, say, $u_A > w_A$ and $u_B < w_B$. For example, let G_A and G_B be the games

	Player 2	
	L	R
L	1	0
R	0	2

G_A

	Player 2	
	L	R
L	-2	0
R	0	-1

G_B

(each being assigned probability 1/2). Their values are $w_A = 2/3$, $w_B = -2/3$. The tree of the game Δ_1 is drawn in Figure 5.

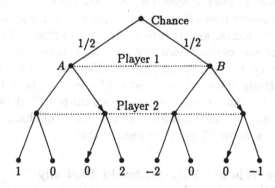

Figure 5. The tree of Δ_1

It is easy to verify that the only optimal strategy for Player 1 in this game is to play right and the only optimal strategy for Player 2 is to play left. (See the arrows in the figure.) The value of Δ_1 is $u = 0$.

Looking at the payoffs for Players 1_A and 1_B, we find $u_A = 0$ and $u_B = 0$ and therefore $u_A < w_A$ whereas $u_B > w_B$. The same numbers are, of course, obtained for Δ_∞ when the average expectation replaces the expected payoff.

Consider again the two alternatives for Player 1 playing Γ_∞, which were discussed at the beginning of this section:

  i. Act as though he himself does not know the choice of chance (i.e., play as if he were playing optimally in Δ_∞).
  ii. Reveal the choice of chance to Player 2 (i.e., play maximin against G_A or G_B at each stage in accordance with the choice of chance).

Suppose Player 1 has to choose among these alternatives after chance has made the decision (which corresponds to the real game we started with); then we are led to the following dilemma:

If chance chooses left, he would prefer (ii), because $u_A < w_A$. If chance chooses right, he would prefer (i), because $u_B > w_B$. But could he really do so effectively in Γ_∞? If he does, and attempts to conceal the choice of chance, Player 2 would recognize that Player 1 is taking the first alternative and would therefore infer that chance has chosen right.

These considerations indicate that there should be other alternatives that, so to say, partially disclose the choice of chance.

In fact, we shall see in this section that the value of Γ_∞ exists and is[6] $1/6$ (instead of 0, which is the value of Δ_∞). Of course, the way in which Player 1 can guarantee himself this value is different from the above alternatives.

Player 2 can quite easily make sure that in playing Γ_∞ he will not pay an expected average payoff greater than $1/6$. All he has to do is choose left at each stage with probability $2/3$, and right with probability $1/3$. Knowing this, Player 1_B would certainly choose R at each stage, and no matter what Player 1_A will do, the expected payoff for the stage will be $\frac{1}{2} \cdot \frac{2}{3} + \frac{1}{2} \cdot \left(-\frac{1}{3}\right) = \frac{1}{6}$.

---

[6] The value itself can also be computed by the general theorem in Section 5.

Thus, the upper limit of the average payoffs for Player 1 is not greater than 1/6, regardless of his strategy choice.

We must still show that Player 1 can guarantee himself an average expected payoff that is at least 1/6. We shall actually find Player 1's optimal strategy; but first we have to compute the optimal strategy for Player 1 and the value of the 1-stage game $\Gamma_1(p)$, for an arbitrary p, $0 \le p \le 1$, (see Figure 6). The normal form of this game is

Player 2

		L	R
	LL	$3p-2$	0
	LR	p	$p-1$
Player 1	*RL*	$2p-2$	$2p$
	RR	0	$3p-1$

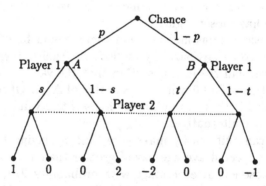

Figure 6. The game $\Gamma_1(p)$

To compute Player 1's optimal strategy in $\Gamma_1(p)$, we consider several cases.

A. Suppose $0 < p < 1/3$; then only the last two strategies of Player 1 are active, and he should play the strategy RL with probability $\dfrac{1-3p}{3(1-p)}$ and RR with probability $\dfrac{2}{3(1-p)}$. The value of the game is

$$v_1(p) = \frac{-2(1-3p)}{3}, \qquad 0 < p < 1/3. \qquad (4.1)$$

In terms of the behavioral strategies described in Figure 6, Player 1 should play right if chance chose left, i.e., $s = 0$; and he should play left with probability $t = \dfrac{1-3p}{3(1-p)}$ if chance chose right.

B. Suppose $1/3 < p < 1$; then the strategies LR and RR are the only active strategies. Player 1's optimal strategies are LR with probability $(3p-1)/3p$ and RR with probability $1/3p$. The value of the game is

$$v_1(p) = \frac{3p-1}{3}, \qquad 1/3 < p < 1. \qquad (4.2)$$

In terms of the behavioral strategies described in Figure 6, Player 1 should play right if chance chose right, i.e., $t = 0$; and he should play left with probability $s = (3p-1)/3p$ if chance chose left.

C. Suppose $p = 1/3$. Player 1 should then play RR; i.e., he should choose right regardless of the choice of chance ($s = 0$, $t = 0$). The value of the game is

$$v_1(1/3) = 0. \qquad (4.3)$$

D. Suppose $p = 0$ or $p = 1$. The values of the games in these cases are $-2/3$ and $2/3$, respectively.

Figure 7 shows the value of $\Gamma_1(p)$ as a function of p. Note that if $p = 1/2$, then $s = 1/3$, $t = 0$, and $v_1(1/2) = 1/6$. Observe also that $v_1(p) > 0$ for $p > 1/3$.

Let us turn now to the game $\Delta_\infty(1/2)$. We must exhibit a strategy σ for Player 1 that guarantees him $1/6$ in Γ_∞. More precisely, a strategy σ such that

$$\liminf_{n \to \infty} \frac{1}{n} \sum_{i=1}^{n} \gamma_i(\sigma, \tau) \geq 1/6 \qquad (4.4)$$

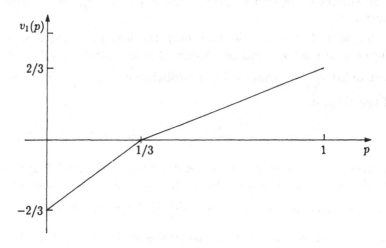

Figure 7. The values of $\Gamma_1(p)$

for *every* strategy τ chosen by Player 2. Here, $\gamma_i(\sigma, \tau)$ is the expected payoff to Player 1 at the i-th stage of Γ_∞, obtained when Player 1 employs σ and Player 2 employs τ. Thus, for a given σ we must determine a strategy τ for Player 2 that minimizes the left side of (4.4).

The key word in the subsequent arguments is the word "every" above. Heuristically speaking, the following ideas will be helpful: a strategy that minimizes the left side of (4.4) is a strategy that Player 2 would have chosen *had he known* that Player 1 is employing σ. We therefore assume that Player 1 commits himself to σ and that Player 2 knows σ and knows that Player 1 is committed to σ. As far as Player 2 is concerned—Player 1 is now nothing but a chance mechanism playing σ and his object is to choose a pure strategy that minimizes (4.4).

As a result of playing σ, there is a choice of L or R at each stage with known probabilities, and by the rules of the game, this choice is revealed at the next stage. Knowing both the probability of the choice and the actual choice, Player 2 can compute the *conditional probabilities* that chance has chosen either vertex A (Game G_A) or vertex B (Game G_B). He can therefore make use of this computation for the next stage. All this amounts to is that Γ_∞ can be regarded as a sequence of 1-stage independent games

$\Gamma_1(p_i)$ (see Figure 8), where s_i, t_i are the (known) probabilities that Player 1 chooses left at the i-th stage, at the vertices A and B, respectively, and p_i is the conditional probability of chance choosing L given the choices of Player 1 prior to Stage i.

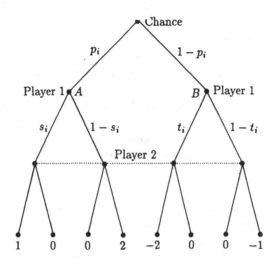

Figure 8. The game $\Gamma_1(p_i)$

Intuitively, $\Gamma_1(p_i)$ is the game that Player 2 believes he is facing at stage i. It is therefore reasonable[7] to expect that the best reply for Player 2 is to choose L or R at each stage i so that the expected payoff for Player 1 in $\Gamma_1(p_i)$ is minimum, where s_i and t_i are the probabilities of Player 1 choosing L, induced by σ at stage i.

To be sure—the strategy that we have just described for Player 2 is *not* an optimal strategy for him in Γ_∞. It is only one of the best replies that Player 2 has *if* Player 1 is committed to σ. Hence it it is a strategy for Player 2 that minimizes the left side of (4.4).

We are now in a position to describe an optimal strategy for Player 1. It is a behavioral strategy: *At each stage i, Player 1 should assume that he is facing the 1-stage game $\Gamma_1(p_i)$ and play optimally accordingly.*[8] Here, the p_i's are the conditional prob-

---

[7]Formally, this follows from Theorem N4 in Postscript e to this chapter (p_2 in (N13) depends on σ but not on τ).(*)

[8]Such a strategy is optimal in this specific game, but not necessarily in other games.(*)

abilities attributed to chance choosing A by a Player 2 who is assumed to know Player 1's strategy and previous moves.

Let us now compute this strategy stage by stage and then determine the expected payoff at each stage if Player 2 answers with his best reply.

At the beginning, Player 1 assumes that he is facing $\Gamma_1(1/2)$. He therefore plays $s_1 = 1/3$, $t_1 = 0$. As a result of this strategy two events might happen: Either he chooses left—the probability of this is $1/6$—or he chooses right. If he chooses left, the second stage is $\Gamma_1(1)$. If he chooses right, the second stage is $\Gamma_1(2/5)$. The situation is summarized in Figure 9.

If Player 1 chooses left, then Player 2 "realizes" that chance has decided upon game A. Thus, Player 1 will continue to play minimax against G_A at each subsequent stage; i.e., $s_i = 2/3$, $i = 2, 3, \ldots$. (His choice at vertex B is irrelevant because this happens with 0 probability.)

If Player 1 chooses right, then the conditional probability attributed by Player 2 to chance choosing A is $2/5$. By our prescription, Player 1 should then play as if he were facing the 1-stage game $\Gamma_1(2/5)$; i.e., $s_2 = 1/6$, $t_2 = 0$. The picture is now as in Figure 10. Thus, if left was chosen, Player 1 will play $s_i = 2/3$ from stage 3 onwards. If right was chosen, Player 1 will play optimally for $\Gamma_1(5/14)$ in the third stage; i.e., $s_3 = 1/15$, $t_3 = 0$.

It can be shown by induction that for $i = 2, 3, \ldots$, the stages look as in Figure 11.

The case not described in this figure is that in which it was revealed in one of the previous stages $2, 3, \ldots, i - 1$ that chance chose A. This occurs with probability

$$1 - \frac{3^{i-1} + 1}{4 \cdot 3^{i-2}} = \frac{3^{i-2} - 1}{4 \cdot 3^{i-2}}. \tag{4.5}$$

At each stage i, Player 1 plays an optimal strategy for a certain game $\Gamma_1(p_i)$ (where p_i depends on the sequence of choices made by Player 1 at the previous stages). As indicated previously, a best reply for Player 2 is to play optimally for the *same* game $\Gamma_1(p_i)$. Therefore, at stage i Player 1 will obtain an expected payoff of $v_1(p_i)$. It follows from the p_i's being conditional probabilities determined by his own strategy, that Player 1's expected payoff for the i-th stage of Γ_∞ is

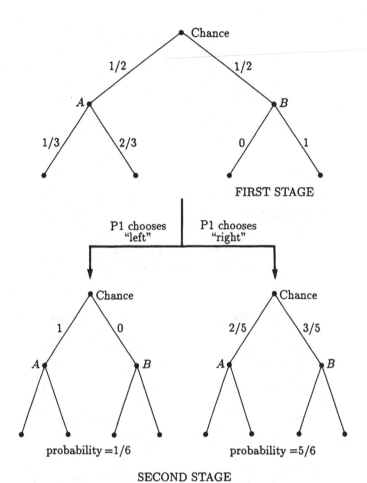

Figure 9. After the first stage

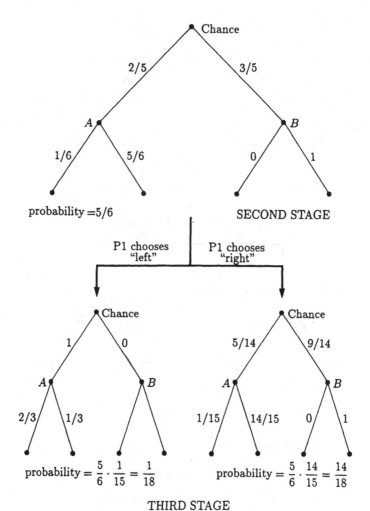

THIRD STAGE

Figure 10. After the second stage

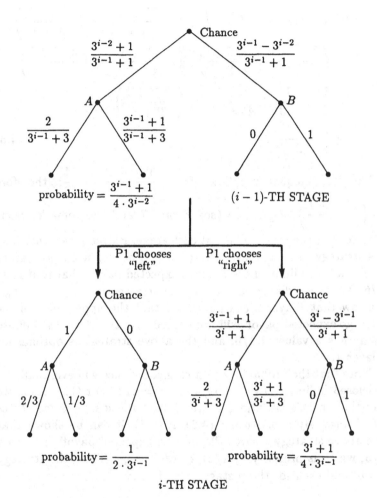

i-TH STAGE

Figure 11. After the $(i-1)$-th stage

$$\text{Prob}\,(p_i = 1) \cdot v_1(1) + \text{Prob}\left(p_i = \frac{3^{i-1}+1}{3^i+1}\right) \cdot v_1\left(\frac{3^{i-1}+1}{3^i+1}\right)$$

$$= \left(\frac{3^{i-2}-1}{4 \cdot 3^{i-2}} + \frac{1}{2 \cdot 3^{i-1}}\right) \cdot \frac{2}{3} + \frac{3^i+1}{4 \cdot 3^{i-1}} \cdot v_1\left(\frac{3^{i-1}+1}{3^i+1}\right)$$

$$= \frac{1}{6} - \frac{1}{2 \cdot 3^i} + \frac{3^i+1}{4 \cdot 3^{i-1}} \cdot v_1\left(\frac{3^{i-1}+1}{3^i+1}\right)$$

$$\geq \frac{1}{6} - \frac{1}{2 \cdot 3^i}. \tag{4.6}$$

The last inequality follows from $\dfrac{3^{i-1}+1}{3^i+1} > \dfrac{1}{3}$; therefore $v_1\left(\dfrac{3^{i-1}+1}{3^{i+1}}\right)$ is positive (see Figure 7 and the remarks referring to it in the text). Thus, at each stage, Player 1 guarantees by his strategy to get at least $1/6 - (2 \cdot 3^i)^{-1}$; hence, he can guarantee in Γ_∞ a lower limit of the average expected payoff that is at least $1/6$. When we discussed the optimal strategy of Player 2 in Γ_∞, we saw that Player 2 can guarantee that the upper limit of the average expected payoff will not exceed $1/6$; therefore, the infinite game has a value of $1/6$, and the above strategy is optimal for Player 1.

Note that the probability that chance's choice will eventually be disclosed is $\lim_{i \to \infty}(3^{i-2}-1)/4 \cdot 3^{i-2} = 1/4$. For this reason we say that in this situation, Player 1 *partially discloses the choice of chance.* By substituting (4.2) in (4.6), it can be shown that the above strategy assures Player 1 an expected payoff of at least $1/6$, which is precisely $v_1(1/2)$, *at each stage.* Thus, the strategy is optimal even for the n-stage game Γ_n.

5. The Main Theorem

In the preceding sections we showed by means of examples that in some cases an optimal strategy for Player 1 in a game Γ_∞ is to refrain from making use of his knowledge of chance's choice; i.e., to play as if he were in the game Δ_∞. In other cases, his optimal strategy makes use of his knowledge, which may result in fully or partially revealing chance's choice to Player 2 (who is supposed to know which strategy Player 1 is using).

The first question that comes to mind is: When should Player 1 play like in Δ_∞ and when not?

Obviously, Player 1 should make use of his knowledge of chance's choice if and only if he can guarantee an average expected payoff that is higher than the value of Δ_1. This brings us to the question of the value of Γ_∞ (if it exists), which is an important question in itself. In this section we answer this seemingly more difficult question, from which the answer to the first question will become apparent.

Let $\Gamma_\infty(p)$ be a general (infinite) game based on two 2-person constant sum games G_A and G_B, as sketched in Figure 12, where the rules are as explained in the previous sections. In particular, Player 1 knows the choice of chance, whereas Player 2 does not.

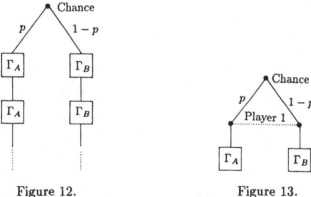

Figure 12.   Figure 13.
The game $\Gamma_\infty(p)$ The game $\Delta_1(p)$

Let $\Delta_1(p)$ be the 1-stage game sketched in Figure 13. Let $u(p)$ be the value of $\Delta_1(p)$ (which is also the value of the infinite game $\Delta_\infty(p)$). It is a continuous function of p. Clearly $u(0) = w_B$ and $u(1) = w_A$, where w_A and w_B are the values of G_A and G_B, respectively.

In general, u is not a concave function, and therefore it may be different from the function cav u defined by

$$\text{cav } u(p) := \min \tilde{u}(p), \qquad 0 \leq p \leq 1, \qquad (5.1)$$

where the minimum is taken over all *concave* functions $\tilde{u}$ such that $\tilde{u}(p) \geq u(p)$ for all p. The function cav u is itself concave; it will be called *the concavification* of u. It is indicated in Figure 14 by a broken line for all the values p where cav $u(p) \neq u(p)$.

THEOREM 5.1. *The value of the game* $\Gamma_\infty(p)$ *exists, and is equal to* cav $u(p)$, *where* cav u *is the concavification of* u.

We outline the proof in the remainder of the section, for simplicity taking only G_A and G_B that are 2×2 matrix games. Player 1's (behavioral) strategy is then an infinite sequence of pairs (s_1, t_1), (s_2, t_2), ..., where s_i, t_i are the probabilities at stage i of Player 1 choosing "left" if chance chose "left" or "right", respectively.[9] Similarly, Player 2's strategy is a sequence $\lambda_1, \lambda_2, \ldots$, where λ_i is the probability of "left" at the i-th stage. The parameters s_i, t_i, λ_i may depend on the actual choices made by both players at the previous stages.

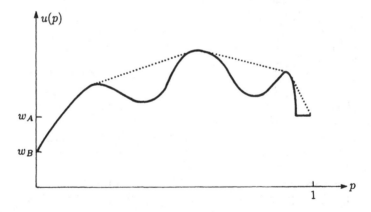

Figure 14. The concavification of $u(p)$

---

[9]By the theorem of Kuhn [1953], generalized to infinite games [Aumann, 1963], we can limit ourselves to behavioral strategies, because ours is a game of perfect recall.

LEMMA 5.2. *Let $0 \leq p^L < p < p^R \leq 1$, or $0 \leq p^R < p < p^L \leq 1$; then there exist probabilities s_1, t_1 for the first stage, such that*

$$\text{Prob} \left\{ \text{chance chose "left"} \; \middle| \; \begin{array}{l} \text{player 1 went left} \\ \text{at the first stage} \end{array} \right\} = p^L, \quad (5.2)$$

$$\text{Prob} \left\{ \text{chance chose "left"} \; \middle| \; \begin{array}{l} \text{player 1 went right} \\ \text{at the first stage} \end{array} \right\} = p^R. \quad (5.3)$$

PROOF: The equations (5.2) and (5.3) are, in fact,

$$p^L = \frac{s_1 p}{s_1 p + t_1(1-p)}, \quad p^R = \frac{(1-s_1)p}{(1-s_1)p + (1-t_1)(1-p)}, \quad (5.4)$$

whose solution is:

$$s_1 = \frac{p^L(p^R - p)}{p(p^R - p^L)}, \quad t_1 = \frac{(1-p^L)(p^R - p)}{(1-p)(p^R - p^L)}. \quad (5.5)$$

Clearly $0 \leq s_1 < 1$ and $0 \leq t_1 \leq 1$. ∎

LEMMA 5.3. *Player 1 can guarantee in $\Gamma_\infty(p)$ average expected payoffs whose lower limit is at least cav $u(p)$.*

PROOF: We shall exhibit a strategy for Player 1 such that even if Player 2 knew it and knew that Player 1 is committed to it, his best reply would still yield Player 1 an average expected payoff whose lower limit is not less than cav $u(p)$.

A. If p is such that cav $u(p) = u(p)$, then Player 1 acts as if he does not know the choice of chance; i.e., plays as if he is playing Δ_1. In other words, he plays at each stage as if he were playing optimally in Δ_1. He then guarantees an average expected value whose lower limit is at least cav $u(p)$.

B. If p is such that cav $u(p) > u(p)$, then there exist p^L and p^R with $0 \leq p^L < p < p^R \leq 1$, such that $u(p^L) = $ cav $u(p^L)$, $u(p^R) = $ cav $u(p^R)$ and $(p^L, \text{cav } u(p^L))$, $(p, \text{cav } u(p))$, and $(p^R, \text{cav } u(p^R))$ are on a straight line (see Figure 15).

A strategy for Player 1 is as follows: Choose s_1 and t_1 satisfying (5.5). If left was played at the first stage, continue as in $\Delta_\infty(p^L)$; i.e., play an optimal strategy for $\Delta_1(p^L)$ at each stage i, $i \geq 2$.

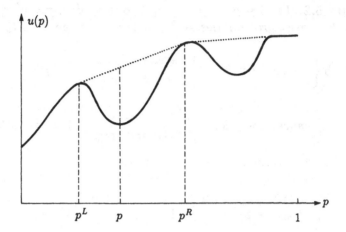

Figure 15. $u(p^L) = \text{cav } u(p^L)$ and $u(p^R) = \text{cav } u(p^R)$

If right was played at the first stage, continue as in $\Delta_\infty(p^R)$; i.e., play an optimal strategy for $\Delta_1(p^R)$ at each stage i, $i \geq 2$.

Player 2, who is assumed to know that Player 1 is committed to this strategy, would decide after the choices of the first stage are revealed to play as in $\Delta_\infty(p^L)$, if at the first stage Player 1 chose left; and as in $\Delta_\infty(p^R)$, if Player 1 chose right. His best reply would still guarantee Player 1 average expected payoffs with lower limit either $u(p^L)$ or $u(p^R)$, according to his choice in the first stage.[10]

The probability that Player 1 chooses left at the first stage is $ps_1 + (1 - p)t_1 =: \alpha$. The probability that he chooses right is $p(1 - s_1) + (1 - p)(1 - t_1) = 1 - \alpha$. Observe that

$$\alpha p^L + (1 - \alpha)p^R = p. \tag{5.6}$$

In other words, p is the center of gravity of the weights α and $1 - \alpha$ attached to p^L and p^R, respectively. Consequently, $(p, \text{cav } u(p))$ is the center of gravity of the same weights attached to the points

---

[10]Whatever Player 1 has gained in the first stage has no effect on the average expected payoffs when Γ_∞ is played.

$(p^L, u(p^L))$ and $(p^R, u(p^R))$, because these points are on a straight line. It follows that

$$\alpha u(p^L) + (1 - \alpha)u(p^R) = \alpha \operatorname{cav} u(p^L) + (1 - \alpha) \operatorname{cav} u(p^R)$$
$$= \operatorname{cav} u(p). \tag{5.7}$$

But the left side of (5.7) is the lower limit of the average expected payoffs for Player 1. We have therefore shown that this lower limit is equal to cav $u(p)$. This concludes the proof. ∎

The relation (5.6) can be interpreted as follows: The (unconditional) expectation of the conditional probability at the second stage that chance has chosen "left" is equal to the original probability that chance has chosen "left". This, of course, can be generalized to an arbitrary stage.

Thus, let p_n be the conditional probability that chance has chosen left, given the choices of Player 1 at stages $1, 2, \ldots, n-1$, and his announced strategy $\{(s_i, t_i)\}$. Then p_n is a random variable taking up to 2^{n-1} possible values, and

$$\operatorname{Exp}(p_n) = p. \tag{5.8}$$

(Here, $p_1 = p$.) We must still show that Player 2 can guarantee that he will not pay an average expected payoff whose expected limit is greater than cav $u(p)$.

We first give this part of the proof for the case treated in Section 2, where G_A and G_B are the games

		Player 2					Player 2	
		L	R				L	R
	L	1	0			L	0	0
Player 1					Player 1			
	R	0	0			R	0	1
		G_A					G_B	

and furthermore $p = 1/2$. We shall later indicate what modifications should be made in the proof of the general case, which is
technically more complicated but uses the same ideas.

Before giving this part of the proof technically, we describe the
idea. It is based on the minimax theorem. If to each strategy
of Player 1, Player 2 can respond so as to guarantee paying at
most 1/4 on the average, then, in a finite game, the minimax
theorem tells us that he has a strategy that guarantees at most
1/4. Therefore, we may assume that Player 1 must announce
his behavior strategy $\{(s_i, t_i)\}$ before the start of the game. If
s_i and t_i differ from each other by "a significant amount" and
"sufficiently often", then Player 2 will be able to deduce chance's
choice with high probability, and the resulting payoff will be close
to 0. Otherwise, s_i and t_i must eventually become and remain
"almost equal." When this happens, Player 2 can play in the resulting game—in which the probabilities are now the conditionals
p_i—as if Player 1 did not know chance's choice either. If Player 2
then plays optimally for the one-shot case, he will get a payoff
of $p_i(1 - p_i)$, which is always at most 1/4. We now turn to the
technical details.

Step 1. We first compute $u(p)$ and $v_1(p)$ for $0 \le p \le 1$. These are
the values of the games whose normal forms are

	L	R
L	p	0
R	0	$1 - p$

	L	R
LL	p	0
LR	p	$1 - p$
RL	0	0
RR	0	$1 - p$

Here, $u(p) = p(1 - p) = \operatorname{cav} u(p),$ and $v_1(p) = \min(p, 1 - p)$ (see
Figure 16). Note that $\operatorname{cav} u(p)$ and $v_1(p)$ are continuous functions of p.

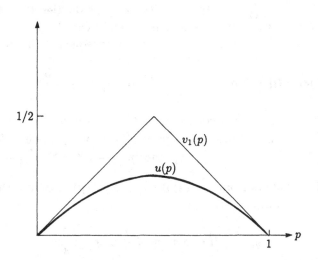

Figure 16. The graphs of $u(p)$ and $v_1(p)$

Step 2. We now assume that in the n-stage game $\Gamma_n(1/2)$, Player 1 announces and commits himself to a (not necessarily optimal) strategy $\{(s_i, t_i)\}$, $i = 1, 2, \ldots, n$, and that Player 2 knows this. A possible reply for Player 2 in $\Gamma_n(1/2)$ would be to answer at each stage i as best as he can, as if it were a 1-stage game based on the conditional probability p_i that chance chose "left". The payoff to Player 1 at stage i (as perceived by Player 2) will then be:

$$
\begin{aligned}
g_i &= \min\{p_i s_i, (1 - p_i)(1 - t_i)\} \\
&= \min\{p_i s_i, (1 - p_i)(1 - s_i) + (1 - p_i)(s_i - t_i)\} \\
&\leq \min\{p_i s_i, (1 - p_i)(1 - s_i)\} + |s_i - t_i| \\
&\leq u(p_i) + |s_i - t_i| \leq 1/4 + |s_i - t_i|, \qquad i = 1, 2, \ldots, n.
\end{aligned}
\tag{5.9}
$$

(The second inequality follows from the fact that if Player 1 plays any $(s_i, 1 - s_i)$ in $\Delta_1(p_i)$, he cannot guarantee more than $u(p_i)$.)

Step 3. It follows from (5.5), adapted to stage i, that

$$
|s_i - t_i| = \left| \frac{(p_{i+1}^R - p_i)(p_{i+1}^L - p_i)}{p_i(1 - p_i)(p_{i+1}^R - p_{i+1}^L)} \right|, \qquad i = 1, 2, \ldots, n, \tag{5.10}
$$

where[11] p_{i+1}^R, p_{i+1}^L are the conditional probabilities that chance chose left, given p_i at the previous stage, in case Player 1's choice at stage i is right or left, respectively. Consequently, in any case,

$$|s_i - t_i| \leq K|p_{i+1} - p_i|, \quad \text{if, say, } \frac{1}{4} \leq p_i \leq \frac{3}{4}, \tag{5.11}$$

where K is a positive constant, and p_{i+1} is either p_{i+1}^R or p_{i+1}^L. Indeed, p_i is a weighted average of p_{i+1}^R and p_{i+1}^L, and it follows that $|p_{i+1}^R - p_{i+1}^L| \geq |p_{i+1}^R - p_i|$ and $|p_{i+1}^R - p_{i+1}^L| \geq |p_{i+1}^L - p_i|$.

Step 4. It follows from the expression for $v_1(p)$ in Step 1 that for each i, $i = 1, 2, \ldots, n$,

$$g_i \leq \frac{1}{4} \text{ if either } p_i \leq \frac{1}{4} \text{ or } p_i \geq \frac{3}{4}. \tag{5.12}$$

Consequently, by (5.11),

$$g_i \leq \frac{1}{4} + K|p_{i+1} - p_i|. \tag{5.13}$$

Step 5. We are interested in $\text{Exp} \sum_{i=1}^n g_i$ and so must estimate the expression

$$\text{Exp} \sum_{i=1}^n |p_{i+1} - p_i|.$$

Fortunately, the conditional probabilities p_i satisfy

$$\text{Exp}(p_i \mid p_1, p_2, \ldots, p_{i-1}) = p_{i-1}, \quad i = 1, 2, \ldots, n. \tag{5.14}$$

Indeed, (5.14) follows from the fact that given $p_1, p_2, \ldots, p_{i-1}$, it is possible to compute $\text{Exp}(p_i)$ by an analogue of (5.6), using p_{i-1} only. A sequence of random variables p_i satisfying (5.14) is known as a *martingale*; and for martingales it may be shown (see, e.g., Doob [1953]) that

$$\text{Exp} \sum_{i=1}^n (p_{i+1} - p_i)^2 = \text{Exp}(p_{n+1} - p_1)^2. \tag{5.15}$$

---

[11] p_{n+1}^R and p_{n+1}^L are meaningful even if the game terminates after n stages.

Since, moreover, p_{n+1} and p_1 are probabilities, it follows that

$$\text{Exp} \sum_{i=1}^{n} (p_{i+1} - p_i)^2 \leq 1. \tag{5.16}$$

Step 6. It follows from (5.13), (5.16) and the Cauchy-Schwarz inequality that

$$\begin{aligned}
\text{Exp} \sum_{i=1}^{n} g_i &\leq \frac{n}{4} + K \, \text{Exp} \sum_{i=1}^{n} |p_{i+1} - p_i| \cdot 1 \\
&\leq \frac{n}{4} + K \, \text{Exp} \sqrt{\sum (p_{i+1} - p_i)^2 \cdot n} \\
&\leq \frac{n}{4} + K\sqrt{n} \, \text{Exp} \sqrt{\sum (p_{i+1} - p_i)^2 + 1} \\
&\leq \frac{n}{4} + K\sqrt{n} \, \text{Exp} \left(\sum (p_{i+1} - p_i)^2 + 1 \right) \\
&\leq \frac{n}{4} + 2K\sqrt{n};
\end{aligned}$$

consequently,

$$\text{Exp} \frac{1}{n} \sum_{i=1}^{n} g_i \leq \frac{1}{4} + \frac{2K}{\sqrt{n}} =: b_n, \tag{5.17}$$

and this expression tends to 1/4 when n tends to infinity.

Step 7. Define the payoff in $\Gamma_n(1/2)$ to be the average payoff for the n stages in the game. By the minimax theorem and (5.17), the value v_n of $\Gamma_n(1/2)$ is not greater than b_n. Let σ_n be an optimal strategy for Player 2 in $\Gamma_n(1/2)$. We now describe an optimal strategy for Player 2 in $\Gamma_\infty(1/2)$: Play σ_1 in the first stage. Play σ_2 in the next two stages. Play σ_3 in the next three stages, etc. Let m be any integer; we shall compute the average expected payoff for m stages. Put $m = 1 + 2 + 3 + \cdots + n + k$, where $0 \leq k < n + 1$. The average expected payoff for m stages is at most

$$\begin{aligned}
q_m &:= \frac{1}{m} (v_1 + 2v_2 + \cdots + nv_n + \frac{k}{2}) \\
&\leq \frac{b_1 + 2b_2 + \cdots + nb_n}{1 + 2 + \cdots + n} + \frac{1}{n},
\end{aligned} \tag{5.18}$$

where, for the last k stages we took the maximum expected payoff in each game; namely, $1/2$. The last term in (5.18) tends to zero as n tends to infinity. The first term is a Cesaro mean of $n(n+1)/2$ terms of the sequence $b_1, b_2, b_2, b_3, b_3, b_3, \ldots$. By (5.17), this sequence tends to $1/4$ as $n \to \infty$; hence $\limsup q_m \leq 1/4$.

We have exhibited a strategy for Player 2 that guarantees that the upper limit of the average expected payoff is at most $1/4$. This and Lemma 5.3 prove Theorem 5.1 for the case of $\Gamma_\infty(1/2)$ treated here.

The proof in the general case is quite similar and we only outline the necessary modifications. In this case p is an arbitrary number between 0 and 1, and G_A and G_B are arbitrary $\mu \times \nu$ matrix games, $\mu, \nu \geq 2$, whose values are w_A and w_B, respectively.

From Step 1 we use only the fact that $\operatorname{cav} u(p)$ and $v_1(p)$ are continuous functions of p that satisfy $v_1(0) = w_B = u(0) = \operatorname{cav} u(0)$ and $v_1(1) = w_A = u(1) = \operatorname{cav} u(1)$. In Step 2 an analogue of (5.9), which is easily derived, is

$$g_i \leq u(p_i) + C\|s_i - t_i\| \leq \operatorname{cav} u(p_i) + C\|s_i - t_i\|, \qquad (5.19)$$

where $s_i = (s_i^1, s_i^2, \ldots, s_i^\mu)$ and $t_i = (t_i^1, t_i^2 \ldots, t_i^\mu)$ are the i-th stage strategies of Player 1_A and Player 1_B, respectively. Now $\|s_i - t_i\|$ is the distance between the vectors s_i and t_i in, say, the maximum norm, and C is μ times a constant that is larger than the absolute value of each entry in G_A and G_B. Furthermore, we note that for each ε there is a δ such that if $p_i \leq \delta$ or $(1 - p_i) \leq \delta$, then

$$g_i \leq \operatorname{cav} u(p_i) + \varepsilon. \qquad (5.20)$$

This can be seen as follows: In any case we have $g_i \leq v_1(p_i)$. If p_i is small then from the continuity of v_1 in p it follows that $v_1(p_i)$ is close to $v_1(0) = \operatorname{cav} u(0)$, and from the continuity of $\operatorname{cav} u$ in p it follows that $\operatorname{cav} u(0)$ is then close to $\operatorname{cav} u(p_i)$. The argument is similar when p_i is close to 1.

One substantive change is made in Step 3: If p_{i+1}^r is the conditional probability of chance choosing left, given that Player 1 has chosen the r-th row at stage i (and given the conditional probability p_i), then

$$p_{i+1}^r = \frac{p_i s_i^r}{p_i s_i^r + (1 - p_i)t_i^r}. \qquad (5.21)$$

Hence,

$$(p_i s_i^r + (1 - p_i)t_i^r)^2(p_{i+1}^r - p_i)^2 = (1 - p_i)^2 p_i^2 (s_i^r - t_i^r)^2. \quad (5.22)$$

If $\delta < p_i < 1 - \delta$, then since $0 \le p_i s_i^r + (1 - p_i)t_i^r \le 1$, by setting $K = C/(\delta(1 - \delta))$ we obtain

$$
\begin{aligned}
(s_i^r - t_i^r)^2 &\le \frac{K^2}{C^2}(p_{i+1}^r - p_i)^2(p_i s_i^r + (1 - p_i)t_i^r)^2 \\
&\le \frac{K^2}{C^2}(p_{i+1}^r - p_i)^2(p_i s_i^r + (1 - p_i)t_i^r) \\
&\le \frac{K^2}{C^2}\sum_r (p_{i+1}^r - p_i)^2(p_i s_i^r + (1 - p_i)t_i^r) \\
&= \frac{K^2}{C^2}\, \mathrm{Exp}((p_{i+1} - p_i)^2|p_i).
\end{aligned}
\quad (5.23)
$$

Since this is true for any r, it follows that

$$\|s_i - t_i\|^2 \le \frac{K^2}{C^2}\, \mathrm{Exp}(p_{i+1} - p_i)^2|p_i.$$

Hence, from (5.19), we obtain

$$
\begin{aligned}
g_i &\le \mathrm{cav}\, u(p_i) + C\|s_i - t_i\| \\
&\le \mathrm{cav}\, u(p_i) + K\sqrt{\mathrm{Exp}(p_{i+1} - p_i)^2|p_i} \\
&\le \mathrm{cav}\, u(p_i) + \varepsilon + K\sqrt{\mathrm{Exp}(p_{i+1} - p_i)^2|p_i},
\end{aligned}
$$

when $\delta < p_i < 1 - \delta$, and this is true also when $p_i \le \delta$ or $p_i \ge 1 - \delta$, because of (5.20). Hence, from the concavity of cav u and of $\sqrt{\ }$, and from $\mathrm{Exp}\, p_i = p$, we obtain

$$\mathrm{Exp}\, g_i \le \mathrm{cav}\, u(p) + \varepsilon + K\sqrt{\mathrm{Exp}(p_{i+1} - p_i)^2}.$$

Using the Cauchy-Schwarz inequality and (5.16), we obtain

$$
\begin{aligned}
\mathrm{Exp} \sum_{i=1}^{n} g_i &\le n(\mathrm{cav}\, u(p) + \varepsilon) + K\sqrt{n}\sqrt{\sum_{i=1}^{n} \mathrm{Exp}(p_{i+1} - p_i)^2} \\
&\le n(\mathrm{cav}\, u(p) + \varepsilon) + K\sqrt{n}.
\end{aligned}
$$

Thus,

$$v_n \leq \text{Exp} \frac{1}{n} \sum_{i=1}^{n} g_i \leq \text{cav } u(p) + \varepsilon + \frac{K}{\sqrt{n}}.$$

Finally, letting $n \to \infty$, we deduce that $\lim_{n \to \infty} v_n \leq \text{cav } u(p) + \varepsilon$. Since this is true for arbitrary ε, we have $\lim_{n \to \infty} v_n \leq \text{cav } u(p)$; and the rest of the proof is as before. ∎

We remark that by a slight modification we can prove, as before, that

$$v_n(p) = \text{cav } u(p) + O\left(\frac{1}{\sqrt{n}}\right). \tag{5.24}$$

Theorem 5.1 remains true also in the more general situation in which chance chooses any of κ alternatives, each leading to a possibly different game. The proof follows the same pattern as when $\kappa = 2$, except that at one stage an induction on κ must be employed.

6. The Optimal Strategy of Player 2

The reader will have observed that Theorem 5.1 was proved without presenting an optimal strategy for Player 2. We shall now present such a strategy for the game treated in Section 2.

Rather than representing the situation as a tree, let us consider a somewhat different approach. We start with a 1-stage game.

Since Player 2 does not know chance's choice, he may regard his outcome[12] as a *pair* of numbers (x, y), where x represents the payoff if he plays against Player 1_A, and y represents the payoff if he plays against Player 1_B. Only at the end does chance reveal its choice. The situation for Player 2 can therefore be described by a bimatrix, an outcome space X and the original p, namely,

---

[12] "Outcome" in this section is to be distinguished from "expected payoff."

$p = 1/2$. In our case, we obtain the following bimatrix and the outcome space of Figure 17.

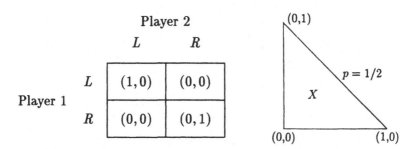

Figure 17.
The outcome space

If $\Delta_1(1/2)$ is being considered, we may say that Player 1, too, is informed of the choice of chance only at the end of the game. Therefore, if (x, y) is the outcome, the expected payoff for Player 1 is $(x+y)/2$. The situation is somewhat different if $\Gamma_1(1/2)$ is being played, because in this case Player 1 knows the choice of chance at the beginning, and at the same time he has to take into account the game as viewed by Player 2. Suppose, for example, that Player 2 announces a mixed strategy $(q, 1-q)$; then Player 1 can answer either L or R, which lead to two points (x_1, y_1) and (x_2, y_2) on the axes in the outcome space. He can also answer by a mixed strategy, in which case he can achieve any point on the straight line segment l joining these points (see Figure 18).

If he wishes, his answer if he is Player 1_A may differ from his answer if he is Player 1_B. Knowing this, Player 2 must regard his actual expected payoff as

$$\max\left\{\frac{x+\eta}{2} : (x, y) \in l \text{ and } (\xi, \eta) \in l\right\}. \tag{6.1}$$

Thus, the expected payoff that Player 2 can guarantee is determined by considering *pairs of points* from a given set. A similar situation holds if an n-stage game is being considered, in which case one adds the vectors obtained as outcomes in each stage. The expected payoff for $\Delta_n(1/2)$ may be obtained by maximizing

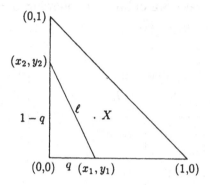

Figure 18. Payoffs against $(q, 1 - q)$

$(x_i + y_i)/2$ at each stage over a certain straight line segment l_i. The expected payoff for $\Gamma_n(1/2)$ may be obtained by maximizing at each stage an expression of the form (6.1) over all the l_i. In the case of an infinite game one considers a *sequence* of *averages* of the two dimensional vectors, i.e., their centers of gravity for $1, 2, 3, 4, \ldots$ stages, and one studies their limit points.

Games with vector outcomes were considered by D. Blackwell [1956], where he gave a criterion for a convex set S in X to be *approachable* by, say, Player 2 when the infinite game is played. By this is meant that Player 2 has a strategy such that with probability 1, the distance between a_i and S approaches 0 as $i \to \infty$, *regardless* of the strategy chosen by Player 1, where a_i is the average of the outcomes up to Stage i. It follows from his criterion that in our game $\Gamma_\infty(1/2)$, the square S of Figure 19 is an approachable set. This square is of size $1/4 \times 1/4$; two of its sides are on the axes and meet at the origin. Fortunately,

$$\max \left\{ \frac{(x + \eta)}{2} : (x, y) \in S, \quad (\xi, \eta) \in S \right\} \le \frac{1}{4}, \qquad (6.2)$$

and since $1/4$ is the value of $\Gamma_\infty(1/2)$, a strategy for Player 2 that would lead the outcomes to a zero distance from S with probability 1 is optimal.

D. Blackwell [1956] describes a class of such strategies, one of which can be stated verbally as follows:

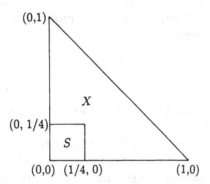

Figure 19. An approachable set

At each stage $i + 1$, Player 2 observes his and Player 1's choices at the previous stages. He then computes the average outcome $(\bar{\xi}_i, \bar{\eta}_i)$ for the first i stages. His intention is to see to it that both $\bar{\xi}_i$ and $\bar{\eta}_i$ will have upper limits that are not greater than $1/4$. This he does as follows:

i. If $\bar{\xi}_i \leq 1/4$ and $\bar{\eta}_i \leq 1/4$, he is satisfied, and can play in any way he wishes at the $(i + 1)$-th stage.

ii. If $\bar{\xi}_i \leq 1/4$ and $\bar{\eta}_i > 1/4$, then Player 1_A is O.K., but Player 1_B is not. Player 2 therefore plays against Player 1_B at the $(i + 1)$-th stage; i.e., he plays L.

iii. Similarly, if $\bar{\xi}_i > 1/4$ and $\bar{\eta}_i \leq 1/4$, Player 2 plays R at the $(i + 1)$-th stage.

iv. If $\bar{\xi}_i > 1/4$ and $\bar{\eta}_i > 1/4$, Player 2 considers the ratio $c := (\bar{\xi}_i - 1/4)/(\bar{\eta}_i - 1/4)$. At stage $i + 1$ he then plays a mixed strategy $(q, 1 - q)$ with $(1 - q)/q = c$. Thus if $c > 1$, then Player 1_A is better off than Player 1_B; and Player 2 will play "more" against him, by playing R with a higher probability than L.

It can be shown that any closed approachable set for which the left side of (6.2) does not exceed $1/4$ must contain the point $(1/4, 1/4)$; therefore, Player 2 cannot play optimally and force, say, Player 1_A to an average expected payoff lower than $1/4$, even if he allows Player 1_B an expected payoff higher than $1/4 = v$.

If p is different from $1/2$, the situation is different! Reasoning similar to the above shows that if both players play optimally in $\Gamma(p)$, Player 1_A will get $(1-p)^2$ with probability 1 and Player 1_B will get p^2 with probability 1.

7. Conclusions

A start has been made toward a theory of games of incomplete information when often repeated.

It was seen that considerations of long-term revelation or concealment of utilities are crucial for understanding the situation. Specifically, we saw that when one of the two players (Player 1) has special information not available to the other (Player 2), then *he can use this information to his advantage only to the extent that he reveals it.*[13] Whether or not such revelation is worthwhile depends on the circumstances, but at least for the class of games considered here we are able to say when it is worthwhile and when it is not. In the examples we examined in Sections 2 and 3, one of two extremes of behavior was optimal for Player 1: he must either make no use whatever of his information, or he must disregard the future, playing each stage as if it was the last one (which allows him to make full use of the information). At one time we conjectured that one of these two extremes of behavior is always optimal, but the example of Section 4 shows that this conjecture is false. However, it follows from the theorem of Section 5 that Player 1 can always play so as to reveal everything he is going to reveal already in the first stage, and then play so as to make no further use of his information.

The most startling conclusion of our investigation is that to understand a situation in which it is known that Player 2's beliefs can be described by a specific subjective probability $p = p_0$ it may be (and usually is) necessary to analyze other situations in which p is different from p_0. Thus, if you know that one of the players in a game places $1/2 - 1/2$ probabilities on a certain conjecture, in order to analyze the situation properly you cannot restrict yourself

---

[13]See Section 3.5 of Chapter Two for a fuller discussion of this principle. "Using" information (partially or fully) is discussed in Subsection A; "revealing it"—in Subsection B. (*)

to the $1/2 - 1/2$ distribution, but *must* consider all other *hypothetical* probability distributions. This surprising conclusion, like the statement italicized in the previous paragraph, is an example of the kind of insight that may eventually have influence on policy-making bodies.

8. Where Do We Go From Here?

All the material presented above concerns situations which may be modelled as nature choosing one of a number of 2-person 0-sum games and informing one player, but not the other, of the game that has been chosen; the chosen game is then repeated a large number of times. From here we can (and should) proceed in two main directions:

a) Extending the theory to a broader class of situations;
b) Completing and deepening the results in the area of this chapter.

In direction (a), the theory should be extended to 2-person 0-sum situations in which there is incomplete information on *both* sides. Also, non-zero sum two-person games, which are typical of bargaining situations, should be considered. An important difference between such games and 0-sum games is that even in the case of complete information, a repeated non-zero sum game leads to outcomes that are very different from those of the nonrepeated game. Typically, repetition pushes the players towards cooperative behavior, even if the framework is non-cooperative. It remains to be seen what effect incomplete information has on this and other non-zero-sum phenomena. Both cooperative and non-cooperative models should be studied. At a later stage, n-person games with $n > 2$ may be studied.

Averaging methods other than the one used here should be investigated; for example, one might look into discounting methods.

The insights that we hope to gain from the non-zero sum study should be applied also to more general situations, in which possibly *different* games are played successively, all involving one or more parameters that are unknown to one of the sides. For example, consider a situation in which the successive stage games are different, all have payoffs in money, and each player's utility for

money is unknown to the other. The question is, to what extent
should such utilities be revealed, or concealed, during the course
of the "grand" game. This is the question that must eventually
be tackled, for it is rarely that the same game is actually repeated
again and again: rather, the players engage in different games, but
often use the same basic considerations in each of many different
situations.

In direction (b), explicit optimal strategies for Player 2 should
be sought for all games in the class considered in this chapter;
up to now they are known only for special games. As we have
seen in Section 6, investigation of these optimal strategies has led
to the conclusion that many of the games under consideration
have a unique value *pair* rather than just a unique value; that
is, a value can be assigned to each of the two types A and B of
Player 1. For example, when $p = 1/4$ in the game considered in
Section 6, and both players use optimal strategies, then type A
must get 1/16 (with probability 1, not only with expectation 1),
and type B must get 9/16. However, such a situation does not
always obtain. This phenomenon looks important and should be
investigated further.

Other aspects that are not yet understood fully concern the relationship between v_1 and $v_\infty (= \text{cav } u)$. In the example of Section
4, we found that Player 1 has an optimal strategy in which he always disregards the future and plays as if he were in a one-stage
game. In other words, Player 2 gains nothing from the repetition,
in contrast to the example of Section 2, in which Player 1 gains
nothing from his extra information. The example of Section 4 also
had the startling property that $v_1 = v_\infty$. There is some reason to
believe that this property is related to that of playing each stage
as if it was the last one, but we have not succeeded in clarifying
this relation (if it exists).

The final problem under heading (b) concerns the second-order
properties of the limiting process. For example, consider again
the problem of Section 5. Rather than considering averages, let
us now consider the sum of the payoffs, so that the value of the
n-stage game is nv_n. We know that $nv_n = n/4 + \text{O}(\sqrt{n})$. Is
this error term the best possible? Note that $\pm\sqrt{n}$ is precisely the
order of magnitude of the fluctuations that one might expect from
probabilistic considerations. This similarity suggests the following

approach to answering the above question: In the n-stage game, Player 1 can guarantee $n/4$ by playing $s_i = t_i = 1/2$ at each stage; i.e., by not using his information. In that case, the observed L-R ratio would differ from 1 by $O(1/\sqrt{n})$. In an optimal strategy, Player 1 would, of course, obtain more by using his information. Thus, he should usually play s_i slightly different from t_i. If this difference is too great too often, then Player 2 would "catch on," and deduce Player 1's type, 1_A or 1_B, with high probability. But if Player 1 keeps the difference between s_i and t_i low enough so that the L-R ratio differs from 1 by $O(1/\sqrt{n})$, then perhaps he could keep Player 2 from "catching on." This would indicate that $O(\sqrt{n})$ is indeed the best possible error term. Is this correct?

POSTSCRIPTS TO CHAPTER ONE

In this chapter we proceeded largely by example; all the ideas for a rigorous general formulation were there, but the treatment was comparatively informal. A formal, general model for the class of games treated here may be found in Chapter Two, Section 3.1, and also in Chapter Four, Section 2. Postscript d below contains a rigorous general proof of the main theorem of this Chapter (Theorem 5.1) that is based on Blackwell's [1956] theory of games with vector payoffs (cf. Section 6). For a formal proof of a more general theorem, based on the ideas of Section 5, see Chapter Four, Section 6. Additional examples and intuitive explanations for the material in this Chapter may be found in Chapter Two.

Since 1966, when this Chapter was written, there has been considerable progress on the open problems discussed in Section 8, "Where do we go from here?"; a large literature has developed. In direction (a), "Extending the theory to a broader class of situations", the theory has been extended to 2-person 0-sum games with incomplete information on both sides, and to non-zero sum 2-person games. These developments will be discussed in detail in Chapters Two, Three, and Five. Another important development that will be discussed below (Chapters Two and Four) concerns the case of imperfect information, at the end of each stage, as to the actual choice of the other side at that stage (sometimes called "imperfect monitoring"). The topic of averaging by discounting has also been investigated; we return to this in Section 6c of Chapter Two ("Repeated Games with Incomplete Information: A Survey of Recent Results").

In direction (b), "Completing and deepening the results", explicit optimal strategies for the uninformed player (Player 2) have been found for all games in the class considered in this chapter (Postscript d). Also, the second order properties of the limiting process—i.e., the error term in the formula (5.24) for the value v_n of the n-stage game—have been thoroughly investigated (Postscript c).

Postscript a is devoted to a discussion of martingales and their relationship to the contents of this chapter. In Postscript b we discuss a simplified (but less constructive) proof of Lemma 5.3 (that Player 1 can assure himself cav $u(p)$, where cav u is the concavification of u). In Postscript e we show that v_n is a non-increasing function of n; this follows from the so-called "recursive structure" of Γ_n—a formula that expresses the function $v_n(p)$ in terms of the function $v_{n-1}(p)$.

In these postscripts, we denote Players 1 and 2 by P1 and P2, respectively.

a. Martingales

Intuitively, underlying this chapter—and indeed, much of the whole book—is the theory of martingales. A *martingale* is defined (Section 5, Step 5) (see Doob [1953]) as a sequence of random variables $x_1, x_2, \ldots$, with $\mathrm{Exp}(x_{i+1} \mid x_i) = x_i$ for each i. If P2 knew P1's mixed strategy in Γ_∞, then the sequence of his posteriors p_i that P1 is really of type A would constitute a martingale.[14] The *martingale convergence theorem* [Doob, 1953] asserts that a

---

[14]See (5.6). Indeed, posterior (conditional) probabilities always form a martingale as more and more information becomes available. Explicitly, let E be an event with probability p, and let S be a signal that may be received about the state of the world. Then the conditional probability of E given the signal S is a random variable that depends on the true state of the world; the expectation of this random variable is p. It follows that if $S_1, S_2, \ldots$ is a sequence of such signals, and $p_{i+1} := \mathrm{Exp}\,\mathrm{Prob}(E|S_1, S_2, \ldots, S_i)$, then the sequence $p_1, p_2, \ldots$ constitutes a martingale.

bounded martingale converges almost surely. It follows that the p_i converge almost surely, since they are bounded by 1. The limit of the p_i is a random variable, which we call p_∞.

The main theorem of this chapter (Theorem 5.1) has two parts: that P1 can get at least cav $u(p)$ and that P2 can hold the payoff down to cav $u(p)$. To prove the latter, we make use of the principle that P1 cannot use his information without revealing it (see footnote 3 below), and that partial use is associated with partial revelation. Explicitly, if at stage i, P1 uses different strategies s_i and t_i depending on whether he is of type A or B, then the posterior probability p_{i+1} will be different from p_i. Moreover if s_i and t_i are *very* different, then p_{i+1} is likely also to be very different from p_i (unless p_i is close to 0 or 1). From $p_i \rightarrow p_\infty$ it follows that p_{i+1} is eventually close to p_i, and hence, unless $p_\infty = 0$ or 1, that s_i and t_i are almost equal; i.e., that P1 plays in a way that is almost independent of his type. He then gets a payoff that is close to the payoff $u(p_i)$ that he could guarantee by playing totally independently of his type, and this, in turn, is close to $u(p_\infty)$. It may be seen that a similar conclusion holds when $p_\infty = 0$ or 1. This reasoning holds for all sufficiently large i, and in Γ_∞, these are what determine the payoff. We thus conclude that the largest expected payoff that P1 can guarantee by any particular mixed strategy is $= \text{Exp}\, u(p_\infty) \leq \text{Exp cav}\, u(p_\infty) \leq \text{cav}\, u(\text{Exp}\, p_\infty) = \text{cav}\, u(p)$, where the first inequality follows from $u \leq \text{cav}\, u$, and the second from the concavity of cav u.

Of course, the above is only meant to be suggestive, it is not a proof. The proof is given in the body of this chapter.

b. Convexity and Concavity as Monotonicity in Information

The probability of a person P for an event E is a random variable that depends on P 's information about the state of the world. Convexity of a function w of P 's probabilities p may be interpreted as a kind of monotonicity of w as a function of the information available to P : the more information, the larger, "on the average", is w.

Explicitly, when P gets more information, his probability p for E is replaced by a distribution of posterior probabilities p' whose expectation is p. Convexity says that for all p and all such distributions p',

$$w(p) = w(\operatorname{Exp} p') \leq \operatorname{Exp} w(p'),$$

which is precisely what we mean by w increasing "on the average". A dual statement applies to concavity.

This fundamental fact yields an alternative proof that P1 can get at least cav $u(p)$ in Γ_∞; i.e., of Lemma 5.3, which says that $\underline{v}_\infty(p) \geq \operatorname{cav} u(p)$, where $\underline{v}_\infty(p)$ is the most that P1 can guarantee in $\Gamma_\infty(p)$ (see Postscript h to Chapter Two for a precise definition). In the body of this chapter, this is proved by explicitly exhibiting a strategy for P1 that guarantees cav $u(p)$. Alternatively, the result follows if one shows that $\underline{v}_\infty(p) \geq u(p)$ and that $\underline{v}_\infty$ is concave in p. That $\underline{v}_\infty(p) \geq u(p)$ follows from the fact that by ignoring his information completely, P1 can always obtain at least $u(p)$. That $\underline{v}_\infty$ is concave means that P2's corresponding payoff $-\underline{v}_\infty$ is convex, and we have just seen that that simply means that P2's value is monotonic in his information: the more information P2 has, the higher (weakly) is his payoff. In a two-person zero sum game, one can never lose by getting more information, and hence $-\underline{v}_\infty$ is indeed convex. Similar methods show that also $v_n \geq \operatorname{cav} u$. For details, see Chapter Four, (7.16).

c. The Error Term

The error term in (5.24) has been thoroughly investigated by Zamir [1972] and by Mertens and Zamir [1976b, 1977a]. Formula (5.24) itself asserts that the error term is always $O(1/\sqrt{n})$. In many cases it is, however, much smaller. For example, in the game of Section 2, the error term has order of magnitude $\log n/n$; and in Games 1 and 2 (below), the order of magnitude is $1/n$. Of course, the error term may vanish identically; for example, in the game of Section 3, $v_n(p) = \operatorname{cav} u(p) = 0$ for all n. A game for which the order of magnitude of the error is $1/\sqrt{n}$ —the largest possible—is Game 3.

−2	0
0	−1

−1	0
0	−2

Game 1

1	0
−1	−2

−2	−1
0	1

Game 2

3	−1
−3	1

2	−2
−2	2

Game 3

All these assertions hold for any p with $0 < p < 1$.

More generally, Zamir has proved the following results, which for simplicity we state only for the case $\kappa = 2$ (two possible stage games). For the formulation for arbitrary κ, see Zamir [1972].

THEOREM N1. *Suppose $u(p)$ is twice differentiable for all p, with a second derivative that is strictly negative and bounded away from zero.*[15] *Then for each p,*

$$v_n(p) = \operatorname{cav} u(p) + O(\log n / n).$$

---

[15] A function f is *bounded away from zero* if there is a positive constant δ such that $|f| \geq \delta$ throughout its domain. Such a function need not be bounded.

THEOREM N2. *Suppose that* $(\text{cav } u(p) - u(p))/(p(1-p))^{3/2}$ *is strictly positive for* $0 < p < 1$, *and is bounded away from zero. Then for each* p,

$$v_n(p) = \text{cav } u(p) + O(1/n).$$

For example, in the game of Section 2, we have $u(p) = \text{cav } u(p) = p(1-p)$; thus $u''(p) = -2$, which is bounded away from zero. Hence Theorem N1 yields an error term of $O(\log n/n)$. In fact, the error term is asymptotic to $\log n/16n$.

In Game 1,

$$u(p) = -\frac{2}{3} - \frac{p(1-p)}{3};$$

thus $\text{cav } u(p) = -2/3$ identically, so we have $\text{cav } u(p) - u(p) = p(1-p)/3$. In Game 2,

$$u(p) = \max\{-p, -(1-p)\};$$

thus $\text{cav } u(p) = 0$ identically, and $\text{cav } u(p) - u(p) = \min\{p, 1-p\}$. In both these cases, therefore, Theorem N2 yields error terms that are $O(1/n)$.

In Game 3, $u(p) = \text{cav } u(p) = 0$ identically for all p. Hence the error term $= v_n(p)$. Mertens and Zamir [1976b] have shown that in this example, $\lim \sqrt{n}v_n(p)$ exists and equals the normal density at the p'th quantile x_p of the normal distribution; i.e.,

$$v_n(p) \sim e^{-x_p^2/2}/\sqrt{2\pi n}$$

as $n \to \infty$, where $\sim$ means "asymptotic to", and x_p is such that

$$p = \frac{1}{\sqrt{2\pi}} \int_{-\infty}^{x_p} e^{-x^2/2} dx.$$

Geometrically, the hypothesis of Theorem N1 implies that u is strictly concave and smooth; since $\text{cav } u$ is always the concavification of u, this implies that $\text{cav } u = u$. The hypothesis of Theorem N2 implies that except at the end points ($p = 0$ and $p = 1$), u lies strictly below $\text{cav } u$ (which implies that $\text{cav } u$ is linear). At the endpoints, the graphs of $\text{cav } u$ and u may meet at positive angles (as in Section 3 and in Game 1), or they may be asymptotic; in the latter case, the hypothesis forbids the asymptotic approach from being too close. For example, the conclusion will not in general hold when cav $u(p) - u(p)$ has order of magnitude p^2 as $p \to 0$.

Theorems N1 and N2, and Game 3, represent three situations that are conceptually very different as far as P1's long-run policy is concerned. The concavity of u in Theorem N1 implies that for the long run, it is positively harmful for P1 to reveal his type, even partially, and hence he had better use his information very sparingly. The situation in Theorem N2 is the precise opposite: since u lies strictly below its concavification cav u, it is vital for the long run that P1 use his information essentially fully, and essentially from the very beginning, even though he thereby reveals it. Indeed, as long as he does not use his information at all, he will be getting $u(p)$ rather than cav $u(p)$; and making only partial use of his information—revealing partially—is like moving to different probabilities q in the interior of the interval, so that $u(q)$ is still considerably smaller than cav $u(q)$. Game 3 represents a situation that in a sense lies exactly inbetween these two extremes: both u and cav u are flat, so from the long-run point of view, it does not matter whether P1 reveals his information or not.

Heuristically, these differences explain why it is plausible that the orders of magnitude of the error terms in Theorems N1 and N2 are smaller than in Game 3. In the situations of Theorems N1 and N2, any revelation or concealment will have a significant, first-order effect on the main term cav $u(p)$ in (5.24) (the asymptotic formula for the value v_n of the n-stage game when n is large). Considerations of maximizing the main term will therefore dominate the thinking of P1; he will not take any action that will prejudice the main term of his payoff. But in Game 3, no amount of revelation or concealment will affect the main term, since $u = $ cav u, and the graph of these functions is a straight line. Therefore P1 may orchestrate the pace of revelation so as to maximize the error term, and that is what leads to the relatively large error term in this game.

The above examples illustrate these ideas. Let us start by taking $p = 1/2$ in Game 2. If the game is played only once and P1 is of type A (the left matrix), then it is optimal for him to play top; for type B, on the other hand, bottom is optimal. Moreover, these strategies are strictly dominating (i.e., strictly better for P1 than

his other choice, no matter what P2 does). Suppose now that the
game is played n times. If P1 makes full use of his information immediately, i.e., plays top or bottom at the first stage, according as
to whether he is of type A or B, then he reveals his information[16]
for all subsequent stages. Thus we are led to a situation in which
the true matrix is common knowledge; therefore, starting at the
second stage, the payoff will be 0 (the value of both the left and
right matrices). But at the first stage itself, P2 does not yet have
the information; he cannot do better than randomizing half-half,
yielding a payoff of 1/2 to P1 for that stage. Since the payoff is
0 at all subsequent stages, the average payoff is $1/2n$, which is
the precise order of magnitude for the error term that is given by
Theorem N2. Thus we see that in this case, P1 cannot do better
than making use of his information immediately, at least insofar
as the order of magnitude is concerned.

The situation in Game 1 is similar, but slightly more subtle. If
it were common knowledge that the left matrix is being played, it
would be optimal for P1 and P2 to use mixed strategies that assign
probabilities 1/3 to "Top" and "Left" respectively; for the right
matrix, these probabilities would be 2/3. In this case, though, it
is not clear what it means for P1 to "make full use of his information immediately". Indeed, if P1 were to use the above mixed
strategy from the very beginning, then his expected payoff at each
stage would be exactly cav $u(p) = -2/3$; i.e., the error term would
vanish completely, and thus P1 would not gain even a second order advantage from his superior knowledge (over and above what
he gets simply by revealing his type to P2). Moreover, he would
not be "revealing fully immediately;" since P1's action at the first
stage depends on his type only probabilistically, P2 would not be
able to deduce P1's type from P1's action with certainty. Assume,

---

[16]We cannot emphasize too heavily that this "revelation", as well as all the
other "revelations" discussed here, are "as if". For P2 actually to deduce
anything about P1's type from P1's actions, he would have to know which
mixed strategy P1 is using in the n-stage game Γ_n; and of course, he does
not in general really know this. What justifies the "as if" argument is the
minimax theorem, according to which an optimal mixed strategy for P1 in Γ_n
assures him at least the value v_n of the game no matter what P2 does, *even if
P2 knows that P1 is using this strategy.* See the discussion just before Step 1
in the proof of Theorem 5.1. In brief, we say that P1 is making a "revelation"
each time that his mixed strategy calls for his two types to behave differently.

for example, that $p = 1/2$ originally. If P1 is really of type A, and the pure choice actually made by his mixed strategy at the first stage is "bottom" (as is more probable), then after the first stage, P2's posterior probability that P1 is indeed of type A is not 1 but $2/3$. The fact that the revelation is not full leads one to think that perhaps the *use* that P1 is making of his information also is not as full as it could be.

And, indeed, while P1 cannot get much more than $-2/3$, he *can* do a little better. By considerations of symmetry, P2 will play half-half at the first stage. Suppose now that with certainty, P1 plays bottom if he is of type A, and top if he is of type B. Then he reveals his type fully, but his expected payoff at the first stage is $-1/2$ rather than $-2/3$. He thus gains $1/6$ over cav $u(p)$ at the first stage, and nothing thereafter; the average, $1/6n$, is again precisely of the order of magnitude predicted by Theorem N2.

Roughly speaking, what is happening in both these examples, as well as in Theorem N2 in general, is the following: As long as P1 fails to make use of his information, he cannot get more than $u(p)$, which is considerably less than the amount cav $u(p)$ that he could be getting. Therefore it is not worthwhile for P1 to postpone making use of his information; he should do so immediately. At the first stage at which P1 does make use of his information, he may gain a one-time advantage (since P2 does not yet have the information at that stage), and this is what leads to the error term of $O(1/n)$.

In actuality, the story is complicated somewhat by the possibility of revelation that is gradual and/or partial. Assume for simplicity that the graphs of u and cav u actually make positive angles with each other at $p = 0$ and $p = 1$; i.e., that $(\text{cav}\, u(p) - u(p))/p(1 - p)$ is bounded away from zero. These conditions ensure that as long as there is any significant deviation from full revelation—any considerable probability that P2's posterior p_i is near neither 0 nor 1—then P1's per stage payoff Exp $u(p_i)$ will be considerably below the amount cav $u(p)$ that he could have gotten by revealing fully immediately. Any failure to make full and immediate use of the information available to P1 is thus punished by an amount whose order of magnitude is $1/n$ times the *total number of stages* during which this information is not fully used. On the other hand, each partial revelation is accompanied by a *one-time* reward, which can change the payoff in Γ_n by at most $O(1/n)$. Under these circumstances, it is obviously not worthwhile for P1 to incur any significant delay in making full use of his information. Therefore about the best that he can do is to reveal fully and immediately, and to take his one-time profit from P2's one-time ignorance. We thus again get $O(1/n)$ for the error term.

The situation in Theorem N1 is in a sense opposite to the above. Because u is strictly concave, revelations cause long-term damage; but like above, they may, and usually do, have one-time rewards. If the error term is to be positive, it can only be as the cumulative result of one or more one-time gains; but such gains can only come as the result of revelations, which cause long-term damage that cancels out much of the one-time gains. This explains the relatively small terror term in this case.

A detailed analysis is, however, more involved in this case than in Theorem N2. One option of P1 is to reveal nothing until the last stage, and only then to make full use of his information. In this way he will make a one-time gain without incurring any long-term damage. But a single one-time gain can only contribute $O(1/n)$ to the error term. An error term of the size indicated by Theorem N1 can only be achieved by making revelations at many stages.

How worthwhile a single revelation is—if at all—depends on two factors: its timing and its "size". The timing of the revelation—how late it comes in the game—has little or no effect on the one-time gain; but from the long-term point of view, the later it comes, the less the damage. The size of the revelation—how much it causes P2's posterior p_i to shift—affects both the one-time reward and the long-term damage. Let us examine each of these two effects separately.

The one-time gain is usually roughly proportional to the distance $\|s_i - t_i\|$ between the i'th stage mixed strategies s_i and t_i of P1$_A$ and P1$_B$; compare (5.9) and (5.19). This, in turn, is $O(\varepsilon_i)$, where ε_i measures the size of the revelation, i.e., by how much the posteriors p_i change between Stages i and $i + 1$; precisely, ε_i may be defined as $\sqrt{\text{Exp}((p_{i+1} - p_i)^2 \mid p_i)}$, the conditional standard deviation of p_{i+1} given p_i (compare (5.11) and (5.23)). Since the payoff in Γ_n is obtained by averaging over all n stages, we conclude that the one-time gain is of order ε_i/n at most.

The long-term damage, on the other hand, is proportional to the loss in conditional expected payoff, $\mathrm{Exp}((u(p_i)-u(p_{i+1))) \mid p_i)$. By expanding u in a Taylor series around p_i, and noting that the linear term disappears (by the martingale condition $\mathrm{Exp}(p_{i+1} \mid p_i) = p_i$), we see that this $\approx (-u''(p_i)/2)\,\mathrm{Exp}((p_{i+1} - p_i)^2 \mid p_i)$, which is of order ε_i^2. The per-stage loss is therefore of order ε_i^2/n. Since $n - i$ stages remain at the time of the revelation, we conclude that the long-term loss is of order $(n - i)\varepsilon_i^2/n$.

Summing up, a revelation can be worthwhile only if the order $(n - i)\varepsilon_i^2/n$ of the loss is not larger than the maximal order ε_i/n of the gain. Thus we must have $\varepsilon_i = O(1/(n - i))$. For the total of all one-time gains we therefore get

$$O\left[\sum_{i=1}^{n-1} \varepsilon_i\right] = O\left[\sum_{i=1}^{n-1} \frac{1}{n-i}\right] = O\left[\sum_{i=1}^{n-1} \frac{1}{i}\right] = O(\log n),$$

and so the average is $O(\log n/n)$. This is the gross; what really interests us is the net, obtained from the gross by subtracting the sum of all the long-term damages. But the net cannot be larger than the gross, so that $\log n/n$ is the maximum order of magnitude for the net as well.

Intuitively, because u is smooth and strictly concave, the per-stage long-term damage from a revelation behaves like the square of its size (Figure 20), whereas the one-time gain is linear in its size. Thus at any given stage, a revelation is likely to be worthwhile if it is sufficiently small. On the other hand, for the long-term damage, the timing is important. Near the beginning of the game, P1 can afford only very small revelations, as he will suffer the long-term damage from them throughout the remainder of the game. As the game progresses, each unit of long-term damage becomes less and less important, and so the revelations can be made larger and larger. Since the gains depend linearly on the sizes

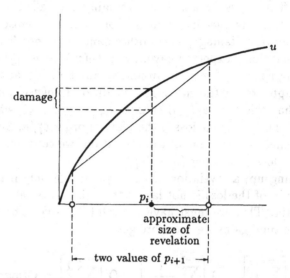

Figure 20. The per-stage long-term damage
from a revelation

of the revelations, we get a series of ever increasing revelations,
which leads to the error term in Theorem N1.

We end this note by a brief discussion of the requirements in
Theorems N1 and N2 governing the behavior of u near the endpoints of the interval $[0,1]$. In Theorem N1 the requirement is that
u'' be bounded away from 0, and in Theorem N2 it is that u should
not approach the linear function cav u too rapidly. The content
of both requirements is that the conditions on u that enable the
proofs to work be maintained throughout the interval. Thus in
Theorem N1, the requirement implies that the order of magnitude of the long-term damage from a single revelation is at least
the square of its size, *uniformly* in the posterior p_i; and in Theorem N2, that any failure to reveal immediately causes damage that
is "considerable", no matter what p is. If these requirements were
not met, then as the posteriors p_i approach the endpoints, one
would approach a situation that is conceptually closer and closer
to that of Game 3 (where u is linear), and this, like in Game 3,
could lead to a larger error term.

Games of the type of Game 3, in which the normal distribution plays a role in the error term, have been investigated further by De Meyer [1989], [1992].

d. Optimal Strategies of the Uninformed Player

In Section 6, an explicit optimal strategy for P2 was presented, for the specific game treated in Section 2. We now show that the same kind of strategy works for any game of the class considered in this Chapter (incomplete information on one side).

Like in the case discussed in Section 6, the idea is for P2 to keep track of the payoffs that each of the two possible types of P1 would get. Thus one is led to a game with vector payoffs in the sense of Blackwell [1956]. One then constructs a vector (x, y) such that the area or "quadrant" to the "southwest" of (x, y) is approachable for P2 in an appropriate sense, and such that the expected payoff $px + (1 - p)y$ from this vector is cav $u(p)$. Any strategy with which P2 can indeed assure approaching this quadrant is optimal for him. Below, we will construct such a strategy explicitly; it is similar to that described in Section 6 for the special case treated there.

As sometimes happens, the treatment becomes both notationally simpler and conceptually more transparent in the more general case, when P1 can be any one of κ types, rather than just two. Thus we consider the game with κ-dimensional vector payoffs, each coordinate representing the payoff to a different type of P1. We use x (rather than (x, y)) to denote such a vector payoff, and p (rather than $(p, 1 - p)$) to denote the vector of initial probabilities (one for each type). Denote by S_x the "orthant" to the "southwest" of x; that is, the set of vectors ξ each of whose coordinates is $\leq$ the corresponding coordinate of x. Call S_x *e-approachable* ("e-" for expectation) if P2 has a strategy τ in Γ_∞ such that for each strategy σ of P1, the expected average vector payoff for the first n stages of Γ_∞ approaches S_x as $n \to \infty$. That S_x is e-approachable means that P2 can force the expected vector payoff in Γ_∞ into S_x. The fundamental result is

THEOREM N3. *S_x is e-approachable if and only if $q \cdot x \geq$ cav $u(q)$ for all probability vectors q (not just the "true" one p).*

Here $q \cdot x := \sum_{k=1}^{\kappa} q^k x^k$ is the overall (scalar) expectation of the vector payoff x when the probabilities of the coordinates (i.e., of the stage games) are given by q.

Before proving Theorem N3, we show how P2 can use it to construct an optimal strategy in $\Gamma_\infty(p)$. First he must construct a vector x for which

$$S_x \text{ is e-approachable and } p \cdot x = \text{cav } u(p). \tag{N1}$$

Once he has such an x, he can use the explicit strategy described below (at the beginning of the "if" part of Theorem N3's proof) actually to e-approach S_x. His expected payment to P1 is then $\leq p \cdot x = \text{cav } u(p)$; and he can do no better than that, as P1 can guarantee at least cav $u(p)$ (e.g., by ignoring his information after a possible one-time "split"; see Lemma 5.2). So this is indeed optimal for P2.

To construct an x satisfying (N1), we start by returning to the case of two stage games ($\kappa = 2$). Since cav u is concave, there is a line $\mathcal{L}$ passing through the point $(p, \text{cav } u(p))$ and supporting the graph of cav u (Figure 21). Define x as the vector whose coordinates are the intercepts of $\mathcal{L}$ with the vertical lines at the endpoints $q = (1, 0)$ and $q = (0, 1)$ of the interval.

To see that this x satisfies (N1), let L be the linear function defined by $L(q) := q \cdot x$. Two points on the line $\mathcal{L}$, namely $((1,0), x^1)$ and $((0,1), x^2)$, lie on the graph of L. Since L is linear, it follows that each point of $\mathcal{L}$ is in the graph of L. In particular, the point $(p, \text{cav } u(p))$ is in the graph of L; that is, $p \cdot x = \text{cav } u(p)$. Moreover, $q \cdot x \geq \text{cav } u(q)$ for all q, as $\mathcal{L}$ supports the graph of cav u; hence, by Theorem N3, S_x is e-approachable. Thus both parts of (N1) are verified.

When cav u is smooth (differentiable) at p, then $\mathcal{L}$ must be tangent to the graph of cav u at p (Figure 21). In that case there is a unique x satisfying (N1), which is easily calculated from p, cav $u(p)$, and the derivative of cav u at p. If cav u has a kink (non-differentiability) at p, then there is a whole range of supporting lines (Figure 22). Each of them determines an x satisfying (N1),

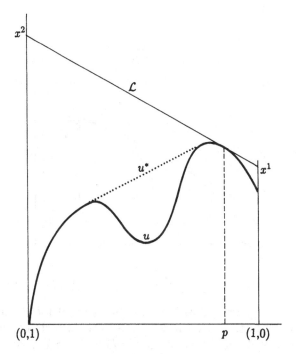

Figure 21. The support $\mathcal{L}$ in the smooth case

i.e., an optimal strategy for P2 in $\Gamma_\infty(p)$; and all such x are determined in this way. In the vector payoff space, the set of all such
x is an interval.

In the general case, when $\kappa > 2$, the procedure is entirely analogous; one must only replace the line $\mathcal{L}$ by a hyperplane. The
intercepts of this hyperplane with the "vertical" lines over the
vertices of the q-simplex are then the coordinates of x.

It should be noted that the idea of e-approachability is entirely
independent of which probability vector actually represents P2's
beliefs. Thus for *every* probability vector p—not just the "true"
one—there is an x such that S_x is e-approachable, and $p \cdot x =$
cav $u(p)$. Consider, for example, the game of Section 2. From
Theorem N3 it follows that P2 can, if he wishes, play to assure that
he will pay no more than $1/9$ to $P1_A$ or $4/9$ to $P1_B$ (Figure 23).
If the initial probabilities were $2/3$ for G_A and $1/3$ for G_B, this
would yield an expectation of $2/9$, which is the value $v_\infty(2/3)$

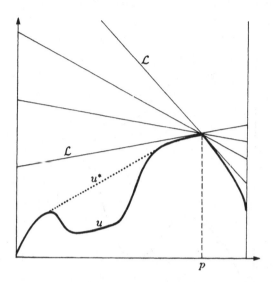

Figure 22. Supports $\mathcal{L}$ in the non-smooth case

of the infinite game; thus it would be optimal for P2 to play in this way. Since the initial probabilities are, in fact, $1/2$–$1/2$, such play would yield an expectation of $5/18$, which is more than the expectation of $1/4$ that P2 (who is the minimizer) can assure; so it is not especially worthwhile for him. But if P2 does for some particular reason want to drive $P1_A$'s payoff down to $1/9$, he *can* do so—at the expense of paying $4/9$ (rather than $1/4$) to $P1_B$. In brief, the set of vector payoffs that P2 can assure in Γ_∞ does not at all depend on the initial probability.

We come now to the

PROOF OF THEOREM N3: Only if: By e-approaching S_x, P2 can assure a payoff $\leq q \cdot x$ in $\Gamma_\infty(q)$. But P1 can assure $\geq u(q)$ by ignoring his information and playing optimally at each stage as if the true probability distribution were q. So $q \cdot x \geq u(q)$ for all q. Hence $q \cdot x \geq$ cav $u(q)$, as $q \cdot x$ is linear in q, and therefore concave.

If:[17] We proceed as in Section 6. At the first stage, P2 makes an arbitrary choice. Subsequently, let ξ_n^k be the average payoff to P1's type k up to[18] stage n. Let ζ_n be the closest point to

---

[17] See the end of the proof for an intuitive sketch.
[18] "Up to" will always mean "up to and including".

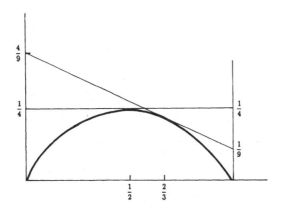

Figure 23. Payoff pairs that P2 can assure

ξ_n in S_x; then at the next stage, P2 plays optimally in $\Delta_1(p_n)$ (the one-shot game in which neither player is informed), where the probability vector p_n is chosen proportional to $\xi_n - \zeta_n$ when $\xi_n \notin S_x$, and is chosen arbitrarily when $\xi_n \in S_x$.

We must show that this strategy assures that the average vector payoff e-approaches S_x. Assume $x = (0, \ldots, 0)$ (otherwise, subtract x^k from each entry of the k'th stage game G^k). Denote the vector payoff at stage n by x_n; let $X_n := x_1 + x_2 + \cdots + x_n$, and define $\hat{X}_n$ by $\hat{X}_n^k := \max(X_n^k, 0)$. Thus $\hat{X}_n$ is in the non-negative orthant of κ-space, and indeed is the closest point in that orthant to X_n. Setting $\hat{\xi}_n := \hat{X}_n/n$, note that $\hat{\xi}_n = \xi_n - \zeta_n$ (Figure 24). We claim that

$$\hat{X}_n \cdot \mathrm{Exp}(x_{n+1} \mid \hat{X}_n) \le 0 \qquad (N2)$$

for all values of $\hat{X}_n$. Indeed, $\hat{X}_n = n\hat{\xi}_n = n(\xi_n - \zeta_n) = \alpha_n p_n$, where α_n is a non-negative scalar. So $\hat{X}_n \cdot \mathrm{Exp}(x_{n+1} \mid \hat{X}_n) = \alpha_n \mathrm{Exp}(p_n \cdot x_{n+1} \mid \hat{X}_n)$. But $\mathrm{Exp}(p_n \cdot x_{n+1} \mid \hat{X}_n)$ is just the expectation of the outcome when P2 plays optimally in $\Delta_1(p_n)$, so it is $\le u(p_n) \le \mathrm{cav}\, u(p_n) \le p_n \cdot x = 0$ (since $x = (0, \ldots 0)$); so (N2) is proved.

Let M be a bound on the absolute values of the entries in the payoff matrices of all the stage games G^k. We claim that

$$\mathrm{Exp}\, \|\hat{X}_n\|^2 \le 3\kappa M^2 n, \qquad (N3)$$

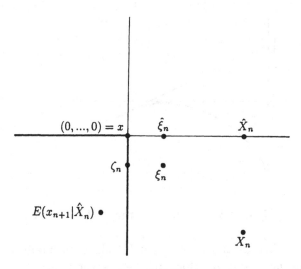

Figure 24. Proof of Theorem N3

where $\| \ \|$ is the euclidean norm. Proceeding by induction, assume (N3) for n. Set $\hat{x}_n := \hat{X}_n - \hat{X}_{n-1}$. Then $|\hat{x}_n^k| \leq |x_n^k|$ for all k, whence $\|\hat{x}_n\| \leq \|x_n\| \leq M\sqrt{\kappa}$; so

$$
\begin{aligned}
\mathrm{Exp}\,\|\hat{X}_{n+1}\|^2 &= \mathrm{Exp}(\|\hat{X}_n + \hat{x}_{n+1}\|^2) \\
&= \mathrm{Exp}(\|\hat{X}_n\|^2 + \|\hat{x}_{n+1}\|^2 + 2\hat{X}_n \cdot \hat{x}_{n+1}) \\
&\leq \kappa M^2(3n+1) + 2\,\mathrm{Exp}(\hat{X}_n \cdot \mathrm{Exp}(\hat{x}_{n+1}|\hat{X}_n)).
\end{aligned}
$$

Thus it suffices to show that $\hat{X}_n \cdot \mathrm{Exp}(\hat{x}_{n+1} \mid \hat{X}_n) \leq \kappa M^2$ for all values of $\hat{X}_n$; so by (N2), that

$$
\hat{X}_n \cdot \mathrm{Exp}((\hat{x}_{n+1} - x_{n+1})|\hat{X}_n) \leq \kappa M^2. \tag{N4}
$$

Now if $\hat{X}_n^k \geq M$, then *a fortiori* $\hat{X}_n^k \geq 0$, so $X_n^k = \hat{X}_n^k \geq M$, so $X_{n+1}^k = X_n^k + x_{n+1}^k \geq M - M = 0$, so $\hat{X}_{n+1}^k = X_{n+1}^k$, so $\hat{x}_{n+1}^k = x_{n+1}^k$, so

$$
\hat{X}_n^k\,\mathrm{Exp}((\hat{x}_{n+1}^k - x_{n+1}^k) \mid \hat{X}_n) = 0 < M^2; \tag{N5}
$$

and if $\hat{X}_n^k < M$, then $\hat{X}_n^k \operatorname{Exp}((\hat{x}_{n+1}^k - x_{n+1}^k)|\hat{X}_n) \leq M \max |x_{n+1}^k|$
$\leq M^2$, since x_{n+1}^k and $\hat{x}_{n+1}^k$ have the same sign. Combining this
with (N5) and summing over k, we obtain (N4), and so (N3) for
all n.

Let δ_n denote the euclidean distance between $\operatorname{Exp} \xi_n$ and S_x.
Since $\zeta_n \in S_x$ and S_x is convex, it follows that $\zeta_n \in S_x$. So

$$\delta_n \leq \|(\operatorname{Exp} \xi_n) - (\operatorname{Exp} \zeta_n)\| = \| \operatorname{Exp}(\xi_n - \zeta_n)\|$$
$$= \| \operatorname{Exp} \hat{\xi}_n \| \leq \operatorname{Exp} \|\hat{\xi}_n\|,$$

by the triangle inequality. By Schwarz's inequality and (N3),

$$(\operatorname{Exp} \|\hat{\xi}_n\|)^2 \leq \operatorname{Exp} \|\hat{\xi}_n\|^2 = \operatorname{Exp} \|\hat{X}_n\|^2/n^2 \leq 3\kappa M^2/n; \quad \text{(N6)}$$

so we conclude that $\delta_n \leq C/\sqrt{n}$, where C is the constant $M\sqrt{3\kappa}$.
This proves Theorem N3. ∎

The idea of the proof is that whenever the average vector payoff
ξ_n is outside S_x, P2 drives it towards S_x; i.e., towards the point ζ_n
in S_x that is nearest to ξ_n (Figure 24). Thus if p_n is a probability
vector with direction $\hat{\xi}_n := \xi_n - \zeta_n$, then P2 uses a stage strategy
that minimizes the component of x_{n+1} (the next stage vector payoff) in the direction p_n. Since we have taken $x = (0, \ldots, 0)$, the
hypothesis of the theorem yields $u(p_n) \leq p_n \cdot (0, \ldots, 0) = 0$; so by
playing optimally in $\Delta_1(p_n)$, P2 can actually force a non-positive
payoff in $\Delta_1(p_n)$. But the payoff in $\Delta_1(p_n)$ is merely the vector
payoff weighted by the p_n^k, i.e., the component of x_{n+1} in the direction p_n. So P2 can force this component to be non-positive.
Thus the sum of payoffs does not increase in the direction of p_n,
so the average decreases.

The technical expression of this idea is (N2), which says that
x_{n+1} is never positively correlated with $\hat{X}_n$. If we could replace[19]
$\hat{X}_n$ by X_n we could deduce, by induction, that the variance of
the sum X_n of the previous x_i is $\leq$ the sum of the variances of
those x_i, and so is $O(n)$; so $\operatorname{Var} \xi_n$ would be $O(n)/n^2 = O(1/n)$.
In fact, we cannot replace $\hat{X}_n$ by X_n; but by doing so, and then
estimating the resulting error ((N4)), we *can* conclude ((N3)) that
$\operatorname{Var} \hat{X}_n = O(n)$, which suffices.

---

[19] Recall that $\xi_n = X_n/n$ and $\hat{\xi}_n = \hat{X}_n/n$.

Note that Theorem N3 provides an independent proof for that part of the main theorem of this chapter according to which P2 can hold the expected payoff down to cav $u(p)$. One can also go in the opposite direction: derive Theorem N3 from the main theorem of this chapter. In fact, Blackwell's [1956] characterization of convex closed approachable sets, and the relations between approachability and excludability proved by him, can all be derived from the main theorem of this chapter. But for an explicit optimal strategy for P2, we must still use the method of Blackwell described above.

The proof has several other implications worth noting. First, in the course of proving e-approachability, we actually prove something stronger, namely Exp $\|\hat{\xi}_n\| \to 0$ (see (N6)). That is, not only does the expectation of the average vector payoff ξ_n approach the corner S_x, but also the expectation of the distance between ξ_n and S_x tends to 0. It follows immediately that ξ_n approaches S_x in probability, i.e., that for each positive ε there is an N such that for all $n > N$, the probability is at least $1 - \varepsilon$ that ξ_n is within ε of S_x. Using Exp $\|\hat{\xi}_n\| = O(1/\sqrt{n})$ (see (N6)), and mimicking the proof of the strong law of large numbers, one can establish the still stronger result that ξ_n approaches S_x with probability 1. This, indeed, is Blackwell's [1956] definition of approachability.

The second implication is the speed of convergence, $O(1\sqrt{n})$. For one thing, this yields an alternative proof for something already proved in the body of the text, namely $v_n - v_\infty = O(1/\sqrt{n})$. But it goes further than that. That $v_n - v_\infty = O(1/\sqrt{n})$ means that P2 can hold P1 to within $O(1/\sqrt{n})$ of v_∞ in the game Γ_n; but in principle, this might require a strategy for P2 that depends on n from the very beginning. The proof of Theorem N3 implies that P2 has a single strategy in Γ_∞ that assures him an expected payoff $\leq v_\infty + O(1/\sqrt{n})$ simultaneously[20] in all the games Γ_n.

---

[20]No such result holds for P1. For example, when u is strictly concave (as in Section 2), P1 cannot guarantee any error term at all for all n simultaneously, as even the slightest one-time "revelation" has a permanent first-order effect.

e. Monotonicity of v_n and the Recursive Structure of Γ_n

It is relatively easy to prove that

$$nv_n + mv_m \geq (n+m)v_{n+m} \qquad \text{(N7)}$$

for all n and m, and from this it follows that

$$v_n \geq \lim v_n \qquad \text{(N8)}$$

for all n. Indeed, (N7) follows from the fact that P2 can play the first n stages in Γ_{n+m} as if he were playing Γ_n, then ignore everything he learned in those stages, and play the last m stages as if he were playing Γ_m. From (N7) we obtain

$$v_n \geq v_{nk} \qquad \text{(N9)}$$

for all n and k, and then (N8) follows if we let $k \to \infty$.

The above derivation of (N8) uses the fact that $\lim v_n$ exists. This, in turn, is a consequence of the main theorem of this chapter, Theorem 5.1, whose proof lies comparatively deep. One can, however, use (N7) directly to give a comparatively simple proof that $\lim v_n$ exists; from this it follows as in Step 7 in the proof of Theorem 5.1 that also v_∞ (the value of the infinite stage game) exists.

To prove that $\lim v_n$ exists, assume without loss of generality that all the entries in the game matrices G_A and G_B are nonnegative; let M be a bound for these entries. Then the sequence $\{v_n\}$ is also bounded by M; hence $\liminf v_n$ exists and is finite. Let $\{n_j\}$ be a sequence such that

$$v_{n_j} \to \liminf v_n \qquad \text{(N10)}$$

as $j \to \infty$. Now for an arbitrary n and a fixed j, write $n = qn_j + r$, where $0 \leq r < n_j$. From (N7) and (N9) it then follows that

$$nv_n \leq qn_j v_{n_j} + rv_r \leq nv_{n_j} + n_j M. \qquad \text{(N11)}$$

Keeping j fixed, divide (N11) by n, and let $n \to \infty$; it follows that $\limsup v_n \leq v_{n_j}$ for all j. Now let $j \to \infty$ and use (N10);

it follows that $\limsup v_n \leq \liminf v_n$, which means that $\lim v_n$ exists, as asserted.

In view of (N8), one may ask whether v_n is monotonically non-increasing as a function of n, i.e., whether

$$v_{n+1} \leq v_n \qquad\qquad (N12)$$

for all n. The answer is "yes", but the proof lies deeper than the above. It was first proved by Stearns in the late sixties, but that proof was never published, even in report form. Given an optimal strategy for P1 in Γ_{n+1}, Stearns constructs a strategy for him in Γ_n that yields him at least as much. Here we present an entirely different proof of (N12), due to Sorin [1979], which is based on the "recursive structure" of Γ_n. This structure is worth exhibiting in its own right, as it plays an important role in many areas of the theory.

THEOREM N4. *For any probability vector* $p = (p^1, p^2, \ldots, p^\kappa)$, *and any* n, *we have*[21]

$$(n+1)v_{n+1}(p) = \max_\sigma \min_\tau [\gamma_1(\sigma, \tau) + \mathrm{Exp}\, nv_n(p_2)], \qquad (N13)$$

where σ *and* τ *range over the strategies of P1 and P2 respectively in* Γ_1 *(the one-stage game),* γ_1 *is the payoff function in* Γ_1, *and* p_2 *is P2's conditional probability vector after the single stage of* Γ_1 *has been played (but before he knows his payoff), given that P1's mixed strategy in* Γ_1 *was indeed* σ, *and given P1's pure choice.*

As usual, p_2 is a random variable, depending on the pure choice made by P1 in accordance with his mixed strategy σ.

For a proof of (N13), see Zamir [1972]. Intuitively, we may suppose that P1 and P2 use optimal mixed strategies $\sigma*$ and $\tau*$ in Γ_{n+1}, which induce mixed strategies σ and τ for the first stage. The expected payoff for that stage is then $\gamma_1(\sigma, \tau)$. Since $\sigma*$ is optimal, P1 may announce it without losing anything; and then after the first stage, P2, having observed the pure choice of P1 at the first stage, will have the probability vector p_2 for the true game being played. After the first stage, the players are faced with an

---

[21]The general formulation presented here is due to Zamir [1972].

n-stage game; and since $\sigma*$ and $\tau*$ remain optimal after the first stage, they must yield an average payoff of $v_n(p_2)$ for those stages, or a total payoff of $nv_n(p_2)$. Thus the total expected payoff for all $n+1$ stages is the expression inside the square brackets on the right side of (N13). The max min of this expression is therefore the value $(n+1)v_{n+1}(p)$ of $(n+1)\Gamma_{n+1}(p)$ (the $(n+1)$-stage game with total rather than average payoff), which is what (N13) asserts.

Sorin's proof of (N12) proceeds by induction. Suppose it has been proved up to but not including n. Then by (N13), the concavity of v_n, the induction hypothesis, the martingale condition $\operatorname{Exp} p_2 = p$ (see (5.8) or Postscript a), and again (N13), we have

$$(n+1)v_{n+1}(p) = \max_\sigma \min_\tau [\gamma_1(\sigma,\tau) + \operatorname{Exp} nv_n(p_2)]$$
$$= \max_\sigma \min_\tau [\gamma_1(\sigma,\tau) + \operatorname{Exp} v_n(p_2) + \operatorname{Exp}(n-1)v_n(p_2)]$$
$$\leq \max_\sigma \min_\tau [\gamma_1(\sigma,\tau) + v_n(\operatorname{Exp} p_2) + \operatorname{Exp}(n-1)v_{n-1}(p_2)]$$
$$= \max_\sigma \min_\tau [\gamma_1(\sigma,\tau) + v_n(p) + \operatorname{Exp}(n-1)v_{n-1}(p_2)]$$
$$= v_n(p) + \max_\sigma \min_\tau [\gamma_1(\sigma,\tau) + \operatorname{Exp}(n-1)v_{n-1}(p_2)]$$
$$= v_n(p) + nv_n(p) = (n+1)v_n(p),$$

and dividing by $n+1$ yields (N12). (The removal of $v_n(p)$ from the max min on the next-to-last line is permitted because $v_n(p)$, unlike $\operatorname{Exp} v_n(p_2)$, does not depend on σ and τ.)

One may begin the induction in the same way; alternatively, one can note that $v_2 \leq v_1$ follows from (N9). This proves (N12).

CHAPTER TWO

REPEATED GAMES WITH INCOMPLETE
INFORMATION: A SURVEY OF RECENT RESULTS

1. Introduction

Two person games with incomplete information are games in which one or both players are not sure of the payoff function. If such games are played in several stages, there is a danger that a party that lacks some information may gather some of it by observing the actions taken by the other party during the various stages. One question that arises, therefore, is to what extent a party should make use of available information, risking revealing it to the other party.

The present chapter surveys results obtained so far on this question. We have confined ourselves to cases in which the stage games are constant-sum and are repeated without change over and over again. Clearly these limitations are met very seldom, if ever, in real life. Nevertheless, in spite of these simplifying assumptions, the results shed some light on the complex problem of revealing information.

Two somewhat contradictory goals have guided us during the preparation of this survey. One goal was to write the chapter in such a way that a person who is not an expert in game theory should be able to get an idea about the nature of our results. The other goal was to formulate precise statements, actually to describe our results rather than to talk about them. The first goal required many compromises, such as dealing with examples instead of, or prior to, formulating theorems, omitting proofs, and using lengthy explanations. The second goal required the use of some mathematical machinery. We hope that the expert will be able to formulate general statements from our description and that the reader who is little acquainted with game theory will still get the main ideas we wish to convey, even if he skips the mathematical parts. Although the chapter is self-contained, the reader is advised to look at Chapter One, where simpler examples are presented and parts of the mathematical arguments are presented in greater detail.

In Section 2 we discuss the problem of revealing information, and its connection with real life situations. We then proceed by constructing a model in which only one party lacks some relevant information (Section 3). Section 4 deals with the case in which both parties lack some information. This case offers new features. Section 5 deals again with the case in which only one party lacks information but, unlike in Section 3, we relax the assumption that the players' moves become known at the end of each stage. In Section 6 we briefly survey open problems and report on some partial results, thereby indicating the direction that, in our opinion, future research should follow.

2. Repeated Games and the Problem of Information

Whenever one wants to apply game theory to real life situations, one has to bear in mind, among other things, two aspects in which classical game theory differs from real life:

i. Unlike a game situation, which is essentially a one-shot affair, a conflict situation in real life usually leads to another conflict situation. Thus, in real life, when one takes actions one should consider not only the immediate payoffs but also the effect that the actions may have on the other conflict situations that will occur in the future.[1]

ii. Unlike in a game situation, in which it is assumed that the players know all the available strategies as well as the payoff functions, in real life each participant usually has only partial knowledge of the strategies available to him and to the other participants; moreover, the actual payoff that results from the possible actions taken by the participants is impossible to determine because of a lack of knowledge of relevant facts.

---

[1] For an account of some attempts to account for this possibility see R. D. Luce and H. Raiffa [1957], Appendix 8.

J. Harsanyi has recently [1967-8] laid the foundations of a *theory of games with incomplete information*, in which he demonstrates that many situations involving missing relevant information can be modeled as classical games (with complete information) involving a chance mechanism.

Concealing or revealing information is often crucial. Military secrets, trade secrets, hiding weaknesses, concealing embarrassing circumstances—these are but a few examples involving information.

The word "secret" can be applied in two different senses, which should not be confused. One type of "secret" is something that you know or possess and others do not. For example, you may possess a certain weapon that other people do not know how to manufacture, or you know how to produce a certain item which others do not know how to produce. We shall not be concerned in this book with such secrets. Another meaning that is often attached to the word "secret" is something that you know or possess which *others do not know that you know or possess*. Contrary to the previous case, where the secret involved the item, this type of secret involves your knowledge or possession of the said item. In this book we shall be interested in this type of secret which, to be precise, we shall call *secret information*. Only in this sense should the word "secret" be understood, unless otherwise specified.

Perhaps one of the most important accomplishments in the art of diplomacy is the ability to handle information during negotiations. In this respect diplomacy has reached a high degree of sophistication. It is not enough simply not to divulge information one wants to hide, or even to supply wrong information. In many cases the opponent can guess the right information, either by detecting a lie, or merely by observing attempts to conceal the said information. How one expresses oneself is sometimes as important as what one says.

But diplomacy is not only the art of negotiating without revealing information—the best way to hide information is perhaps not to negotiate at all; the main object of diplomacy is to reveal, or partially reveal, information in such a way as to make it possible to gain both immediate profits and a better position in the next stage of negotiations. It is often said that the purpose of the

Geneva conferences[2] was not only to reach agreements on various aspects of disarmament—important though such agreements may be—but also to let the parties know each other better, clear up misunderstandings, build trust and find a common language—in the hope that this will pave the way to an improved world situation. Thus, the Geneva conferences furnish an example where partial information disclosure is tied both to immediate profits and to better negotiation positions in the future.

Concealing information and revealing information are tied together in many other real life situations—not only in diplomacy. Indeed, *in order to make use of the fact that it is not known that one is in possession of a certain item or piece of knowledge, one often has to reveal that one possesses this item or piece of knowledge.*

If a country A, for example, is in possession of a certain weapon and no other country knows this, and if under no circumstances will any other country get to know that this weapon is available to country A, then country A would be just as well off if it did not possess the weapon. For country A could benefit from the weapon either if she employed it in a certain military action, or if she announced that she had the weapon (thereby deterring enemies). In both cases it would become known that the weapon is available to country A.

A manufacturer can benefit from knowing how to manufacture a certain item either by manufacturing it or by patenting it, in which case it is no longer a secret that he knows how to manufacture the item.

Let it be said at once: We do not claim that all secret information should eventually be announced. On the contrary; quite often it is better to conceal forever the fact that one is in possession of certain information. In this case, however, it seems that one would often be just as well off if one does not have the information at all. To illustrate this argument, suppose that Ford knows how to make a car which lasts 100 years, and no one else knows that Ford has this capability. It is conceivable that it is not to the advantage of Ford to make such a car, nor even to

---

[2] A series of arms control conferences involving the United States and the Soviet Union that took place during the sixties.(*)

announce that such knowledge exists. Inasmuch as this situation prevails forever, Ford would be just as well off if it lacked the knowledge. But suppose that after a while some other company starts to manufacture better cars; it may then be of advantage to Ford to use its knowledge. In this case, of course, everyone will become aware of the fact that Ford can produce good cars.

We summarize: Sometimes it does not pay to make use of the fact that it is not known that one possesses a certain knowledge or item. Sometimes it pays. But it seems that if such use is made, then often the very use makes others aware of the secret information.

Recall that we consider here only the information that one possesses of a certain piece of knowledge or a certain item. A secret of the other kind—where, say, one has exclusive knowledge of some process—can be used without being revealed. If one is capable of producing, say, everlasting watches, then he can benefit by manufacturing them in sealed cases which, if tampered with, destroy the mechanism.

One is tempted to formulate the following principle: One can make use of the fact that it is not known that one possesses a certain knowledge or a certain item only by revealing it. This principle, however, is not always true.

EXAMPLE.[3] Suppose that a country is in the business of selling heavy water. Suppose that this country discovers a method of producing heavy water by a cheaper method. She can then produce the heavy water inexpensively, thereby making profits, and yet keep it secret that such knowledge is available to her. This is done by selling at the old price the same quantities and investing the additional profits only in such enterprises that can be kept secret from the rest of the world. (For example, in better education, if the amount invested in education is never disclosed.) Thus profits are made, and the fact that the country possesses the know-how is not revealed because every action taken, which is different from the actions taken by that country before discovering

---

[3]We owe this example to Hanna Maschler (oral communication).

the cheap method of production, remains unknown to the other countries.[4]

The ideas presented thus far are heuristic in nature, and even the concepts are only vaguely defined. We shall see in the next sections how these ideas develop from precise mathematical models, where an exact meaning will be given not only to phrases like "revealing" or "concealing" information, but also to phrases such as "partially revealing" information. In Chapter Three, R. Stearns treats also the problem of measuring the information that is revealed. These models will help us decide in which context and under what interpretation the above principle is correct. Later we shall discuss situations where this principle is incorrect.

The models in this work consist of 2-person constant-sum games—called *stage games*—which are to be played over and over again by the same two players. Assuming that there is incomplete information on the payoff function—either on the part of one player alone or on the part of both players—we shall see that it might be profitable for a player to reveal part of the information that he has at a certain stage, in order to gain more profits at later stages. Harsanyi's model will be used in order to find optimal strategies (if they exist) for the repeated games, and we shall then characterize how much information should be revealed when playing optimally, and what gains the revelation produces.

Some insights that may be obtained from the mathematical results will also be discussed.

3. Lack of Information on One Side—Stage Games in Normal Form

3.1. The Model

The following is a description of a repeated game with incomplete information.

---

[4]One reason for concealing such information is that, once it is revealed, research in that direction would intensify, and thus the chance of others to discover a similar method within a short time would increase.

Consider a constant-sum two-person game (in normal form) that is being played over and over again. We assume that one of the players, Player 1, knows precisely the payoffs that result from the choices of strategies by both players, whereas Player 2 is ignorant about these payoffs. Both players, however, know the available strategies on each side.

As he is ignorant of the payoff function, Player 2 assumes that it can be any of a number κ of possibilities, which, for simplicity, we assume to be finite. He also attaches a probability distribution $p^0 = (p_1^0, p_2^0, \ldots, p_\kappa^0)$ on the various possible alternatives $G_1, G_2, \ldots, G_\kappa$. This distribution represents his belief on the likelihood of each game to be the true game.[5]

The point of view of Player 2 can therefore be summarized by the diagram of Figure 1.

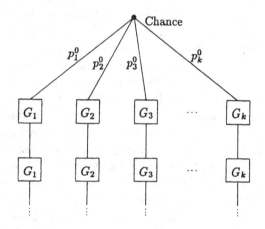

Figure 1. The point of view of Player 2

In addition, Player 2 knows that Player 1 knows on which branch they are playing.

We emphasize that only one of the games $G_1, G_2, \ldots, G_\kappa$ is being played over and over; Player 1 knows which one, and Player 2 has only a probability distribution over the alternatives. We shall

---

[5] We assume that $p_k^0 > 0$, $k \in \{1, 2 \ldots, \kappa\}$.

call the games $G_1, G_2, \ldots, G_\kappa$ *stage games* and the game actually being played the *true stage game*.

All the stage games are described by matrices having the same number of rows and the same number of columns. The entries represent the payoffs to Player 1. At each stage Player 1 picks a row, and, independently, Player 2 picks a column. At the end of each stage the entry from the *true* stage game is credited[6] to the "bank account" of Player 1 and deducted from the "bank account" of Player 2.

The players are never allowed to look at their own or their opponent's bank accounts,[7] but at the end of each stage it is announced which row and which column were picked.[8] Thus, Player 1 is able to figure out the balance in his bank account at each stage but Player 2 can only compute his expected balance. We assume that Player 1 knows the payoffs in $G_1, G_2, \ldots, G_\kappa$ and also the beliefs of Player 2; i.e., the vector $(p_1^0, p_2^0, \ldots, p_\kappa^0)$. Player 2 knows the payoffs in $G_1, G_2, \ldots, G_\kappa$. Finally, we assume that both players know the description stated so far.[9] This concludes the description of the repeated game with incomplete information.

By Harsanyi's theory, a game of complete information but involving a chance move can represent our situation of incomplete information on the part of Player 2. It is the following:

First "chance" makes a lottery with probability distribution p^0. According to the results of the lottery, both players then play one of the stage games $G_1, G_2, \ldots, G_\kappa$ infinitely often. Chance informs Player 1 of the result of the lottery but does not release this information to Player 2. After each stage the rows and columns that were picked at that stage are announced. Roughly speaking, Figure 1, which was used to explain Player 2's point of view, should, according to Harsanyi, be regarded by *both* players as a

---

[6] A negative credit means a decrease in the bank account.

[7] Otherwise Player 2 would be able, in general, to deduce which is the true stage game by looking at his gain or loss at a particular stage. (This will always be the case if the payoffs at corresponding entries of the stage games are all different.)

[8] We shall later relax this requirement.

[9] Including this sentence. Therefore, Player 1 knows that Player 2 knows that Player 1 knows the p^0 attributed by Player 2 to the various possibilities, etc.(*)

game representing the true situation together with the above description of the information given to each player. Let us call this game $\Gamma_\infty(p^0)$. Suppose that $\Gamma_\infty(p^0)$ has a value,[10] and let σ and τ be optimal strategies for Players 1 and 2, respectively; then these strategies generate strategies for the game with incomplete information as follows: Player 2 should play τ and Player 1 should play σ_k, where σ_k is generated from σ after chance chose the stage game G_k. Harsanyi proves, thereby justifying his model, that the pair (σ_k, τ) is in equilibrium, in the sense that no player in the game with incomplete information can improve himself by alone switching to another strategy. And vice versa, if strategy pairs $(\sigma_1, \tau), \ldots, (\sigma_\kappa, \tau)$ exist that are in equilibrium in the games with incomplete information when the stage games are $G_1, G_2, \ldots, G_\kappa$, respectively, then $\Gamma_\infty(p^0)$ has a value and (σ, τ) are optimal strategies, where σ is a strategy in Γ_∞ which tells Player 1 to play σ_k if chance chooses move k, $k = 1, 2, \ldots, \kappa$.

Thus, in order to analyze the incomplete information game, it is enough to find out whether $\Gamma_\infty(p^0)$ has a value and if so, to characterize its optimal strategies.

The description thus far is not complete if we do not state what the strategy spaces are and what the value of $\Gamma_\infty(p^0)$ means.

Let us, therefore, start by introducing the concept of *a history* of a play of the game. Formally, a history is a sequence of pairs $((s_1, t_1), (s_2, t_2), \ldots)$, where $s_1, s_2, \ldots$ are numbers chosen from the set $\{1, 2, \ldots, \mu\}$ and are called the *moves* of Player 1 at stages $1, 2, \ldots$ and $t_1, t_2, \ldots$—the *moves* of Player 2—are numbers chosen from the set $\{1, 2, \ldots, \nu\}$; here, μ is the number of rows and ν is the number of columns of each stage game. This history is interpreted as stating that at stage i, $i = 1, 2, \ldots$, Player 1 picks the s_i-th row and Player 2 picks the t_i-th column. An n-stage history, denoted Δ_n, is a history truncated after stage n. The set of all possible Δ_n's is denoted $\mathcal{L}_n$.

A strategy[11] for Player 2 is a rule telling Player 2 at each stage what probability he should choose for each row at each stage, as a function of the history that took place at prior stages.

---

[10]In a sense that will subsequently be defined precisely.

[11]We restrict ourselves to behavioral strategies. Since $\Gamma_\infty(p^0)$ is a game of

Thus, a strategy for Player 2 can be denoted by $\tau = (\tau^1, \tau^2, \ldots)$, where, for $i = 1, 2 \ldots$, τ^i is a probability distribution over the set $\{1, 2, \ldots, \nu\}$ that depends on the history Δ_{i-1}.

A strategy for Player 1 is a similar rule (concerning the rows instead of the columns), except that it may also depend on the choice of chance, which is known to Player 1. It can therefore be denoted by $\sigma = (\sigma^1, \sigma^2, \ldots, \sigma^\kappa)$, where $\sigma^k = (\sigma^{k1}, \sigma^{k2}, \ldots)$, $k = 1, 2, \ldots, \kappa$, is a sequence of probability distributions over the set $\{1, 2, \ldots, \mu\}$, and each σ^{ki} is a function of Δ_{i-1}.

Each pair of strategies (σ, τ) determines a probability distribution over the histories in $\mathcal{L}_n$, for each positive integer n.

Denote by $w(\Delta_n)$ the probability that an n-stage history Δ_n will arise, given (σ, τ). Such an n-stage history gives rise to an expected payoff, during the first n stages, of

$$\gamma^*(\Delta_n) = \sum_{k=1}^{\kappa} \sum_{i=1}^{n} p_k^0 g^k(s_i, t_i), \qquad (3.1)$$

where $\Delta_n = \big((s_1, t_1), \ldots, (s_n, t_n)\big)$, and $g^k(s_i, t_i)$ is the entry in the s_i-th row and t_i-th column of the matrix G_k.

Thus, a pair of strategies (σ, τ) determines an expected average payoff

$$\gamma_n(\sigma, \tau) = \frac{1}{n} \sum_{\Delta_n \in \mathcal{L}_n} w(\Delta_n) \gamma^*(\Delta_n), \qquad (3.2)$$

which represents the expected payoff per game for Player 1 for n stages. Minus this sum represents the expected payoff per game for Player 2. In general, as n goes to infinity, the sequence $(\gamma_1(\sigma, \tau), \gamma_2(\sigma, \tau), \ldots)$ need not converge. Nevertheless, one can define a value for $\Gamma_\infty(p^0)$ as follows:[12]

---

perfect recall, it follows from Aumann [1964], which generalizes Kuhn [1953], that such a restriction involves no loss of generality.

[12]The definition in the original paper required only that $\inf_\tau \gamma(\sigma^0, \tau) \geq v(\Gamma_\infty(p^0)) \geq \sup_\sigma \gamma(\sigma, \tau^0)$. We made the change in order to conform to the definition in other chapters. Of course, a value under the present definition is also a value in the original sense.(*)

DEFINITION 3.1 A number v is called *a value* for $\Gamma_\infty(p^0)$, and is denoted $v\big(\Gamma_\infty(p^0)\big)$, if there exists a pair of strategies (σ_0, τ_0) in $\Gamma_\infty(p^0)$, (called *optimal strategies*) such that for every $\varepsilon > 0$ there is a positive n_0, having the property that for every pair of strategies (σ, τ) for $\Gamma_\infty(p^0)$, and every $n > n_0$, we have

$$\gamma_n(\sigma_0, \tau) + \varepsilon \geq v \geq \gamma_n(\sigma, \tau_0) - \varepsilon. \tag{3.3}$$

In the remaining part of this section we propose to prove that $\Gamma_\infty(p^0)$ always has a value and to describe the optimal strategies for both players. In order to do so, we must first introduce the 1-shot game $\Delta_1(p)$.

3.2. Description of $\Delta_1(\mathbf{p})$

First "chance" chooses one of the κ alternatives $1, 2, \ldots, \kappa$ according to the probability distribution p. If alternative k has been chosen, both players play G_k once. Chance does not inform *either player* of the result of his choice.

First Intuitive Reason for Studying $\Delta_1(\mathbf{p})$

In $\Gamma_\infty(p)$ Player 1 knows something that Player 2 does not know; namely, the choice of chance. If one wishes to find out what he can gain from this knowledge, it is natural to compare the value of $\Gamma_\infty(p)$ with the value of a game $\Delta_\infty(p)$ differing from $\Gamma_\infty(p)$ only in that in $\Delta_\infty(p)$ chance does not inform any of the players of the outcome of the lottery.

It can easily be shown that the value of $\Delta_\infty(p)$ is the same as the value of $\Delta_1(p)$. As a matter of fact, an optimal strategy for each player for the game $\Delta_\infty(p)$ is to play at each stage a maximin strategy for $\Delta_1(p)$.

Second Intuitive Reason for Studying $\Delta_1(\mathbf{p})$

In the previous reason we argued that $\Delta_1(p)$ serves us in finding

out what Player 1 can do if he *does not know* more than Player 2
about the repeated game. We now argue that $\Delta_1(p)$ serves us also
in finding out what Player 1 can do if he decides *not to reveal* to
Player 2 anything that he knows about the choice of chance.

3.3. Revealing Information

The word "reveal" needs some explanation:[13] Suppose you saw
a man running out of a house with a bloody knife in his hand.
You enter the house and find a dead person who obviously was
stabbed a few minutes earlier. Most probably you would assume
that the man who was running is the killer. But suppose now that
you happen to know the man personally and you know that he is
a noble man, highly respected among his friends. You would then
assume that probably, like you yourself, he happened to enter the
house and see the corpse and now he is running to call the police.
Out of shock and panic, perhaps you would reason, he took the
knife in order to convince the police that someone was stabbed.
This example serves to explain that actions alone do not reveal
anything. They only serve to alter whatever *a priori* beliefs you
had at the beginning. For the first man you attached a relatively
high probability that he could kill somebody (even before you saw
the corpse). For the noble man this probability was very low.
The action—running with a knife—has changed both probabilities; the new probabilities—called *conditional probabilities*—are
now very high for the first man, but still low for the second. We
conclude: the thing that actions reveal is a new set of conditional
probabilities based on the *a priori* probabilities.

The word "reveal" that we use in this book is related to the
above everyday usage but it is not quite the same. Player 2 has
a priori probabilities, namely the probability distribution on the
choice of chance. He also knows the actions taken by Player 1 at
the end of each stage, but this knowledge does not enable him to
compute new conditional probabilities unless he knows the strategy that Player 1 employed, or unless he has formed for himself in

---

[13]We owe this way of explaining the intuitive meaning of conditional probabilities to H. Kuhn (oral communication).

a different way some *a priori* probability distribution about the choices of Player 1 (as functions of the choice of chance).

Here, *whenever we talk about revealing the choice of chance, we shall assume*[14] *that Player 2 knows the strategy employed by Player 1.* If this is the case then one can compute the conditional probabilities on the choice of chance. For example, if in $\Gamma_\infty(p^0)$, at the first stage, Player 1 chooses row j, and if his strategy contains the probabilities $\sigma_j^{11}, \sigma_j^{21}, \ldots, \sigma_j^{\kappa 1}$, then at the end of this stage, Player 2 would conclude that the conditional probability that chance chose alternative k from $1, 2, \ldots, \kappa$ is

$$\frac{p_k^0 \sigma_j^{k1}}{p_1^0 \sigma_j^{11} + p_2^0 \sigma_j^{21} + \cdots + p_\kappa^0 \sigma_j^{\kappa 1}}. \tag{3.4}$$

Here, σ_j^{k1} is the probability of choosing the j-th row in the first stage, given that chance chose k.

In addition to providing an explanation for the meaning of the word "reveal", these conditional probabilities serve also a very important mathematical goal: One way to compute what a given strategy σ^* guarantees Player 1 in n stages is to assume that Player 2 knows that σ^* is being used, computes at each stage a new set of conditional probabilities, and chooses at each stage a column that yields him the highest expected payoff. The average of these n expected payoffs is the amount that σ^* guarantees Player 1. We use this method in many of the proofs.

Note that expression (3.4) equals p_k^0 if $\sigma_j^{11} = \sigma_j^{21} = \cdots = \sigma_j^{\kappa 1}$. In general,[15] the condition $\sigma^1 = \sigma^2 \ldots = \sigma^\kappa$ is necessary and sufficient in order that for all k, the derived conditional probabilities will be equal to the probabilities on the choice of chance at the

---

[14]If Player 1 had only one optimal strategy, then this assumption would have been quite reasonable, because a wise Player 2 would be able to compute the optimal strategy. It turns out that in our games Player 1 has, in general, many optimal strategies. For this reason, we consider arguments about "making use of one's own extra information" to be more basic and more convincing than arguments involving "revealing information". Nevertheless, arguments using the revealing aspect of a strategy do throw light on the results and therefore we use them.

[15]For this statement to be correct it is necessary to assume that the vector p^0 is strictly greater than 0 in all coordinates.

beginning. Accordingly, a strategy $\sigma = (\sigma^1, \sigma^2, \ldots, \sigma^\kappa)$ for Player 1 is called *non-revealing* if and only if $\sigma^1 = \sigma^2 = \ldots = \sigma^\kappa$. Thus, the game $\Delta_\infty(p)$ is nothing but the game $\Gamma_\infty(p)$ in which Player 1 restricts himself to non-revealing strategies.

   The above two interpretations of $\Delta_\infty(p)$ serve to show that in the games that we consider here, *the only way for Player 1 to make use of his knowledge of the choice of chance is to use a revealing strategy.*[16] The validity of this statement follows from (3.4) and from the fact that the rules of the game $\Gamma_\infty(p^0)$ require that at the end of each stage the actions of Player 1 be announced.

3.4. The Main Theorem

The reader should observe that at the beginning of the section the distribution p^0 on the choice of chance was a vector of fixed numbers $(p_1^0, p_2^0, \ldots, p_\kappa^0)$, whereas, as soon as we discussed the 1-shot game $\Delta_1(p)$, p was assumed to be a variable probability distribution $p = (p_1, p_2, \ldots, p_\kappa)$. This was done on purpose; for in order to find the value of $\Gamma(p^0)$ at a particular distribution p^0, it is necessary to compute the values of $\Delta(p)$ for *all* the distributions p. This is manifested in the theorem which we are now able to state:

THEOREM 3.2. *The value of $\Gamma_\infty(p^0)$ exists and is given by*

$$v_\infty(p^0) = \operatorname{cav} u(p^0). \tag{3.5}$$

Here, $u(p)$ is the value of $\Delta_1(p)$ (which is also the value of $\Delta_\infty(p)$, as stated above), and $\operatorname{cav} u$ is the least concave function that is at least equal to u at all distributions p.

   Before discussing this central theorem, let us treat a numerical example of a repeated game with incomplete information.

---

[16]More precisely, a strategy such that if Player 2 knows that it is employed, there is a positive probability that by observing the actions of Player 1, Player 2 can derive conditional probabilities on the choice of chance which are different from the original probabilities.

EXAMPLE 3.3. Suppose Player 2 thinks that Player 1 can be only one of two "types": "red" or "blue" ($\kappa = 2$). Suppose also that Player 2 attaches equal probabilities to the two possibilities; that is, he places $p_1^0 = p_2^0 = 1/2$. If Player 1 is the red type, let the stage game be

Player 2

Player 1

0	1	1	3
0	1	0	3

If Player 1 is the blue type, let the stage game be

Player 2

Player 1

3	0	1	0
3	1	1	0

Looking at the numbers, one observes the following:

i. If Player 2 knew which type his opponent is, he could guarantee himself not to pay more than 0 at each stage. Simply, he would always choose the 1-st column if he were to play against a red Player 1 and choose the 4-th column if he were to play against a blue Player 1. Consequently, if Player 1 reveals his type completely,[17] then he guarantees himself only an expected average payoff of zero.

---

[17]I.e., uses a strategy such that if Player 2 knew the strategy that Player 1 is using, he could deduce after a finite number of stages that the conditional probabilities are either $(0, 1)$ or $(1, 0)$, according to the true type of Player 1.

ii. For a 1-shot game, Player 1 would act optimally if he chooses the first row when he is red and chooses the second row when he is blue, since these rows (weakly) dominate the other rows in the corresponding game. However, this choice cannot be used at each stage in[18] $\Gamma_\infty(1/2)$, because this is a completely revealing strategy: If Player 2 knew that this strategy is being used, he would realize after the first stage what the choice of chance was.

iii. Let us see what Player 1 can guarantee if he decides to use a non-revealing strategy. In this case $\Delta_1(p_1)$ is a combination of the two games with probability $p = (p_1, p_2)$:

Player 2

Player 1

$3p_2$	p_1	1	$3p_1$
$3p_2$	1	p_2	$3p_1$

Routine computation shows that the value $u_1(p)$ of the game $\Delta_1(p)$ is:

$$u_1(p) = \begin{cases} 3p_1, & 0 \le p_1 \le 2 - \sqrt{3}, \\ 1 - p_1(1 - p_1), & 2 - \sqrt{3} \le p_1 \le \sqrt{3} - 1, \\ 3(1 - p_1), & \sqrt{3} - 1 \le p_1 \le 1. \end{cases} \quad (3.6)$$

Figure 2 shows a graph of this function (as a function of p), from which one sees immediately that

$$\text{cav } u_1(p) = \begin{cases} 3p_1, & 0 \le p_1 \le 2 - \sqrt{3}, \\ 6 - 3\sqrt{3}, & 2 - \sqrt{3} \le p_1 \le \sqrt{3} - 1, \\ 3(1 - p_1), & \sqrt{3} - 1 \le p_1 \le 1. \end{cases} \quad (3.7)$$

The broken horizontal segment in Figure 2 is that part of the

---

[18]We shall write $\Gamma_\infty(1/2)$ for $\Gamma_\infty(1/2, 1/2)$ and, in general, $\Gamma_\infty(p_1)$ for $\Gamma_\infty(p_1, p_2)$. A similar shortcut applies to $\Delta_1(p_1)$. If $p = (p_1, p_2)$ we shall also write $\Delta_1(p)$, $\Gamma_1(p)$, $u(p)$, etc. for $\Delta_1(p_1)$, $\Gamma_1(p_1)$, $u(p_1)$, etc.

graph of cav u_1 that is different from u_1.

By Theorem 3.2, the value of $\Gamma_\infty(1/2)$ in this example is $v_\infty(1/2) = 6 - 3\sqrt{3}$. This is greater than the value of $u_1(1/2)$, which is equal to $3/4$, and consequently it cannot be guaranteed by a non-revealing strategy. We have seen before that $v_\infty(1/2)$ also cannot be guaranteed by a completely revealing strategy, because such a strategy guarantees only 0. We shall return to this example later, when we discuss the optimal strategies.

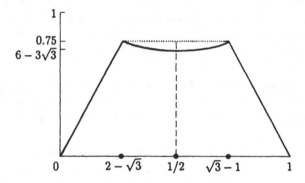

Figure 2. u_1 and its concavification

Note that besides stating that a value for $\Gamma_\infty(p^0)$ exists, Theorem 3 reduces the computation of this value to a computation of a value of a 1-shot game with a variable parameter p. Various techniques are known for solving finite constant-sum games, whereas very little is known about computing a value of an infinite game, when such a value exists. The fact that $v_\infty(p)$ (for a variable parameter p) is equal to the concavification of $u_1(p)$ encourages us to search for additional situations where increase in knowledge achieves a "smoothing effect".

3.5. The Optimal Strategy of Player 1

We start by formally stating one of many optimal strategies for Player 1 for the game described in Example 3.3 (or, equivalently, for Harsanyi's representation of this game). We shall then characterize the optimal strategies for all the games of this section.

Two coins are prepared. One of them, which we name the "red coin", has a probability $2 - \sqrt{3}$ of "heads". The other—the "blue coin"—has a probability $\sqrt{3} - 1$ of "heads". If Player 1 is the red type he flips the red coin. If he is the blue type he flips the blue coin. *This is the only time Player 1 makes use of his knowledge of his type.* In other words, only in picking the coin do the actions of the two types differ.

If the coin turns out "heads", Player 1 plays at each stage a maximin strategy of the game $\Delta_1(2 - \sqrt{3})$. If the coin turns out "tails", Player 1 plays at each stage a maximin strategy of the game $\Delta_1(\sqrt{3} - 1)$. This concludes the description of his strategy.

In order to find out what this strategy guarantees, let us ask ourselves what Player 2 could do if he *knew* that Player 1 employs this strategy.

By "knew" we mean that he knew the description stated above, including the probabilities of the coins, but not, of course, which coin was picked up. It also means that he knew whether the coin fell on heads or on tails, because this could be deduced to any level of significance by observing Player 1's actions for a while. (The maximin strategies for $\Delta_1(2 - \sqrt{3})$ and $\Delta_1(\sqrt{3} - 1)$ are different.)

Knowing all this information, Player 2 could deduce a new set of conditional probabilities on the choice of chance; namely,

$$\begin{cases} p_1 = 2 - \sqrt{3}, & \text{if heads comes about,} \\ p_1 = \sqrt{3} - 1, & \text{if tails comes about.} \end{cases} \tag{3.8}$$

Since from now on Player 1 is committed to a non-revealing strategy, a best response for Player 2 would be to play at each stage a minimax strategy for $\Delta_1(2 - \sqrt{3})$ or $\Delta_1(\sqrt{3} - 1)$, according to the fall of the coin. Thus, at each stage Player 2 pays an expected amount of $u_1(2 - \sqrt{3}) = u_1(\sqrt{3} - 1) = 6 - 3\sqrt{3}$ at most. As a result, Player 1's strategy guarantees him $v_\infty(1/2)$.

A. First Intuitive Interpretation of Player 1's Optimal Strategy

Let us call Player 1 *the policy maker*. Let us suppose that instead of himself playing the game, he sends another person to play the game for him. We shall call this person *the negotiator*.

The optimal strategy simply states that the policy maker should fool his own negotiator to some extent. Instead of briefing him and telling him which type of policy maker he is, he only tells him either that the probability of being the strong type is equal to $2 - \sqrt{3}$, or that it is equal to $\sqrt{3} - 1$. He must also instruct the negotiator to assume that Player 2 knows this fact. However, the policy maker is not free to choose which information he should pass to the negotiator. He has to flip the right coin and pass on that information that the coin prescribes.

This strategy of fooling one's own negotiator, or, rather, not telling him all the things one knows, seems strange at first. One can imagine how angry a diplomat would feel if he is sent on a mission and later finds out that some very relevant facts were purposely kept secret from him by the policy maker, or at least, were played down and vaguely stated. And yet, such situations do occur from time to time (not necessarily because the policy maker has used an optimal strategy). One encounters cases when a diplomat strongly denies a certain claim and discovers later that he himself was not told the full story. Would that diplomat be capable of denying the claim so forcefully had he known the facts? Let us draw an analogy from a different level: Suppose a man has committed a crime for which little evidence is available. What lawyer will better serve him? One who knows that he has committed the crime or one who does not?

As we have just said, such situations are known in the history of mankind. However, in our opinion it is really impressive that

i. such strategies appear in a mathematical model and, moreover, seem crucial for an optimal strategy;

ii. neither complete disclosure nor complete concealment of secret information from one's negotiator is, in general, an optimal strategy;

iii. at least in our games, there exists a random mechanism that prescribes what partial information should be disclosed to the negotiator; and that

iv. in our case it was possible to characterize completely the type of information that should be disclosed to the negotiator and the extent to which it should be revealed.

B. Second Intuitive Interpretation of Player 1's Optimal Strategy

We shall now make an assumption that Player 2 knows the strategy Player 1 is using while playing $\Gamma_\infty(1/2)$. This means that Player 2 knows what probability distribution Player 1 will use at each stage if he is the red type and what—if he is the blue type.[19] Knowing this, and knowing the actions of Player 1, Player 2 is able to compute a set of conditional probabilities on the choice of chance.

In this case, therefore, we can analyze the revealing aspect of the optimal strategy. Player 2, from his point of view, will deduce with probability $1/2$ that the probability that he is facing the red player is $2 - \sqrt{3}$ and with probability $1/2$ he will deduce that the probability that he is facing the red player is $\sqrt{3} - 1$. (This computation has been done before.) To see that this is a revealing strategy let us compute the conditional probabilities given that Player 1 is, say, the red type. In this case, the probability that Player 2 will deduce that Player 1 is red with probability $\sqrt{3} - 1$ is equal to $\sqrt{3} - 1 \sim 0.7$ and the probability that Player 2 will deduce that Player 1 is red with probability $2 - \sqrt{3}$ is equal to $2 - \sqrt{3} \sim 0.3$. Thus, with probability 0.7, Player 2 will attribute to the truth a higher probability than he had originally (a change from $1/2$ to $\sqrt{3} - 1$) and with probability 0.3 he will attribute a lower probability to the truth than he had originally[20] (a change from $1/2$ to $2 - \sqrt{3}$).

---

[19] As has been pointed out before, this assumption is unrealistic in our model: Player 1 has many optimal strategies. For example, he may play erratically and independently of his type for a while and then flip a coin, say, at the 103rd stage. Or he may decide to flip coins (with different probabilities of falling on heads) several times, each time revealing to his negotiator more and more information (but never more than and eventually exactly what is disclosed in the strategy described before). Nevertheless, this reasoning is valid if the rules of the game require Player 1 to disclose his strategy, and at least it analyzes what can happen in the worst case when, say by spying, Player 2 discovers the strategy.

[20] On the "average", therefore, his information will be better—he will "know more". To formalize these ideas, one must define an appropriate measure of "quantity of information" and show that it increases. See Stearns's results in Chapter Three.(*)

We see that an optimal strategy for Player 1 is a revealing strategy, but it is only *partially revealing*. Neither does Player 2 necessarily get a better estimate of the true situation (he gets it with probability 0.7 approximately—not 1), nor does he get the full information (he gets a new probability of $\sqrt{3} - 1$ or $2 - \sqrt{3}$, and both are strictly between 0 and 1.)

Combining the two interpretations of Player 1's optimal strategy we see that in this example *it pays Player 1 to make partial use of his knowledge about his type* (it is partial in the sense that he does not tell his negotiator the full story), *but in order to make such use he must use a strategy that partially reveals his type. Moreover, whatever he reveals to his negotiator—that much exactly he must reveal to Player 2 if Player 2 knows the strategy he employs.*

Thinking from the revealing, or rather the concealing, aspect of an optimal strategy, we can recommend again: If the policy maker does not wish to reveal something to his opponent he should not reveal that information to his negotiator. Indeed, there are two possibilities: Either the actions of the negotiator will not change after being given the secret information; then why does he need that information to begin with? Or, he may act differently as a result of the briefing, in which case the opponent may sense this and deduce that information which the policy maker wishes to conceal from him. We shall later see cases where these recommendations are wrong.

REMARK. If one plays a 1-shot game $\Gamma_1(1/2)$ whose stage games are the games of Example 3.3, one finds that the optimal strategy for Player 1 reveals conditional probabilities for Player 1 that are outside the interval $[2 - \sqrt{3}, \sqrt{3} - 1]$. In other words, the optimal strategy for $\Gamma_1(1/2)$ cannot be used as a part of an optimal strategy for $\Gamma_\infty(1/2)$ because it reveals too much. Thus, we have here an example of a situation in which one should reveal information but also sacrifice some payoff from the intermediate stages of the game.

The optimal strategy for Player 1 for a general repeated game with incomplete information on the part of Player 2, as described

in the previous section, is of the same nature as the one treated
in Example 3.3.

Let $\Gamma_\infty(p^0)$ be Harsanyi's representation as discussed in Section 2. Let $u(p)$ be the value for the game $\Delta_1(p)$ in which both
players do not have the information on the choice of chance.

There exist vectors $p^1, p^2, \ldots, p^s$, $s \leq \kappa$, where κ is the number
of the stage games, such that there exist unique positive weights
$x^1, x^2, \ldots, x^s$ summing to 1 with

$$x^1 p^1 + x^2 p^2 + \cdots + x^s p^s = p^0 \qquad (3.9)$$

and

$$x^1 u(p^1) + x^2 u(p^2) + \cdots + x^s u(p^s) = \operatorname{cav} u(p^0). \qquad (3.10)$$

It is possible to arrange lotteries similar to the coins discussed
in the above example so that an observer who knows the nature
of the lotteries, as well as the outcome, will find that the conditional distributions over the choices of chance that he computes
are always elements of the set $\{p^1, p^2, \ldots, p^s\}$. Since the *a priori*
distribution is p^0 and since the weights in (3.9) are unique, such an
observer will find with probability x^i the conditional distribution
p^i over the choices of chance, $i = 1, 2, \ldots, s$. An optimal strategy
for Player 1 is to perform one of these lotteries (depending on the
choice of chance, which he knows) and after performing the lottery behave as if he himself is facing the game $\Delta_1(p^i)$, where p^i is
the resulting probability distribution over the choices of chance.
By (3.10), this strategy guarantees Player 1 an expected payoff of
$\operatorname{cav} u(p^0)$.

As in Example 3.3, this strategy is a method of partially using one's own extra information (by performing one of several
lotteries), after which Player 1 behaves as if he himself does not
know the choice of chance, except that he places on the choice of
chance a conditional probability distribution, which depends on
the outcome of the lottery. As in the example above, this strategy of Player 1 can be regarded as a partially revealing strategy
for a Player 2 who knows the strategy and can therefore compute
for himself the conditional probabilities by observing Player 1's
actions.

3.6. The Optimal Strategy of Player 2

In computing what a strategy for Player 1 guarantees we assumed that Player 2 knows the strategy employed by Player 1 and answers the best he can. Such an assumption is nothing but a mathematical device designed to find out what Player 1's strategy actually guarantees; i.e., what is the worst thing that can happen to Player 1 if he employs that strategy. Such knowledge is inadmissible when one describes Player 2's own strategy and computes his level of safety, because there is nothing in the rules of the game that specifies that Player 1 must use a certain strategy even if that strategy is known to be optimal. Since this remark is crucial to the understanding of the present chapter, let us illustrate it by the following simple example:

Consider the 2-person constant-sum game

Player 2

Player 1

1	0
0	1

In this example Player 1 has a unique optimal strategy; namely, to choose the first row and second row with equal probabilities. A best reply for Player 2 is, e.g., to choose the first column.[21] One sees that Player 1's strategy guarantees an expected payoff of 1/2. But choosing the first column, although it is a best reply for the specific optimal strategy of Player 1, is *not* an optimal strategy for Player 2. Indeed, choosing the first column guarantees Player 2 not to pay more than 1 (i.e., the worst possible result in the game), because a best reply by Player 1 for such a strategy is to choose the first row.

Since we now cannot assume that Player 2 knows Player 1's strategy, we cannot assume that he learns anything about the distribution over the choices of chance, because without knowing

---

[21] Actually any strategy for Player 2 in this example is a best reply.

the opponent's strategy, Player 2 cannot compute any conditional probability.

Let us therefore analyze what information he does receive at each stage. We shall do this for the game treated in Example 3.3:

0	1	1	3
0	1	0	3

G_1

3	0	1	0
3	1	1	0

G_2

Suppose that at a certain stage Player 1 chose the first row and Player 2 chose, say, the first column. Since by the rules of the game Player 2 learns these moves at the end of the stage, he will then note that if G_1 was the true stage game he was paying 0 and if G_2 was the true stage game he was paying 3. We summarize this information by the ordered pair $(0, 3)$. Other pairs would obtain if the moves of the players were different. Plotting all the possible pairs we obtain the vertices in Figure 3.

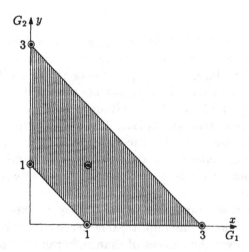

Figure 3. From the point of view of Player 2

Thus, at the end of each stage Player 2 knows which of the points encircled in the figure was hit. If at the first n stages these points were (x_1, y_1), (x_2, y_2), $\ldots$, (x_n, y_n), he can compute the average

$$(\xi_n, \eta_n) = \left(\frac{1}{n}(x_1 + x_2 + \cdots + x_n), \frac{1}{n}(y_1 + y_2 + \cdots + y_n)\right),$$

which is a point in the shaded area in Figure 3. Player 2 also knows that if G_1 is the true stage game, then Player 1 will try to push the average to the right as far as he can, and if G_2 is the true stage game, then Player 1 will try to push the average upward as far as he can.

Thus, from the point of view of Player 2, he is playing a game with *vector payoffs*, knowing at the same time that Player 1 is interested in one of the coordinates, which is his true payoff, and this coordinate is unknown to Player 2.

A theory for playing repeated constant-sum games with vector payoffs was developed by D. Blackwell [1956]. Blackwell calls a set S in the payoff vector space *approachable for Player 2* if Player 2 has a strategy for the repeated game such that no matter what Player 1's strategy is, the distance of the average vector payoff from S tends to 0 with probability 1. In that paper Blackwell proves that a necessary and sufficient condition for a convex compact set S to be approachable for Player 2 in the infinite shot game is that it is not excludable by Player 1 in the *1-shot* game.[22] He also describes the optimal strategy, i.e., the strategy which enforces the approachability in the infinite-shot game.

Consider again the game in our example, treated as a repeated game with vector payoffs.

Player 2

Player 1	(0,3)	(1,0)	(1,1)	(3,0)
	(0,3)	(1,1)	(0,1)	(3,0)

---

[22]I.e., that Player 1 has no strategy for the 1-shot game which forces the outcome outside of S, regardless of what Player 2's reply is.

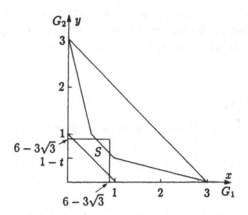

Figure 4. An approachable set

Let S be the intersection of the shaded area in Figure 3 with the quarter-plane whose upper right corner is $(6 - 3\sqrt{3}, 6 - 3\sqrt{3})$ (see Figure 4).

In order to check whether this set is approachable for Player 2, we can ask ourselves whether for each strategy $(t, 1-t)$ of Player 1 there exists a strategy (y_1, y_2, y_3, y_4) for Player 2 such that the expected payoff in a 1-shot game lies in S. Looking for all possible strategies (y_1, y_2, y_3, y_4) for a fixed $(t, 1 - t)$, one finds that the expected payoffs that result form the convex hull of the points $(0, 3)$, $(1, 1 - t)$, $(t, 1)$, $(3, 0)$ (see the shaded area in Figure 4). It is easy to establish that this convex hull always intersects S. Consequently, S is approachable for Player 2.

Suppose now that Player 2 actually uses a strategy which, with probability 1, forces the average to S; then, whatever the true stage game is, both coordinates will not be greater than $6 - 3\sqrt{3}$, and therefore the combination of the coordinates in the ratios p^0, $1 - p^0$, which is what Player 2 expects to pay Player 1, will not be greater than $6 - 3\sqrt{3}$. Thus, for $2 - \sqrt{3} \leq p^0 \leq \sqrt{3} - 1$ (see Figure 2) this strategy is optimal for Player 2. (For other values of p^0 there are other approachable sets, which generate optimal strategies for Player 2.)

Our aim now is to state results that show that for each repeated game with incomplete information as described in Section 2, there exists an approachable set for Player 2 that generates an optimal strategy for him.

Let $\Gamma_\infty(p^0)$ be an arbitrary repeated game with incomplete information on the part of Player 2 as described in Section 2. Let $\Delta_1(p)$ be the corresponding 1-shot game in which both players lack the information on the choice of chance (with a variable distribution p). Let $u(p)$ be the value of $\Delta_1(p)$. We know already that cav $u(p) = v_\infty(p)$, where $v_\infty(p)$ is the value of $\Gamma_\infty(p)$. A point x^0 in the vector payoff space will be called an *exposed point* with respect to p^0 and the function cav $u(p)$, if

$$p^0 \cdot x^0 = \text{cav } u(p^0),$$

$$p \cdot x^0 \geq \text{cav } u(p), \quad \text{for all } p.$$

The main result in establishing that there is an appropriate approachable set for Player 2 is that *an exposed point always exists*. We have two proofs for this result. One is based on the main theorem of Section 3 and the other does not make use of that theorem.

If $x^0 = (x_1^0, x_2^0, \ldots, x_\kappa^0)$ is an exposed point, then the intersection of the orthant

$$\left\{ y \colon y_1 \leq x_1^0,\, y_2 \leq x_2^0,\, \ldots,\, y_\kappa \leq x_\kappa^0 \right\}$$

with the convex hull of the vector payoffs determined by the stage games G_1, G_2, ..., G_κ is the required approachable set. This assertion is proved by using one of Blackwell's criteria for approachability.[23]

4. Lack of Information on Both Sides

4.1. The Model

So far, lack of information has been assumed for only one player. When both players lack some information, the problems become more complicated and new phenomena arise. According to Harsanyi [1967-8], any 2-person finite constant-sum game with incomplete information can be represented by the following model:[24]

---

[23] For a complete proof of these assertions, see Postscript d to Chapter One.(*)
[24] For simplicity we assume that there are only finitely many possibilities for each player.

There is given an $\alpha \times \beta$ array of 2-person constant-sum games in normal form, having the same number of rows and the same number of columns and arranged in a rectangular form as follows:

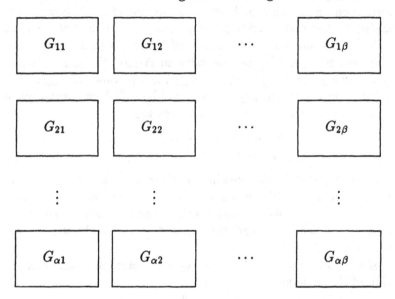

Player 1 is told in which row the true game lies but he is not told which of the games in that row is actually being played. Player 2 is told in which column the true game lies but he is not told which of the games in that column is the true game.

Player 1 associates to the various alternatives a probability matrix

$$
\begin{array}{cccc}
q_{11} & q_{12} & \cdots & q_{1\beta} \\
q_{21} & q_{22} & \cdots & q_{2\beta} \\
\cdots & \cdots & \cdots & \cdots \\
q_{\alpha 1} & q_{\alpha 2} & \cdots & q_{\alpha\beta}
\end{array}
$$

with

$$\sum_{j=1}^{\beta} q_{ij} = 1, \qquad i = 1, 2, \ldots, \alpha,$$

$$q_{ij} \geq 0, \qquad i = 1, 2, \ldots, \alpha, \ j = 1, 2, \ldots, \beta.$$

The interpretation is that if he is told that the true game is in the i-th row, then he associates a probability q_{ij} to the possibility that the true game is in the j-th column. The above matrix is known[25] to Player 2.

Similarly, Player 2 associates to the various alternatives a probability matrix

p_{11}	p_{12}	$\cdots$	$p_{1\beta}$
p_{21}	p_{22}	$\cdots$	$p_{2\beta}$
$\vdots$	$\vdots$		$\vdots$
$p_{\alpha 1}$	$p_{\alpha 2}$	$\cdots$	$p_{\alpha\beta}$

with

$$\sum_{i=1}^{\alpha} p_{ij} = 1, \qquad j = 1, 2, \ldots, \beta,$$

$$p_{ij} \geq 0, \qquad i = 1, 2, \ldots, \alpha, \ j = 1, 2, \ldots, \beta,$$

meaning that if he is told that the true game is in the j-th column, then he believes that the probability that the true game lies in the i-th row is p_{ij}. This matrix is known also to Player 1. Finally, it is assumed that both players are acquainted with the description so far.

---

[25]This is no loss of generality. Harsanyi shows that the case when a player does not know what his opponent thinks can be reduced to the situation described here. (See Example 4.1.)

This is, therefore, a description of a 1-shot game with incomplete information on the part of both players. We will, however, be interested in the infinite-shot game, which differs from the previous description only in that the true game G_{ij} is repeated infinitely often. As in the previous section, we shall refer to the various games G_{ij} as *stage games* and we shall assume that at the end of each stage, the moves of both players are revealed, but the payoffs are credited to the "bank accounts", without telling the amounts to the players.

The first difficulty one encounters when one wants to represent this game as a classical game involving a chance move is that it is not at all clear what moves should be attached to chance, and with what probabilities. Harsanyi [1967–8] distinguished two cases: the consistent case and the inconsistent case.

The Consistent Case

Suppose given a matrix

a_{11}	a_{12}	$\cdots$	$a_{1\beta}$
a_{21}	a_{22}	$\cdots$	$a_{2\beta}$
$\cdots$	$\cdots$	$\cdots$	$\cdots$
$a_{\alpha 1}$	$a_{\alpha 2}$	$\cdots$	$a_{\alpha\beta}$

with $a_{ij} \geq 0$ for all i, j,

$$\sum_{i=1}^{\alpha} \sum_{j=1}^{\beta} a_{ij} = 1, \tag{4.1}$$

$$\frac{a_{ij}}{a_{i1} + a_{i2} + \cdots + a_{i\beta}} = q_{ij}, \quad \text{all } i, j, \tag{4.2}$$

$$\frac{a_{ij}}{a_{1j} + a_{2j} + \cdots + a_{\alpha j}} = p_{ij}, \quad \text{all } i, j. \qquad (4.3)$$

Such a matrix is called a *joint probability distribution*. In this case, Harsanyi claims, the players should regard the true stage game as drawn from a lottery that assigns probability a_{ij} to the game G_{ij}. Chance then informs Player 1 of the index i and Player 2 of the index j. It turns out that the matrices (q_{ij}) and (p_{ij}) are nothing but the conditional probabilities on the choice of chance given the i-th index and the j-th index, respectively.[26] After chance makes its choice and the players are informed of the respective indices, the true stage game is played over and over, and at the end of each stage the moves (but not the payoffs) are announced.

The Inconsistent Case

If no such matrix (a_{ij}) exists, then it is no longer clear how to incorporate chance into a representation of the game with incomplete information. Harsanyi [1967-8] reports a suggestion made by R. Selten of a representation involving $\alpha + \beta$ players engaged in a non-constant-sum game involving chance. We wish to present here a different representation involving only two players engaged in a non-constant-sum game.

THE GAME FOR PLAYER 1. Choose strictly positive numbers $\gamma_1, \gamma_2, \ldots, \gamma_\alpha$ whose sum is 1. Player 1 should consider himself as playing the following game: First, chance performs a lottery involving $\alpha\beta$ alternatives (i, j). The probability of choosing the alternative (i, j) is $\gamma_i q_{ij}$. Chance then informs Player 1 of the i-th index, and Player 2—of the j-th index. If (i, j) is chosen, Player 1 should imagine that both players now play the game G_{ij} (once if we are dealing with a 1-shot game, infinitely often if we are dealing with the repeated game). The above rules described in normal form (stage by stage in the repeated game) constitute the payoff matrix for Player 1.

THE GAME FOR PLAYER 2. Choose positive numbers $\delta_1, \delta_2, \ldots, \delta_\beta$ whose sum is 1. Player 2 should consider himself as playing the following game: First, chance performs a lottery involving

---

[26] Harsanyi proves that if the matrix (a_{ij}) exists, it is essentially unique.

an $\alpha \times \beta$ array of alternatives (i,j). The probability of choosing
the alternatives (i,j) is $\delta_j p_{ij}$. Chance then informs Player 1 of
the i-th index and Player 2 of the j-th index. If (i,j) is chosen,
Player 2 should imagine that both players now play the game G_{ij}
(once, or infinitely often, as the case may be). These rules, described in normal form (stage by stage in the repeated game),
constitute the payoff matrix for Player 2.

Both games together form a 2-person non-constant-sum game.

EXAMPLE 4.1. One of the two games

1	0
0	0

G_1

0	0
0	1

G_2

is being played. Player 1 knows which; Player 2 is not sure. However, Player 1 does not know precisely what Player 2 thinks. He
believes that with probability 1/4 Player 2 assigns equal probabilities to G_1 and G_2, and with probability 3/4 Player 2 assigns
probabilities 1/3 and 2/3 to G_1 and G_2.[27] According to Harsanyi,
the game with incomplete information can be described by the
matrix of games

1	0
0	0

1	0
0	0

0	0
0	1

0	0
0	1

---

[27]Tacitly, it is assumed that Player 2 indeed thinks in one of these ways and
that all this is common knowledge.

and of beliefs

1/4	3/4
1/4	3/4

1/2	1/3
1/2	2/3

The beliefs are clearly inconsistent. Our suggestion is to represent the situation by the two trees in Figures 5 and 6 (for the 1-shot case).

In normal form, the games are

$\frac{1}{4}\gamma + \frac{3}{4}\gamma$	$\frac{1}{4}\gamma$	$\frac{3}{4}\gamma$	0
$\frac{1}{4}\gamma + \frac{3}{4}\gamma$	$\frac{1}{4}\gamma + \frac{3}{4}(1-\gamma)$	$\frac{3}{4}\gamma + \frac{1}{4}(1-\gamma)$	$\frac{1}{4}(1-\gamma) + \frac{3}{4}(1-\gamma)$
0	0	0	0
0	$\frac{3}{4}(1-\gamma)$	$\frac{1}{4}(1-\gamma)$	$\frac{1}{4}(1-\gamma) + \frac{3}{4}(1-\gamma)$

Game for Player 1

and

$\frac{1}{2}\delta + \frac{1}{3}(1-\delta)$	$\frac{1}{2}\delta$	$\frac{1}{3}(1-\delta)$	0
$\frac{1}{2}\delta + \frac{1}{3}(1-\delta)$	$\frac{1}{2}\delta + \frac{2}{3}(1-\delta)$	$\frac{1}{3}(1-\delta) + \frac{1}{2}\delta$	$\frac{1}{2}\delta + \frac{2}{3}(1-\delta)$
0	0	0	0
0	$\frac{2}{3}(1-\delta)$	$\frac{1}{2}\delta$	$\frac{1}{2}\delta + \frac{2}{3}(1-\delta)$

Game for Player 2

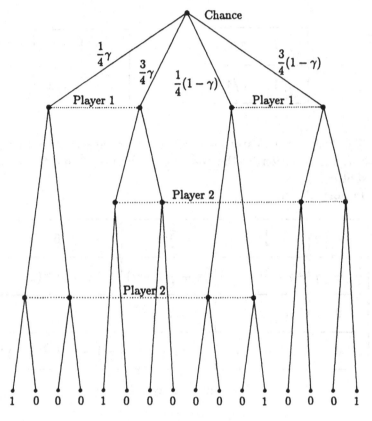

Figure 5. Game for Player 1

Combined, they form a 2-person non-constant-sum game.

The justification for the above representation lies in the fact that if both players play an equilibrium strategy pair with respect to the representation game, then in the original game with incomplete information, neither player can benefit by deviating alone to another strategy, regardless of which game G_{ij} is the true one. The converse is also true: If a strategy pair is such that regardless of which G_{ij} is the true game, a player cannot benefit by departing from it alone in the game with incomplete information, then this strategy pair is an equilibrium pair in the representation suggested above.

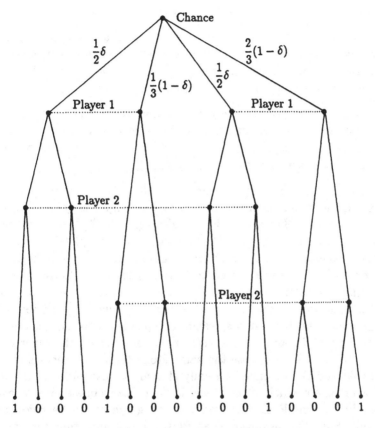

Figure 6. Game for Player 2

REMARK 4.2. The expected payoffs that result from the representation are different from those that are expected if the game of incomplete information is being played, but the effect is only up to multiplying each matrix G_{ij} by a constant (possibly different for each player). It is easy to modify the representation so as to avoid even this slight discrepancy.

REMARK 4.3. The same representation applies if the games G_{ij} are themselves non-constant-sum games. One should note, in this case, that the entries for Player 1 from each G_{ij} should be listed as the payoffs in the game for Player 1 and the entries for Player 2 from each G_{ij} should be listed as payoffs in the game for Player 2.

REMARK 4.4. The consistent case is, of course, a particular case of the inconsistent case. In this case we obtain Harsanyi's representation if we choose $\gamma_i = a_{i1} + a_{i2} + \cdots + a_{i\beta}$, $i = 1, 2, \ldots, \alpha$ and $\delta_j = a_{1j} + a_{2j} + \ldots + a_{\alpha j}$, $j = 1, 2, \ldots, \beta$.

REMARK 4.5. We have seen that there are, in fact, many representations. These depend on the choice of the γ_i's, and δ_j's. Except for the consistent case (see Remark 4.4) we cannot at present recommend any particular one among them.

REMARK 4.6. One might wonder why we arrive at a non-constant-sum game in the inconsistent case even though the games G_{ij} are constant-sum. The answer is that although the G_{ij}'s are constant-sum games the interests of the players are not completely opposed, due to the fact that the players evaluated the situation inherently differently. We are indebted to Harsanyi for the following illuminating example: Two stones lie on a table. One of them is a plain stone and the other—a precious stone. Two players participate in the game and their strategies are independently to choose one of the stones. If both choose different stones then each player gets his stone. If they choose the same stone then the precious stone is sold and the revenue is equally shared by both players. If both players knew which of the stones is the precious one their interests would be completely opposed and the game would be constant-sum. Suppose, however, that Player 1 is completely convinced that stone A is the precious one, whereas his opponent is completely convinced that stone B is the precious one. Clearly, the beliefs are inconsistent. In this case the interests are not at all opposing. Player 1's interest is to possess stone A and Player 2's interest is to possess stone B and both can have their wish. No wonder that a representation of this situation is a non-constant-sum game.

4.2. The Independent and the Dependent Cases

Throughout the remainder of this section we shall deal only with the consistent case. This case can be subdivided into two subcases:

The independent case and the dependent case.

Recall that in the consistent case chance chooses one of the pairs (i,j). The probability of choosing (i,j) is a_{ij}. The independent case is that in which chance chooses i and j independently. More formally, we have:

DEFINITION 4.7. A consistent case will be called *independent* if there are non-negative numbers $p_1, p_2, \ldots, p_\alpha, q_1, q_2, \ldots, q_\beta$ with

$$p_1 + p_2 + \cdots + p_\alpha = 1, \qquad q_1 + q_2 + \cdots + q_\beta = 1, \qquad (4.4)$$

$$a_{ij} = p_i q_j, \qquad i = 1, 2, \ldots, \alpha, \qquad j = 1, 2, \ldots, \beta. \qquad (4.5)$$

The interpretation is that chance chooses i according to the distribution $(p_1, p_2, \ldots, p_\alpha)$ and, independently, j according to the distribution $(q_1, q_2, \ldots, q_\beta)$.

In the remainder of this subsection we shall show that each game with incomplete information in the dependent case is equivalent to a game with incomplete information in the independent case. Rather than stating a general theorem to this effect, we shall show by means of an example how to transform a dependent case to an equivalent independent case.

EXAMPLE 4.8. Consider the stage games

1	2
3	4

5	6
7	8

9	10
11	12

13	14
15	16

and the joint probability distribution

1/4	1/8
0	5/8

which represents a dependent case. We would like to transform this game—at first the 1-shot case—into an equivalent game in which the joint probability matrix is

1/4	1/4
1/4	1/4

which is an independent case. (Any matrix with strictly positive entries representing an independent case will do). Examining the tree (Figure 7), which describes Harsanyi's representation of the original game, we find that it can be replaced by a similar tree (Figure 8) which differs from the first one only by the probability distribution on the choice of chance and by the payoffs at the end of the tree. These payoffs, however, are chosen in such a way that along corresponding paths[28] the product of the probability and the payoff remains the same.

This being the case, it follows that for each pair of pure strategies both trees yield the same expected payoff and therefore both games are, in fact, the same game. Going back to the original game with incomplete information, we see that it is equivalent to the game

---

[28] From the origin to a payoff.

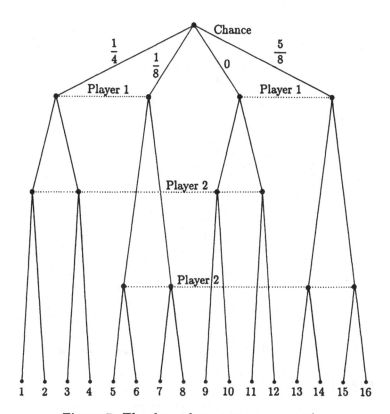

Figure 7. The dependent case representation

1	2
3	4

$2\frac{1}{2}$	3
$3\frac{1}{2}$	4

0	0
0	0

$32\frac{1}{2}$	35
$37\frac{1}{2}$	40

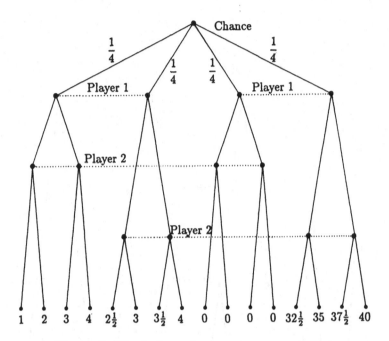

Figure 8. The independent case representation

with joint probability matrix

1/4	1/4
1/4	1/4

It is also true that the original infinite shot game is equal to the infinite shot game based on these stage games, and the independent joint probability matrix.

Thus, without loss of generality, we shall assume in the remainder of this section that we are in the independent case.

4.3. Conditions Under Which a Value Exists

Let $\Gamma_\infty(q^0, p^0)$ be a Harsanyi representation of a consistent independent game with incomplete information on both sides. Here, $q^0 = (q_1^0, q_2^0, \ldots, q_\beta^0)$ is the probability distribution over the columns of the stage games, and $p^0 = (p_1^0, p_2^0, \ldots, p_\alpha^0)$ is the distribution over the rows of the stage games.

Generalizing the considerations of the previous section, we may define the game $\Delta_1(q, p)$, which is a 1-shot game (with variables q and p similar to $\Gamma_1(q, p)$, except that chance does not reveal at all either the index i or the index j. Denote by $u_1(q, p)$ the value of $\Delta_1(q, p)$.

Before proceeding with the analysis, we need some notation: Let u be any function defined on pairs (q, p) of probability distributions. We shall denote by $\operatorname{cav}_p u$ the smallest function on such pairs that is concave in p and is not smaller than u at each point (q, p). Similarly, $\operatorname{vex}_q u$ will denote the greatest function that is convex[29] in q which is not greater than u at each point (q, p). $\operatorname{cav}_p u(q, p)$ will denote the value of $\operatorname{cav}_p u$ at (q, p); similarly, $\operatorname{vex}_q u(q, p)$ will denote the value of $\operatorname{vex}_q u$ at (q, p). Finally, $\operatorname{vex}_q \operatorname{cav}_p u(q, p)$ will denote the value of $\operatorname{vex}_q \operatorname{cav}_p u$ at (q, p); the notation $\operatorname{cav}_p \operatorname{vex}_q u(p, q)$ has a similar meaning. In a similar fashion, we define $\operatorname{cav}_p v$ and $\operatorname{vex}_q w$ for functions v and w defined on single probability distributions p and q, respectively.

Let us look at $\Gamma_\infty(q^0, p^0)$ from the point of view of Player 1. He may, if he wishes, draw lotteries at the beginning, which depend on the index i known to him. Then, having observed the outcome, he may proceed to play a game $\Gamma_\infty^*(q^0, p^1)$ in which he himself does not know the choice of chance. But in this game, p^0 is replaced by p^1—the conditional probability distribution over the rows of stage games as computed by a Player 2 who is assumed to know the nature of these lotteries and to observe the outcome. Since the outcome of the lotteries on the rows (the i index) is unknown to both players, and since both players place on these lotteries the conditional probability distribution p^1, one can combine the games in each column with the probability distribution p^1 and thus

---

[29]Convexification rather than concavification is used for q because Player 2 wants to minimize the payoff.

arrive at a game $\Gamma_\infty^{**}(q^0)$. This game is of the type discussed in the previous section, except that now Player 2 has all the information and Player 1 only has a probability distribution on the choice of chance. Thus, Player 1 can play a Blackwell's strategy and guarantee himself

$$\underset{q}{\text{vex}}\, u_1^{**}(q^0). \tag{4.6}$$

Here, $u_1^{**}(q)$ is the value of the game $\Delta_1^{**}(q)$, which differs from $\Gamma_1^{**}(q)$ by the requirement that Player 2 also does not know the choice of chance on the columns (the j index). Note that $\Delta_1^{**}(q)$ is precisely the game $\Delta_1(q, p^1)$. Thus, inasmuch as a conditional probability p^1 arises, Player 1 can guarantee himself

$$\underset{q}{\text{vex}}\, u_1(q^0, p^1). \tag{4.7}$$

However, by lotteries Player 1 cannot assure any specific p^1. He can only assure a distribution of p's whose expectation is p^0. Choosing that distribution that yields him the highest expected payoff, Player 1 can guarantee by this type of strategy the amount

$$\underset{p}{\text{cav}}\,\underset{q}{\text{vex}}\, u_1(q^0, p^0). \tag{4.8}$$

In a similar fashion we can show that Player 2 can guarantee himself

$$\underset{q}{\text{vex}}\,\underset{p}{\text{cav}}\, u_1(q^0, p^0). \tag{4.9}$$

We therefore arrive at

THEOREM 4.9. *If*

$$\underset{p}{\text{cav}}\,\underset{q}{\text{vex}}\, u_1(q^0, p^0) = \underset{q}{\text{vex}}\,\underset{p}{\text{cav}}\, u_1(q^0, p^0), \tag{4.10}$$

then the game $\Gamma_\infty(q^0, p^0)$ has a value $v_\infty(q^0, p^0)$, namely the common value of the two expressions in (4.10).

Naturally one wants to know if (4.10) always holds. The answer is negative, as the following example—constructed together with R. Stearns—shows:

EXAMPLE 4.10. Let $\Gamma_\infty\big((1/2,1/2);(1/2,1/2)\big)$ be defined by the stage games

1	2	0		-1	0	2
-1	2	0		1	0	2
1	2	0		1	0	2
-1	2	0		-1	0	2

1	0	2		-1	2	0
-1	0	2		1	2	0
-1	0	2		-1	2	0
1	0	2		1	2	0

with the joint probability distribution

1/4	1/4
1/4	1/4

i.e., $q^0 = (\frac{1}{2},\frac{1}{2})$, $p^0 = (\frac{1}{2},\frac{1}{2})$.

Combining the rows with probability distribution $(p, 1-p)$ and the columns with probability distribution $(q, 1-q)$ we obtain that the game $\Delta_1(q, p)$ is defined by the matrix

$2q - 1$	$2(1-q)(1-p) + 2qp$	$2p(1-q) + 2q(1-p)$
$-2q + 1$	$2(1-q)(1-p) + 2qp$	$2p(1-q) + 2q(1-p)$
$2p - 1$	$2(1-q)(1-p) + 2qp$	$2p(1-q) + 2q(1-p)$
$1 - 2p$	$2(1-q)(1-p) + 2qp$	$2p(1-q) + 2q(1-p)$

The value $u_1(q, p)$ of this game is given in the various regions of Figure 9, for $0 \leq q, p \leq \frac{1}{2}$. This determines the value for the other probabilities q, p, because it is symmetric about the lines $q = \frac{1}{2}$ and $p = \frac{1}{2}$. The boundaries of the various regions are given by equating the payoffs in the neighboring regions.

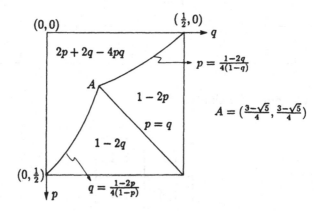

Figure 9. The payoffs in the various regions

Figures 10 and 11 result from computing $\mathrm{cav}_p \, \mathrm{vex}_q \, u_1(q,p)$ and $\mathrm{vex}_q \, \mathrm{cav}_p \, u_1(q,p)$. Again, there is a complete symmetry in the values of these functions about $q = \frac{1}{2}$ and $p = \frac{1}{2}$. Thus, in this example

$$\underset{p}{\mathrm{cav}} \, \underset{q}{\mathrm{vex}} \, u_1\Big(\frac{1}{2}, \frac{1}{2}\Big) = \frac{1}{2}, \qquad (4.11)$$

$$\underset{q}{\mathrm{vex}} \, \underset{p}{\mathrm{cav}} \, u_1\Big(\frac{1}{2}, \frac{1}{2}\Big) = \frac{\sqrt{5}-1}{2}. \qquad (4.12)$$

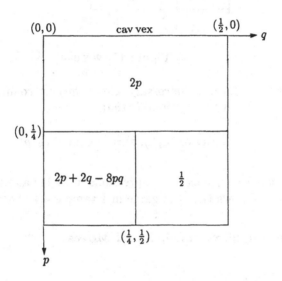

Figure 10. cav vex

Therefore, by the above strategies Player 1 can guarantee that he will receive at least $1/2$ and Player 2 can guarantee that he will not pay more than $(\sqrt{5}-1)/2$.

One can therefore ask if there are other strategies for one or both players that can guarantee better results. The answer is negative. In Chapter Three, R. Stearns proves the following:

THEOREM 4.11. *No strategy for Player 1 guarantees that he will receive more than* $\mathrm{cav}_p \, \mathrm{vex}_q \, u_1(p,q)$, *and no strategy for Player 2 guarantees that he will pay less than* $\mathrm{vex}_q \, \mathrm{cav}_p \, u_1(p,q)$.

Combining this with Theorem 4.9, we obtain

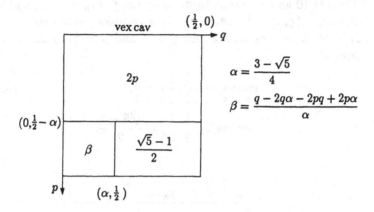

Figure 11. vex cav

THEOREM 4.12. *A necessary and sufficient condition that the game* $\Gamma_\infty(q,p)$ *have a value is that*

$$\operatorname*{cav}_{p}\operatorname*{vex}_{q} u_1(q,p) = \operatorname*{vex}_{q}\operatorname*{cav}_{p} u_1(q,p).$$

In particular, since the expressions in (4.11) and (4.12) are not equal, it follows that the game in Example 4.10 has no value.

5. Incomplete Knowledge of Moves

5.1. Examples

Up to now, we have assumed that the stage games are given in normal form (i.e., represented by matrices), and at the end of each stage the moves of the players are announced. It has been pointed out to us by R. Selten that if the stage games are given in extensive form (i.e., represented by trees), then the information one obtains by knowing which terminal was reached (but not in which stage game) is not the same information that one obtains from the equivalent normal form, when moves are announced. We shall present here a few examples, assuming (as in Section 3) that there is lack of information only on one side, that of Player 2. In the following subsections we formulate a model and state, without proof, a theorem that characterizes the value in these cases. For a full analysis of this kind of game, see Chapter Four.

EXAMPLE 5.1. Consider the following stage games (Figure 12):

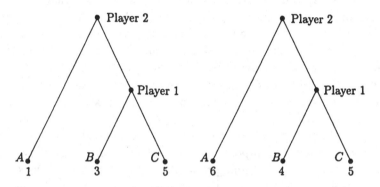

Figure 12. Incomplete knowledge of moves

In each game, Player 2 chooses between two alternatives, L and R, and, similarly, Player 1 chooses between two alternatives L and R. The choices are made independently. If Player 2 chooses L, the payoff is determined, regardless of the choice made by Player 1. It is 1 in the case of G_1 and 6 in the case of G_2. If Player 2 chooses R, the payoff depends on the move of Player 1. It is 3 and 4 in games G_1 and G_2, respectively, if Player 1 chooses L, and it is 5 if Player 1 chooses R. At the end of each stage the players are informed which of the vertices A, B, or C in the above figure was reached, but Player 2 is not informed in which of the games he was playing. Thus, if Player 2 chose L, he will not be able to deduce the move chosen by Player 1.

Transforming each game into normal form, we obtain the matrices

1	3
1	5

G_1

6	4
6	5

G_2

But it must be noted that if a result is reached in the first column, Player 2 is not informed of the move made by Player 1 (in addition to not knowing which of the two stage games is being played).

This situation is somewhat different from the situation discussed in Section 3, and we are interested in knowing whether the results of Section 3 can be generalized to this situation. At the moment we are interested in finding out what types of strategies for Player 1 may reveal something about the choice of chance (in Harsanyi's model). Obviously, if Player 1 chooses L at each stage with probabilities in G_1 equal to the probabilities in G_2, then he neither makes use of the information that he possesses nor does he reveal any further information to Player 2—even if Player 2 knew these probabilities. These are non-revealing strategies just as they were in Section 3. Suppose now that at a certain stage Player 1 decides to employ different probabilities in G_1 and G_2. Does he reveal something? The answer depends on the move of Player 2 at that stage. If he goes left he will not find out what was the move chosen by Player 1, and therefore his conditional probability on the choice of chance will not be different from his conditional probability at the previous stage. But Player 2 may choose to go right, in which case he will find out Player 1's move and he will be able to deduce a conditional probability different from the previous one. Since we are interested in finding out what a given strategy for Player 1 can guarantee, i.e., what is the worst thing that can happen to Player 1 if he uses that strategy, and since the loss that Player 2 may possibly suffer in one stage by going right does not matter in the infinite shot game $\Gamma_\infty(1/2)$, we shall still say that the strategy for Player 1 in this game, which uses different probabilities for G_1 and G_2 at any stage, is a *revealing strategy*. In this example, therefore, the non-revealing strategies are precisely those that were described in Section 3.

EXAMPLE 5.2. Consider the two stage games of Figure 13:
Rules of the stage game: Player 1 makes a choice from two alternatives L and R. Having made the choice, Player 1 is required to make a second choice from two alternatives L and R. Player 2 is told which moves were made by Player 1 only if they were either LL or RR. If Player 1 chose either RL or LR, Player 2 is told only that Player 1 made his moves, whereupon he is required to

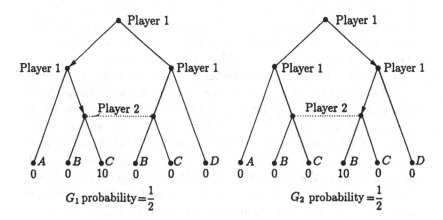

Figure 13. Using one's information without revealing anything

make a choice from two alternatives L and R. If Player 1 chooses
RR or LL he gets 0 in each of the two stage games, regardless of
Player 2's choices. If he chooses RL in the first stage game and LR
in the second stage game he again gets 0, regardless of Player 2's
choices. The only case in the first stage game in which he does
not get 0 is if he chooses LR *and* Player 2 chooses R. He then
gets 10 from Player 2. Similarly, the only case in the second stage
game in which Player 1 does not get 0 is if he chooses RL *and*
Player 2 chooses L. At the end of each stage the players simply
remember whatever they knew or did during the play of the stage
game. They are also told that the play of the stage game has
ended. Thus, Player 1 knows everything, whereas the information
for Player 2 is illustrated by capital letters at the terminals of Figure 13. For example, if the players have reached a terminal marked
B, then Player 2 does not know whether it has been reached via
the choices LRL or RLL and he also does not know which of the
two stage games is the true one. Note that if Player 2 knew which
of the two stage games is the true one he could reduce the payoff
to zero (by going L in the first stage game and going R in the
second one). Note also that if Player 1 is committed to actions
in which he himself does not know the choice of chance—i.e., to
using the same strategy in both stage games—then the only sen-
sible thing for him to do is to use combinations of LR and RL.

In fact, it can easily be proved that under the restriction of using the same strategy in both stage games, the only optimal strategy for Player 1 is to mix LR and RL with equal probabilities. This strategy guarantees him $\frac{10}{4} = 2\frac{1}{2}$ in Harsanyi's model.

But Player 1 can do much better! He *can make use* of the fact that he knows the choice of chance and yet *reveal nothing* to his opponent. For example, he can choose at each stage to go LR if he is in the first stage game and RL if he is in the second stage game. (This strategy is described by arrows in the figure). Since Player 2 cannot distinguish between RL and LR, his conditional probabilities on the choice of chance will remain $(1/2, 1/2)$. Thus, in this example Player 1 can profit by making use of his knowledge and, contrary to the situation discussed in Section 3, he can do so without revealing anything about the true stage game.

If we write the games in normal form we obtain

	L	R
LL	0	0
LR	0	10
RL	0	0
RR	0	0

G_1

	L	R
LL	0	0
LR	0	0
RL	10	0
RR	0	0

G_2

The information pattern at the end of each stage being[30]

	L	R
LL	a	d
LR	b	e
RL	b	e
RR	c	f

IG_1

	L	R
LL	a	d
LR	b	e
RL	b	e
RR	c	f

IG_2

Here, we have used two additional matrices to represent information. Equal symbols in these matrices indicate places that Player 2 cannot distinguish. For example, if the players hit a square with e at the end of a stage, Player 2 knows that he was in one of four squares, but he does not know which one.

EXAMPLE 5.3. In this example (Figure 14), the information concerning the terminals at the end of the stage may depend on the stage game. For instance, if Player 2 chooses R and Player 1 chooses L and the true game is G_1, then Player 2 is told that if the true game is G_1, Player 1 has chosen L and if the true game is G_2, Player 1 has chosen R. In matrix notation, the stage games are

	L	R
L	0	0
R	0	10

G_1

	L	R
L	10	0
R	0	0

G_2

---

[30] IG_j means: the information pattern of G_j, $j = 1, 2$.

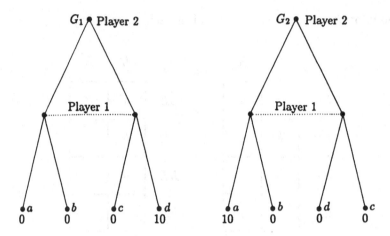

Figure 14. Every pure strategy is revealing

and the information pattern is

	L	R
L	a	c
R	b	d

IG_1

	L	R
L	a	d
R	b	c

IG_2

The interesting aspect of this example is that Player 1 has no non-revealing *pure* strategy. Indeed, if his pure strategy is to choose L in both games, and Player 2 knows this, then he can find out chance's choice by choosing R. If he is told c, he deduces that the true stage game is G_1; otherwise, it is G_2. Similarly, choosing R in both games identifies the choice of chance if Player 2 chooses R. Suppose now that Player 1 uses the following pure strategy: Go L if G_1 is the true game, go R if G_2 is the true game. In this case Player 2, who is assumed to know that this strategy is being used, can choose L and he will identify the true game to be G_1 if he is told a and G_2 if he is told b. In the same fashion one shows that R on G_1 and L on G_2 is a revealing strategy.

But Player 1 has a non-revealing *mixed strategy*. Indeed, if Player 1's strategy in *both* games is to choose L with probability $1/2$ and to choose R with probability $1/2$, then no matter what information Player 2 gets, the conditional probability on the choice of chance is equal to the original *a priori* probability. Here, although the non-revealing strategy prescribes the same procedure for both stage games, if Player 1 wants to reveal nothing about the choice of chance, it is not enough that he acts as if he himself does not know the choice of chance. He must restrict himself to the mixed strategy $(1/2, 1/2)$. Note that if the choice of chance is completely revealed, Player 2 can reduce the expected average payoff to 0; whereas the non-revealing strategy, above, guarantees 2.5.

EXAMPLE 5.4. The stage games are any games, and at the end of each stage nothing is announced. Player 2 knows only his own actions. The information pattern (for Player 2) looks as follows:

a	b	c	$\ldots$
a	b	c	$\ldots$
a	b	c	$\ldots$
$\cdot$	$\cdot$	$\cdot$	
$\cdot$	$\cdot$	$\cdot$	
$\cdot$	$\cdot$	$\cdot$	

IG_1

a	b	c	$\ldots$
a	b	c	$\ldots$
a	b	c	$\ldots$
$\cdot$	$\cdot$	$\cdot$	
$\cdot$	$\cdot$	$\cdot$	
$\cdot$	$\cdot$	$\cdot$	

IG_2

Player 1's optimal strategy is to act at each stage as if he is facing a 1-shot game. Nothing that he does reveals anything about the

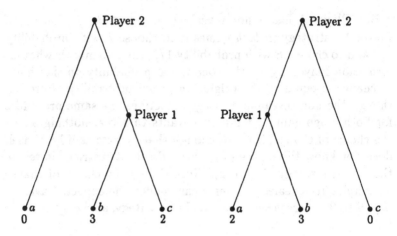

Figure 15. Using one's own information
conceals type

choice of chance. Note that with such a strategy he makes full use
of his information.

EXAMPLE 5.5. This example resembles Example 5.1, except that
the trees are different (see Figure 15). Both games yield 2×2
matrices.

	L	R
L	0	3
R	0	2

G_1

	L	R
L	2	0
R	3	0

G_2

If Player 2 remembers his own moves, then the information pattern at the end of each stage is

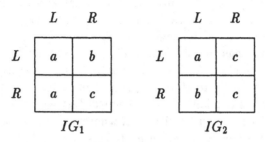

$$IG_1 \qquad\qquad\qquad IG_2$$

The interesting feature of this example is that if terminal b is ever reached, Player 2 will immediately know the choice of chance. In fact, if Player 2 went R, the true stage game must be G_1 and if he went L, the true stage game must be G_2. Thus, the only non-revealing strategy for Player 1 is to move R if the true stage game is G_1 and to move L if the true stage game is G_2. (This strategy is illustrated by arrows in the figures).

This feature is diametrically opposed to the situation we encountered in Section 3. *In order to conceal information, Player 1 must make full use of the information.*

Note that it is advantageous to conceal information, because if Player 2 knew the true stage game he could guarantee not to pay more than 0.

Since this example represents a situation in which the results of Section 3 are not valid, it is worthwhile to describe a somewhat oversimplified realistic situation where the same information pattern may arise:

A manufacturer (Player 1) has two plants A and B, manufacturing two related but different goods. He has a contract with an agent in which he undertakes to produce for him these goods with a specific quality. Since one cannot inspect the finished items without destroying them (say, they are produced in sealed boxes), the manufacturer allows the agent to inspect any one of his plants but only once (or—to make it a repeated game—once for each shipment). Upon inspecting, the agent may perform a chemical test. Somehow, perhaps through spying, the agent learns that the manufacturer has found a way to produce a low quality of merchandise that will not be discovered by the chemical test. The source of this information failed to specify the good concerned (and the manufacturer knows precisely what knowledge is known to the agent). Can the manufacturer cheat and at the same time not reveal which good can be manufactured with low quality and not be detected by the chemical test?

The agent has two strategies (at each stage): to inspect plant A or to inspect plant B. The manufacturer has two strategies (if he decides to cheat): to cheat in plant A or to cheat in plant B. G_1 represents a situation where a chemical test would fail at plant A, whereas G_2 represents a situation where a chemical test would fail at plant B. The information pattern is

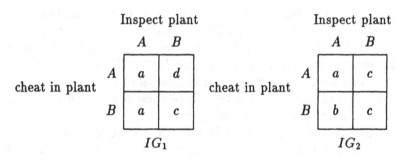

The following is a non-revealing strategy for the manufacturer: Cheat in that plant in which you can overcome the chemical test. This is a strategy in which Player 1 makes full use of the information that Player 2 lacks. Any other strategy, such as deciding by flipping a coin which plant to choose for cheating does not guarantee that Player 2 will not discover which good can be produced at a low quality and escape the chemical test. For example, if the agent ever detects a violation, say at A, he learns not only that the manufacturer cheated but also that his method for concealing violations does not work in plant A and so does work in plant B.

EXAMPLE 5.6. It is very easy to construct an example in which Player 1 has no non-revealing strategy whatsoever. One simply labels the information sets differently in each of the stage games, as in the information pattern

	L	R
L	a	b
R	a	c

IG_1

	L	R
L	d	e
R	d	e

IG_2

Note that in this example Player 2 will always be ignorant of the move taken by Player 1 if G_2 is the true stage game. He will also be ignorant if the true stage game is G_1 and he moved L. However, he will always be able to tell which is the true stage-game. This example represents a repeated game in which the *rules of the game* specify that the true stage game is announced after the first stage.

A more sophisticated example is the following:

EXAMPLE 5.7. Consider the information pattern

	κ	λ	ρ	σ
$x\,\alpha$	a	c	e	h
$y\,\beta$	b	d	e	g
$z\,\gamma$	i	j	f	h

IG_1

	κ	λ	ρ	σ
$r\,\alpha$	b	c	f	g
$s\,\beta$	a	d	f	h
$t\,\gamma$	i	j	e	g

IG_2

A strategy for Player 1 in a stage is to play in G_1 rows α, β, γ with probabilities x, y, z, respectively and in G_2 to play rows α, β, γ with probabilities r, s, t, respectively. If $x \neq r$ or $y \neq s$ or $z \neq t$, then by playing λ and observing the resulting information set, there is a positive probability that Player 2 can deduce conditional

probabilities that are different from the *a priori* probabilities.[31]
Therefore, $x = r$, $y = s$ and $z = t$. However, if $x \neq s$ or $y \neq r$, then
by playing κ, there is again a positive probability that Player 2
will deduce a different conditional probability. Therefore, $x = s$,
$y = r$. Similarly $x + y = t$ and $x + z = s$. All these equalities are
impossible to fulfill and therefore none of Player 1's strategies is
non-revealing.

5.2 The Model

In order to simplify the representation we shall now assume that
there are only two stage games. Let us stress, however, that the
results can be generalized to any number of stage games. In the
remainder of this section we shall describe some general results on
repeated games in which the moves are not necessarily revealed
at the end of each stage. We shall also sketch some of the proofs.
Note that the situation in Section 3 is a particular case of the
situation described here.

As in Section 3, we assume that one of two 2-person constant-
sum stage games, G_1 and G_2, is repeated infinitely often. We assume that Player 1 knows which game is being played and Player 2
associates a probability distribution $p^0 = (p_1^0, p_2^0)$ to the possibilities that G_1 and G_2 are the true stage games. Each stage game
is an $m \times n$ matrix whose entries are known to both players.

We assume[32] that Player 1 knows at the end of each stage what
moves were made by both players at this and the previous stages.

Contrary to Section 3, we assume here that Player 2 remembers
only his own previous moves[33] and receives only partial information about the moves of Player 1. More precisely, we assume that
a partition of the set of cells in both matrices into so-called *information sets* is given, and Player 2 is told at the end of each stage

---

[31] For example, if $x \neq y$, and Player 2 gets the signal c, he will deduce a
different probability distribution on the choice of chance.

[32] No such assumption is made in the more general treatment in Chapter Four.(*)

[33] We conjecture that even this requirement can be relaxed. However we do
not wish here to consider situations in which a player forgets his own moves.
(They do occur if a player is actually a group of people, say it is a country,
and there is a lack of communication between them.)

at which information set the outcome fell in this and the previous stages. Thus, the information pattern can be represented as two $m \times n$ matrices IG_1 and IG_2, whose entries a_{ij} and b_{ij} are taken from a set of letters $\{a, b, c, \ldots, z\}$, such that two cells may contain the same letter only if they belong to the same column either in the same or in the two matrices; i.e.

$$a_{i_1 j_1} = a_{i_2 j_2} \implies j_1 = j_2, \qquad (5.1)$$

$$b_{i_1 j_1} = b_{i_2 j_2} \implies j_1 = j_2, \qquad (5.2)$$

$$a_{i_1 j_1} = b_{i_2 j_2} \implies j_1 = j_2. \qquad (5.3)$$

A *history* h for Player 2 is a sequence $h = (\alpha_1, \alpha_2, \alpha_3, \ldots)$, where $\alpha_j \in \{a, b, \ldots, z\}$, $j = 1, 2, 3 \ldots$; it *takes place* during a certain play if, after the first, second, $\ldots$ stages the outcomes are $\alpha_1, \alpha_2, \ldots$, respectively. A *$k$-stage history* $h_k = (\alpha_1, \alpha_2, \ldots, \alpha_k)$, $k = 1, 2, 3, \ldots$, is such a sequence truncated to k elements.

It will sometimes be convenient to talk also about a 0-*stage history* h_0, which is an empty sequence representing the start of play.

A *history* e for Player 1 is a sequence of pairs $e = ((\mu_1, \nu_1), (\mu_2, \nu_2), \ldots)$, $\mu_i \in 1, 2, \ldots, m$, $\nu_i \in 1, 2, \ldots, n$, $i = 1, 2, 3, \ldots$, and we say that the history *took place* if Player 1 chose the moves $\mu_1, \mu_2, \ldots$ and Player 2 chose the moves $\nu_1, \nu_2, \ldots$ in the first, second, $\ldots$ stages, respectively.

Similarly, we talk about a *k-stage history* e_k, which is a history truncated to k pairs, $k = 1, 2, \ldots$, and we talk about the 0-stage history e_0 for Player 1 which represents the start of play.

A k-stage history h_k uniquely determines Player 2's moves $\nu_1, \nu_2, \ldots, \nu_k$ in the first k stages. It also determines two sets, $M_1(h_k)$ and $M_2(h_k)$, which are the moves that could have been taken by Player 1 in the first k stages if the true stage game had been G_1 or G_2, respectively. If $h_k = (\alpha_1, \alpha_2, \ldots, \alpha_k)$ then

$$M_1(h_k) = \{(\mu_1, \ldots, \mu_k) \mid a_{\mu_1 \nu_1} = \alpha_1, \ldots, a_{\mu_k \nu_k} = \alpha_k\}, \qquad (5.4)$$

$$M_2(h_k) = \{(\mu_1, \ldots, \mu_k) \mid b_{\mu_1 \nu_1} = \alpha_1, \ldots, b_{\mu_k \nu_k} = \alpha_k\}. \qquad (5.5)$$

A strategy for Player 2 is a sequence $\left(\lambda^1(h_0), \lambda^2(h_1), \lambda^3(h_2), \ldots \right)$ of probability distributions over the set of columns $\{1, 2, \ldots, n\}$, where the k-th distribution is a function of the $(k-1)$-stage history h_{k-1} that took place.

A strategy[34] for Player 1 is a pair of sequences $(\sigma^1(e_0), \sigma^2(e_1),$ $\sigma^3(e_2),\ldots), (\tau^1(e_0), \tau^2(e_1), \tau^3(e_2),\ldots)$ of distributions over the rows $\{1, 2, \ldots, m\}$. The interpretation is that if G_1 $[G_2]$ is the true stage game, and if Player 1's history e_{k-1} took place in the first $k-1$ stages then Player 1 will use the distribution $\sigma^k(e_{k-1})$ $[\tau^k(e_{k-1})]$ at the k-th stage.

Suppose we are given a strategy $\lambda = (\lambda^1, \lambda^2, \ldots)$ for Player 2 and a strategy $(\sigma, \tau) = ((\sigma^1, \sigma^2, \ldots), (\tau^1, \tau^2, \ldots))$ for Player 1, both known to Player 2. Then Player 2 is still not capable of computing Player 1's probability distributions over moves in the k-th stage game, $k \geq 2$, because these distributions depend on the previous moves of Player 1, which are not known to Player 2. All he can do is form an expectation over all possible moves of Player 1 in the first $k-1$ stages which lead to the history h_{k-1} that he knows; i.e., over all the elements of $M_1(h^{k-1})$ and $M_2(h^{k-1})$. In other words, Player 2 must consider the *expected distributions* s^k, t^k, defined by

$$s^k = \frac{\sum_{\mu^{k-1} \in M_1(h_{k-1})} \text{Prob}(\mu^{k-1}, \nu^{k-1}) \sigma^k(\mu^{k-1}, \nu^{k-1})}{\sum_{\mu^{k-1} \in M_1(h_{k-1})} \text{Prob}(\mu^{k-1}, \nu^{k-1})}, \quad (5.6)$$

$$t^k = \frac{\sum_{\mu^{k-1} \in M_2(h_{k-1})} \text{Prob}(\mu^{k-1}, \nu^{k-1}) \tau^k(\mu^{k-1}, \nu^{k-1})}{\sum_{\mu^{k-1} \in M_2(h_{k-1})} \text{Prob}(\mu^{k-1}, \nu^{k-1})}. \quad (5.7)$$

Here, $\mu^{k-1} = (\mu_1, \mu_2, \ldots, \mu_{k-1})$ and $\nu^{k-1} = (\nu_1, \nu_2, \ldots, \nu_{k-1})$, $k = 1, 2, 3, \ldots$. The sequence ν^{k-1} is completely determined by the history h_{k-1}.

One can regard $(s, t) \equiv ((s^1, s^2, \ldots), (t^1, t^2, \ldots))$ as a new strategy for Player 1, with the interpretation that s^k $[t^k]$ is the probability distribution at the k-th stage whenever the history e_{k-1} implies a history h_{k-1} and the true stage game is G_1 $[G_2]$. Obviously, such a distribution is a function of h_{k-1} only.

---

[34]Note that we are making use of the fact that the information that Player 1 gets is standard; namely, that at each stage he knows all moves made. Otherwise, the histories $e_1, e_2, \ldots$ are not known to him.(*)

LEMMA 5.8. *The strategy (σ, t) for Player 1 is equivalent to the corresponding strategy (s, t) in the sense that at each stage they both lead to the same expected payoff for each strategy λ of Player 2, and for each λ, both yield the same probability that any k-stage history h_k takes place. Moreover, as far as Player 2 is concerned, they generate the same expected probability distribution over Player 1's moves at each stage.*

PROOF: The last part has already been proved by (5.6) and (5.7). It follows from the definitions of s and t that the probabilities for the occurrence of each history h_k are equal under both strategies. Finally, since the expected payoffs are bilinear in the probabilities of choosing rows and columns, it follows that the expected payoffs are also equal at each stage under both strategies. ∎

Note that (s, t) depends only on Player 2's history h. When Player 1 plays (σ, τ), Player 2 makes the same observations[35] as those he would have made had Player 1 played (s, t). Therefore, Player 2's conditional probabilities on Player 1's type when Player 1 plays (σ, τ) are the same as what they would have been had Player 1 played (s, t). By Lemma 5.8, nothing changes in the payoffs if Player 1 actually plays (s, t) instead of (σ, τ). In view of this, we say from now on that Player 1 *uses* (s, t) when he plays (σ, τ).

5.3. Revealing Information

If Player 1 plays a strategy $(s, t) = ((s^1(h_0), s^2(h_1), \ldots),$ $(t^1(h_0), t^2(h_1), \ldots))$ and Player 2 plays a strategy $\lambda = (\lambda^1(h_0), \lambda^2(h_1), \ldots)$, then the probability that history h_k results, given that $G_1[G_2]$ is the true stage game is

$$w(h_k|G_1) =$$
$$\Big[\sum_{\mu_1 : a_{\mu_1 \nu_1} = \alpha_1} s^1_{\mu_1}(h_0) \Big] \Big[\sum_{\mu_2 : a_{\mu_2 \nu_2} = \alpha_2} s^2_{\mu_2}(h_1) \Big] \ldots \Big[\sum_{\mu_k : a_{\mu_k \nu_k} = \alpha_k} s^k_{\mu_k}(h_{k-1}) \Big] \cdot$$
$$\lambda^1_{\nu_1}(h_0) \lambda^2_{\nu_2}(h_1) \ldots \lambda^k_{\nu_k}(h_{k-1}),$$

$$(5.8)$$

---

[35] The letters in the information matrix.

$$w(h_k|G_2) =$$
$$\Big[\sum_{\mu_1 : b_{\mu_1 \nu_1} = \alpha_1} t^1_{\mu_1}(h_0) \Big] \Big[\sum_{\mu_2 : b_{\mu_2 \nu_2} = \alpha_2} t^2_{\mu_2}(h_1) \Big] \dots \Big[\sum_{\mu_k : b_{\mu_k \nu_k} = \alpha_k} t^k_{\mu_k}(h_{k-1}) \Big] \cdot$$
$$\lambda^1_{\nu_1}(h_0) \lambda^2_{\nu_2}(h_1) \dots \lambda^k_{\nu_k}(h_{k-1}).$$

$$(5.9)$$

Here, $h_k = (\alpha_1, \alpha_2, \dots, \alpha_k)$, and the signal α_j lies in the column ν_j in at least one of the matrices IG_1 and IG_2.

The expression

$$w(h_k) = p^0_1 \ w(h_k|G_1) + p^0_2 w(h_k|G_2) \qquad (5.10)$$

is the *a priori* probability that history h_k will take place.

If history h_k takes place and Player 2 knows both (s,t) and λ, he can compute the conditional distribution $(p^0_1(h_k), p^0_2(h_k))$ on the choice of chance. It is given by $p^0_1(h_0) = p^0_1$, $p^0_2(h_0) = p^0_2$, and

$$p^0_1(h_k) = \frac{p^0_1 w(h_k|G_1)}{p^0_1 w(h_k|G_1) + p^0_2 w(h_k|G_2)}, \qquad (5.11)$$

$$p^0_2(h_k) = \frac{p^0_2 w(h_k|G_2)}{p^0_1 w(h_k|G_1) + p^0_2 w(h_k|G_2)}, \qquad (5.12)$$

$$k = 1, 2, \dots$$

Note that the conditional probabilities do not depend on λ.

Our first concern is to determine what strategies of Player 1 do not reveal any new information on the choice of chance; i.e., for what strategies $p^0_1(h_k) = p^0_1$, for all histories h_k, and all choices $\lambda^1, \lambda^2, \dots, \lambda^k$, that occur with positive probability.

Clearly, this requirement is met if $p^0_1 = 0$ or $p^0_1 = 1$, regardless of Player 1's strategy. If, however, $0 < p^0_1 < 1$, it is met if and only if $w(h_k|G_1) = w(h_k|G_2)$ (see (5.11)) or, by (5.8) and (5.9), if and only if

$$\sum_{\mu | a_{\mu\nu} = \alpha} s^k_\mu(h_{k-1}) = \sum_{\mu | b_{\mu\nu} = \alpha} t^k_\mu(h_{k-1}), \qquad (5.13)$$

for all the histories h_{k-1}, $k = 1, 2, \dots$ and for all signals α. Relation (5.13) motivates the following:

DEFINITION 5.9. A strategy $((s_1, s_2, \ldots, s_m), (t_1, t_2, \ldots, t_m))$ of Player 1 in the 1-shot game will be called *non-separating* if

$$\sum_{\mu: a_{\mu\nu} = \alpha} s_\mu = \sum_{\mu: b_{\mu\nu} = \alpha} t_\mu, \text{ all } \alpha. \qquad (5.14)$$

We have just proved:

LEMMA 5.10. *If $p_1^0 = 0$ or $p_1^0 = 1$, Player 1 does not reveal any information, regardless of the strategy he employs. If $0 < p_1^0 < 1$, Player 1 reveals no information if and only if at each stage he uses a non-separating strategy.*

Verbally stated, a strategy of Player 1 in the 1-shot game is non-separating iff, for any pure strategy of Player 2, one reaches the same information sets in both stage games with equal probabilities.

Note that the set of non-separating strategies is compact and convex. It may be empty (see Examples 5.6 and 5.7). Like in Section 3, we can now define the game $\Delta_1(p)$, which is the one-shot game in which chance makes a lottery with distribution p, of the result of which he informs Player 1 but not Player 2. If the first alternative comes through, game G_1 is played; otherwise— game G_2 is played. Unlike in $\Gamma_1(p)$, Player 1's strategies in $\Delta_1(p)$ are limited to non-separating ones. The game $\Delta_1(p)$ is defined only if the set of non-separating strategies is not empty. We shall denote by $u_1(p)$ the value of $\Delta_1(p)$. Clearly, in $\Gamma_\infty(p^0)$, Player 1 can guarantee himself[36] $u_1(p^0)$ by simply playing at each stage the optimal strategy for $\Delta_1(p^0)$. Moreover, if $p^0 = (0, 1)$ or $p^0 = (1, 0)$ he can guarantee for himself $v_1(p_0)$ by simply playing at each stage an optimal strategy for $\Gamma_1(p^0)$. In general, he can guarantee himself more, as we shall see in the next subsection.

5.4. The Main Theorem

A theorem analogous to the main theorem in Section 3 is not quite straightforward. One reason is that in the model discussed in Section 3, "withholding information" was synonymous with "acting

---

[36] If $\Delta_1(p^0)$ exists.

as if one does not know such information". This is no longer true
in the model used in this section, as all the examples of subsection
5.1 show. One question that arises when one tries to generalize
the results of Section 3 is, which of these two aspects is the crucial one. It turns out that the "non-revealing" aspect is the aspect
which lends itself to generalization. Another factor that slightly
complicates matters is the special role of the distributions $(1,0)$
and $(0,1)$. If p^0 is one of these distributions and if Player 1 wishes
not to reveal any further information, he does not have to restrict himself to non-separating strategies. All the information is
already revealed and nothing further can be deduced, regardless
of his method of play.[37] Finally, as Examples 5.6 and 5.7 show,
sometimes there is no way for Player 1 to hide information.

Nevertheless, one can cope with all the complications by replacing the function $u_1(p)$ with the slightly different function

$$\tilde{u}_1(p) = \begin{cases} u_1(p), & \text{if } 0 < p_1 < 1, \\ v_1((0,1)), & \text{if } p = (0,1), \\ v_1((1,0)), & \text{if } p = (1,0). \end{cases} \quad (5.15)$$

Here, $v_1(p)$, $p = (0,1)$ or $p = (1,0)$, is the value of the 1-shot
game $\Gamma_1(p)$ (i.e., the value of G_2 or G_1, respectively). Note that
if non-separating strategies do not exist, $\tilde{u}_1(p)$ is only defined for
$p = (0,1)$ and $p = (1,0)$. We then have the following:[38]

THEOREM 5.11. *The game $\Gamma_\infty(p)$, which is Harsanyi's representation of the game with incomplete information described in subsection 5.2, has a value. The value of this game is given by*

$$v_\infty(p^0) = \text{cav } \tilde{u}_1(p) \text{ at } p = p^0. \quad (5.16)$$

Note that if no non-separating strategy exists then the graph of
cav $\tilde{u}_1(p)$ is a straight line segment joining $v_1((0,1))$ and $v_1((1,0))$.

---

[37]This complication did not arise in Section 3, because there $\Gamma_1(p^0)$ and
$\Delta_1(p^0)$ were the same game for $p^0 = (0,1)$ and for $p^0 = (1,0)$.
[38]The original paper contained a sketch of the proof of Theorem 5.11. Since
Chapter Four contains a full analysis of a more general problem, including a
complete proof, this sketch is omitted here. (*)

6. Further Problems

In this section we shall list a few of the problems in this subject that should be studied further.

A. So far, all the stage games were assumed constant-sum. It is important to find out in what way the results can be extended to non-constant-sum stage games. In most real life situations the stage games are not constant-sum.

B. It is unnatural to assume that the same game is repeated over and over again. Inasmuch as there are repetitions in real life situations, one passes from one stage game to a similar stage game which is not quite the same. One would like to know under what conditions our conclusions can be extended when the stage games are not identical.

C. Even though the rules of the stage games remain the same from stage to stage, it is unnatural to assume that the payoffs remain the same. A "physical" payoff today would be valued by a person more than the same payoff in the far future. We have started to work on a model where a discount factor is imposed on the payments of the stage games. So far we have examined only the example of the two stage games

1	0
0	0

0	0
0	1

where the payoff of the repeated game is defined as

$$v_r(p^0) = (1-r) \cdot \sum_{k=0}^{\infty} A_k r^k \, , \qquad (6.1)$$

where A_k is the true stage game payoff at the k-th stage, and $0 < r < 1$. For such games a value always exists and one would like to compute it. In this example we succeeded in finding recursion

formulas for $r \leq 1/3$ from which one can compute the value at
each rational point. It turns out that, unlike when there is no
discount, there is no explicit simple formula that expresses the
value of the game for each p. In fact, we found that $v_r(p)$ for
$r < 1/3$ is a concave continuous function with no derivative at
any rational p other than $p = (0,1)$ and $p = (1,0)$. These results
so far are fragmentary.

POSTSCRIPTS TO CHAPTER TWO

a. Incomplete Information on Both Sides: $\lim v_n$

Theorem 4.10 says that when there is incomplete information on
both sides, the game $\Gamma_\infty(q,p)$ has a value $v_\infty(q,p)$ if and only
if $\mathrm{cav}_p\,\mathrm{vex}_q\,u(q,p) = \mathrm{vex}_q\,\mathrm{cav}_p\,u(q,p)$ ("cav vex = vex cav" for
short). The question arises whether $v_n(q,p)$ may perhaps have
a limit even when $v_\infty(q,p)$ does not exist. This question arose
already in 1967, when this chapter was written, and the authors
of this book tried hard to solve it, without success. It was solved
by Mertens and Zamir [1972], who proved that the limit does
indeed exist in all these games, that it lies between cav vex and
vex cav, and that the error term, like in the case of incomplete
information on one side, is $O(n^{-1/2})$.

b. Incomplete Information on Both Sides: The Limit of the Discounted Values

When the game is infinite but the payoffs are discounted at a
positive rate, then considerations of compactness and continuity
imply that the value exists. Here, too, one may ask what happens
to the value as the discount rate goes to zero. In their [1972] paper,
Mertens and Zamir showed that this limit also exists, and equals
$\lim v_n$ (where v_n, as always, denotes the value of the undiscounted
n-stage game).

See Postscript f for a conceptual comparison of the discounted
model with other models of long repetition.

c.   The Conceptual Distinction Between Γ_∞ and Γ_n: Generalities

The previous note raises the question as to the intuitive meaning of v_∞ vis-a-vis $\lim v_n$. This is part of the wider topic of the conceptual distinction between infinite-stage games and limits of finite-stage games, as well as other models of long repetitions, a matter of importance also in areas not covered in this book (such as non-zero sum repeated games of complete information).

The most vital difference between the two models lies in the strategies that they admit. The game Γ_n has a definite duration n, on which the players can base their strategies. Indeed, optimal strategies in Γ_n may be quite different for different n. In Γ_∞, on the other hand, the strategies are by definition independent of n. Thus Γ_∞ reflects properties of the games Γ_n that hold "uniformly" in the duration n; it is a model for long repetitions that abstracts away from their durations.

The definition[39] of optimal strategy in Γ_∞ nicely reflects these themes of duration-independence and uniformity. By using an optimal strategy in Γ_∞ (if there is one), a player guarantees in one fell swoop that in any sufficiently long finite truncation, the outcome will not be appreciably worse[40] for him than v_∞. Optimal strategies in Γ_∞ are approximately optimal[41] in each Γ_n, the approximation getting better and better as n grows; and, this approximate optimality is achieved uniformly, using the same strategy[42] for all n.

---

[39] Section 3.1 of this chapter and Section 5 of Chapter Four.

[40] More precisely, any optimal strategy σ for P1 in Γ_∞ guarantees him that no matter at what stage n the game ends, his average payoff will be at least $v_\infty - \varepsilon_n$, where $\varepsilon_n \to 0$ (ε_n depends on n only—not on P2's strategy). Thus P1 does not have to concern himself with the duration of the game, if he is willing to forego ε_n. A similar statement holds for P2. (For the definition of value and optimality in Γ_∞, see Section 3 of this chapter and Section 5 of Chapter Four. See also the discussion in Postscript h below.)

[41] ε_n-optimal (guaranteeing $v_n - \varepsilon_n$), where $\varepsilon_n \to 0$.

[42] It follows that if v_∞ exists, then so does $\lim v_n$, and they are equal. As we have seen, the converse is false; the existence of v_∞ tells us more than that of $\lim v_n$. (The other side of this coin is that when v_∞ does not exist, then $\lim v_n$ gives us information about the game that could not have been gotten by analyzing Γ_∞).

In brief, Γ_∞ embodies the idea of duration-free strategies in Γ_n, and optimality in Γ_∞ means approximate optimality in all the games Γ_n simultaneously.

Several interpretations or views of Γ_∞ flow from this characterization. The first has to do with ignorance of the duration of the game. Both v_∞ and $\lim v_n$ represent the results of strategic interaction in games that are repeated "many" times; they say something about long repetitions, without reference to just *how* long they are; identify "long-term" properties, properties that hold for *all* sufficiently long repetitions.

Now the idea of the "long term" can be understood either from the analyst's or from the players' viewpoint. The former is represented by limiting properties, as $n \to \infty$, of the solutions of Γ_n. Thus $\lim v_n$, since it is independent of n, tells the analyst something about repetitions that are "long," without his having to know how long. But $\lim v_n$ is only meaningful as the limit of values of games whose duration is precisely known to the *players*. If the analyst is asked, "can you say something useful about the value of a long repetition without being told how long?", he can answer, "yes, *I* don't need to know the duration n in order to tell you that the value is approximately $\lim v_n$. But the *players* need to know n. Don't tell me, tell them; how they play may depend crucially on their knowing the duration".

Suppose, on the other hand, that we wish to model the "long term" from the players' viewpoint: To analyze a situation in which the players themselves know only that the game is "long"— without any clear idea of *how* long. In that case, since they don't know n, they can't use strategies depending on n; and then Γ_∞ is the appropriate model.

Strictly speaking, one should treat such situations by modelling the players' uncertainty about the length of the game explicitly.[43]

---

[43]One can always model the players' uncertainty about the duration of the game, about their uncertainty about each others' uncertainty, etc., as follows: Nature initially chooses not only the stage game, but also the duration n of the repetition. Each of the two players then gets partial (and usually different) information about nature's choice; play then proceeds. The game ends after the chosen duration n—which may not be known to either player beforehand—is reached; the payoff is the average payoff over the n stages. In the consistent case (Section 4), this is a zero-sum game; that it has a value follows from familiar compactness arguments (the usual product topology on

Practically, though, there is a limit to the amount of detail that can usefully be put into a model, or indeed that the players can absorb or take into account. Thus one may think of Γ_∞ as reflecting a kind of bounded rationality, in which the information of the players about the length of the game and about each other's thinking on this subject is so complex and vague that they cannot make use of it, or purposely ignore it.

In two-person zero-sum games with complete information on one side, the analyst's and the player's view of the long term lead to roughly similar results (Chapters One and Four), though there are important second-order differences (Postscript c to Chapter One). But in other cases, the results may be strikingly different. For example, when there is incomplete information on both sides, $\lim v_n$ always exists, but v_∞ need not[44] (Postscript a above). This means that if the analyst knows that the players are rational and know the duration of the game,[45] then he can say approximately what the outcome will be; and this is so even though *he* does *not* know the duration, but knows only that it is "long". But if the players themselves do not know the duration of the game, then nothing definite can be said about the outcome, even approximately; all

the pure strategy spaces is compact, and the expected payoff is continuous in this topology; therefore the value exists by standard minimax theorems on topological spaces, like Ville [1938]).

When the expected duration is finite, one may construct a different model by defining the payoff as total rather than average payoff, normalized by dividing by the expected duration. A particular instance of this is obtained from the usual discounted model (with fixed discount rate δ), by reinterpreting $1 - \delta$ as the probability, at any stage, of continuing at least one more stage. The normalized expected payoff then corresponds to the present value of the discounted payoff stream. In this model, too, the above argument shows that the value exists. (When the expected duration is infinite, then in all but the most degenerate cases, the absolute value of the total payoff has infinite expectation, making meaningful analysis difficult.)

[44] Historically, Zamir [1973b] was the first to prove that there is a multi-stage game in which $\lim v_n$ exists but v_∞ does not; but his example was not a repeated game in the sense of this book. Non-existence of v_∞ implies that it is impossible to play even approximately optimally in Γ_n without making essential use of n.

[45] More precisely, that the rationality of the players and the duration of the game is commonly known to the players (see Aumann [1987]).

that can be said is that in the long run, it will lie between cav vex and vex cav (see Postscript d).

A second view of Γ_∞ is as a convenient vehicle for expressing long-run optimal *behavior* (rather than payoff). We have seen that when the players know the duration, $\lim v_n$ expresses long-run or limiting optimal (min max) payoff. But even then, Γ_∞ provides a much more convenient and appropriate framework for the expression of long-run behavior than the sequence of the Γ_n.

An optimal strategy in Γ_∞ may be viewed as a kind of limiting optimal strategy for finite games; it tells one approximately how to act in a long finite game, in much the same way that $\lim v_n$ tells one approximately how much to expect. Thus if one wants to know not only how *much* one can get in an indefinitely long repetition, but also *how* to get it, one should look at Γ_∞.

Third, the bounded rationality view of Γ_∞, mentioned before in the context of uncertainty about the duration n of the game, applies also when n is fixed and commonly known; the players may simply be unable or unwilling to enter into the complexities of basing their strategies on the duration. It is not just a matter of taking account of an additional parameter; it is also that optimal strategies in Γ_n are usually much more complex and difficult to describe than optimal strategies in Γ_∞.

A fourth view of Γ_∞, which may be considered another variation on the bounded rationality theme, is as follows. Rather than playing optimally in each separate situation, real players often develop rules of thumb that work well in general, but not necessarily always.[46] An important function of game theory is to explain real behavior in terms that are qualitative rather than exact; to predict, or explain, such rules of thumb. To be useful, rules of thumb

---

[46]This is related to the evolutionary interpretation of game theory (e.g., Maynard Smith [1982]), in which optimal behavior comes about not because of conscious maximization, but simply by survival of the fittest. Like genes, modes of behavior propagate themselves in various ways; tautologously, it is the successful ones that survive. But in order to propagate itself, a mode of behavior must have a certain universality; if it applies to too small a class of situations, it will not be used sufficiently often to survive. Of course, simplicity helps in successful propagation. Both universality and simplicity point to the infinite-stage model when seeking successful rules of thumb for playing multi-stage games.

must be simple and uncluttered, and apply in wide classes of situations. In repeated games, one way of achieving such simplicity is to abstract away from the length of the game; and indeed most (though not all[47]) of the significant qualitative insights that have been gleaned from research on repeated games of incomplete information have come from Γ_∞.

Fifth, optimal strategies in Γ_∞ often possess a kind of stationarity property. "Stationarity" implies a lack of dependence on the serial number of the stage.[48] Its most extreme form is when the players do the same thing at each stage; more generally, it involves some translation invariance. When there is complete information on one side, then after the initial randomization, the informed player in Γ_∞ indeed does the same thing at each stage; and whereas this is not so for the uninformed player, the Blackwell strategy prescribes that he, too, should play by a rule that makes use only of a fairly simple statistic[49] of the past history, and does so in a stationary way. This is not at all so for Γ_n, where the optimal strategies make essential use of the stage number.

Finally, we mention the view of Γ_∞ that seems most obvious, namely as a game that literally has infinitely many stages, with payoff to be thought of as the limiting average of the payoff to the individual stages. Intuitively, this reflects play that continues "indefinitely"; where one plays as if there will always be a tomorrow.

Looking at Γ_∞ in this way, we see that what a player does at any particular stage doesn't directly affect his payoff *at all*. There literally is all the time in the world to do anything you might want to do; time, far from being money, is essentially free. This sometimes lends the analysis of Γ_∞ a slightly disconcerting never-never quality. But by the same token, it gives the analysis "elbow-room": frees it from picayune considerations that affect only a small number of stages, thus allowing it to concentrate on long-term effects.

While this view is certainly valid, we have not stressed it because it misses the more significant aspects of Γ_∞, and might give the

---

[47]See the discussion of the error term in Postscript c to Chapter One.

[48]This, of course, is quite different from duration-independence.

[49]The stage number is used in figuring, for each type of the informed player, the average of the payoffs up to the present.

false impression that play in Γ_∞ is only concerned with the distant future, is never relevant to the present.

To summarize: The approximate payoff when a sufficiently long game is played optimally is $\lim v(\Gamma_n)$; strategies in Γ_n usually depend crucially on the duration n of the game. In Γ_∞, strategies are by definition independent of the duration; and if v_∞ exists, there are strategies that are approximately optimal simultaneously for all finite durations. This leads to the following six interpretations of Γ_∞: First, as a repeated game whose length, while large, is not known to the players; second, as expressing limiting optimal behavior (rather than payoff) in long finite games; third, as a bounded rationality model where taking account of n is too complex for the players; fourth, as leading to qualitative rules of thumb for play; fifth, as expressing a form of stationarity; and sixth, as a model of play that continues "indefinitely," with no fixed last stage.

The bottom line, both conceptually and in practice, is that v_∞ is a simpler and more direct tool than $\lim v_n$ for the study of repeated games.

d. The Conceptual Distinction Between Γ_∞ and Γ_n: Incomplete Information

The previous note applies to all repeated games, whether of complete or incomplete information. In the specific case of incomplete information, more can be said. Optimal play in Γ_n often calls for the players to play differently near the beginning of the game, near its middle, and near its end; to use—and thereby "reveal"—their information gradually, in such a way so that by the time it is all revealed, the game is over (some illustrations of this kind of strategy may be found in the discussion of the error term in Postscript c to Chapter One). This is impossible in Γ_∞ since the martingale convergence theorem (Postscript a to Chapter One) implies that the brunt of any revelations must come within a finite number of stages, which have no appreciable effect on the payoff. Thus unlike in the finite-stage case, essentially all information that is going to be revealed, must be revealed before the players make their payoff-relevant decisions.

When the information is complete on one side, these considerations result only in a second-order difference[50] between v_n and v_∞. But when there is incomplete information on both sides, the effect is first order. Both players wish to make use of their information; but they know that by doing so, they will reveal it. The question is, who will reveal first. If P2 waits to reveal until P1 has done so, the outcome is cav vex; if P1 waits to reveal until P2 has done so, the outcome is vex cav. When cav vex $\neq$ vex cav, the result is that in Γ_∞, each player will want to wait for the other to make his revelation before making use of his own information; and each can afford to wait arbitrarily long for the other one, since no finite number of stages affects the payoff in any appreciable way. Thus the game may be compared to that of "Pick the larger integer," which has no value.

In Γ_n, on the other hand, neither player can afford to wait until the other has revealed his information before making use of his own; the payoff counts at each stage, and if the players do not make use of their information now, they may lose by it. Some kind of gradual simultaneous revelation therefore becomes optimal, and this is reflected in the optimal strategies for Γ_n. But though $\lim v(\Gamma_n)$ exists, the optimal strategies in Γ_n need not converge to strategies that are in any sense optimal in Γ_∞. Indeed, in many games the revelation is spread more or less over the entire period of the game; so for any fixed number of stages, the "amount of revelation" that takes place within that fixed number of stages tends to 0 as the total number n of stages tends to infinity. In the limit, therefore, no revelation ever takes place, and this is in general not optimal.

e. Non-Zero Sum Games

Though non-zero sum games play no role in the body of this chapter, they do in Chapter Five, and it is convenient to include them in the present discussion of modelling.

Most of what we said in Postscript b above applies also to non-zero sum games, of complete as well as of incomplete information.

---

[50]Since $v_n \to v_\infty$ in this case.

Like there, Γ_∞ should be thought of as a framework for formulating the idea of a strategy that is independent of the duration of the game; and an equilibrium in Γ_∞, as an approximate equilibrium simultaneously in all Γ_n, the approximation getting better and better as n grows.[51]

In Postscript c we saw that in zero sum games, the infinite-stage approach may lead to fewer equilibrium payoffs[52] than the limiting approach (none rather than one), but never to more. This is not so in non-zero sum games, even of complete information. In the repeated prisoner's dilemma, for example, there is only one equilibrium payoff in Γ_n—namely the "greedy"[53] one—no matter how large n is. But by the "Folk Theorem" (Chapter Five, Section 3), all feasible individually rational payoffs are equilibrium payoffs in Γ_∞. This phenomenon is closely related to Radner's [1986] "ε-equilibrium" analysis of the finitely repeated prisoner's dilemma;[54] equilibrium points in Γ_∞ represent a limiting form of ε-equilibria in finite repetitions.

However, it should be pointed out that the prisoner's dilemma is atypical in this respect. Benoit and Krishna [1985] have shown that for non-zero sum repeated games of complete information,

---

[51] Formally, a strategy profile ("tuple") is an equilibrium in Γ_∞ if and only if for some sequence of ε_n tending to 0, each of its n-stage truncations is an ε_n-equilibrium in Γ_n (i.e., no player can gain more than ε_n by deviating; cf. Radner [1986]).

[52] Vectors of payoffs (payoff profiles) to equilibrium points.

[53] We prefer "friendly" to describe the action sometimes called "cooperative" in the one-shot Prisoner's Dilemma, and "greedy" for the one sometimes called "defect" or "double-cross". The term "cooperative" has other meanings in game theory; that they are related—but not identical—to the one under discussion only makes matters worse. "Defect" and "double-cross" have the connotation of someone who has agreed to something and then reneges, which need not at all be so in the Prisoner's Dilemma.

[54] Radner's results imply that for every positive ε, there is an N such that if $n \geq N$, then the n-fold repetition of the prisoner's dilemma has an ε-equilibrium whose payoff is the "friendly" one. If equilibrium is defined as above (three footnotes back), this says precisely that the cooperative payoff is an equilibrium payoff of the infinitely repeated prisoner's dilemma. More generally, with this definition of equilibrium in infinitely repeated games, the Folk Theorem implies that for every finite game G, every feasible individually rational payoff x of G, and every positive ε, there is an N such that if $n \geq N$, then the n-fold repetition of G has a ε-equilibrium whose payoff is x.

the set of equilibrium payoffs in Γ_∞ is equal to the Hausdorff limit of the sets of equilibrium payoffs in Γ_n, whenever the stage game G has an equilibrium payoff that yields each player more than his maxmin.

f. Discounting

In addition to v_∞ and $\lim v_n$, there are two other specific models of "long" repetitions that warrant discussion. The first is the limit of the values v^δ of the discounted games Γ^δ as the discount rate δ goes to 0 (see Postscript b). In most ways, this is conceptually closer to $\lim v_n$ than to v_∞. Strictly speaking, the games Γ^δ do not have a finite duration. But since "time is money"—since one discounts the value of later stages—total time is "value-wise" finite. In a sense, therefore, one can speak of "half[55] the game being over," which is perhaps the crucial property of the $\lim v_n$ approach.

Like in Γ_n, optimal strategies in the discounted game Γ^δ usually depend strongly on the parameter—in this case, the discount rate δ. Therefore most of the above discussion applies when Γ^δ is substituted for Γ_n; in particular, Γ^δ, like Γ_n, is not as well suited as Γ_∞ for studying optimal long-term behavior. Also like in Γ_n— and unlike in Γ_∞—what the players do at each stage of Γ^δ affects their payoff in an important way.

On the other hand, discounted games Γ^δ are like Γ_∞—and unlike Γ_n—in that they have no fixed, commonly known last stage. In addition to its innate implausibility, this feature of Γ_n often[56] creates unnatural terminal effects that propagate themselves backwards and grossly distort the analysis, like in the hangman's paradox or the finitely repeated prisoner's dilemma. Another way in which Γ^δ resembles Γ_∞ rather than Γ_n is that it admits strategies with some kind of stationarity property (see Postscript b), a feature that has been heavily used by almost all writers on discounted repeated (and other sequential) games.[57]

---

[55] Or any other proportion.

[56] Especially in non-zero sum games.

[57] Such as Shapley [1953], Mayberry [1967], Bewley and Kohlberg [1978], Radner [1985], Fudenberg and Maskin [1986], and Abreu [1988].

g. Continuous Time

Finally, one may treat long repetitions by modelling time as bounded and continuous, like the unit interval [0,1]. The large literature on Differential Games, pioneered by Isaacs [1965], works exclusively with continuous time. In economics, continuous time games have been used by Case [1979], Simon and Stinchcombe [1989], and others. In the context of repeated games, Sorin [1989] has used them as a tool in solving games with a "non-recursive structure" (Postscript i to Chapter Four). This kind of model is like $v(\Gamma_\infty)$ in some ways and like $\lim v(\Gamma_n)$ in others. It is like Γ_∞ in that the payoff to no individual stage appreciably affects the total payoff; also in that optimal strategies may be thought of as representing limiting optimal behavior in long finite games. It is like Γ_n in that there is a definite duration, so that one can talk about having gone through half (or some other definite proportion) of the game's duration. Complexity-wise, it is between Γ_∞ and Γ_n; optimal strategies are more complex than in Γ_∞, but less than in Γ_n. Though the unit interval does have a last point, terminal effects do not propagate themselves backwards, so that in that respect, the model is more like Γ_∞ than Γ_n. A disadvantage is that a direct definition of "strategy" is a matter of some difficulty. On the whole, the model appears quite attractive, and deserves more study than it has received.

h. Alternative Definitions of Value, Maxmin, and Minmax in Γ_∞

The value v_∞ defined in the text[58] has been called[59] the *uniform value*, because each player can play so that his average expected payoff tends, uniformly in what the other player does, to something no worse than the value; i.e., so that he gets—and subsequently remains—within any given ε of v_∞ (or better) by a stage n_0 that depends on ε only, not on the other player's strategy.

---

[58]Section 3.1 of this chapter and Section 5 of Chapter Four.
[59]By Hart [1985], Sorin [1990], and others.

For an alternative, call v the *nonuniform* or lim exp *value* of Γ_∞ if there are σ_0, τ_0 such that for all σ, τ,

$$\liminf \gamma_n(\sigma_0, \tau) \geq v \geq \limsup \gamma_n(\sigma, \tau_0);$$

here and subsequently, σ_0, τ_0, σ, τ denote mixed strategies in Γ_∞, and γ_n is the expected average payoff for the first n stages. Thus P1, by playing σ_0, guarantees that he will eventually get and remain within any given ε of the value (or better); but how long it takes may depend on P2's srategy τ, not only on ε.

Clearly the uniform value is "stronger" than the nonuniform one, in the sense that every uniform value is also a nonuniform value. Thus existence of the uniform value is in principle harder to achieve; it "says more" than existence of the nonuniform value. On the other hand, the nonuniform value might conceivably exist for larger classes of games; but though theoretically possible, in practice this does not happen, at least for the games considered in this book. Since use of the nonuniform value would have weakened our conclusions without broadening our hypotheses, we adopted the uniform definition.

In Chapter Three, though, Stearns adopts the nonuniform definition. We use his results in this chapter to show that if the uniform value exists, then cav vex = vex cav. This is justified because as just noted, existence of the uniform value implies existence of the "weaker" nonuniform value.

We also prove the converse, that cav vex = vex cav implies the existence of a uniform value (Theorem 4.9). That proof does not use Stearns's result.[60] Thus we may conclude that cav vex = vex cav if and only if the uniform value exists (Theorem 4.11).

Even when the uniform value does not exist, we may define the *uniform maxmin*, (or simply *maxmin*) $\underline{v}_\infty$ of Γ_∞ as the largest number v such that for each $\varepsilon > 0$ there is an n_0 and a σ_0 such that for all $n \geq n_0$ and all τ, we have $\gamma_n(\sigma_0, \tau) \geq v - \varepsilon$. Dually, the *uniform minmax* (or simply *minmax*) $\overline{v}_\infty$ of Γ_∞ is the smallest v

---

[60]The optimal strategies used in the proof of Theorem 4.9 may be seen to satisfy the uniformity condition. They combine the "splitting" strategy used by the informed player in games of complete information on one side, with the "Blackwell" strategy used by the uninformed player; and each of these components has the requisite uniformity property.

such that for each $\varepsilon > 0$ there is an n_0 and a τ_0 such that for all $n \geq n_0$ and all σ, we have $\gamma_n(\sigma, \tau_0) \leq v + \varepsilon$. One may also use "nonuniform" definitions, as follows:

$$\underset{\approx}{v}_\infty := \max_\sigma \min_\tau \liminf_n \gamma_n(\sigma, \tau), \quad \tilde{\tilde{v}}_\infty := \min_\tau \max_\sigma \limsup_n \gamma_n(\sigma, \tau),$$

$$\underset{\sim}{v}_\infty := \max_\sigma \min_\tau \limsup_n \gamma_n(\sigma, \tau), \quad \tilde{v}_\infty := \min_\tau \max_\sigma \liminf_n \gamma_n(\sigma, \tau).$$

Conceptually, $\underset{\sim}{v}_\infty$, $\underset{\approx}{v}_\infty$, and $\tilde{v}_\infty$ reflect P1's viewpoint. If he does not know P2's strategy, then $\underset{\sim}{v}_\infty$ is the largest payoff that he can guarantee within some stated time, and $\underset{\approx}{v}_\infty$ is the largest payoff that he can guarantee eventually getting. If he does know P2's strategy, then $\tilde{v}_\infty$ is the largest payoff that he can guarantee eventually getting. From these definitions it follows that

$$\underset{\sim}{v}_\infty \leq \underset{\approx}{v}_\infty \leq \begin{array}{c} \tilde{v}_\infty \\ \underset{\sim}{v}_\infty \end{array} \leq \tilde{\tilde{v}}_\infty \leq \overline{v}_\infty,$$

since a guarantee is at least as difficult to achieve uniformly as nonuniformly (the inequalities apply both to $\tilde{v}_\infty$ and to $\underset{\sim}{v}_\infty$). Theorem 4.9 shows that P1 can guarantee cav vex uniformly, i.e., that cav vex $\leq \underset{\sim}{v}_\infty$. The result of Stearns (Chapter Three) shows that even nonuniformly, P1 cannot guarantee more than cav vex, i.e., that $\underset{\approx}{v}_\infty \leq$ cav vex. Mertens and Zamir [1980] prove the stronger result that P2, when he knows P1's strategy, can drive P1's payoff down to at most cav vex, i.e., that $\tilde{v}_\infty \leq$ cav vex. Thus

$$\underset{\sim}{v}_\infty = \underset{\approx}{v}_\infty = \tilde{v}_\infty = \text{cav vex} \quad \text{and} \quad \overline{v}_\infty = \tilde{\tilde{v}}_\infty = \tilde{v}_\infty = \text{vex cav}.$$

Finally, we briefly mention two additional definitions for the value of Γ_∞, yielding what may be called "exp lim" values. The first is defined and discussed in Section 5 of Chapter Four; as shown there, it is fraught with difficulties that render it unsatisfactory. The other (e.g., Forges [1985, 1988], Hart [1985], Lehrer [1989, 1990]) uses measurable Banach limits to overcome these difficulties.

i. Incomplete Information on Both Sides: The Dependent Case

In the text (Section 4.2) we showed how the dependent case can always be reduced to the independent one. Nevertheless, one may ask whether in the dependent case, one could carry out the analysis directly, without using the reduction. Mertens and Zamir [1972, 1980] showed how this can indeed be done in a natural way.

To describe their method, for each probability distribution a on the set K of possible stage games, let $X(a)$ $(Y(a))$ denote the set of all those distributions b on K that induce the same posterior probabilities on K for P1 (P2) as a does. Let Δ be the $(\kappa - 1)$-dimensional simplex of all probability distributions on K. Note that $X(a)$ and $Y(a)$ are convex and compact; indeed, each is the intersection of a hyperplane with Δ. Now for any function u on Δ, denote by $\mathrm{cav}_X u$ the smallest function on Δ that is $\geq u$ on Δ and is concave on each of the sets $X(a)$. Similarly, denote by $\mathrm{vex}_Y u$ the largest function on Δ that is $\leq u$ on Δ and is convex on each of the sets $Y(a)$. The reader may verify that if u is continuous, then both $\mathrm{cav}_X u$ and $\mathrm{vex}_Y u$ exist and are themselves continuous.

As elsewhere in this book, denote by $u(a)$ the value of the one-shot game when neither player is given any information (other than the commonly known initial distribution a). Then the maxmin[61] of Γ_∞ is $\mathrm{cav}_X \mathrm{vex}_Y u(a)$, and its minmax[62] is $\mathrm{vex}_Y \mathrm{cav}_X u(a)$. It follows that $\lim v_n$ lies between these two values (see Postscript a).

A relatively transparent case is that of four stage games G_{ij}, where each of i and j can take on two values (say 1 and 2), P1 knows i but not j, and P2 knows j but not i. Setting $a = (a_{11}, a_{12}, a_{21}, a_{22})$, where a_{ij} denotes the initial probability of G_{ij}, we find that $X(a)$ is the set of all probability distributions on K of the form $(ra_{11}, ra_{12}, sa_{21}, sa_{22})$, where r and s are non-negative; similarly for $Y(a)$, but with $(ra_{11}, sa_{12}, ra_{21}, sa_{22})$. Thus the endpoints of $X(a)$ may be viewed as the conditional distributions of a given the rows (P1's information); and those of $Y(a)$, as the conditional distributions of a given the columns (P2's information). For

---

[61] maxmin and minmax are as defined in Postscript h.
[62] Recall $\mathrm{cav}\,\mathrm{vex}\,u(a) := (\mathrm{cav}\,\mathrm{vex}\,u)(a)$, and similarly for $\mathrm{vex}\,\mathrm{cav}$.

example, if $a = (.1, .2, .3, .4)$, then $X(a)$ is the segment connecting $(1/3, 2/3, 0, 0)$ to $(0, 0, 3/7, 4/7)$, and $Y(a)$ is that connecting $(1/4, 0, 3/4, 0)$ to $(0, 1/3, 0, 2/3)$.

Geometrically, the simplex Δ of all possible distributions a is a tetrahedron, whose vertices are the G_{ij} themselves.[63] Denote by E_i. the edge of Δ connecting the vertices G_{i1} and G_{i2}, and by $E_{\cdot j}$ the edge connecting G_{1j} and G_{2j}. If a is in the interior of the simplex, then $X(a)$ is a straight line segment through a whose two endpoints lie on the two edges E_1. and E_2.. This geometrical property determines $X(a)$ uniquely: If there were two such segments, then since a lies on both, they would determine a plane containing two skew edges of a tetrahedron, and no such plane exists. Similarly, $Y(a)$ is the unique segment through a connecting the edges $E_{\cdot 1}$ and $E_{\cdot 2}$. Note that each point on the edges E_i. $(E_{\cdot j})$ of the simplex corresponds to a game in which P2 (P1) knows which G_{ij} is being played.

For each point a in the simplex, let $Z(a)$ denote the union of all the segments $Y(a')$, where a' ranges[64] over $X(a)$. Then it may be seen that for each a'' in $Z(a)$, both $X(a'')$ and $Y(a'')$ are included in $Z(a)$. It follows that both $\text{cav}_X \text{vex}_Y u(a)$ and $\text{vex}_Y \text{cav}_X u(a)$ are determined by the behavior of u on $Z(a)$ only; thus $Z(a)$ may be called the "relevant" surface for a. When a is in the interior of the simplex, then $Z(a)$ is a doubly ruled hyperboloid containing the four edges E_1., E_2., $E_{\cdot 1}$, $E_{\cdot 2}$ of the tetrahedron (Figure 16). The hyperboloids $Z(a)$ constitute a foliation of the interior of the simplex, i.e., they cover the interior entirely and are disjoint there.

When a is in the relative interior of a face of the simplex, then $Z(a)$ is that face. This happens if and only if precisely one of the G_{ij} has initial probability $a_{ij} = 0$. If, say, $a_{22} = 0$, then one of the endpoints of the segments $X(a)$ is the vertex G_{21} of the simplex, and one of the endpoints of $Y(a)$ is G_{12} (Figure 17).

The remaining cases—when a lies on an edge of the simplex—are degenerate in the sense that they do not really represent incomplete information on both sides. The analysis of these cases is left to the reader.

---

[63]I.e., the distributions that assign probability 1 to some G_{ij}.

[64]An equivalent definition of this set $Z(a)$ is as the union of all the $X(a')$, where a' ranges over $Y(a)$.

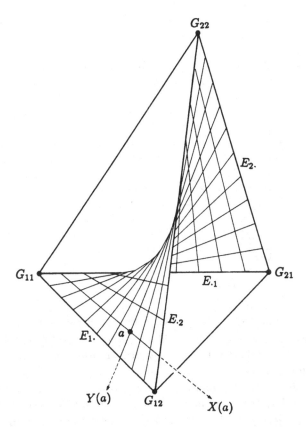

Figure 16. The Hyperboloid $Z(a)$

Note that all the "independent" a—those obeying (4.5)—together constitute just *one* of the surfaces $Z(a)$; thus a is independent if and only if it is in $Z(1/4, 1/4, 1/4, 1/4)$. It follows that when a is independent, $\text{vex}_Y \text{cav}_X u(a)$ and $\text{cav}_X \text{vex}_Y u(a)$ depend on $u(a')$ for all the independent a', but for no other a'.

j. Incomplete Information on One-and-a-Half Sides

In Example 4.1, one of the players knows which stage game is the true one, but does not know the probability distribution of the uninformed player as to the true stage game. That example

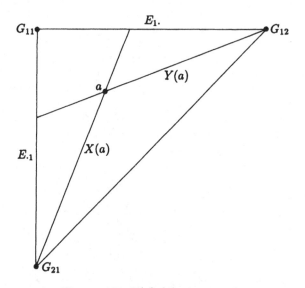

Figure 17. $Z(a)$ when $a_{22} = 0$

involved inconsistent beliefs; the question arises whether similar examples can be constructed with consistent beliefs, and if so, what can be said about the existence or non-existence of v_∞ in such games.

In [1985], Sorin and Zamir constructed a class of such examples, and showed that for some of them, v_∞ does not exist. Consider the following game (there is no need to specify the matrix on the lower right, as it is anyway assigned probability 0):

5	−3
0	0

5	−3
0	0

1/4   1/2

1/4   0

−3	5
0	0

Payoff matrices   Probability distribution
                                      on the matrices

Game 1

As usual, P1 knows in which row the true game is, and P2 knows
the column. Since the two entries in the top row are the same,
it follows that P1 knows which is the true game being played.
What he does not know is the probability that P2 assigns to this
game. If nature chose the right column, then also P2 knows the
true game for sure; if the left column was chosen, then P2 assigns
half-half probabilities to the two possible games. In either case,
P1 does not know whether or not P2 knows the true game, and
assigns probability 1/2 to each of those two possibilities. This
entire description[65] is commonly known.

To understand the situation, let us start by recalling why P1,
who in any case knows the true game, should care what P2 thinks
about it. The reason is that P1 can take advantage of P2's ignorance only if he knows its extent. Denote the games in the top
and bottom rows by A and B respectively. If P1 knew P2's probabilities, then he could get an expected payoff of 1 when they are
half-half (by playing top always), and 0 when P2 knows the true

---

[65]Including this sentence itself. It is, however, not necessary to specify this,
because it can be proved that whenever something is commonly known, it is
commonly known that it is commonly known.

game (by playing bottom always), for an average of 1/2. But he does not know. If he plays top, and P2's probabilities are indeed half-half, he will of course still get 1. But if P2 knows the true game, then by playing right, he can drive the payoff to -3, which will more than wipe out P1's profit. To be sure, this is not an optimal strategy for P2, as it will reveal his information, and so bring us back to the first case (when P1 knows exactly what P2 thinks). But it does show that P1 cannot guarantee 1/2—or indeed even a positive amount—just by playing top always. What he *can* guarantee—and for that matter, what P2 can guarantee—is not obvious.

In fact, we will see that P1 cannot guarantee more than 0, but P2 cannot hold him down to less than the average payoff of 1/2 that he could get if he knew what P2 thought.

More generally, suppose A and B are two matrix games of the same size. Consider the following game:

A A		a_{11} a_{12}
B B		a_{21} a_{22}

Payoff matrices	Probability distribution a on the matrices

Game 2

Nature chooses one of the four corners in the array on the left, with the probability distribution a on the right. P1 is informed of the row chosen by nature, and P2 of the column; the corresponding game is then played repeatedly. Thus (in general) P1 knows whether A or B is being played, while P2 does not; but P1 does not know the probability that P2 ascribes to each of A and B. Such games will be called *games of incomplete information on one and a half sides*. Sorin and Zamir [1985] prove the following general theorem:

THEOREM N1. *For games with incomplete information on one and a half sides, the minmax*[66] $\bar{v}_\infty$ *of* Γ_∞ *equals the value of the game* $\hat{\Gamma}_\infty$ *obtained from* Γ_∞ *by informing both players (rather than just P2) of the column chosen by nature.*

IDEA OF PROOF: In $\hat{\Gamma}_\infty$, after the column is revealed to both players, there is complete information for P1. Thus depending on the column chosen, two games are possible, each having a value. So $\hat{\Gamma}_\infty$, too, has a value, namely the expectation of the two possible values.

To show that $\bar{v}_\infty = \text{val}(\hat{\Gamma}_\infty)$, note first that $\bar{v}_\infty \leq \text{val}(\hat{\Gamma}_\infty)$ is obvious, since P1 can only gain from more information. The other half—that P1 cannot be prevented in Γ_∞ from getting as much as in $\hat{\Gamma}_\infty$—seems at first rather surprising. See the above discussion of Game 1.

To understand this phenomenon, we use two facts: First, that in guaranteeing $\bar{v}_\infty$ (his security level), P2 can reveal immediately whatever he will reveal eventually, without waiting for prior revelations from P1 (see Postscript d). Second, that he cannot use what he does not reveal.

Thus when P2 makes his revelations, P1 has not yet revealed anything. After P2 has revealed everything he ever will, it is still possible that he knows more about his own probabilities for A and B than P1 does, but he must never use this additional information! He must act as if he didn't have it, no matter what P1 subsequently does. Thus after P2's revelations, and before P1's, the situation is essentially one of complete information for P1, with P2's probability p'_A for[67] A taken as if he himself had forgotten what he did not reveal.

How much, then, should P2 actually reveal? The final payoff, of course, depends on p'_A, indeed is concave in p'_A. Conceptually, the concavity means that the less information P2 has (or more accurately, uses), the better the outcome is for P1 (see Postscript b to Chapter One). But the better it is for P1, the worse it is for P2. So P2 should use—and thereby reveal—all the information

---

[66] See Postscript h.

[67] We use p'_A because p_A refers to P2's probability if he forgets all private information immediately, before revealing anything.

he has, right at the beginning of the game! This is precisely what
the theorem says.

The argument hinges on the fact that P2's private information
is about his own probabilities only. And it is valid only because
we are dealing with the minmax $\bar{v}_\infty$. In other contexts—e.g. for
the maxmin $\underline{v}_\infty$ or for $\lim v_n$—P2 can indeed effectively exploit
P1's ignorance about his probabilities for A and B. Thus Sorin
and Zamir demonstrate $\underline{v}_\infty < \bar{v}_\infty$ whenever the payoff matrices
are those of Game 1 and the probability a_{22} vanishes, even though
the other probabilities a_{ij} may be different from those of Game 1.
They also calculate $\lim v_n$ for all these games, and show that it is
strictly between $\underline{v}_\infty$ and $\bar{v}_\infty$. In particular, it is strictly smaller
than $\bar{v}_\infty$, which means that in the sense of $\lim v_n$, P2 *can* use his
private information effectively.

PROOF: We start by analyzing $\hat{\Gamma}_\infty$. For all p in $[0,1]$, let

$$\tilde{u}(p) := \text{the value of the one-shot game } pA + (1-p)B. \quad \text{(N1)}$$

For brevity, set

$$\tilde{u}^* := cav_p\tilde{u}. \quad \text{(N2)}$$

Given any distribution a as in Game 2, set

$$q_j := a_{1j} + a_{2j}, \ p_A := a_{11} + a_{12}, \text{ and } p|j := a_{1j}/q_j; \quad \text{(N3)}$$

thus the total probability of column j is q_j, the total probability
of the game A is P_A, and the conditional probability of A, given
that column j was chosen, is $p|j$. Now let a be the initial distribu-
tion on K in the game Γ_∞. Revealing the column to both players
is equivalent to having nature choose one of two games, each of
complete information for P1, and telling both players which game
it chose. In the first, it is common knowledge that P2 assigns
probability $p|1$ to A and $1 - (p|1)$ to B, so the value of this game
is $\tilde{u}^*(p|1)$. Similarly the value of the second is $\tilde{u}^*(p|2)$. The prob-
abilities of the two games are q_1 and q_2, so

$$\Gamma_\infty \text{ has the value } q_1\tilde{u}^*(p|1) + q_1\tilde{u}^*(p|2). \quad \text{(N4)}$$

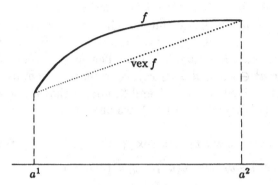

Figure 18. Convexification of a concave function

For future reference, note that if f is a concave function on a segment $[a^1, a^2]$, then its convexification[68] vex f is linear, so

$$\text{vex } f(\theta a^1 + (1 - \theta)a^2) = \theta f(a^1) + (1 - \theta)f(a^2), \qquad (\text{N5})$$

whenever $0 \leq \theta \leq 1$ (Figure 18).

To prove that $\bar{v}_\infty = \text{val}(\hat{\Gamma}_\infty)$, we set $G_{11} = G_{12} = A$ and $G_{21} = G_{22} = B$. For each distribution a on the G_{ij}, let $X(a)$ be the segment defined in Postscript i (see Figure 16); its endpoints $a^A \in E_1$ and $a^B \in E_2$ represent the conditional distributions of a given A and B, and so assign probability 1 to A and B respectively. Thus for each $p \in [0, 1]$, the point $pa^A + (1 - p)a^B$ in $X(a)$ assigns total probability p to A and $(1 - p)$ to B; therefore, since the function u gives the value of the one-shot game when neither player gets any private information, it follows from (N1) that $\tilde{u}(p) = u(pa^A + (1 - p)a^B)$. Thus $p \to pa^A + (1 - p)a^B$ defines a one-one linear mapping from $[0,1]$ onto $X(a)$ that sends $\tilde{u}$ to $u|X(a)$, and so also the concavification $\tilde{u}^*$ of u to the concavification of $u|X(a)$. Since this mapping also sends p_A to a, it follows that[69]

$$\text{cav}_X\, u(a) = \tilde{u}^*(P_A) = \tilde{u}^*(a_{11} + a_{12}).$$

---

[68] The largest function pointwise $\leq f$.

[69] Since by definition, $\text{cav}_X\, u(a)$ is the value at a of the concavification of $u|X(a)$.

From this it follows that $\text{cav}_X u$ is concave not only on each $X(a)$, but actually on the entire simplex. Hence its restriction to $Y(a)$, which we call f, is also concave. Hence $\text{vex} f$, as the convexification of a concave function, is linear. The endpoints of $Y(a)$, which we denote $a^1 \in E_{\cdot 1}$ and $a^2 \in E_{\cdot 2}$, represent the conditional distributions of a given columns 1 and 2; noting that $a = q_1 a^1 + q_2 a^2$, and using (N5), (N3), and (N4), we obtain

$$\bar{v}_\infty = \text{vex}_Y \text{cav}_X u(a) = \text{vex} f(a) = q_1 f(a^1) + q_2 f(a^2) =$$
$$q_1 \text{cav}_X u(a^1) + q_2 \text{cav}_X u(a^2) = q_1 \tilde{u}^*(p|1) + q_2 \tilde{u}^*(p|2) = \text{val}(\hat{\Gamma}_\infty).$$

This completes the proof of Theorem N1. ∎

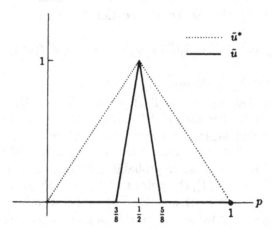

Figure 19. $\tilde{u}$ and $\tilde{u}*$

For Game 1, $\tilde{u}$ and $\tilde{u}^*$ are depicted in Figure 19. For the distribution a of Game 1, the relevant surface $Z(a)$ (Postscript i) is a face of the simplex (Figure 20), $p|1 = 1/2$, $p|2 = 1$, and $q_1 = q_2 = 1/2$. Therefore (N4) yields

$$\bar{v}_\infty = \text{val}(\hat{\Gamma}_\infty) = q_1 \tilde{u}^*(p|1) + q_2 \tilde{u}^*(p|2)$$
$$= (1/2)1 + (1/2)0 = 1/2. \tag{N6}$$

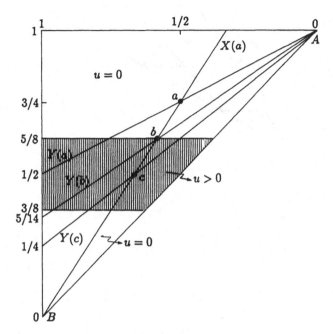

Figure 20. $Z(a)$ for Game 1

Next, we calculate the maxmin $\underline{v}_\infty$ of Γ_∞. From Figures 19 and 21, we see that u vanishes except in the strip that is hatched in Figure 20. We claim that

$$\operatorname{vex}_Y u(a') = 0 \text{ for each } a' \text{ in } X(a). \qquad (\text{N7})$$

Indeed, if a' is above the strip, then $0 \leq \operatorname{vex}_Y u(a') \leq u(a') = 0$. If a' is the point b at which $X(a)$ intersects the upper boundary of the strip (Figure 20), then the endpoints of $Y(a')$ ($= Y(b)$) are outside the strip, which implies that $\operatorname{vex}_Y u(a') = 0$; *a fortiori* this is so if a' is below b (like c in Figure 20). This yields (N7), whence

$$\underline{v}_\infty = \operatorname{cav}_X \operatorname{vex}_Y u(a) = 0.$$

From this and (N6) it follows that our game indeed has no value.

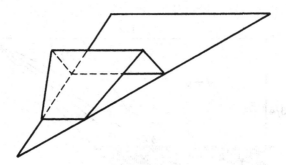

Figure 21. The graph of u

CHAPTER THREE

A FORMAL INFORMATION CONCEPT FOR GAMES
WITH INCOMPLETE INFORMATION

In situations of repeated games with incomplete information, there are two considerations which the players' strategies must take into account. One of these is of course the payoff, and the other is information. The information is important because a player's strategic opportunities to assure certain payoff levels are dependent on the information disclosed on previous plays. Examples of how information changes can affect the players' payoff expectations were illustrated in Chapter One. The optimal strategies for these games were most easily understood in terms of informal references to "information", although the derivations and proofs were expressed without reference to any concept of information. In this chapter we will develop a mathematical measure of such information and apply it to the model of the previous chapters. In doing this, we show that a measure of information can be used as a formal mathematical tool in game theory in addition to being a useful heuristic.

In order to qualify for the title "measure of information", a proposed measure must exhibit some of the properties we ordinarily attach to "information" as interpreted in a game theory context. In this regard, there are three criteria that we consider minimal for any "information measure" to satisfy:

(1) It must be meaningful to talk about the expected information revealed by given strategy choices after some n repetitions of the game.

(2) The expected information cannot decrease as the repetitions unfold. In particular, the expected information after n repetitions cannot be more than the expected information after $n + 1$ repetitions.

(3) The expected information must change significantly if a player's estimate of the situation changes significantly.

For the present application, there are a variety of measures which satisfy these conditions, and we will choose one to satisfy the following additional condition:

(4) The change of information after changes in the situation should be equal to the information in these changes.

These criteria cannot be tested unless one has a specific game model in mind and has selected an appropriate domain space for the measure. To this end, we now define the class of games of interest here.

Throughout the chapter, we will assume a game Γ represented by a seven-tuple

$$\Gamma = (T_1, \overline{p}, T_2, \overline{q}, M_1, M_2, \pi),$$

where T_1, T_2, M_1, and M_2 are finite sets, $\overline{p}$ and $\overline{q}$ are probability vectors over the sets T_1 and T_2, respectively, and π is a mapping of $M_1 \times M_2 \times T_1 \times T_2$ into the real numbers.

Set T_1 represents the possible types of Player 1 which (Player 2 believes) might participate in the game,[1] and component $\overline{p}_t$ of $\overline{p}$ for t in T_1 represents (what Player 2 believes to be) the probability that the Player 1 actually playing the repeated series of games is of type t. Similarly,[2] (Player 1 believes that) Player 2 may be any type in T_2, and $\overline{q}$ is the initial distribution on these types. The theory of Harsanyi suggests that it is reasonable for the players to behave as if an initial lottery on the players' types actually occurred using these probabilities.

Sets M_1 and M_2 consist of the pure strategies available to Players 1 and 2, respectively, in a single play of the game.[3] We call the elements of these sets *choices*, as we wish to reserve the word "strategy" for options in the supergame. During each repetition of the game, Player 1 chooses an element m_1 in M_1, Player 2 chooses an element m_2 in M_2, and then the players are informed as to which m_1 and m_2 were selected. Later we will discuss some

---

[1] These are the α rows at the beginning of Chapter Two, Section 4.(*)

[2] The set T_2 is the set of β columns at the beginning of Chapter Two, Section 4.(*)

[3] These are, respectively, the set of rows and the set of columns of the games G_{ij} of Chapter Two, Section 4.(*)

generalizations, where less information is released. The number $\pi(m_1, m_2, A, B)$ is the utility Player 1 of type A attaches[4] to choices m_1 and m_2 when Player 2 is of type B. Player 2 is assumed to attach utility $-\pi$.

We define the payoff to Player 1 to be the lim inf as $n \to \infty$ of the expected average payoff to Player 1 during the first n repetitions. The payoff to Player 2 is defined to be the lim sup as $n \to \infty$ of the expected average payoff. Thus, roughly speaking, Player 1 is trying to maximize and Player 2 to minimize the average value of π.

A *history* h is a finite sequence of elements from $E = M_1 \times M_2$. If $h_1 = e_{1,1} \ldots e_{1,n}$ and $h_2 = e_{2,1} \ldots e_{2,m}$, then we let $h_1 h_2$ be the concatenated sequence

$$e_{1,1} \ldots e_{1,n} e_{2,1} \ldots e_{2,m}.$$

The set of all histories is represented by E^*. A *behavioral strategy* for Player 1 is a mapping σ_1 of $E^* \times T_1$ into the space of probability vectors over the set M_1. Similarly,[5] a behavioral strategy σ_2 for Player 2 is a mapping of $E^* \times T_2$ into the space of probability vectors over M_2. For any other strategy, an equivalent behavioral strategy σ can be found[6] by computing $P_m(h, t)$, the conditional probability that a player of type t will choose m after history h, and letting $P_m(h, t)$ be the probability assigned by t. Thus no generality is lost by considering only behavioral strategies.

Now let us return to the information question. Suppose that the players are using known strategies σ_1 and σ_2 and that a certain history h has occurred. From σ_1, σ_2, and h, it is possible to compute conditional probabilities about the type of Player 1 and the type of Player 2. These conditional probability vectors are the basic objects of information we wish to measure. This information is generally not available to the players, as they do not usually know their opponents' strategy; but this information must (in

---

[4]These are the entries a_{ij} of the corresponding stage game matrices of Chapter Two, Section 4.(*)

[5]It is convenient in this chapter to denote the strategies σ_1, σ_2, rather than σ, τ as in other chapters.(*)

[6]This statement can be justified formally by Aumann's extension of Kuhn's theorem on extensive games with perfect recall (see Aumann [1964]).

theory) be considered to be available to our opponent if we propose a method of choosing strategies, for we must assume that the opponent has read our theory and can compute our strategy for himself.[7] If this knowledge gives the opponent an advantage over what he could otherwise assure himself, then the game will have no value. We show later that this may in fact happen for games of the form previously defined.

The problem is now to assign a measure $\Phi(p)$ to each conditional probability vector $p = (p_1 \ldots p_\nu)$, indexed over a set of types $T = \{1, \ldots, \nu\}$ such that our criteria for "information" are satisfied. To this end, we define the measure Φ by

$$\Phi(p) = \sum_T p_t^2.$$

In addition to characterizing the information in a given present situation in terms of a conditional probability vector, it is also desirable to characterize the anticipated situation some k repetitions in the future. One possibility is to represent this future situation as a probability distribution w on the set of histories of length k, where $w(h)$ represents the probability that the next k events add a string of outcome events h to the present history. It is also natural to represent the future situation by the probability distribution over the space of conditional probability vectors that these k repetitions generate. Although many of our results are stated in terms of the underlying histories, the second representation is generally more convenient due to its simplicity. Also, a distribution on the space of conditional probability vectors is the more natural generalization of a conditional probability vector. Motivated by these needs, we now generalize the measure independently of the particular game context.

DEFINITION 1. If T is a finite set, let $P(T)$ be the space of probability vectors over T. If D is a function[8] with finite support

---

[7]See, e.g., the material following (4.4) in Chapter One.(*)

[8]Usually D will represent a probability distribution, i.e., its values will be nonnegative and sum to one. At this point it is convenient to keep the definition general.

mapping $P(T)$ into the real numbers, then we define the information $\Phi(D)$ in D by

$$\Phi(D) = \sum_p D(p) \sum_T p_t^2.$$

DEFINITION 2. For each p in $P(T)$, let U_p be the probability distribution over $P(T)$ which is one at p and zero elsewhere.

Our original definition of Φ is now seen to be embedded in the new one as

$$\Phi(p) = \Phi(U_p).$$

The new Φ is simply the expected value of the old.

Our primary interest is in measuring the information in probability distributions that arise in the following way:

DEFINITION 3. If (w, g, H, T) is a quadruple such that H and T are finite sets, w is a probability distribution on H, and g is a mapping of H into $P(T)$, then the probability distribution D of $P(T)$ into the reals, defined by

$$D(p) = \sum_{\{h \in H:\ g(h) = p\}} w(h),$$

will be called the distribution *determined by* (w, g, H, T).

The support for distribution D will be no larger than the size of H. In this chapter, the sets H will be certain sets of histories. The information in such a D may be computed directly from the underlying histories as follows:

LEMMA 4. *If D is the distribution determined by (w, g, H, T), then*

$$\Phi(D) = \sum_H \sum_T w(h) g_t^2(h).$$

PROOF: Substituting Definition 3 into Definition 1, we get

$$\Phi(D) = \sum_p \left(\sum_{\{h \in H:\ g(h) = p\}} w(h) \right) \sum_T p_t^2,$$

which, after applying the distributive law, has the same terms as given by the lemma. ∎

DEFINITION 5. For any probability distribution D on $P(T)$ with finite support, we define the *center* $c(D)$ of D to be the vector in $P(T)$ defined by the equation

$$c(D) = \sum_p pD(p),$$

and we define the distribution $\overline{D}$ by

$$\overline{D} = U_{c(D)}.$$

Note that the vector $c(D)$ is always a probability vector; we will let $c_t(D) = \sum_p p_t D(p)$ represent the t-th component. An alternative method of computing $c(D)$ and $\overline{D}$ in terms of histories is given by the following:

LEMMA 6. *If the probability distribution D is determined by (w, g, H, T), then*

$$c_t(D) = \sum_H w(h)g_t(h).$$

PROOF: As in Lemma 4, this is immediate from the definitions. ∎

In order to relate these concepts to the game situation, we introduce some additional notation relative to the game Γ as defined above. For all $k \geq 0$, let H_k be the set of histories in E^* of length k. We let the symbol "ε" represent the null history, so $H_0 = \{\varepsilon\}$. We suppose further that strategies σ_1 and σ_2 are specified for Players 1 and 2, respectively. For each h in E^* and each t_1 in T_1, we let $g_{t_1}(h)$ be the conditional probability that Player 1 is of type t_1 after history h. We let $g(h)$ be the corresponding probability vector. The probabilities $g_{t_1}(h)$ depend only on σ_1. Similarly we define conditional probabilities $g'_{t_2}(h)$ for Player 2, which depend only on σ_2. By definition $g(\varepsilon) = \overline{p}$, the starting probabilities for Player 1, and $g'(\varepsilon) = \overline{q}$. For all k and all h in H_k, we let $w(h)$ be the probability that the first k repetitions of Γ result in history h. The function w can be defined inductively by $w(\varepsilon) = 1$ and

$$w(h(m_1, m_2)) = w(h) \sum_{T_1} \sum_{T_2} g_{t_1}(h)g'_{t_2}(h)\sigma_1(h, t_1)_{m_1}\sigma_2(h, t_2)_{m_2},$$

where $\sigma_1(h, t_1)_{m_1}$ is the probability that Player 1 of type t_1 will pick choice m_1, $\sigma_2(h, t_2)_{m_2}$ is similarly defined for Player 2, and $h(m_1, m_2)$ is history h concatenated with the length one history (m_1, m_2). For all $k \geq 0$, let D_k be the probability distribution determined by (w, g, H_k, T_1). A symmetric definition could be made for Player 2 but this is not required for what follows here.

The notation of the previous paragraph extends to conditional situations as follows: for all h in E^* such that $w(h) \neq 0$ and all h_k in H_k, let

$$w(hh_k \mid h) = w(hh_k)/w(h),$$

and let D_k^h be the distribution determined by $(w(hh_k \mid h), g(hh_k), H_k, T_1)$, where the first two components are interpreted as functions of h_k.

The weight $w(hh_k \mid h)$ is just the conditional probability of hh_k given h (i.e., the probability that history h_k will follow h), and D_k^h represents the distribution of conditional probability vectors k stages after history h. The distribution D_k is a special case of D_k^h; namely, $D_k = D_k^\epsilon$. The distributions represent the anticipated results of future stages (given σ_1 and σ_2) to be made after an initial history h. The relation of these distributions to their centers is given by the following:

THEOREM 7. *For all histories h and non-negative integers k,*

$$\overline{D}_k^h = U_{g(h)}$$

and

$$c(D_k^h) = g(h).$$

PROOF: The results follow because

$$c_t(D_k^h) = \sum_{H_k} w(hh_k \mid h) g_t(hh_k) = g_t(h).$$

The first equality is from putting the definition of D_k^h into Lemma 6. The expression $w(hh_k \mid h)g_t(hh_k)$ is the conditional probability of the event that Player 1 is of type t and history h_k follows history h. These events partition the event that Player 1 is type t after history h. By the laws of probability, summing these expressions over all h_k in H_k gives the probability that Player 1 is of type t after history h, and this probability is $g_t(h)$ by definition. ∎

COROLLARY 8. $\overline{D}_k = U_{\overline{p}}$ and $c(D_k) = \overline{p}$.

PROOF: Use the theorem with $h = \varepsilon$. ∎

The importance of the theorem is that if distribution D represents an anticipated situation, then $\overline{D}$ may be considered as the present situation, and the change of information may be represented by the expression

$$\Phi(D) - \Phi(\overline{D}).$$

A second useful property is the following combination rule:

THEOREM 9. *For all histories h in E^* and non-negative integers k and l,*

$$D_{k+l}^h = \sum_{H_k} w(h_k) D_l^{hh_k}.$$

PROOF: For any p in $P(T_1)$, the function on the left has value

$$\sum_{\{h_k h_l \in H_{k+l}: g(hh_k h_l) = p\}} w(hh_k h_l \mid h),$$

the right-hand side has value

$$\sum_{H_k} w(h_k) \sum_{\{h_l \in H_l: g(hh_k h_l) = p\}} w(hh_k h_l \mid hh_k),$$

and these are equal on a term-to-term basis due to the fact that

$$w(hh_k h_l \mid h) = w(h_k) w(hh_k h_l \mid hh_k).$$

∎

COROLLARY 10. $D_{k+l} = \sum_{H_k} w(h_k) D_l^{h_k}$.

PROOF: Take $h = \varepsilon$. ∎

The principal method of manipulating these expressions is given by the next two lemmas, which hold independent of the game context.

LEMMA 11. *If $a(h)$ is a real number and D^h is a distribution with finite support for all h in the finite set H, then*

$$\Phi(\sum_H a(h)D^h) = \sum_H a(h)\Phi(D^h).$$

PROOF: This is the distributive law applied to Definition 1. ∎

LEMMA 12. *If D is the distribution determined by (w, g, H, T) and*

$$\Delta_t(h) = g_t(h) - c_t(D)$$

for t in T and h in H, then

$$\phi(D) - \phi(\overline{D}) = \sum_T \sum_H w(h)(\Delta_t(h))^2.$$

PROOF: By Lemma 4, $\Phi(D) - \Phi(\overline{D})$ equals

$$\sum_T \sum_H w(h)g_t^2(h) - \sum_T (\sum_H w(h))c_t^2(D),$$

which, by definition of Δ_t, equals

$$\sum_T \left[\sum_H w(h)(c_t(D) + \Delta_t(h))^2 - \left(\sum_H w(h)\right) c_t^2(D) \right],$$

which expands to give

$$\sum_T \left[2c_t(D)\sum_H w(h)\Delta_t(h) + \sum_H w(h)\Delta_t^2(h) \right].$$

By Lemma 6, definition of $\Delta_t(h)$, and $\sum_H w(h) = 1$:

$$c_t(D) = \sum_h w(h)g_t(h) = \sum_H w(h)(c_t(D) + \Delta_t(h))$$

$$= c_t(D) + \sum_H w(h)\Delta_t(h).$$

Therefore, $\sum_H w(h)\Delta_t(h) = 0$ and thus our last expression for $\Phi(D) - \Phi(\overline{D})$ reduces to that stated in the lemma. ∎

Because the $w(h)$ are always non-negative, the change of information is always non-negative. Furthermore, if we represent the change between D and $\overline{D}$ by the probability distribution defined on the space of zero-sum vectors over T and determined by w, Δ, and H, then Lemma 12 says that the change of information is equal to the information in the change.

An alternative to the equation of Lemma 12 is the equation

$$\Phi(D) - \Phi(\overline{D}) = \frac{1}{2} \sum_T \sum_{H_1} \sum_{H_2} w(h_1)w(h_2)(g_t(h_1) - g_t(h_2))^2,$$

which is stated without the intermediate concept $\Delta_t(h)$. Since we do not plan to use this variation here, we shall not prove it.

Now we want to derive an expression for the change of information between the k-th and $k+l$-th repetition of the game. To this end we define $\Delta_t(h, l)$ for h in H_{k+l} and t in T_1 as follows:

$$\Delta_t(h, l) = g_t(h_k h_l) - g_t(h_k),$$

where h_k in H_k and h_l in H_l are the histories which satisfy $h = h_k h_l$.

THEOREM 13. *For all k and l,*

$$\Phi(D_{k+l}) - \Phi(D_k) = \sum_T \sum_{H_{k+l}} w(h)(\Delta_t(h, l))^2.$$

PROOF: By Corollary 10, $\Phi(D_{k+l}) - \Phi(D_k)$ is equal to

$$\Phi(\sum_{H_k} w(h_k)D_l^{h_k}) - \Phi\left(\sum_{H_k} w(h_k)U_{g(h_k)}\right).$$

By Lemma 11, this may be rewritten as

$$\sum_{H_k} w(h_k)\left[\Phi(D_l^{h_k}) - \Phi(U_{g(h_k)})\right],$$

and since $U_{g(h_k)} = \overline{D}_l^{h_k}$ by Theorem 7, we can apply Lemma 12 and get

$$\sum_{H_k} w(h_k) \sum_T \sum_{H_l} w(h_k h_l \mid h_k) \Delta_t^2(h_k h_l, l).$$

Rearranging this expression, we get

$$\sum_T \sum_{H_k} \sum_{H_l} w(h_k) w(h_k h_l \mid h_k) \Delta_t^2(h_k h_l, l).$$

Since $w(h_k) w(h_k h_l \mid h_k) = w(h_k h_l)$, this becomes

$$\sum_T \sum_{H_k} \sum_{H_l} w(h_k h_l) \Delta_t^2(h_k h_l, l),$$

which is equal to the expression in the theorem, because each h in H_{k+l} is equal to a unique $h_k h_l$ and vice versa. ∎

COROLLARY 14. *If*

$$H_\Delta(k, l) = \{h \in H_{k+l} : \mid \Delta_t(h, l) \mid \geq \Delta \text{ for some } t \in T\},$$

then

$$\sum_{H_\Delta(k,l)} w(h) \leq \frac{\Phi(D_{k+l}) - \Phi(D_k)}{\Delta^2}.$$

PROOF:

$$\Phi(D_{k+l}) - \Phi(D_k) \geq \sum_T \sum_{H_\Delta(k,l)} w(h) \Delta_t^2(h, l) \geq \Delta^2 \sum_{H_\Delta(k,l)} w(h).$$

∎

We are now in a position to test the measure against the four conditions stated in the beginning.

(1) We have defined the measure so that expected information is meaningful. Lemma 11 illustrates this point.

(2) The expression in Theorem 13 is always non-negative and so the information cannot decrease. Since the measure is bounded above by 1, we can treat information as a finite resource which a player may release during the repetitions of the game.

(3) We interpret the significance of a change in situation to be the probability that at least one component of the conditional probability vector changes by at least some small amount Δ. In Corollary 14, we see that this significance times Δ^2 bounds the change of information from below, thus insuring a proportionally significant change in information.

(4) If we extend Φ to be defined over distributions on zero-sum vectors, namely, define $\Phi(\Delta) = \sum w(h)\Delta^2$. Theorem 13 says that the change of information is equal to the information in the changes.

We are now ready to apply our information measure to the solution of game Γ. For all p in $P(T_1)$ and q in $P(T_2)$, let $U(p,q)$ be the ordinary minmax value of the zero-sum matrix game in which M_1 and M_2 are the sets of pure strategies, and the payoff matrix element corresponding to pair (m_1, m_2) is given by

$$\sum_{T_1 \times T_2} p_{t_1} q_{t_2} \pi(m_1, m_2, t_1, t_2).$$

This game, a "one-shot game", represents the situation where each player selects a move in ignorance of his own type. Note that $U(p,q)$ is continuous.

For any function $f(p)$ mapping $P(T)$ into the real numbers, we define $\text{cav}_p f(p)$ to be the smallest concave function greater than or equal to f. When f is continuous, the Carathéodory Theorem says that for each p, there is a probability distribution D_p on $P(T)$ such that the support at D_p has a size equal to the size of T, $c(D_p) = p$, and

$$\text{cav}_p f(p) = \sum_{p'} f(p') D_p(p').$$

It is shown in Chapter Two that a player with initial distribution p can effectively change the initial situation into a situation represented by such a D_p, by choosing strategies which depend only on the history and the result of some initial type-dependent lottery. Similarly, for any function $f(q)$ defined for q in $P(T)$, let $\text{vex}_q f(q)$ be the largest convex function smaller than or equal to f. The Carathéodory theorem and the above result apply dually here. We can now state the main theorem about Γ.

THEOREM 15. *The most Player 1 can assure himself in the repeated game* Γ *is the value of the function*

$$\operatorname*{cav}_{p} \operatorname*{vex}_{q} U(p,q)$$

evaluated at the initial probabilities $\bar{p}$ *and* $\bar{q}$ *and the minimum loss Player 2 can assure himself is the value of the function*

$$\operatorname*{vex}_{q} \operatorname*{cav}_{p} U(p,q)$$

evaluated at $\bar{p}$ *and* $\bar{q}$.

PROOF: For any probability distribution p on T_1, define a payoff function $\bar{\pi}_p$ by

$$\bar{\pi}_p(m_1, m_2, t_2) = \sum_{T_1} p_{t_1} \pi(m_1, m_2, t_1, t_2).$$

Let $\Gamma(p)$ be the repeated game where Player 1 has only one type, Player 2 again has type set T_2 and initial distribution $\bar{q}$, M_1 and M_2 are as before, and the one stage payoff is $\bar{\pi}_p$. The game $\Gamma(p)$ is of the form analyzed in Chapter One.

A strategy for Player 1 to ensure the cav vex value can be described as follows:

Player 1 divides into various conditional type probabilities according to the distribution $D_{\bar{p}}$ which achieves the cav of vex U. This division is accomplished as described in Chapter One by an initial type-dependent lottery. If the resulting conditional probabilities of this initial move are given by vector $\hat{p}$, then Player 1 defends as if he were playing the repeated game $\Gamma(\hat{p})$.

By Section 5 of Chapter Two, the value of $\Gamma(\hat{p})$ is the value of the function

$$\operatorname*{vex}_{q} U(p,q),$$

evaluated at $\hat{p}$ and $\bar{q}$ and so the expected value (before the initial lottery) is simply cav vex U evaluated at $\bar{p}, \bar{q}$.

To show that Player 1 can assure himself no more than this amount, we must find a counter-strategy σ_2 for Player 2 for each proposed strategy σ_1 of Player 1 and every $\delta > 0$, such that this counter-strategy holds Player 1 within δ of the cav vex value. Such a strategy can be described (somewhat informally) as follows:

Player 2 finds a pure type-independent strategy for some initial k repetitions such that his information is very close (depending on δ) to the supremum of the information he could ever possibly obtain against σ_1. After these initial repetitions have resulted in some h_k in H_k, Player 2 computes the conditional probability vector $g(h_k)$ and then plays an optimal strategy for $\Gamma(g(h_k))$.

A more formal description of σ_2 will follow shortly. We first discuss briefly why σ_2 gets within δ of the cav vex value.

The expected payoff in Γ after history h_k in H_k will be compared to a play of $\Gamma(g(h_k))$ where Player 1 plays the type independent strategy $\overline{\sigma}_1$ defined by

$$\overline{\sigma}_1(h) = \sum_{T_1} g_{t_1}(h_k h)\sigma_1(h_k h, t_1).$$

for all h in E^*. Corollary 14 says that $g(h_k h)$ is close to $g(h_k)$ with high probability if $\Phi(D_{k+l}) - \Phi(D_k)$ is small, and a detailed examination of the equations for the expected payoff will show that the result of Γ at stage $k + l$, when Player 1 uses σ_1, is very close to the average of the payoffs to $\Gamma(g(h_k))$ at stage l, when Player 1 uses $\overline{\sigma}_1$; and so the overall result cannot be more than cav vex $U + \delta$.

A symmetric argument gives the vex cav expression for Player 2. The formal construction of σ_2 is as follows:

Let

$$\Phi_{\max} = \sup_{\tau \in \Sigma_2} \lim_{k \to \infty} \Phi(D_{k,\tau}),$$

where Σ_2 is the set of strategies for Player 2, and $D_{k,\tau}$ is the distribution D_k on T_1 after k moves when strategies σ_1 and τ are used. Choose two small positive numbers Δ_1 and Δ_2 such that

$$\left(\Delta_1 + \frac{\Delta_2}{\Delta_1^2}\right) \cdot b \cdot a \leq \delta,$$

where a is the largest absolute value of numbers is the range of π and b is the number of elements in T_2.

By definition of $\Phi_{\max}$, there exists a strategy $\overline{\tau}$ and an integer k such that

$$\Phi_{\max} - \Phi(D_{k,\overline{\tau}}) \leq \Delta_2.$$

Let τ^k be a strategy for the k-repetition game such that τ^k maximizes $\Phi(D_{k,\tau^k})$ when Player 1 makes his moves according to σ_1. We can assume τ^k is type-independent because for any given type-dependent strategy $\overline{\tau}^k$, Player 2 can see which type t gets the most information, and then do just as well by choosing $\tau^k(h, t') = \overline{\tau}^k(h, t)$ for all $h \in H_k$ and $t' \in T_1$. We can also assume τ^k is pure because $\Phi(D_{k,\tau})$ is a linear function of τ (an application of Lemma 11). By choice of τ^k,

$$\Phi(D_{k,\tau^k}) \geq \Phi(D_{k,\tau})$$

for all $\tau \in \Sigma_2$, and so

$$\Phi_{\max} - \Phi(D_{k,\tau^k}) \leq \Delta_2.$$

Letting τ_p be Player 2's optimal strategy for the game $\Gamma(p)$, we define our counter-strategy σ_2 as follows:

$$\sigma_2(h, t) = \tau^k(h, t) \quad \text{when } |h| \leq k,$$

$$\sigma_2(h_k h, t) = \tau_{g(h_k)}(h, t) \quad \text{for } h_k \in H_k \text{ and } h \in E^*,$$

where $|h|$ represents the length of h.

The expected payoff l stages after history h_k in H_k must be compared with the expected payoff to the game $\Gamma(g(h_k))$ when Player 1 plays $\overline{\sigma}_1$ as defined above.

The repeated game $\Gamma(g(h_k))$ for strategies $\overline{\sigma}_1$ and $\tau_{g(h_k)}$ will have functions $\overline{g}$, $\overline{g}'$, and $\overline{w}$ defined in the same way as g, g', and w are defined for Γ. Since Player 1 has only one type t in $\Gamma(g(h_k))$, $\overline{g}_t(h) = 1$ for all h. Since the first k moves by Player 2 are type independent, $g'(h_k) = \overline{g}'(\varepsilon)$ and then $g'(h_k h) = \overline{g}'(h)$ for all h in E^* since $\sigma_2(h_k h, t_2)$ and $\tau(h, t_2)$ are defined to be identical for all h and t_2.

We next show that $\overline{w}(h) = w(h_k h, h_k)$ whenever $w(h_k) \neq 0$. This can be proved by induction starting with $h = \varepsilon$, where $\overline{w}(\varepsilon) = w(h_k \mid h_k) = 1$. Assuming it is true for history h, we need to prove it for history $h(m_1, m_2)$ for any m_1 in M_1 and m_2 in M_2. Using the inductive defining formula given earlier,

$$\overline{w}(h(m_1, m_2)) = \overline{w}(h) \sum_{T_2} \overline{g}'_{t_2}(h)\overline{\sigma}_1(h)_{m_1}\tau(h_1, t_2)_{m_2}.$$

The induction hypothesis says $\overline{w}(h) = w(h_k h)/w(h_k)$. Using this relationship, the relationship between $\overline{g}'$ and g', the relationship between τ and σ_2, and the definition of $\overline{\sigma}_1$, the right hand side is seen to be equivalent to

$$(w(h_k h)/w(h_k))\cdot$$

$$\left[\sum_{T_2} g'_{t_2}(h_k h) \left[\sum_{T_1} g_{t_1}(h_k h)\sigma_1(h_k h, t_1)_{m_1}\right] \sigma_2(h_k h, t_2)_{m_2}\right].$$

By using the distributive and commutative laws, this expression becomes

$$\frac{\left[w(h_k h)\sum_{T_1}\sum_{T_2} g_{t_1}(h_k h)g'_{t_2}(h_k h)\sigma_1(h_k h, t_1)_{m_1}\sigma_2(h_k h, t_2)_{m_2}\right]}{w(h_k)}.$$

The expression in brackets is just $w(h_k h(m_1, m_2))$ and we get the desired conclusion that

$$\overline{w}(h(m_1, m_2)) = w(h_k h(m_1, m_2))/w(h_k) = w(h_k h(m_1, m_2) \mid h_k).$$

For any non-null history h, let (m_1, m_2) be the last pair of choices in h (i.e., $h = h'(m_1, m_2)$ for some h') and let $\pi(h, t_1, t_2) = \pi(m_1, m_2, t_1, t_2)$ for all t_1 in T_1 and t_2 in T_2. Using this notation, the expected payoff to Player 1 at stage $k + l$ under strategies σ_1 and σ_2, is given by the expression

$$\sum_{H_k}\sum_{H_l}\sum_{T_1}\sum_{T_2} w(h_k h_l)g_{t_1}(h_k h_l)g'_{t_2}(h_k h_l)\pi(h_k h_l, t_1, t_2).$$

Replacing $g_{t_1}(h_k h_l)$ by $g_{t_1}(h_k) + \Delta_{t_1}(h_k h_l, l)$, the expression can be written as the sum of two parts, namely (part 1)

$$\sum_{H_k}\sum_{H_l}\sum_{T_1}\sum_{T_2} w(h_k h_l)g_{t_1}(h_k)g'_{t_2}(h_k h_l)\pi(h_k h_l, t_1, t_2).$$

and (part 2)

$$\sum_{H_k}\sum_{H_l}\sum_{T_1}\sum_{T_2} w(h_k h_l)\Delta_{t_1}(h_k h_l, l)g'_{t_2}(h_k h_l)\pi(h_k h_l, t_1, t_2).$$

Part 1 can be written as $\sum_{H_k} w(h_k)R(h_k)$ where

$$R(h_k) = \sum_{H_l}\sum_{T_2} w(h_k h_l | h_k)g'_{t_2}(h_k h_l)\sum_{T_1} g_{t_1}(h_k)\pi(h_k h_l, t_1, t_2).$$

We want to show $R(h_k)$ is equal to the expected result $E(h_k)$ of stage l in the game $\Gamma(g(h_k))$ when strategies $\overline{\sigma}_1$ and $\tau_{g(h_k)}$ are used.

For any non-null history h, let (m_1, m_2) be the last pair in h and define

$$\overline{\pi}_{g(h_k)}(h, t_2) = \overline{\pi}_{g(h_k)}(m_1, m_2, t_2).$$

Using this notation, the expected result $E(h_k)$ can be given by the expression

$$E(h_k) = \sum_{H_l}\sum_{T_2} \overline{w}(h_l)\overline{g}'(h_l)_{t_2}\overline{\pi}_{g(h_k)}(h_l, t_2).$$

We already know that $\overline{w}(h_l) = w(h_k h_l)$ and $\overline{g}'_{t_2}(h_l) = g'(h_k h_l)$. Thus to prove $R(h_k) = E(h_k)$, we need only show

$$\overline{\pi}_{g(h_k)}(h_l, t_2) = \sum_{T_1} g_{t_1}(h_k)\pi(h_k h_l, t_1, t_2).$$

Whatever pair of choices (m_1, m_2) ends history h_l also ends $h_k h_l$ and so the last equation can be rewritten

$$\overline{\pi}_{g(h_k)}(m_1, m_2, t_2) = \sum_{T_1} g_{t_1}(h_k)\pi(m_1, m_2, t_1, t_2),$$

which is true by definition of $\overline{\pi}$.

Since $R(h_k) = E(h_k)$, we conclude that

$$\sum_{H_k} w(h_k)R(h_k)$$

is the average result of all the subgames that result from the outcomes of the first k moves. Thus the average part 1 over all
stages is precisely the expected value if Player 1 uses the type-
independent strategies $\overline{\sigma}_1$ after the first k moves. The theorem is
proven if "part 2" above is small.

Part 2 can be rewritten as

$$\sum_{H_k}\sum_{H_l}\sum_{T_1} w(h_k h_l)\Delta_{t_1}(h_k h_l, l)\left[\sum_{T_2} g'_{t_2}(h_k h_l)\pi(h_k h_l, t_1, t_2)\right].$$

The absolute value of this expression is bounded by

$$\sum_{H_k}\sum_{H_l}\sum_{T_2} w(h_k h_l)\mid \Delta_{t_1}(h_k h_l, l)\mid a,$$

or, more simply, by

$$a\sum_{H_{k+l}}\sum_{T_2} w(h)\mid \Delta_{t_2}(h, l)\mid.$$

Let $H' = \{h \in H_{k+l}: \mid \Delta_t(h, l)\mid \geq \Delta_1$ for some t in $T_2\}$ and let
$\overline{H}' = H_{k+l} - H'$. By Corollary 14 and $\mid \Delta_{t_2}(h, l)\mid \leq 1$,

$$\sum_{H'}\sum_{T_2} w(h)\mid \Delta_{t_2}(h, l)\mid \leq \frac{\Phi(D_{k+1}) - \Phi(D_k)}{\Delta_1^2}b \leq \frac{\Delta_2}{\Delta_1^2}b.$$

Using $\sum_{\overline{H}'} w(h) \leq 1$ and $\mid \Delta_{t_2}(h, l)\mid \leq \Delta_1$ for h in $\overline{H}'$,

$$\sum_{\overline{H}'}\sum_{T_2} w(h)\mid \Delta_{t_2}(h, l)\mid \leq \Delta_1 \cdot b.$$

Thus $\sum_{H_{k+l}}\sum_{T_2} w(h)\mid\Delta_{t_2}(h, l)\mid \leq \left(\Delta_1 + \Delta_2/\Delta_1^2\right)b$ and thus
part 2 sums to at most δ. In the limit, Player 2 has limited
Player 1 to within δ of

$$\sum_p D_{k,\tau}(p)\operatorname*{vex}_q U(p, q),$$

which cannot be greater than cav vex U. ∎

COROLLARY 16. *The game Γ does not generally have a value.*

PROOF: cav vex U can sometimes be smaller than vex cav U (see Example 4.10 in Chapter Two). ∎

Speaking very loosely, the game lacks a value because it is to each player's advantage to release the information he plans to release later in the game than his opponent. This is very much like the game of picking the largest number, a game which also has no value. The proof itself is, we feel, ample demonstration that "information" can be effectively treated as a formal concept and tool. The remainder of this chapter discusses a couple of topics related to more general use of these concepts.

GENERALIZATION OF Γ. There are three directions in which Γ might be generalized, and we will discuss briefly how the information measure might apply to each of these.

One generalization is to allow an initial joint probability distribution[9] on $T_1 \times T_2$ instead of the independent distributions p on T_1 and q on T_2. These games can already be solved under the present theory, since these games all are equivalent to other games with independent probabilities. These equivalent games are obtained by changing the payoff entries and the probabilities in a compensating manner so that the overall payoff function is the same and the new probabilities independent. Although these games are thereby included under the present theory, we still lack a clear idea as to what information means in these transformed cases.

Another direction for generalization is to introduce more complex relationships between the players' moves and the information given to each player after each repetition. Again the players would have a limited amount of information to reveal and the many type vs. many type situation should reduce to the many vs. one.[10] The principal problem would thus appear to be the solution to the many vs. one case. Chapter Four has some results in this direction.

The game should also be generalized using other payoff functions for the supergame. Since the information is defined independent of payoff, the measure will still be defined. However, the trick

---

[9] See Postscript i to Chapter Two.(*)
[10] See Postscript f to Chapter Four. (*)

of first maximizing information and then maximizing the payoff
will not usually be applicable.

GENERALIZATION OF Φ. There remains the question as to what
initial choices of $\Phi(p)$ would have sufficed to prove Theorem 15
and satisfied criteria 1 to 3. Actually, any strictly convex function of p would have been sufficient, although the argument would
generally require compactness arguments instead of the clean algebraic arguments of Theorems 9 and 13. Convexity is required
to satisfy condition 2, and strict convexity for condition 3. However, if we also insist that Φ be symmetric and that the change of
information depend only on the changes in p (a weaker condition
than condition 4), then our choice is the only one possible, except
for $a\Phi + c$.

The more fundamental question, as to the choice of Φ, is to
understand more clearly the class of problems in which the basic
information object is a conditional probability vector, and to extend the information concept when more complex situations must
be measured.

CHAPTER FOUR

REPEATED GAMES OF INCOMPLETE INFORMATION: THE ZERO-SUM EXTENSIVE CASE

1. Introduction

This chapter is concerned with a situation in which a two-person zero-sum game is repeatedly played between two players, but only one of the two knows exactly which game is being played, i.e., what the rules are and what the payoff function is. More precisely, let G_k be a finite set of two-person zero-sum games (known to both players). Consider a game Γ played as follows: First chance chooses one of the games G_k, using a fixed probability distribution known to both players. Player 1 is informed which game G_k was chosen by chance, but Player 2 is not informed of chance's choice. The game G_k is then played a large number of times. During each play, each player collects some information (for example, about the moves of the other player) that he may use on subsequent plays. This information need not include the payoffs obtained at previous stages. The players need not be informed of the payoff at the end of each play; the payoff may, so to say, be held in escrow indefinitely.

Naturally, Player 2 is interested in finding out which game is being played. Though he is not necessarily explicitly informed about this, he may be able to draw some reasonable inferences, for example from the information that he can collect and remember about the choices of Player 1 during the course of the various plays. Player 1, on the other hand, may be interested in concealing which game is being played, and may try to confuse his opponent and lead him astray by making choices that are not necessarily to his own (i.e., Player 1's) best short-term interests. It is this interplay between the short and long-term interests of Player 1, and the information that Player 2 gradually accumulates, that forms the crux of the investigation in this chapter. Formally, the question will be treated by asking what is the value and what are the optimal strategies in the game Γ described above; after we have found the answers to these formal questions, we can present intuitive interpretations.

2. Motivation

Traditionally, Game Theory has been concerned with games in which before the start of play, all players are informed of the rules of the game and the payoff function. They know, so to say, which game is being played; they have a complete description of the game, either in the extensive form [1] or in the strategic form.[2] Such games are called games of *complete* information; this concept is to be sharply distinguished from the concept of games of *perfect* information, in the classical sense of Zermelo [1912], Von Neumann-Morgenstern [1944] and Kuhn [1953]. A game of perfect information is a game in extensive form, in which the players know at any stage of the play exactly which alternatives were chosen at all previous moves.

Game Theory has been criticized for its exclusive concern with games of complete information.[3] It has been pointed out that very often one might wish to model a real-life conflict situation, in which the participants (players) do not know the payoff functions of the other players, and might not even know their own; moreover they often do not know what moves (or strategies) are available to the other players. Usually each player can form some estimate on both these counts, but this estimate is often far from a certainty. The situation is complicated by the fact that not only are the players uncertain as to which game is being played, but also as to the beliefs of the other players; and it becomes very difficult to see through the complex interactions of beliefs, beliefs about beliefs, and so on.

---

[1] The "extensive form" is a complete formal description, which corresponds closely to the usual notion of the "rules" of the game.

[2] The "strategic form", sometimes called the "normal form", summarizes the significant facts about the game, in an array whose rows correspond to the strategies of Player 1, whose columns correspond to the strategies of Player 2, and whose entries correspond to the outcomes. The phrase "strategic form" was introduced by Shapley at the Princeton Games Conference in 1965.

[3] For example, see Luce and Raiffa [1957], p.49.

Recently, Harsanyi [1967–8] has shown how a large class of games of incomplete information can be modelled as games of complete information. This present chapter deals with a class of models, derived according to that procedure of Harsanyi, wherein the information of one of the two sides is complete.

3. The Mathematical Model

The games G_k will be called "stage games," as distinguished from Γ, which will be called the "supergame." Each of the repeated plays of a stage game which make up the supergame will be called a "stage" (of the supergame).

It is most convenient to use the strategic form for describing the stage games, with certain modifications that will make it more suitable for our problem. Chief among these is a device for describing the information that each player collects during a play of a stage game, or more precisely that information that is remembered by him and can be used on subsequent stages. To the extent that the stage games involve chance, it is important that this be explicitly taken into account, and not "averaged out," because information revealed by chance on one play may be used on all subsequent plays.

In the introduction we stated that the supergame is constructed by repeating the stage game a "large number" of times. Formally, we shall consider two models: in one, we first calculate the value of a supergame Γ_n consisting of exactly n repetitions of the stage game, and then ask about the asymptotic behavior of this value as n tends to infinity; in the other, we consider at once a supergame Γ_∞ with infinitely many stages.

To avoid trivialities, one must assume that Player 2 has the same strategy space in all the stage games; otherwise, he could obtain information about which stage game was chosen by chance, from the strategy space that is presented to him.

Formally, then, the n-stage supergame Γ_n consists of a positive integer n (the number of stages); a finite set T called the *stage strategy space* for Player 2; two finite sets H^1 and H^2 called *information spaces* (for Players 1 and 2 respectively); a finite set K

(chance's possible choices), together with a fixed probability distribution on K; and for each $k \in K$, an object G_k called a *stage game*, consisting of the following:

(i) a finite set R_k together with a fixed probability distribution on R_k (the strategy space for chance in the stage game G_k);

(ii) a finite set S_k (the strategy space for Player 1);

(iii) a real-valued function g_k defined on $R_k \times S_k \times T$ (the *payoff function*, which is both the gain to Player 1 and the loss to Player 2);

(iv) two functions h_k^1 and h_k^2 defined on $R_k \times S_k \times T$, with values in the information spaces H^1 and H^2 respectively. (These describe the information that each of the two players recalls from the play of each stage, and can use on subsequent stages.)

The supergame Γ_n is played as follows:

Step 1: Chance chooses a member k of K, in accordance with the fixed probability distribution on K (known to both players). Player 1, but not Player 2, is informed of k.

Step 2: Chance chooses a member r_1 of R_k, in accordance with the fixed probability distribution on R_k (chance's first-stage strategy).

Step 3: Player 1 chooses a member s_1 of S_k (his first stage strategy).

Step 4: Player 2 chooses a member t_1 of T (his first stage strategy).

Step 5: Player 1 is informed[4] of $h_k^1(r_1, s_1, t_1)$, and Player 2 of $h_k^2(r_1, s_1, t_1)$.

Steps 2, 3, 4, and 5 describe the first stage. These steps are repeated again and again. For the i-th stage we have:

Step 4i-2: Chance chooses a member r_i of R_k, in accordance with the fixed probability distribution on R_k (chance's i-th stage strategy). This choice is stochastically independent of chance's choices during the other stages. (Of course, in general the

---

[4]In addition to the information that he has on K. (*)

probabilities will depend on chance's original choice of k).

Step 4i-1:   Player 1 chooses a member s_i of S_k (his i-th stage strategy).

Step 4i: Player 2 chooses a member t_i of T (his i-th stage strategy).

Step 4i+1:   Player 1 is informed of $h_k^1(r_i, s_i, t_i)$ and Player 2 of $h_k^2(r_i, s_i, t_i)$.

Except for the information implicit in h_k^1 and h_k^2, no information regarding the choices r_i, s_i and t_i is ever revealed to anybody.

At the end of the n-th and last stage (i.e., step $4n+1$), Player 1 receives the amount[5] $\sum_{i=1}^n g_k(r_i, s_i, t_i)/n$ from Player 2. Before the end of the last stage, the payoffs are not revealed (except as the functions h_k^1 and h_k^2 imply).

The model assumes that information obtained in any step by means of the functions h_k^1 or h_k^2 can be used on all subsequent steps. (This means that s_i, Player 1's i-th stage strategy, may depend on the values of h_k^1 in stages before the i-th, and that t_i, Player 2's i-th stage strategy, may depend on the values of h_k^2 in stages before the i-th.)

The above is essentially a description of the n-stage supergame[6] Γ_n in extensive form, although the strategic form was used for the stage games that form the "building-blocks" of the supergame.

To describe Γ_n in strategic form, we need only describe the set of pure strategies for each player, and show how to specify the resulting payoff. A pure strategy s for Player 1 consists of a sequence of pure strategies, one for each stage:

$$s = (s_1, s_2, \ldots, s_n),$$

---

[5] Division by n is a matter of normalization to permit easy comparison of the values of Γ_n for different n.

[6] The above description, in which the set of chance's choices was placed at the beginning of the stage, is not a loss of generality. Suppose the stage game is given as a tree, in which chance moves are scattered all over. We can always regard chance as a separate player, and convert the game to the strategic form, where the players play simultaneously and the order of writing their moves is irrelevant. (*)

where each of those pure stage strategies may depend on k (i.e., which stage game was chosen by chance in Step 1) and on the values attained by h_k^1 at *previous* stages:[7]

$$s_i = s_i \left(k, h_k^1(r_1, s_1, t_1), \ldots, h_k^1(r_{i-1}, s_{i-1}, t_{i-1})\right).$$

A pure strategy t for Player 2 is analogous:

$$t = (t_1, \ldots, t_n),$$

where each of those pure stage strategies may depend on the values attained by h_k^2 at previous stages:

$$t_i = t_i \left(h_k^2(r_1, s_1, t_1), \ldots, h_k^2(r_{i-1}, s_{i-1}, t_{i-1})\right).$$

We do not permit t_i to depend explicitly on k, since we have assumed that Player 2 is not explicitly informed of k.

The manner in which a pair of pure strategies (s, t) defines the stage strategies s_i, t_i, for $i = 1, \ldots, n$, is obvious; chance then determines a pure strategy r in the supergame, with

$$r = (r_1, \ldots, r_n),$$

where r_i is a pure strategy for chance in the i-th stage game. Those stage strategies r_i, s_i, t_i then determine the payoff $g_k(r_i, s_i, t_i)$ in the i-th stage, and the i-th stage expected payoff $g_i(r_i, s_i, t_i)$.

Mixed strategies, σ for Player 1 and τ for Player 2, may be defined in the usual way as mixtures of pure strategies.

This completes the formal description of Γ_n. The description of play in Γ_∞ is similar, except that there is an infinite sequence of stages; the payoff to the infinite-stage supergame is, however, a somewhat more complicated matter, and we postpone discussing it until after we have given some illustrations.

---

[7]Formally, we even permit a player to forget actions he himself took in the past. In fact, this does not affect the analysis or the results.

4. Examples

Although the general model defined above allows the stage games
to be indexed by any finite set K, all of our examples will take
$K = \{1, 2\}$.

In fact, each of the examples of this section permits each G_k
to be defined as a 2×2 matrix game; each example dictates that
chance, in step 1, selects $k = 1$ with probability $1/2$, $k = 2$ with
probability $1/2$; and each example has $R_k = \{1\}$ for both $k = 1$
and $k = 2$ (no chance moves after step 1).

EXAMPLE 1. The 2×2 matrices of the stage games are:

$$
G_1 = \begin{array}{|c|c|} \hline 2 & 0 \\ \hline 0 & 1 \\ \hline \end{array}
\qquad \text{and} \qquad
G_2 = \begin{array}{|c|c|} \hline 1 & 0 \\ \hline 0 & 2 \\ \hline \end{array}
$$

Each occurs with probability $1/2$ and after each stage both players
are informed of the row and column that were chosen. In this
example $K = \{1, 2\}$, with probability $1/2$ assigned to each of the
members of K; $S_k = T = \{1, 2\}$ for both k in K, $H^1 = H^2 =
\{(1, 1), (1, 2), (2, 1), (2, 2)\}$; R_k is trivial (i.e., $R_k = \{1\}$) for both
k in K);

$$
g_k(r, s, t) = \begin{cases} 2, & \text{if } k = s = t, \\ 1, & \text{if } k \neq s \text{ and } s = t, \\ 0, & \text{otherwise;} \end{cases}
$$

and

$$
h_k^1(r, s, t) = h_k^2(r, s, t) = (s, t) \text{ for both } k \text{ in } K.
$$

One way of representing the information function $h_k^2(r, s, t)$ is to introduce two matrices A_k, $k = 1, 2$, where[8]

$$
A_1 = \begin{array}{|c|c|} \hline a & b \\ \hline c & d \\ \hline \end{array} \quad \text{and} \quad A_2 = \begin{array}{|c|c|} \hline a & b \\ \hline c & d \\ \hline \end{array}
$$

Here, a stands for $(1, 1)$, b for $(1, 2)$, c for $(2, 1)$ and d for $(2, 2)$. The interpretation is that at each stage, when the players find themselves in a square at a stage game, a caller tells Player 2 the letter corresponding to the same square in the information matrix—in A_1, if chance chose $k = 1$, and in A_2 otherwise.

We need not have bothered to represent $h_k^1(r, s, t)$; as we shall see later, only the space H^2 and the functions h_k^2 really play any role in the analysis (but see Postscript a to this chapter).[9]

Short-run naïve considerations would seem to indicate that Player 1 should play $(1/3, 2/3)$ at each stage if the stage game is G_1, and $(2/3, 1/3)$ if the stage game is G_2. Since these strategies are different, Player 2 could eventually[10] discriminate between the two strategies and infer whether game G_1 or G_2 is being played. Since $v(G_1) = v(G_2) = 2/3$, such a policy (of using his information) would enable Player 1 to guarantee himself an expectation of $2/3$.

But Player 1 could do better by *ignoring* his information. He would then act as if he were participating in the game

$$
\frac{1}{2}G_1 + \frac{1}{2}G_2 = \begin{array}{|c|c|} \hline 3/2 & 0 \\ \hline 0 & 3/2 \\ \hline \end{array}
$$

---

[8]In general, A_1 and A_2 are different matrices.
[9]It is precisely this point which makes the games with incomplete information on both sides so much more complex, and has prevented us from achieving the same success in this case (see Chapter Two).
[10]i.e., with a very high probability, if n is sufficiently large.

and playing it optimally. This would enable him to guarantee to himself an expectation of $3/4$, which is larger than $2/3$.

EXAMPLE 2. In this example we again have $K = \{1, 2\}$ (i.e., there are two stage games), $R_1 = R_2 = \{1\}$ (there are no chance moves after the first one), and the stage games are as follows:

$$
G_1 = \begin{array}{|c|c|} \hline 1 & 0 \\ \hline 0 & 1 \\ \hline \end{array}
\quad \text{and} \quad
G_2 = \begin{array}{|c|c|} \hline -1 & 0 \\ \hline 0 & 1 \\ \hline \end{array}
$$

Each occurs with probability $1/2$, and after each stage, each player is informed of the row and column chosen *and also of the payoff.* Here,

$$S_k = T = \{1, 2\} \text{ for both } k \text{ in } K;$$

$$H^1 = H^2$$
$$= \{(1, 1, (-1)), (1, 1, (1)), (1, 2, (0)), (2, 1, (0)), (2, 2, (1))\};$$

$$
g_k(r, s, t) = \begin{cases} 1 & \text{if } s = t = 2, \\ 1 & \text{if } s = t = k = 1, \\ -1 & \text{if } s = t = 1,\ k = 2, \\ 0 & \text{if } s \neq t; \end{cases}
$$

and $h_k^1(r, s, t) = h_k^2(r, s, t) = (s, t, g_k(r, s, t))$.

The information pattern (for Player 2) in this example has the form

$$
A_1 = \begin{array}{|c|c|} \hline a & b \\ \hline c & d \\ \hline \end{array}
\quad \text{and} \quad
A_2 = \begin{array}{|c|c|} \hline e & b \\ \hline c & d \\ \hline \end{array}
$$

(compare Example 1).

This example is what Rosenfeld [1964] calls an "adaptive competitive decision process"; in fact this particular example appears on p. 81 of his paper. More generally, any repeated game with complete information on one side only, where both players are told of the rows, columns and payoffs, is an "adaptive competitive decision process with unequal information"; in fact we get all such processes in which one side has complete information. All such processes can be solved by using the results of this chapter, in the sense that we can find an expression for the value of the game, and a good strategy for each player. What Rosenfeld calls the "equal information case" corresponds to a situation in which neither Player 1 nor Player 2 is informed of chance's choice of k, and can also be easily solved by using the methods of this chapter. The more general unequal information case, in which on the two sides there is partial – but different – information as to which k chance chose, is much more complicated, and only fragmentary results have been obtained on it (see Chapter Three).[11]

Let us return to the specific example under discussion, Example 2. If chance chooses G_1, and Player 1 plays optimally in G_1, he will play $(1/2, 1/2)$: the value $v(G_1)$ is $1/2$. If chance chooses G_2, and Player 1 plays optimally in G_2, he will play $s = 2$; the value $v(G_2)$ is 0. Because these strategies are different, Player 1's policy "play an optimal strategy in the stage game that is actually chosen" is almost sure eventually to reveal k to Player 2. The expectation to Player 1 if he pursues this policy is $(1/2) \cdot (1/2) + (1/2) \cdot 0 = 1/4$. Thus, for large n, Player 1 can only ensure himself an average payoff per stage of $1/4$ if he exploits (and thereby reveals) his information.

On the other hand, if Player 1 wishes to conceal k from his opponent, what can he do? The answer, in the long run, is clear: if his policy is playing $s = 1$ a positive proportion of the time, then Player 2 can eventually discover[12] k. So he must play $s = 2$ almost always. In this case, player 2 can always hold him down to a 0 average payoff by choosing $t = 1$.

So it seems that for large n, Player 1 must reveal, and the payoff is $1/4$. But for small n this argument does not hold; in

---

[11]The general case has in the meantime been completely solved. See Postscript g. (*)

[12]With probability approaching 1 as n increases.

particular, for $n = 1$, Player 1 may ensure an expected payoff of at least $1/2$ by choosing $s = k$.

EXAMPLE 3. In this example it is convenient to describe the stage games in extensive form, as in Figure 1. The numbers at the branch-points of the trees represent the players to whom the respective moves belong; the numbers at the terminal (bottom) vertices represent the payoffs. The games are of perfect information; we assume also that both players are informed, at the end of each stage, as to which terminal was reached.[13] Each game occurs with probability $1/2$.

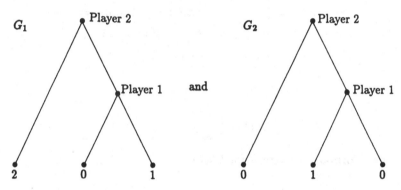

Figure 1. The trees for Example 3

In strategic form, we obtain the payoff matrices

$$G_1 = \quad \begin{array}{c|c|c|} & L & R \\ \hline L & 2 & 0 \\ \hline R & 2 & 1 \\ \hline \end{array} \quad \text{and} \quad G_2 = \quad \begin{array}{c|c|c|} & L & R \\ \hline L & 0 & 1 \\ \hline R & 0 & 0 \\ \hline \end{array}$$

Formally, we have $K = \{1, 2\}$, with probability $1/2$ for each member of K; $S_k = T = \{L, R\}$ for both k in K (each player has two

---

[13] But, for Player 2, not in which stage game.

strategies, denoted by L for "left" and R for "right", and we write LR for (L, R), etc);

$$H^1 = \{LL, LR, RL, RR\};$$
$$H^2 = \{L, LR, RR\};$$
$$R_k \text{ is trivial for both } k;$$

(L alone means that Player 2 chose "left".)

$$g_k(r, s, t) = \begin{cases} 2 & \text{when } k = 1 \text{ and } t = L, \\ 1 & \text{when } t = R \text{ and} \\ & \quad \text{either } k = 1 \text{ and } s = R, \\ & \quad \text{or } k = 2 \text{ and } s = L, \\ 0 & \text{otherwise;} \end{cases}$$

$$h_k^1(r, s, t) = (s, t),$$

$$\text{and } h_k^2(r, s, t) = \begin{cases} L & \text{when } t = L, \\ sR & \text{when } t = R. \end{cases}$$

The information pattern for Player 2 is

$$A_1 = \begin{array}{|c|c|} \hline a & b \\ \hline a & d \\ \hline \end{array} \quad \text{and} \quad A_2 = \begin{array}{|c|c|} \hline a & b \\ \hline a & d \\ \hline \end{array}$$

5. The Infinite-Stage Game and its Relation to the n-Stage Games

The formal description of play in Γ_∞ is exactly the same as in the Γ_n (Section 3), except that there is an infinite sequence of stages. In the definition of the payoff to Γ_∞, however, we run into difficulties. A natural way to define the payoff would be by

$$\lim_{n\to\infty} \left(\sum_{i=1}^{n} g_k(r_i, s_i, t_i)/n \right). \tag{5.1}$$

Unfortunately, this limit may not exist, as may easily be verified. Fortunately, though, it is still possible to define the notion of value. Indeed, each pair σ, τ of mixed strategies of players 1 and 2 in Γ_∞ determines an expected payoff for each stage of Γ_∞. The average of the first n such payoffs will be denoted $\gamma_n(\sigma, \tau)$, and will be called the n-th stage payoff in Γ_∞. We now define a number $v(\Gamma_\infty)$ to be the *value* of Γ_∞ if there is a pair of mixed strategies σ_0, τ_0 in Γ_∞ (called *optimal strategies*) such that for every $\varepsilon > 0$ there is a positive integer n_0 such that for every pair (σ, τ) of mixed strategies in Γ_∞ and every $n > n_0$, we have

$$\gamma_n(\sigma_0, \tau) + \varepsilon \geq v(\Gamma_\infty) \geq \gamma_n(\sigma, \tau_0) - \varepsilon. \tag{5.2}$$

It is clear that there can be at most one such value.

Let us denote the value of the n-stage games by $v(\Gamma_n)$ or v_n for short; since these are finite games with well-defined payoffs, there is of course no difficulty in defining their value.

PROPOSITION A. $v(\Gamma_\infty)$ and $\lim_{n\to\infty} v(\Gamma_n)$ *both exist, and are equal.*

The proof of Proposition A appears in Section 7. The common numerical value of these two quantities will be denoted v_∞.

Still another possibility for defining the value of Γ_∞ is to define the *lower payoff* and *upper payoff* in the extensive form of Γ_∞ by replacing the "lim" operator in (5.1) by "lim inf" and "lim sup", respectively. We could then try to define v to be the value of Γ_∞ if Player 1 has a strategy in Γ_∞ that guarantees an expected lower payoff[14] that is $\geq v$, and Player 2 has a strategy that guarantees an expected upper payoff that is $\leq v$. This, however, does not

---

[14]Exp lim inf, which is not the same as lim inf Exp.

work. Consider the case in which there are two stage-games, with matrices

$$G_1 = \boxed{\begin{array}{c|c} 0 & 1 \end{array}} \quad \text{and} \quad G_2 = \boxed{\begin{array}{c|c} 1 & 0 \end{array}}$$

and probability $1/2$ for each game, each player being informed after each stage which column was chosen by Player 2. Player 1, of course, has no choice in the game. Now if Player 2 plays left and right in alternating blocks of rapidly increasing length (for example, the n-th block could have length 2^{n^2}), then the lower payoff will be 0 no matter what chance did; hence Player 1 cannot guarantee a higher expected lower payoff. On the other hand, it is clear that Player 2 cannot depress the expected upper payoff to less than $1/2$. So even in this very simple case, the value in this strong sense does not always exist.

6. Statement of the Main Theorem: The Value of the Infinite-Stage Game

The purpose of this section is to give an "explicit" expression for v_∞, in terms of the stage games and the other parameters of the supergame. This constitutes the main theorem of this chapter. Only the statement will be given in this section; the proof appears in subsequent sections.

The one-stage game Γ_1 plays a central role in the statement of our theorem. A mixed strategy σ of Player 1 in Γ_1 is called *non-separating* if, for every strategy τ of Player 2, it induces the same probability distribution on $h_k^2(r, s, t)$ for all k that occur with positive probability. The definition is not affected if we restrict the strategies τ of Player 2 to be pure strategies; therefore, for simplicity, we do so.

Intuitively, σ is non-separating if Player 2 can get no hints about which game is being played (in addition to what he knows already) from the information available to him at the end of the (first and only) stage, *even if he knows that Player 1 is indeed playing σ*. The simplest examples of non-separating strategies occur in games of the type described in Example 1 of Section 4. In this game not only does Player 2 have the same strategy space in all the stage games, but so does Player 1; furthermore, the only information Player 2 retains from the play of previous stages is the stage strategy chosen by Player 1. In such games, the non-separating strategies for Player 1 in Γ_1 are exactly those in which Player 1 "ignores his information about which game is being played", i.e., chooses the same strategy regardless of which stage game was selected by chance. In general, though, there is no clear relationship between "ignoring information" and "non-separating"; indeed, there are even games in which non-separating strategies require the use of one's information (Chapter Two, Example 5.5).

The game Γ_1 is finite, with a finite number of pure strategies for each player. Hence its space of mixed strategies for Player 1 is finite-dimensional, and one may ask about the subset of this space consisting of the non-separating strategies. The answer is

PROPOSITION B. *The non-separating strategies of Player 1 in Γ_1 form a convex compact polyhedron in the space of all mixed strategies of Player 1.*

PROOF: The proof of this proposition is so simple that it is not worthwhile to postpone it. It is convenient to denote a probability distribution by a formal sum. Thus if ξ^i are (not necessarily distinct) elements of a set Ξ and x_i are non-negative numbers summing to 1, then $\sum_i^* x_i \xi^i$ denotes that probability distribution in which the probability assigned to a particular member ξ of Ξ is the sum of all those x_i for which $\xi^i = \xi$; the star in $\sum^*$ is to remind us that the sum is formal.

A pure strategy for Player 2 in Γ_1 is simply a member t of T. A pure strategy for Player 1 is a function σ that assigns to each k in K a member $\sigma(k)$ of S_k. For each k in K, chance's probability distribution on R_k may be denoted $\sum_j^* a_{jk} r^{jk}$, where r^{jk} ranges over R_k. Now let K' be the set of k in K that occur with positive probability, and let $\{\sigma^1, \sigma^2, \ldots, \sigma^m\}$ be the set of all (distinct) pure strategies of Player 1. Then a mixed strategy $\sum_i^* x_i \sigma^i$ is non-separating if and only if for all t in T and all k and l in K',

$$\sum_{i,j}^* x_i a_{jk} h_k^2(r^{jk}, \sigma^i(k), t) = \sum_{i,j}^* x_i a_{jl} h_l^2(r^{jl}, \sigma^i(l), t). \quad (6.1)$$

This equality between formal sums is equivalent to a number of linear equalities in the x_i, one for each distinct value of h_k^2 and h_l^2 appearing in (6.1); the coefficients of the x_i in these linear equalities are linear combinations of the a_{jk} and the a_{jl}. All these equalities for all t in T and all k and l in K', together with $\sum_i x_i = 1$ and the inequalities $x_i \geq 0$, determine a compact convex polyhedron. This completes the proof of Proposition B. ∎

It is to be particularly noted that we can explicitly write down the linear inequalities that define the polyhedron of non-separating strategies. From this it follows that we can also explicitly calculate the extreme points of this polyhedron.

We now define an auxiliary game Δ_1 in strategic form as follows: For Player 1, the mixed strategies in Δ_1 are the non-separating mixed strategies of Player 1 in Γ_1. For Player 2, the mixed strategies in Δ_1 are all the mixed strategies of Player 2 in Γ_1. The payoff is defined in the obvious way from the payoffs in Γ_1.

Δ_1 has been obtained from Γ_1 by restricting Player 1 to using only non-separating strategies. It can easily be represented as a finite matrix game, by defining the pure strategies of Player 1 to be the extreme points of the polyhedron of non-separating strategies. The pure strategies for Player 2 are as in Γ_1, and so is the payoff.

Incidentally, it may well happen that Player 1 has *no* non-separating strategies in Γ_1, and hence no strategies at all in Δ_1. In that case the game Δ_1 remains undefined.[15]

We digress to define the concept of "concavification". Let C be a subset of a euclidean space, f a bounded real function defined on C. Denote the convex hull of C by C^*. The *concavification* of f, denoted f^* or cav f, is the minimum of all concave functions on C^* that are $\geq f$ on C; in symbols

$$f^*(x) := \text{cav } f = \min\{g(x) : g \text{ is defined and concave on } C^*$$
$$\text{and } g(y) \geq f(y) \text{ for all } y \text{ in } C\}.$$

---

[15]It is possible to view Δ_1 as a kind of degenerate "null game", in which Player 1 has no strategies. Player 2, of course, has the same strategies as before. As the maximum of the empty set is conventionally taken to be $-\infty$, it follows that we may take the value ($= \min \max = \max \min$) of Δ_1 to be $-\infty$. It may be seen that this alternative approach leads to the same results as that of the text.

This minimum always exists; to see this, note that the infimum certainly exists, and that the infimum is itself concave.

Now for each k in K, let p_k be the probability that chance chooses k, and let p be the κ-dimensional vector of all the p_k (where κ is the cardinality of K). The set of all p forms a simplex P of dimension $\kappa - 1$. It turns out that in order to calculate v_∞, one must consider values of p other than the originally given one, i.e., one must consider p as a parameter that varies over all of P. We shall therefore adopt the notations $\Gamma_n(p)$, $\Gamma_\infty(p)$, $\Delta_1(p)$, $v_\infty(p)$, and so on.

Let Q be the set of all those points p in P for which $\Delta_1(p)$ is defined. Define a function u on Q by $u(p) =$ the value of $\Delta_1(p)$. Note that each of the unit vectors $(1, 0, \ldots, 0), (0, 1, 0, \ldots, 0), \ldots$, is in Q; for when p is a unit vector, then only one k in K occurs with positive probability, so every strategy of Player 1 in Γ_1 is trivially non-separating. It follows that $Q^* = P$, and since u is clearly bounded, it follows that the concavification u^* of u is defined on all of P.

THEOREM C (MAIN THEOREM). *For all p in P, $v_\infty(p) = u^*(p)$.*

The proof of Theorem C is given in the next section.

7. Proof of the Main Theorem

In this section we will prove both Proposition A (Section 5 of this chapter) and Theorem C (Section 6 of this chapter). First we will prove Theorem C, and part of Proposition A; namely,

$$\lim_{n \to \infty} v_n(p) = u^*(p);$$

and then the other part of Proposition A,

$$v(\Gamma_\infty) = \lim_{n \to \infty} v_n(p).$$

PROOF OF THEOREM C: We start the proof by showing that

$$v_n(p) \le u^*(p) + o(1). \tag{7.1}$$

In this proof we make strong use of the minimax theorem; i.e., in constructing Player 2's strategy we use Player 1's strategy.

To simplify the notation, write $g(k, r, s, t)$ for $g_k(r, s, t)$, and $h^2(k, r, s, t)$ for $h_k^2(r, s, t)$. Without loss of generality, assume that

$$g(k, r, s, t) \geq 0$$

for all k, r, s, t; at certain points this slightly simplifies the argument.

In Section 3 it was assumed that the players recall all information once obtained; i.e., Player 1 recalls the value of k, and Players 1 and 2 recall the values of the information functions h^1 and h^2 respectively. However, if we view the game as presented in Section 3 as a game in extensive form, it does not follow that it is of perfect recall, since it was not explicitly assumed that the players recall their own previous choices. Now, according to results of Dalkey [1953], the strategic form—and a fortiori the value—of a game remains essentially unchanged if we assume that each player recalls his own previous moves. Formally, therefore, we may and will assume that the choices of each player in a given stage are included in the information that is made available to him at the end of that stage. In particular, it follows that

$$t_1 \neq t_2 \implies h^2(k_1, r_1, s_1, t_1) \neq h^2(k_2, r_2, s_2, t_2) \qquad (7.2)$$

for all values of the parameters.[16] ∎

Before going further, we establish some conventions of terminology. It will be convenient to use the language of random variables. Thus k will denote the random variable that indicates the choice k of chance in step 1 of Γ_n. The expectation operator will be denoted by Exp, and conditions by a vertical stroke $|$; thus conditional expectations will be denoted Exp ($|$). If x is a random variable with values in a finite set X, then the *distribution* of x is defined to be the vector

$$\chi = (\chi^x)_{x \in X}, \qquad \text{where } \chi^x = \text{Prob}\,(x = x).$$

---

[16] We need the assumption of perfect recall in order to be able to use behavior strategies for determining the values of the games. Of course, if previous moves are not remembered, the players will have to use mixed strategies to achieve these values.

We will also make use of the notion of "conditional random variable." Let Ω be a probability space, $\mathbf{x}$ a random variable on Ω, Λ an event of positive probability. Then the conditional random variable $\mathbf{x} \mid \Lambda$ is defined to be $\mathbf{x}$ restricted to Λ, where on Λ we impose the measure $\mathrm{Prob}\{\cdot \mid \Lambda\}$. These definitions are consistent with the standard definitions and interpretations of conditional expectations and conditional probabilities; for example, it makes no difference whether one reads $\mathrm{Exp}(\mathbf{x} \mid \Lambda)$ as the conditional expectation, given Λ, of the (unconditional) random variable $\mathbf{x}$, or as the (unconditional) expectation of the conditional random variable $\mathbf{x} \mid \Lambda$; and similarly for conditional probabilities. It is also true that if f is any function defined on a product space $X_1 \times X_2 \times \dots$, and $\mathbf{x}_1, \mathbf{x}_2, \dots$ are random variables with values in $X_1, X_2, \dots$, respectively, then

$$f(\mathbf{x}_1, \mathbf{x}_2, \dots) \mid \Lambda = f(\mathbf{x}_1 \mid \Lambda, \mathbf{x}_2 \mid \Lambda, \dots).$$

Let us now consider the one-stage game Γ_1, which, as we shall see, plays a particularly important role in the analysis. We have already defined $\mathbf{k}$; recall that the set of k in K that occur with positive probability is denoted K'. Next, denote by $\mathbf{r}$ the random variable that indicates the member of $\bigcup_k R^k$ chosen by chance; note that $\mathbf{r} \in R^\mathbf{k}$. Now let us be given mixed strategies for Players 1 and 2 in Γ_1. These strategies can be thought of as random variables $\mathbf{s}$ and $\mathbf{t}$, with values in $\bigcup_k S^k$ and T, respectively, which indicate the choices of Players 1 and 2, respectively; note that $\mathbf{s} \in S^\mathbf{k}$. The variables $\mathbf{k}$, $\mathbf{r}$, and $\mathbf{s}$ are in general mutually dependent; on the other hand, $\mathbf{t}$ is independent of the triple $(\mathbf{k}, \mathbf{r}, \mathbf{s})$, and for given $k \in K'$, the variables $\mathbf{r} \mid k$ and $\mathbf{s} \mid k$ are independent.

The distributions of $\mathbf{k}$ and $\mathbf{t}$ will be denoted p and τ, respectively; thus $p^k = \mathrm{Prob}\{\mathbf{k} = k\}$ and $\tau^t = \mathrm{Prob}\{\mathbf{t} = t\}$. In the case of $\mathbf{r}$ and $\mathbf{s}$, we are more interested in the conditional distributions given k. It is, however, equivalent and more convenient to deal with the distribution of the joint variable $(\mathbf{k}, \mathbf{r}, \mathbf{s})$. This distribution will be denoted α; thus

$$\alpha^{krs} = \mathrm{Prob}\{\mathbf{k} = k \text{ and } \mathbf{r} = r \text{ and } \mathbf{s} = s\},$$

where α^{krs} is defined if and only if $r \in R^k$ and $s \in S^k$.

These notations for the distributions will be retained throughout this section.

For $h \in H^2$, $t \in T$, and $k, l \in K'$, define

$$\Theta^h(t, k) = \text{Prob}\{h^2(\mathbf{k}, \mathbf{r}, \mathbf{s}, t) = h \mid \mathbf{k} = k\},$$

and

$$\overline{\Theta}^h(t) = \text{Prob}\{h^2(\mathbf{k}, \mathbf{r}, \mathbf{s}, t) = h\} = \sum_{k \in K'} p^k \Theta^h(t, k).$$

By definition, Player 1's strategy is non-separating if and only if

$$\Theta^h(t, k) = \Theta^h(t, l)$$

for all $h \in H^2$, $t \in T$, and $k, l \in K'$. This is equivalent to

$$\Theta^h(t, k) = \overline{\Theta}^h(t)$$

for all $h \in H^2$, $t \in T$, and $k \in K'$, and this in turn is equivalent to

$$\text{Prob}\{\mathbf{k} = k \text{ and } h^2(\mathbf{k}, \mathbf{r}, \mathbf{s}, t) = h\} = p^k \overline{\Theta}^h(t), \qquad (7.3)$$
$$\text{whenever } h \in H^2, t \in T, k \in K.$$

(Note that we have written K rather than K'; if $p^k = 0$, the condition holds in any case). Now, for fixed h, t, and k, the two sides of (7.3) can be explicitly expressed in terms of the distribution α; thus whether or not Player 1's strategy is non-separating depends on α only. This justifies us in applying the adjective "non-separating" to distributions α as well as to strategies; α is non-separating if and only if (7.3) holds. Note that the expressions appearing on the two sides of (7.3) are continuous functions of α.

Recall that P denotes the set of all possible distributions of chance's choice $\mathbf{k}$, i.e., the set of all vectors $p = (p^k)_{k \in K}$ with $p^k \geq 0$ and $\sum p^k = 1$. Similarly, denote by A the set of all possible distributions α of $(\mathbf{k}, \mathbf{r}, \mathbf{s})$; that is, A contains all vectors $\alpha = (\alpha^{krs})$ where the index ranges over all k, r, and s with $r \in R^k$ and $s \in S^k$, such that $\alpha^{krs} \geq 0$ and $\sum \alpha^{krs} = 1$. The sets P and A are simplices in euclidean space of dimensions κ and

$\sum_k |R^k| \cdot |S^k|$, respectively.[17] On the simplices P and A we impose the metrics obtained from the ordinary euclidean norm $\| \quad \|$ on these euclidean spaces.

Let NS denote the subset of A consisting of non-separating distributions. From the fact that both sides of (7.3) are continuous functions of α, we deduce

LEMMA 1. *NS is a closed subset of A.*

Now, for given $\mathbf{k}$, $\mathbf{r}$, $\mathbf{s}$, and $\mathbf{t}$, let $\mathbf{h}$ denote the random variable that indicates the information received by Player 2 after the single stage of Γ_1 is completed; that is,

$$\mathbf{h} = h^2(\mathbf{k}, \mathbf{r}, \mathbf{s}, \mathbf{t}).$$

If $h \in H^2$ is such that $\mathbf{h} = h$ has positive probability, let $p(h)$ denote the distribution of $\mathbf{k} \mid \{\mathbf{h} = h\}$; thus

$$p^k(h) = \text{Prob} \{\mathbf{k} = k \mid \mathbf{h} = h\}.$$

The vector $p(h)$, which is in P, represents Player 2's *a posteriori* estimate of nature's choice of k, after he has received the information from one play of the game. If h is allowed to vary at random, then this vector becomes a random variable $p(\mathbf{h})$. Now define

$$e = \text{Exp}\left(\|p(\mathbf{h})\|^2 - \|p\|^2\right).$$

Using the function h^2, it is easy to write down an explicit expression for e in terms of α and τ; thus

$$e = e(\alpha, \tau).$$

The function $e(\alpha, \tau)$ is continuous in both variables simultaneously. To see this, we need only observe that

$$e = \sum_{h \in H^2} \text{Prob} \{\mathbf{h} = h\} \cdot \left(\|p(h)\|^2 - \|p\|^2\right);$$

---

[17]The dimensions of the simplices are, of course, lower by 1.

for a given h, the summand corresponding to h is certainly continuous at each point (α_0, τ_0) at which $\text{Prob}\{\mathbf{h} = h\} > 0$. But at a point (α_0, τ_0) at which $\text{Prob}\{\mathbf{h} = h\} = 0$, this summand is also continuous, since as $(\alpha, \tau) \to (\alpha_0, \tau_0)$, the factor $\|p(h)\|^2 - \|p\|^2$ remains bounded, whereas $\text{Prob}\{\mathbf{h} = h\} \to 0$. Therefore, each summand is everywhere continuous, so $e(\alpha, \tau)$ is also continuous.

Note that

$$e = \text{Exp}\left(\|p(\mathbf{h})\|^2 - \|p\|^2\right) = \text{Exp}\left(\|p(\mathbf{h}) - p\|^2\right). \qquad (7.4)$$

Indeed, it is easily verified (cf. (5.8) of Chapter One) that

$$\text{Exp } p(\mathbf{h}) = p;$$

from this it follows that

$$\begin{aligned}
\text{Exp}\left(\|p(\mathbf{h}) - p\|^2\right) &= \text{Exp}\left(\|p(\mathbf{h})\|^2\right) - 2p \cdot \text{Exp } p(\mathbf{h}) + \|p\|^2 \\
&= \text{Exp}\left(\|p(\mathbf{h})\|^2\right) - \|p\|^2 \\
&= \text{Exp}\left(\|p(\mathbf{h})\|^2 - \|p\|^2\right),
\end{aligned}$$

as claimed. ∎

LEMMA 2. *Let τ be given; assume that $\tau^t > 0$ for all $t \in T$. A necessary and sufficient condition that α be non-separating is that*

$$e(\alpha, \tau) = 0.$$

PROOF: Formula (7.2) implies that there exists a function f, defined on H^2, with values in T, such that

$$f\left(h^2(k, r, s, t)\right) = t \qquad (7.5)$$

for all k, r, s, and t. From this it follows that

$$\begin{aligned}
h^2(\mathbf{k}, \mathbf{r}, \mathbf{s}, t) = h &\Longrightarrow f\left(h^2(\mathbf{k}, \mathbf{r}, \mathbf{s}, t)\right) = f(h) \\
&\Longrightarrow t = f(h).
\end{aligned}$$

Hence, if $t \neq f(h)$, then $h^2(\mathbf{k}, \mathbf{r}, \mathbf{s}, t) = h$ cannot occur, from which it follows that

$$\text{Prob} \{\mathbf{k} = k \text{ and } h^2(\mathbf{k}, \mathbf{r}, \mathbf{s}, t) = h\} = 0$$

for all $k \in K$, and also that

$$\overline{\Theta}^h(t) = 0$$

whenever $t \neq f(h)$. Consequently (7.3) is automatically satisfied for $t \neq f(h)$. It then follows that α is non-separating if and only if (7.3) holds when t is restricted to be equal to $f(h)$; i.e., if and only if

$$\text{Prob} \{\mathbf{k} = k \text{ and } h^2 ((\mathbf{k}, \mathbf{r}, \mathbf{s}, f(h)) = h\} = p^k \overline{\Theta}^h (f(h)) \qquad (7.6)$$

for all $h \in H^2$ and $k \in K$.

Next, by (7.4), $e = 0$ if and only if

$$p^k(h) = p^k$$

for all $h \in H^2$ with $\text{Prob} \{\mathbf{h} = h\} > 0$, and all $k \in K$. This is equivalent to

$$\text{Prob} \{\mathbf{k} = k \text{ and } \mathbf{h} = h\} = p^k \, \text{Prob} \{\mathbf{h} = h\} \qquad (7.7)$$

for all such h and all k; but since (7.7) is in any case satisfied when $\text{Prob} \{\mathbf{h} = h\} = 0$, it follows that $e = 0$ if and only if (7.7) holds for all $h \in H^2$ and $k \in K$. The proof of the lemma will therefore be complete if we can show that for all h and k, formulas (7.6) and (7.7) are equivalent.

From (7.5) it follows that

$$\mathbf{h} = h \iff \mathbf{h} = h \text{ and } \mathbf{t} = f(h)$$
$$\iff h^2 (\mathbf{k}, \mathbf{r}, \mathbf{s}, f(h)) = h \text{ and } \mathbf{t} = f(h).$$

Since $(\mathbf{k}, \mathbf{r}, \mathbf{s})$ and $\mathbf{t}$ are independent, it follows that

$$\text{Prob} \{\mathbf{k} = k \text{ and } \mathbf{h} = h\}$$
$$= \text{Prob} \{\mathbf{k} = k \text{ and } h^2 (\mathbf{k}, \mathbf{r}, \mathbf{s}, f(h)) = h \text{ and } \mathbf{t} = f(h)\}$$
$$= \text{Prob} \{\mathbf{k} = k \text{ and } h^2 (\mathbf{k}, \mathbf{r}, \mathbf{s}, f(h)) = h\} \tau^{f(h)},$$

and that

$$p^k \operatorname{Prob}\{\mathbf{h} = h\} = p^k \operatorname{Prob}\{h^2(\mathbf{k}, \mathbf{r}, \mathbf{s}, f(h)) = h \text{ and } \mathbf{t} = f(h)\}$$
$$= p^k \overline{\Theta}^h(f(h)) \tau^{f(h)}.$$

Thus (7.7) is obtained from (7.6) by multiplying both sides by $\tau^{f(h)}$, and since $\tau^{f(h)} > 0$ (see the statement of the lemma), the desired equivalence is established. This completes the proof of the lemma. ■

The distance between a closed set B in a euclidean space and a point x in the same space will be denoted $\|x - B\|$.

LEMMA 3. *Let τ be given, and assume that $\tau^t > 0$ for all t. Then for each $\xi > 0$ there is an $\eta > 0$ such that for all α,*

$$e(\alpha, \tau) < \eta \Longrightarrow \|\alpha - NS\| < \xi.$$

REMARK. The distance on the right side of the implication is defined because NS is closed (Lemma 1).

PROOF: Suppose not; then there is a $\xi > 0$ and a sequence $\{\eta_j\}$ tending to 0, such that for each j there is an α_j such that

$$e(\alpha_j, \tau) < \eta_j \text{ and } \|\alpha_j - NS\| \geq \xi.$$

Since A is compact, the α_j have a limit point α_0, which we may as well assume is a limit. Since $\|\alpha - NS\|$ and $e(\alpha, \tau)$ are both continuous functions of α, it follows that

$$e(\alpha_0, \tau) = 0 \text{ and } \|\alpha_0 - NS\| \geq \xi. \tag{7.8}$$

The first formula of (7.8) implies, by Lemma 2, that $\alpha_0 \in NS$, whereas the second implies that $\alpha_0 \notin NS$; this contradiction proves Lemma 3. ■

Let $\mathbf{s}$ be given. A pure strategy t_0 of Player 2 is called a *best reply to* $\mathbf{s}$ if it minimizes the expected payoff $\operatorname{Exp}(\mathbf{k}, \mathbf{r}, \mathbf{s}, t)$ over all t in T. For $0 \leq \varepsilon \leq 1$, Player 2's strategy $\mathbf{t}$ is said to be an *ε-best reply* to $\mathbf{s}$ if there is a pure strategy t_0 that is a best reply to $\mathbf{s}$, such that $\mathbf{t}$ takes the value t_0 with probability $1 - \varepsilon + (\varepsilon/|T|)$, and takes all other values in T with probability $\varepsilon/|T|$ each. Note that if $\varepsilon > 0$ and $\mathbf{t}$ is an ε-best reply to $\mathbf{s}$, then $\tau^t > 0$ for all t, so τ satisfies the conditions of Lemmas 2 and 3.

LEMMA 4. *Let*
$$C = \max g(k, r, s, t),$$

the maximum being taken over all $k \in K$, $r \in R^k$, $s \in S^k$, *and* $t \in T$. *Then for each* $\varepsilon > 0$, *there is a* $\delta > 0$, *such that for all choices of* $(\mathbf{k}, \mathbf{r}, \mathbf{s})$ *(i.e., for all* α*), if* $\mathbf{t}$ *is an* ε-*best reply to* $\mathbf{s}$, *and if* $e(\alpha, \tau) < \delta$, *then*

$$\text{Exp } g(\mathbf{k}, \mathbf{r}, \mathbf{s}, \mathbf{t}) \le u(p) + (1 + C)\varepsilon.$$

PROOF: It is easy to write an explicit formula for $\text{Exp } g(\mathbf{k}, \mathbf{r}, \mathbf{s}, \mathbf{t})$ in terms of α and τ (when $\mathbf{t}$ is not necessarily an ε-best reply); say

$$\text{Exp } g(\mathbf{k}, \mathbf{r}, \mathbf{s}, \mathbf{t}) = d(\alpha, \tau).$$

Note that d is continuous in all its variables.

Let

$$b(\alpha) = \min_{\tau} d(\alpha, \tau);$$

that minimum value is assumed when τ is the distribution of some pure strategy, i.e., when $\tau^t = 1$ for a certain value t of $\mathbf{t}$, and $= 0$ for all others. The function b is continuous on A, since it is the minimum of a finite number of continuous functions, arising from letting τ vary over all distributions of pure strategies. Now when $\alpha \in NS$, Player 1's strategy is non-separating, and by the definition of $u(p)$, Player 2 has a strategy that yields a payoff $\le u(p)$; i.e.,

$$\alpha \in NS \implies b(\alpha) \le u(p). \tag{7.9}$$

On the other hand, if τ is the distribution of a $\mathbf{t}$ that is an ε-best reply to $\mathbf{s}$, then it may be verified that

$$d(\alpha, \tau) \le b(\alpha) + C\varepsilon. \tag{7.10}$$

Now let $\psi = \psi(\varepsilon)$ be the modulus of uniform continuity of b, and, for the given ε and τ, let the ξ of Lemma 3 be $\psi(\varepsilon)$. We then obtain an η from Lemma 3; set $\delta = \eta$. It then follows that there is an $\alpha_0 \in NS$ such that

$$\|\alpha - \alpha_0\| < \psi(\varepsilon),$$

and hence
$$|b'(\alpha) - b(\alpha_0)| < \varepsilon.$$

But by (7.9),
$$b(\alpha_0) \leq u(p);$$

hence, by (7.10), if $e(\alpha, \tau) < \eta$, then

$$d(\alpha, \tau) \leq b(\alpha) + C\varepsilon \leq b(\alpha_0) + \varepsilon + C\varepsilon \leq u(p) + (1 + C)\varepsilon;$$

this completes the proof of Lemma 4. ∎

We now return to the proof of (7.1). Let ϕ be an arbitrary mixed strategy of Player 1 in Γ_n, i.e., a random variable whose values are pure strategies. The strategy ϕ will remain fixed throughout.

Given the strategy ϕ, we will construct a behavior strategy for Player 2 that yields a payoff (to Player 1) that is $\leq u^*(p) + o(1)$. Since every behavior strategy is equivalent to a mixed strategy, this is sufficient, by the minimax theorem, to prove (7.1).

First we will construct, for each ε with $0 < \varepsilon \leq 1$, a behavior strategy ψ^ε for Player 2; afterwards we will make an appropriate choice of ε. The construction will be inductive, on the stage i. As we shall see, there is no particular difference between the beginning of the induction and the i'th stage; we will therefore proceed at once to the latter.

Suppose we have defined ψ^ε for the first $i-1$ stages. Let $t_1, \ldots,$ t_{i-1} indicate the choices of Player 2 for stages $1, \ldots, i-1$, and let $s_1, \ldots, s_{i-1}, s_i$ indicate the choices of Player 1 for stages $1, \ldots,$ $i - 1, i$, when Players 1 and 2 play in accordance with ϕ and ψ^ε, respectively; Player 1's choice is defined for one more stage than Player 2's, since his strategy is defined for the whole game, and enables him to respond at the i-th stage to Player 2's previous choices. Let $r_1, \ldots, r_i$ indicate the choices of nature for the first i stages. We have $t_j \in T$, $s_j \in S^k$, $r_j \in R^k$. Define

$$h_j = h^2(k, r_j, s_j, t_j)$$

for $j = 1, \ldots, i - 1$; h_j is the information Player 2 gleans from the j-th stage and it is, of course, a random variable.

Suppose, now, that $h_1, \ldots, h_{i-1}$ is a sequence of members of H^2, and consider an event of the form

$$\Lambda \equiv \Lambda_i \equiv \{\mathbf{h}_1 = h_1, \ldots, \mathbf{h}_{i-1} = h_{i-1}\}.$$

Such an event is called a *history*, or, more precisely, an *i-stage history*; it represents the information Player 2 has garnered up to (but not including) stage i. The set of all i-stage histories with positive probability is denoted $\mathcal{L}_i$.

The i-stage history that actually occurs is, of course, itself a random variable; it is denoted Λ_i.

In order to define the i-th stage of the behavior strategy ψ^ε, we must define, for each i-stage history $\Lambda \in \mathcal{L}_i$, a random variable $\mathbf{t}_i^\Lambda$ that indicates Player 2's choice of a member of T at the i-th stage. Define $\mathbf{t}_i^\Lambda$ as a conditional random variable, with domain Λ, that is an ε-best reply to $\mathbf{s}_i | \Lambda$ in the one-stage game defined by $\mathbf{k} | \Lambda$ and $\mathbf{r}_i | \Lambda$. For the first stage, of course, Λ is the trivial event (the whole probability space), and we have $\mathbf{s}_1 | \Lambda = \mathbf{s}_1$ and $\mathbf{k} | \Lambda = \mathbf{k}$.

Now define a random variable[18] $\mathbf{t}_i$ by specifying that $\mathbf{t}_i | \Lambda = \mathbf{t}_i^\Lambda$ for all i-stage histories Λ. Thus, $\mathbf{t}_i$ is the unconditional random variable defining Player 2's choice at stage i. This completes the inductive definition of ψ^ε.

For each Λ in $\mathcal{L}_i$, let $p(\Lambda)$, $\alpha_i(\Lambda)$ and $\tau_i(\Lambda)$ denote the distributions of $\mathbf{k} | \Lambda$, $(\mathbf{h}, \mathbf{r}_i, \mathbf{s}_i) | \Lambda$ and $\mathbf{t}_i | \Lambda$, respectively. Clearly, $p(\Lambda_i)$ is a random variable, which we denote $\mathbf{p}_i$. The vector $\mathbf{p}_i$ is Player 2's estimate, just before stage i, of the stage game being played; note that $\mathbf{p}_1 = p$.

Let $\Lambda \in \mathcal{L}_i$ be an i-stage history, and let $h \in H^2$ be such that Prob $\Lambda \cap \{\mathbf{h}_i = h\} > 0$. Then, by analogy with the definition of $p(h)$ in the one-stage case, we may write

$$p(\Lambda)(h) = p(\Lambda \cap \{\mathbf{h}_i = h\});$$

note that $p(\Lambda)(h)$ is the distribution of $(\mathbf{k} | \Lambda) | \{\mathbf{h}_i = h\}$, which equals $\mathbf{k} | (\Lambda \cap \{\mathbf{h}_i = h\})$. Now

$$\text{Exp}\left(\|p(\Lambda)(\mathbf{h}_i | \Lambda)\|^2 - \|p(\Lambda)\|^2\right) = e\left(\alpha_i(\Lambda), \tau_i(\Lambda)\right).$$

---

[18]Whose domain is the whole probability space Ω.

Hence, recalling that $p(\Lambda_i) = \mathbf{p}_i$, noting that

$$p(\Lambda_i)(\mathbf{h}_i) = \mathbf{p}_{i+1},$$

and setting

$$\mathbf{e}_i \equiv e\big(\alpha_i(\Lambda_i), \tau_i(\Lambda_i)\big),$$

we obtain

$$
\begin{aligned}
\mathrm{Exp}&\big(\|\mathbf{p}_{i+1}\|^2 - \|\mathbf{p}_i\|^2\big) \\
&= \sum_{\Lambda \in \mathcal{L}_i} \mathrm{Exp}\big(\|p(\Lambda)(\mathbf{h}_i|\Lambda)\|^2 - \|p(\Lambda)\|^2\big) \, \mathrm{Prob}\,\Lambda \\
&= \sum_{\Lambda \in \mathcal{L}_i} e\big(\alpha_i(\Lambda), \tau_i(\Lambda)\big) \, \mathrm{Prob}\,\Lambda \\
&= \mathrm{Exp}\, e\big(\alpha_i(\Lambda_i), \tau_i(\Lambda_i)\big) \\
&= \mathrm{Exp}(\mathbf{e}_i).
\end{aligned}
$$

Hence,

$$
\begin{aligned}
\kappa > \mathrm{Exp}(\|\mathbf{p}_{n+1}\|^2) - \|p\|^2 &= \sum_{i=1}^{n} \mathrm{Exp}(\|\mathbf{p}_{i+1}\|^2 - \|\mathbf{p}_i\|^2) \\
&= \sum_{i=1}^{n} \mathrm{Exp}\,\mathbf{e}_i.
\end{aligned}
\tag{7.11}
$$

For given $\varepsilon > 0$, choose $\delta > 0$ in accordance with Lemma 4. Then it follows from (7.11) that

$$\mathrm{Exp}\,\mathbf{e}_i \leq \varepsilon\delta \tag{7.12}$$

for at least $n - \dfrac{\kappa}{\varepsilon\delta}$ of the numbers $i = 1, \ldots n$. Now if (7.12) holds, then

$$\mathrm{Prob}\,(\mathbf{e}_i \geq \delta) \leq \varepsilon. \tag{7.13}$$

Moreover, since the value of $\mathbf{e}_i$ depends on the value of Λ_i only, it follows that for each $\Lambda \in \mathcal{L}_i$, either $\Lambda \implies \mathbf{e}_i < \delta$ or $\Lambda \implies \mathbf{e}_i \geq \delta$.

In the first case, it follows from Lemma 4 and the definition of $t_i|\Lambda$ that

$$\mathrm{Exp}\big(g(\mathbf{k}, \mathbf{r}_i, \mathbf{s}_i, \mathbf{t}_i)|\Lambda\big) = \mathrm{Exp}\, g(\mathbf{k}|\Lambda, \mathbf{r}_i|\Lambda, \mathbf{s}_i|\Lambda, \mathbf{t}_i|\Lambda)$$
$$\leq u\big(p(\Lambda)\big) + (1+C)\varepsilon < u^*\big(p(\Lambda)\big) + (1+C)\varepsilon.$$

In the second case we clearly have

$$\mathrm{Exp}\big(g(\mathbf{k}, \mathbf{r}_i, \mathbf{s}_i, \mathbf{t}_i)|\Lambda\big) \leq C \leq u^*\big(p(\Lambda)\big) + (1+C)\varepsilon + C.$$

Hence, by (7.13) and the concavity of u^*, we have

$$\mathrm{Exp}\, g(\mathbf{k}, \mathbf{r}_i, \mathbf{s}_i, \mathbf{t}_i) = \sum_{\Lambda \in \mathcal{L}_i} \mathrm{Exp}\big(g(\mathbf{k}, \mathbf{r}_i, \mathbf{s}_i, \mathbf{t}_i)|\Lambda\big)\, \mathrm{Prob}\,\Lambda$$
$$\leq \sum_{\Lambda \in \mathcal{L}_i} u^*\big(p(\Lambda)\big)\, \mathrm{Prob}\,\Lambda + (1+C)\varepsilon + C\varepsilon$$
$$\leq u^*\bigg(\sum_{\Lambda \in \mathcal{L}_i} p(\Lambda)\, \mathrm{Prob}\,\Lambda\bigg) + (1+2C)\varepsilon$$
$$= u^*\big(\mathrm{Exp}\, p(\Lambda_i)\big) + (1+2C)\varepsilon$$
$$= u^*(p) + (1+2C)\varepsilon.$$

Since the above derivation depends on (7.12), which fails to hold for at most $\dfrac{\kappa}{\varepsilon\delta}$ of the i's, we deduce that

$$\mathrm{Exp}\left(\frac{1}{n}\sum_{i=1}^{n} g(\mathbf{k}, \mathbf{r}_i, \mathbf{s}_i, \mathbf{t}_i)\right) \leq u^*(p) + (1+2C)\varepsilon + \frac{\kappa}{n\varepsilon\delta}C.$$

Since the left side of this formula is precisely the payoff to Γ_n, we have shown that for every strategy of Player 1 in Γ_n there is a strategy of Player 2 that yields a payoff (to Player 1) that is $\leq$ the right side of the above formula; hence

$$v_n(p) \leq u^*(p) + (1+2C)\varepsilon + \frac{\kappa}{n\varepsilon\delta}C.$$

Letting $n \to \infty$, we deduce

$$\limsup_{n \to \infty} v_n(p) \leq u^*(p) + (1+2C)\varepsilon;$$

but since ε is arbitrary, it follows that

$$\limsup_{n\to\infty} v_n(p) \leq u^*(p).$$

This proves (7.1).

Next, we will show that for all n,

$$v_n(p) \geq u^*(p). \tag{7.14}$$

First, we show that

$$v_n(p) \geq u(p), \tag{7.15}$$

whenever $u(p)$ is defined, i.e., whenever Player 1 has at least one non-separating strategy. To this end, we describe a specific strategy for Player 1 that yields him a payoff $\geq u(p)$ in Γ_n. This strategy consists of playing each stage as if it was a one-stage game, and in this one-stage game playing what we may call an "optimal non-separating" strategy; i.e., a strategy that is optimal in $\Delta_1(p)$. It then follows from (7.4) and Lemma 2 that

$$p = \mathbf{p}_1 = \mathbf{p}_2 = \cdots = \mathbf{p}_n.$$

Hence, since Player 1's strategy is optimal in $\Delta_1(p)$, it follows that the payoff at each stage is $\geq u(p)$ no matter what Player 2 does. Hence the n-stage average payoff is also $\geq u(p)$, and (7.15) is established.

To deduce (7.14) from (7.15), it is sufficient to show that $v_n(p)$ is concave, i.e., that for all n,

$$v_n(\beta p + (1 - \beta)q) \geq \beta v_n(p) + (1 - \beta)v_n(q), \tag{7.16}$$

whenever $p, q \in P$ and $0 \leq \beta \leq 1$. To prove (7.16), we consider two auxiliary games Γ' and Γ'', defined as follows: both games start with nature making a choice between two alternatives, say "right" or "left"; the choice is made with a probability β for "right" and $1 - \beta$ for "left". If the choice was "right", then nature chooses a member k of K in accordance with the probabilities p; if it was left—in accordance with the probability q. So far the description of the games Γ' and Γ'' was identical; they are to be distinguished in this way: in Γ', Player 2 is informed of neither of the choices of nature; in Γ'', he is informed of the choice of "left" or "right", but not of the subsequent choice of a k in K. (Player 1 is in both cases informed of both choices.) The players then continue to play for n stages as in the definition of Γ_n. Then the value of Γ' is $\geq$ the value of Γ'', since in Γ' Player 2 has less information, and hence fewer pure strategies. But the value of Γ' is precisely the left side of (7.16), and the value of Γ'' is the right side; this completes the proof of (7.16), and hence by (7.15), that of (7.14). Combining (7.14) with (7.1), we deduce

$$\lim_{n \to \infty} v_n(p) = u^*(p). \tag{7.17}$$

This completes the proof of Theorem C. ∎

PROOF OF PROPOSITION A: In order to prove Proposition A, it only remains for us to show that

$$v(\Gamma_\infty) = u^*(p). \tag{7.18}$$

To this end, using the notation of Section 5 above, note first that there is a strategy σ_0 for Player 1 in Γ_∞ such that for all strategies τ for Player 2 and whenever $u(p)$ is defined, we have, for all n,

$$\gamma_n(\sigma_0, \tau) \geq u(p); \tag{7.19}$$

this strategy is obtained, as in the proof of (7.15), by letting Player 1 play in every stage a strategy that would have been optimal in $\Delta_1(p)$. Then

$$\sup_\sigma \inf_\tau \inf_{n=1}^{\infty} \gamma_n(\sigma, \tau) \geq u(p); \tag{7.20}$$

and then by an argument similar to that used above in proving (7.16) and deducing (7.14), it follows that we may replace $u(p)$ by $u^*(p)$ on the right side of (7.20). Hence there is a strategy σ_0 such that for all τ and n,

$$\gamma_n(\sigma_0, \tau) \geq u^*(p). \tag{7.21}$$

To complete the proof of (7.18), we must find a strategy τ_0 of Player 2 that will satisfy the right side of formula (5.2) when we substitute $u^*(p)$ for $v(\Gamma_\infty)$. We already know that Player 2 can hold Player 1 down to $u^*(p) + o(1)$ in Γ_n. The strategy τ_0 for Player 2 will be as follows: first he plays optimally in Γ_1. Then, for the next two steps, he ignores the information received in Γ_1, and plays optimally in Γ_2. This brings him to the fourth stage. He now ignores all information previously received, and plays optimally in Γ_3 for stages 4, 5, and 6. If he continues in this way, it is not difficult to verify, using (7.1), that (5.2) is indeed satisfied. This completes the proof of Proposition A. ∎

POSTSCRIPTS TO CHAPTER FOUR

a. Monotonicity of v_n and the Informed Player's Information Matrices

In Postscript e to Chapter One we showed that v_n is monotonically non-increasing in n when the information is standard (i.e., when each side knows which pure choices were made by the other side at all previous stages). This could be intuitively understood as follows: The information that P1 gets after each stage about P2's actions is of no importance, since P1 already knows which game is actually being played, and so has nothing substantive to learn from P2. On the other hand, P2 does not know which game is being played, and so has much to learn from P1's actions at previous stages. Indeed, a major theme of this book is that an informed player often reveals information by his actions; an uninformed one, of course, cannot. Thus each additional opportunity to exchange information would appear to be in P2's favor. There is an exchange of information at the end of each stage, and since there are more stages in Γ_{n+1} than in Γ_n, one may expect that P2 gains at least as much information in Γ_{n+1} as in Γ_n; this should lead to a payoff that is at least as good for him (i.e., no higher).

There is nothing about this reasoning that is specific to standard information; it appears to apply equally well to the more general context of this chapter. One may therefore conjecture that monotonicity continues to hold when the information is non-standard. *This, however, is not correct*: Lehrer [1987] has exhibited a game with non-standard information matrices in which $v_1 > v_2 < v_3 > v_4$.

The reader is referred to Lehrer's original paper for details of his ingenious example. Here we wish to discuss its conceptual implications only; specifically, we will try to find where the intuitive reasoning outlined above went awry.

Our reasoning was based on the contention that "the information that P1 gets after each stage about P2's actions is of no importance, since P1 already knows which game is actually being played, and so has nothing substantive to learn from P2." In much the same words, this contention also appears in the discussion in Section 4 where we explain why, in presenting our examples, we do not exhibit or even specify the information matrices of P1. Taken at face value, it would seem to imply that v_n does not depend on P1's information matrices; that two games of the class considered in this chapter that are identical in all respects except for P1's information matrices must have the same value. This, however, is not correct; Lehrer's example itself provides a counterexample. In his example as it stands, $v_2 = 3$, whereas $v_2 = 4$ if P1 is given standard information. An earlier example of the same phenomenon was given by Kohlberg [1975, p.23]. The dependence of v_n on P1's information lies at the heart of Lehrer's example, and we must understand it before going to the issue of non-monotonicity.

Formally, there is no problem. The set of P1's pure strategies in Γ_n depends on his information. If he does not know whether P2 went right or left at the previous stage, he cannot use this information in his strategy; his strategy must then prescribe the same actions whether P2 went right or left. With a smaller set of pure strategies, it is of course logically possible for the value to be different.

But the question we are raising is not a logical one. Rather, we are trying to *understand* what is going on. Granted, P1 cannot base his actions on distinctions that he cannot observe. But why should he *want* to? What does he *care* whether P2 went right or left? He already knows everything exogenous that there is to know, so what can he learn from P2's actions at previous stages? In a repeated game of complete information—when both sides know the game being played—the sets of pure strategies in the multi-stage game also formally depend on the information matrices. Yet in that case it is clear that the information matrices are utterly irrelevant; it is enough for each player simply to play minimax separately at each stage,[19] he can just ignore what the other player did at previous stages. This makes good sense, because both players are informed, so neither has anything substantive to learn from the other. Why shouldn't the same phenomenon hold for the informed player in a game of incomplete information?

And indeed, the phenomenon does hold for Γ_∞, as asserted in the discussion in Section 4 that we cited above; v_∞ is indeed independent of P1's information matrices, in the precise sense indicated there. But why doesn't the same intuitive reasoning apply to v_n?

To understand this, let us backtrack and reexamine the case of standard information. The fact is that even there, P1 cannot totally ignore P2. It is very important for P1 to know the parameter p that tells him what P2 is thinking about the game actually being played, and indeed P1 plays differently for different values of p. The effect of the incomplete information is not only that P2 can learn from P1's actions, but also that P1 can exploit P2's ignorance. To do this effectively, he must know as much as possible about the extent of P2's ignorance; the more he knows about it, the better he will be able to exploit it.

Here is where P1's information about P2's moves enters the picture. We know that P2's information about the true game— his posterior assessment of p—depends on P1's moves at previous stages.[20] When P2's information matrices are not standard, it is possible that he will not know what P1's moves at previous stages

---

[19] For the expected payoff this is immediate, both in the n-stage game and in the infinite-stage game (in any of the senses indicated in Section 5). In an infinite-stage game of this kind (repeated two-person zero-sum game of complete information), it may further be shown that each player can guarantee that with probability 1, the lim inf of his average payoff is at least the value (for him) of the one-stage game; but this is a more delicate matter (one can, for example, use Blackwell's [1956] theory).

[20] At the risk of infuriating the reader, we remind him once more of the "as if" nature of this reasoning. See, for example, the second footnote in Postscript c to Chapter One.

were. In that case, P2's assessment of p will depend on whatever information he does have about P1's moves—i.e., on the signals he received from his information matrix. But then when P1's information matrices are not standard, it is possible that P1 will not know what P2's signals were. Therefore it is possible that P1 will not know P2's current assessment of p. Thus P1's assessment of P2's assessment of the true game being played—which is crucial for the value of the game—depends not only on P2's information matrices, but also on P1's.

In brief, P1's informational advantage over P2 in the case of standard information lies not only in his knowledge of the true game being played, but also in his knowledge of what P2 thinks about it. The latter is lost when the information is non-standard, and that explains the dependence of v_n on P1's information matrices.

It also explains the non-monotonicity. The situation is essentially one of two-sided incomplete information. P2 does not know what game is being played, and P1 does not know what P2 thinks about what game is being played. Both parameters have an important bearing on the value of the game. The situation is conceptually similar to that of "incomplete information on one-and-a-half sides," which we discussed in Postscript j to Chapter Two; and as we saw there, those games behave much like games with incomplete information on both sides, where one certainly cannot expect monotonicity.

In Lehrer's specific example, one of three possible games is being played. At the end of the first stage, P2 receives information (from his information matrix) that enables him to rule out one of the three games. With this information, he can lower the payoff considerably in the second stage. P1, however, does not know what information P2 has received, and so does not know which of the three games P2 has ruled out (of course P1 knows the true game, and knows that P2 cannot have ruled it out; but that still leaves two possibilities). If P1 knew which game P2 has ruled out, he could anticipate P2's second stage strategy, and use his private knowledge of the identity of the true game effectually to counteract this strategy; but he does not, and so cannot, and so v_2 is rather low, and in particular $< v_1$. Now in order to achieve the second-stage lowering of the payoff, P2 must in effect reveal which game he has ruled out; in the third stage, therefore, P1 can indeed counteract P2's strategy, and so the payoff goes back up. If at the second stage of Γ_3, P2 were to try to ignore his information—in order to avoid revealing it[21]— then he would lose so much at that stage that the average payoff for all 3 stages would again be $> v_2$.

Some of the subtlety of the example may be apparent from the above description. But not all. The reader is invited to try to reconstruct it; he will find it no easy task, even after reading the above.

Lehrer raises the possibility that v_n is always non-increasing from some point on; but this remains unresolved.

The perspicacious reader will have realized that the discussion six paragraphs back ("Here is where...") is valid only if neither P1 nor P2 have standard information. So perhaps when the information of either P1 *or* P2 is standard, monotonicity holds after all. This is indeed correct. The point is that in either case, what P2 *observes* is common knowledge (though P1 may not know what P2 *does*). It is these observations that determine P2's posteriors, and their being common knowledge is precisely what gives the game its recursive structure (see Theorem N4 in Postscript e to Chapter One). Since the proof of monotonicity is based on the recursive structure, our assertions follow.

Using the recursive structure, one can indeed show that when P2's information is standard, v_n is independent of P1's information matrices. Intuitively, the reason is that P1 then knows that P2 knows what he (P1) has done, and for the reasons indicated above (see especially the seventh paragraph of this note), P1 really does not particularly care what P2 does.

The corresponding statement in the reverse situation is of course incorrect: When P1's information is standard, then v_n, and even v_∞, do depend strongly on P2's information.

We stress again that though P1's information matrices may affect v_n, they cannot affect v_∞ (see the body of the chapter). Indeed, even when P1 has standard information, P2 can hold him down to $u^*(p)$ in $\Gamma_\infty(p)$; and when P1's information is not standard, he can still achieve $u^*(p)$. When there are only finitely

---

[21]Observe how the shoe has leaped to the other foot! Now it is P2—the "uninformed" player—who is considering ignoring his information so as not to reveal it.

many stages, P1 can usually achieve more than $u^*(p)$, and then *how* much more may depend on his assessment of P2's posteriors. But to achieve $u^*(p)$, he need not concern himself with P2's posteriors.

In Lehrer's example, each of P1's types has a different information matrix, and P2 has yet another. Recently, Yareev [1994] constructed an example with non-monotonic values in which all types of P1 have the same information matrix. Moreover, the information matrices of both P1 and P2 can be derived from a single matrix just by adding, for each player, the information on the move he himself made.

b. Remembering One's Own Moves

In Section 7 we quoted the result of Dalkey [1953], according to which the strategic form of a game—and *a fortiori* the value—remain essentially unchanged if we assume that each player remembers his own moves. Intuitively, the reason is that each pure strategy prescribes what the player does at each information set. Therefore if the player knows which pure strategy he is using, he knows the choices that that strategy prescribes for all previous information sets, and therefore what he did at those information sets; and this is so even if the extensive form of the game does not allow him explicitly to remember this information. A mixed strategy, of course, is a probability combination of pure strategies; when a player uses a mixed strategy, he eventually picks some pure strategy, and then the same reasoning applies as before.

The reasoning does not, however, work for behavior strategies; the theorem of Kuhn [1953] (about optimal behavior strategies in games of perfect recall) does not apply to games in which the extensive form does not allow a player to remember what he previously did. Thus, though the value of the game is the same as if he did remember, this value may not be achievable in behavior strategies.

c. Optimal Strategies for the Uninformed Player

The strategy described for P2 in Postscript d to Chapter One was based on P2 keeping track of the payoffs for each type of P1. In the case treated in this chapter, P2 need not know which pure strategy was chosen by P1 at the previous stage, and therefore he may not be able to calculate these payoffs. This appears to block the way to extending the previous method to the current case.

In [1975], E. Kohlberg did succeed in obtaining such an extension. For details of his method, as well as an intuitive overview, the reader is referred to the original paper.

d. The Case When P2 Knows His Payoff

This is an instance of what Rosenfeld [1964] calls an "adaptive competitive decision process;" see the discussion of Example 2 in Section 4. Baños [1968], and subsequently Megiddo [1980] showed that in this case, P2 can guarantee to himself (in the long run) the value of the stage game actually being played, in spite of the fact that he does not know what it is. Neither Baños's proof, nor the simpler proof of Megiddo, use the results of this book.

J. F. Mertens [1987] has pointed out that the Baños-Megiddo theorem follows from the results of this chapter. Indeed, saying that P2 can guarantee to himself (in the long run) the value of the stage game actually being played, is equivalent to saying that $v_\infty(p) = u^*(p)$ is a linear function of p. Thus to prove the Baños-Megiddo result (restricted, for simplicity, to $\kappa = 2$), it is sufficient to show that $u^*(p) = pu(1) + (1 - p)u(0)$. To do so, note that for any $0 < p < 1$, any non-revealing strategy of P1 must yield, against any strategy of P2, the same payoff in G_1 as in G_2 (since P2 is informed of his payoff). Hence the payoff for each non-revealing strategy is independent of p, and therefore also the value $u(p)$ of the game in which P1 restricts himself to non-revealing strategies is a constant that is independent of p. This constant must be $\leq$ each of the values of G_1 and G_2 (since in playing G_1 and G_2, P1 is not restricted to non-revealing strategies). Now the values of G_1 and G_2 are $u(0)$ and $u(1)$, so it follows (see Figure 2)

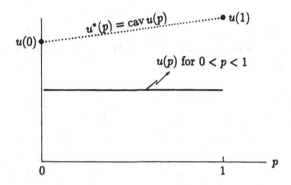

Figure 2. The case when P2 knows his payoff

that the graph of u^* is simply the straight line connecting $(0, u(0))$ to $(1, u(1))$, as asserted.

Note that any optimal strategy for P2 necessarily yields him the value of G_1 if that is the game being played, and the value of G_2 if that is the game being played.[22] Thus such a strategy is independent of the value of the parameter p; P2 does not make any actual use of this parameter. This is what the term "non-Bayesian" in the title of Megiddo's paper means; it is not important what P2's prior probability assessment is, or indeed even that he has such an assessment. (Compare the remark just before the proof of Theorem N3 in Postscript d to Chapter One.)

e. The Error Term

Postscript c to Chapter One was devoted to the error term in the asymptotic formula for v_n when the information is standard. Here we summarize what is known about the error term in the general information case discussed in this chapter.

---

[22] If, say, it would not guarantee $v(G_1) = u(0)$ when G_1 is the true game, then P1 could play in G_1 to get a higher payoff, and in G_2 to get the value $v(G_2) = u(1)$; the result would be larger than $pu(1) + (1 - p)u(0) = v_\infty(p)$, contrary to the assumption that the strategy in question is optimal for P2 in Γ_∞.

In the body of Chapter One, we showed that in the standard information case, the error term is $O(n^{-1/2})$. Already this basic result is incorrect in the general information case. Indeed, consider the game [Zamir, 1973] with the following payoff and information[23] matrices:

8	3	-1
8	-3	1

8	2	-2
8	-2	2

a	c	d
b	c	d

a	c	d
b	c	d

Game 1

For this game, the error term is of the order of magnitude $n^{-1/3}$ exactly. To understand this, note the similarity of this game to Game 3 in Postscript c to Chapter One. It will be recalled that the error term in that game had the largest possible order of magnitude—namely $n^{-1/2}$—for games with standard information. Game 1 is derived from that game by giving P2 no information at all if he makes use of his center or right columns, which are the only ones present in the original game. The only way that P2 can get any information is by playing his left column, and this costs him dearly—each time he does so he must pay 8, which is considerably more than the maximum he would have to pay in either of the other columns. Thus the example is obtained by taking a standard information game that from the point of view of the

---

[23]P2's information matrices are as displayed. For P1, one can either specify the same information matrices, or, what comes to the same thing, full information about P2's actions.

error term is worst possible for P2, and making it still worse by making information very expensive for him.

In the positive direction, Zamir [1973] showed that if P1 and P2 have the same information matrices and $\kappa = 2$ (two stage games), then $v_n(p) = u^*(p) + O(n^{-1/6})$; and that if, in addition, there are no non-separating strategies (for $0 < p < 1$), then the error term is $O(n^{-1/4})$. Mertens [1972] showed that if each player's information matrices are independent of the true stage game (though P1's may be different from P2's), then the error term is $O(n^{-1/4})$; this result applies also to the case of two-sided incomplete information discussed in Postscript f below. In [1987, p.22], Mertens reported that this can be improved to $O(n^{-1/3})$, which is best possible (because of Game 1).

f. Incomplete Information on Both Sides

The result that v_∞ exists if and only if cav vex = vex cav (Chapter Three, and Section 4 of Chapter Two), and that about the existence of lim v_n (Postscript a to Chapter Two) have both been extended from the standard information case treated in Chapter Two to the non-standard information case treated in this chapter. The definition of non-separating strategy generalizes naturally to the case of two-sided incomplete information; using this generalization, the statement of the results is the same as before: v_∞ exists if and only if cav vex = vex cav (Mertens and Zamir [1980]), and lim v_n always exists (Mertens [1972]). In both cases, it is assumed that each player has only one information matrix, which is independent of the stage game chosen by chance; in this sense the extensions are more restricted than the results of this chapter. Like here, P1's information matrix may be different from P2's.

As with standard information, these results may be stated directly for the dependent case—without first reducing it to the independent case (see Postscript i to Chapter Two)—using the appropriate generalization of the "cav vex = vex cav" condition.

When the information matrices of the players may depend on the stage game (i.e., on k), there are no general results. Some specific classes of games of this type are treated in the ensuing notes.

g. Both Players Have Incomplete Information and Know Their Own Payoffs

This is the most general case of Rosenfeld's "adaptive competitive decision process"; see Postscript d above. The results and methods of Baños, Megiddo, and Mertens adduced there imply that each player can in the long run guarantee to himself the value of the stage game actually being played, though he may not know what it is. It follows that both v_∞ and $\lim v_n$ exist, and equal the expected value of the true stage game.

h. Identical Information

By this we mean that the players initially have the same information about the identity k of the stage game, and after each stage, they have the same information. This may be described as follows: First chance chooses a stage game G_k, where k is distributed according to a commonly known probability distribution; neither player gets any private information about chance's choice. The chosen game G_k is then repeated. The information matrices H_k, which are identical for the two players, tell each player which pair of actions was chosen at the previous play, and may also give the players additional information about which k was chosen; that is, the H_k may be different for different k, and each one assigns different letters to different action pairs.

This situation was treated by Kohlberg and Zamir [1974], who showed that v_∞ and $\lim v_n$ exist and are equal, and characterized their common value. To understand their method, consider first the case of two stage games, G_1 and G_2, with initial probabilities p and $1-p$. The information matrices always assign different letters to different action pairs; and for some action pairs—let us call them "informative"—they also assign different letters to $k = 1$ and 2. If an informative pair is played at any stage, then the identity k of the true stage game becomes and remains commonly known; so from that stage on, both players can guarantee the value, val G_k, of the true stage game. On the other hand, until the first time an informative action pair is played, the players assign the same probabilities p and $1 - p$ to $k = 1$ and 2 that they did initially.

Define $v^* := \mathrm{Exp\,val}\,G_k = p\,\mathrm{val}\,G_1 + (1 - p)\,\mathrm{val}\,G_2$, and $G^* :=$ $\mathrm{Exp}\,G_k = pG_1 + (1 - p)G_2$. Consider now a sequential game Γ^* played as follows: play G^* repeatedly until the first stage at which an informative action pair is played, if ever; after that, give the same payoff v^* at each stage. The reader may convince himself that Γ^* is equivalent to the original game Γ. This reduces the original problem to that of analyzing games of the form Γ^*.

Partial results on such games were first obtained by Zamir in his thesis [1970]. In [1974], Kohlberg showed that v_∞ and $\lim v_n$ exist and are equal for all games of the form Γ^*, and this implies the above result (when there are two stage games). At about this time, it was realized that the games Γ^* are particular instances of "stochastic games" in the sense of Shapley [1953]. Shapley had demonstrated the existence of a value for all stochastic games in the discounted case (i.e., for each fixed finite discount); but whether v_∞ and $\lim v_n$ exist remained an open question. Motivated by the above application to repeated games, Bewley and Kohlberg [1976a] managed to prove that $\lim v_n$ exists for all stochastic games, as does the limit of the (appropriately normalized) values of the discounted games as the discount rate δ tends to 0; their methods were quite novel, in that they involved complex function theory (Puiseux series) and mathematical logic (Tarski's principle for real closed fields). In a companion paper [1976b], they applied these methods to obtain asymptotic expressions for the value v_n of an n-stage stochastic game as $n \to \infty$, as well as for the value of the discounted game as $\delta \to 0$. But though they tried hard, and obtained important partial results [1978], they were unable to prove that v_∞ exists for all stochastic games. This difficult problem was finally solved (positively) by Mertens and Neyman [1981].

The case of κ stage games, $\kappa > 2$, reduces to that of $\kappa = 2$. Consider, for example, three stage games G_1, G_2 and G_3, with probabilities p_1, p_2, and p_3, and information matrices

	L	R
L	a	b
R	c	d

H_1

	L	R
L	a	e
R	g	d

H_2

	L	R
L	a	f
R	c	h

H_3

As long as both players play L, they get no information about k. But as soon as they play any other action pair, they do get information about k; as above, we call such action pairs "informative". Suppose that (R, R) is the first informative action pair played at any stage. If the true value of k is 3, then both players will henceforth know this, so we may take the payoff from then on as val G_3. If $k = 1$ or 2, then both will know *this*, but they will not know which one of these alternatives holds (i.e., whether $k = 1$ or $k = 2$). From that stage on, therefore, the players are faced with a stochastic game Γ^* of the type analyzed above, with $\kappa = 2$. We already know how to solve this type of game, so we may assume that from then on, the players receive the value of this game, which we denote v^{12}. A similar analysis applies if the first informative action pair played is (L, R) or (R, L).

Thus we are led to the following stochastic game, which can be solved by the methods we cited: Play Exp G_k as long as no informative action pair is played. If an informative pair is ever played, and (R, R) is the first such pair, pay $(p_1 + p_2)v^{12} + p_3$ val G_3 at all subsequent stages; if (R, L) is first, pay $(p_1 + p_3)v^{13} + p_2$ val G_2 at all subsequent stages, where v^{13} is defined analogously to v^{12}; if (L, R) is first, pay p_1 val $G_1 + p_2$ val $G_2 + p_3$ val G_3 at all subsequent stages.

A similar inductive procedure solves all such games, for any k.

i. Games Without a Recursive Structure

Consider the repeated game with payoff and information matrices

−1	2
2	−4

−4	2
2	−1

a	b
b	b

b	b
b	a

Game 2

it being assumed that nature initially chooses one of the two stage games, with probability 1/2 each, and informs *neither* player of its choice; and that the information matrices are the same for both players, the information they contain coming *in addition* to what each player knows about his own choice of action.

In all the repeated games treated in the main text, the players' "incomplete information"—their initial uncertainty about the identity k of the true stage game (taken to include their uncertainty about each others' uncertainty about k)—can be described by a single commonly known prior probability distribution p on K (i.e., on the stage games), and a commonly known pair $(\mathcal{P}^1, \mathcal{P}^2)$ of partitions of K, where $\mathcal{P}^i$ specifies[24] i's private information about k. In most[25] of the repeated games treated above, if P1 and P2 play commonly known mixed strategies, their uncertainty about k continues to be describable in this way[26] after each stage,

---

[24] Explicitly, if k's true value lies in the element P of $\mathcal{P}^i$, then i knows that k's true value lies in P, and knows no more about k (other than the prior p).

[25] Indeed, all except the games of Lehrer and Yareev discussed in Postscript a above.

[26] By a probability distribution on K and partitions of K.

though the probability distribution p and the partitions $\mathcal{P}^i$ may change from stage to stage (the $\mathcal{P}^i$ can only get finer). This accounts for the recursive formula in Theorem N4 in Postscript e to Chapter One, and implicitly, it underlies much of the foregoing analysis.

In Game 2, this is no longer true. The initial uncertainty of the players can be described by $K = \{L, R\}$, the prior probability distribution p that assigns probability $1/2$ to each element of K, and the "totally non-informative" partitions $\mathcal{P}^1 = \mathcal{P}^2 = \{K\}$. But already after the first stage, it is impossible to describe the players' uncertainty about k in this way. Suppose, for example, that it is commonly known that both players play each of their stage strategies with probability $1/2$ at the first stage. Suppose, moreover, that in actuality, P1 played "top" at the first stage, and that P2 played "right". Both players will get the signal b. The reader can check that P1's posterior for $k = L$ is $1/3$, but that P2 assigns probabilities half-half to P1's posterior for $k = L$ being $1/3$ or $2/3$. This kind of situation is not representable by a probability distribution on and partitions of $K = \{L, R\}$; a larger "state space" is needed. To describe a state in this larger space, it is necessary to specify not only the initial choice of k, but also the actions of the players; and the more stages have been played, the more states are necessary to give a full description of the current uncertainty of the players about k.

In spite of the difficulties associated with such games, Mertens and Zamir [1976a] succeeded in showing that $\underline{v}_\infty = \underset{\approx}{v}_\infty = \underset{\sim}{v}_\infty$ and $\overline{v}_\infty = \overset{\approx}{v}_\infty = \tilde{v}_\infty$ (see Postscript h to Chapter Two) for all games whose information structure[27] is identical to that of Game 2; and they exhibited relatively simple explicit strategies[28] that in the limit guarantee $\underline{v}_\infty$ for P1 and $\overline{v}_\infty$ for P2. Moreover for the particular payoff matrices of Game 2, they showed that $\overline{v}_\infty > \underline{v}_\infty$, just as in Example 4.10 of Chapter Two. Waternaux [1983] generalized their results to other 2×2 information matrices, and later

---

[27] The *information structure* consists of the information matrices, the initial probabilities on K, and the information partitions of K.

[28] Each strategy of P1 is a mixture of three components: in the first, he always plays Top; in the second, always Bottom; the third is an i.i.d. sequence of mixtures of Top and Bottom.

[1983p] to a much larger class[29] of games, with arbitrary κ and matrix size. Using some of the ideas introduced by Waternaux, and the framework of a continuous time model (Postscript g to Chapter Two), Sorin [1989] broke new ground by demonstrating the existence of lim v_n in all[30] games of this class.

---

[29] Consisting of games in which the signal given by the information matrix either fully reveals k to both players, or gives no information at all to either player. (Game 2 is an instance of this.)

[30] This had not previously been known even for Game 2.

CHAPTER FIVE

REPEATED GAMES OF INCOMPLETE INFORMATION: AN APPROACH TO THE NON-ZERO-SUM CASE

1. Introduction

Game theory is meant to construct and analyze models that resemble real life situations in which conflicts of interests among people are involved. As such, classical game theory suffers from two serious drawbacks:

(i) It assumes that the players possess a full evaluation of the strategy spaces, the actual outcomes and their utility payoffs to all the participants, and that they know precisely what information is available to the other participants.

(ii) A real-life conflict situation is seldom a one-shot affair. Usually one conflict leads to another, whose nature may depend on the way past conflicts were resolved.

Recently, J. C. Harsanyi [1967-8] developed a theory of *games with incomplete information*, which analyzes situations in which the participants do not possess a full assessment of the nature of the game. This theory resolves, at least theoretically, many of the difficulties raised in (i) above.

Unfortunately, very little appears in the literature concerning the difficulties raised in (ii), especially if, in addition to participating in a sequence of conflicts, the participants also do not possess a full assessment of the nature of the conflicts. How should a person who has, say, extra knowledge take advantage of such knowledge? How should an ignorant player guess information known to an opponent by observing his opponent's actions in past conflicts? Should a player with extra knowledge make use of it for short-run profits, risking revealing such information, or should he conceal or partially conceal such information in order to gain profits in the future? These are some of the questions that arise and, at present, game-theoretic tools seem incapable of answering them.

In order to come to grips with these problems we construct in this chapter, and in the previous chapters, the simplest models in which the above problems still arise. We made many simplifying assumptions in order to be able to analyze and solve these games, hoping that the nature of the solutions would yield insight into more complex situations which at present do not permit a precise mathematical treatment.

Specifically, the simplifying assumptions made in the present chapter are:

(1) that only two players are involved in the game;
(2) that incomplete information is on the part of one player only;
(3) that the sequence of games being played consists of repetitions of the same game.

With these assumptions we arrive at the 2-person infinitely repeated game with incomplete information on the part of one player. The problems mentioned above are still present in this game, namely: how should the player with the lack of information try to guess the information by observing past moves of his opponent? What information should be concealed by the player who has the information and how should the information be used to the advantage of the player who possesses it, recognizing that information may be revealed when it is used?

A further simplifying assumption can be made; namely, to limit oneself to constant-sum games, i.e., games in which the interests of the players are strictly opposed.

The constant-sum case was studied in chapters 1, 2, and 4 where, in general, we were able to describe optimal strategies for the players and compute the value of the repeated game, all in terms of entities connected with one-shot games. Apart from a few problems of minor importance one can say that this case is completely solved. In Chapters Two and Three, the constant-sum case was treated also for the case in which both players have incomplete information. It was shown there that a value for the game need not always exist, and a criterion was given to distinguish between games which have a value and games which do not.

It turns out that although many ideas that were helpful in the constant-sum case can be used in the present chapter, the results for the non-constant-sum case, treated here, look quite different. Many new phenomena present themselves, which pose completely new (and more difficult) problems.

Allowing for non-constant-sum games, but requiring that complete information be provided to both players, we find cases treated in Aumann [1959], [1960], [1961], [1967]. Roughly speaking, it was shown there that the fact that the game is repeated both *enables* and *encourages* the players to cooperate. The relevant results of those papers are summarized in Section 3 of this chapter.

Quite surprisingly, the presence of incomplete information may hinder cooperation even if cooperation is actually desired by both players. The reason is that although the player who has the information may find it beneficial to release it and his opponent also profits from such information, the opponent cannot believe the informed player, knowing that if the situation were different—which he considers a realistic possibility—the informed player would have told him the same story, since he would have benefitted from cheating. This interesting phenomenon, which did not occur in any of the cases treated previously, is studied in Section 5 of this chapter. It is a phenomenon that can occur only in non-zero-sum games, and that has received little past attention from game theorists.

Any formal discussion of how people do behave, or how they should rationally behave, is necessarily based on a formal *solution concept*, which can often be regarded as a definition of "rational behavior" in the circumstances being studied. We study in this chapter the set of outcomes that constitute *equilibrium payoffs*. An equilibrium payoff can be viewed as the outcome of an agreement between the players, when the agreement is such that no player would benefit by unilaterally deviating from it. Section 2 is devoted to a short survey of their nature and their merits.

Our goal was to determine the whole set of equilibrium payoffs of our repeated games, but, unfortunately, we have not succeeded in determining all of them. We know that the equilibrium payoffs form a convex set (Section 7) and we did succeed in finding an important subset which can be described by entities concerning one-shot games. Yet we know (Section 8) that the subset we could identify need not exhaust all the equilibrium payoffs. The reason is that sometimes equilibrium payoffs can only be reached by quite complicated agreements involving successive partial revelations of the information by the informed player, where the nature of these revelations depends on outcomes of lotteries controlled by both players. We did succeed in determining the nature of simple agreements involving partial revelation of information, and we did succeed in providing examples that use agreements involving intricate plans, but we have not yet succeeded in putting bounds on the amount of intricacy that may be needed.[1] We believe that these examples open up important new fields of further research. We also believe that the analysis does provide significant insight concerning people's behavior under a sequence of repeated conflicts when the information is incomplete.

Two partly conflicting goals guided the style in which this chapter is written. On the one hand, we hoped that non-mathematicians could appreciate the results, without being distracted by the proofs. For this purpose, we have given many verbal descriptions, examples, and interpretations of the results. On the other hand, we wished to give mathematicians the flavor of the arguments used in the proofs, so we have included many of the proofs and more technical discussions. It is also our hope that game theorists will be able to build further on the groundwork that we have laid.

2. Equilibrium Points and Equilibrium Payoffs in a 2-Player One-Shot Game

A (finite) 2-player game can be represented by a pair of $m \times n$ matrices. The rows of each matrix represent the pure strategies of Player 1, the columns represent the pure strategies of Player 2, the entries in the first matrix are the payoffs to Player 1, and the entries in the second matrix represent the payoffs to Player 2. Alternatively, one may write the two matrices as a single matrix whose entries are two-component vector payoffs, where the first component is the payoff to Player 1 and the second component is the payoff to Player 2. If each number in Player 2's payoff matrix is the negative of the corresponding number in Player 1's payoff

---

[1]This problem has since been solved. See Postscripts c–f to this chapter.(*)

matrix, then the game is called zero-sum. In this chapter we shall be concerned mainly with non-zero-sum games.

The rules of the game specify that each player chooses a pure or mixed[2] strategy from which the expected payoff can then be determined. Game theory distinguishes various degrees of agreements that are allowed in pre-play communication. A game that allows all varieties of agreement is called a *cooperative game*. In this case the players are allowed pre-play communication in which *binding agreements* can be made if the players so wish. Such agreements can involve *correlated strategies*; namely, the players may agree to follow the outcome of a single lottery that decides a strategy for each player.

It follows from these rules that the players in a cooperative game can agree on any payoff vector in the convex hull of the entries of the vector matrix of the game. We present an example.

EXAMPLE 2.1. (The Battle of the Sexes.) In the single-matrix form the game looks like this:

$$\begin{array}{cc}
 & \text{Player 2} \\
 & F \qquad\quad C
\end{array}$$

		F	C
	F	2, 1	−1, −1
Player 1	C	−1, −1	1, 2

The name "battle of the sexes" originated from a situation reported in R. D. Luce and H. Raiffa [1957]: A husband and wife must decide independently how to spend the evening. The husband (Player 1) would like to see a football game, and the wife (Player 2) would prefer to attend a concert performance. Above all, however, it is important for them to spend the evening together. If the first and second rows for the husband mean "I go to the football game" and "I go to the concert", respectively, and if

---

[2]A mixed strategy can be physically realized by conducting a lottery with prescribed probabilities that determines which pure strategy (row or column) will be used.

the first and second columns for the wife have the same meanings, then the vectors in the matrix represent their utility payoffs.[3]

In a cooperative game the players may cooperate in achieving any of a large set of outcomes. For example, in the "battle of the sexes" the players can agree on any payoff vector of the shaded region in Figure 1. On which payoff vector they will actually agree—that is a question belonging to the domain of the *solution concepts*. Some theories, like the Nash bargaining theory, provide a unique answer. (For this example, the Nash solution yields the point $(1\frac{1}{2}, 1\frac{1}{2})$.) Other theories hold that the data are not sufficient to provide a unique outcome, but that the actual outcome depends on other factors such as the bargaining ability of the players. It is safe, perhaps, to say that the actual agreement will be in the *core* of the game, which is the set of outcomes that share the following properties:

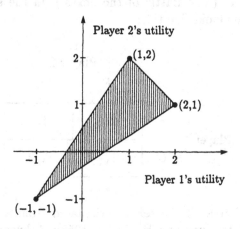

Figure 1. The set of outcomes that can be reached by correlated strategies for the game "battle of the sexes".

---

[3] Actually, the payoffs in square CF should be lower than the payoffs in square FC, because they represent a situation in which the husband not only spends the evening alone but also attends a concert, and the wife suffers similarly.(*)

(i) Each outcome in the core gives each of the players at least the amount that he can guarantee for himself (*individual rationality*).

(ii) For each outcome in the core there does not exist a payoff vector that can be agreed upon and is strictly preferred by each of the players (*group rationality*).

In our example, the core consists of the line segment joining the points $(1, 2)$ and $(2, 1)$.

The essential feature of cooperative games is the possibility of making binding agreements. The opposite extreme is the *noncooperative game* in which agreements may perhaps be made, but they are not binding; i.e., the players can violate them if they wish. There are, of course, solution concepts with various degrees of cooperation between these two extremes. It is sometimes claimed that business situations are examples of cooperative games because agreements are enforced by contracts or by the fear of risking one's good reputation, whereas political situations are examples of noncooperative games because governments sometimes reverse their decisions and ignore their commitments without fear of punishment or loss of reputation. It is probably true that the mechanisms that *enforce* international agreements are both more erratic and more complex than those that enforce business agreements.

One can classify noncooperative games according to the degree of pre-play communication that is allowed. We list a few cases:

a. *The noncooperative game without pre-play communication.* This is the classical noncooperative game as originally conceived by Nash [1951]. The rules of playing the game specify that the players should choose their strategies independently.

b. *The noncooperative game with pre-play communication, where correlated strategies are forbidden.* In this case, the players may talk prior to playing the game, they may agree on strategies that will be played by each player (but such agreements can be violated if a player so desires), and they are not allowed to decide by a joint lottery which strategies will be adopted by the players.

In this chapter the noncooperative games are of this kind.

c. *The noncooperative game with pre-play communication, where correlated strategies are permitted.* In this case, the following type of pre-play communication is allowed: "Let us flip a coin—if it shows heads, each of us will play one specified mixed strategy; if it shows tails, each of us will play another specified mixed strategy."[4]

When attempting to analyze the possible outcomes of a noncooperative game, it seems advisable to answer the following questions and in this order:

(i) What payoff vectors can be obtained, either with or without agreement?

(ii) What agreements are likely to remain unviolated?

(iii) Which of the agreements found in (ii) are likely to be chosen eventually?

The answer to (i) for noncooperative games with pre-play communication and permitted correlated strategies (Case c) is the same as in the cooperative case; namely, any point in the convex hull of the vector payoffs can be agreed upon. In the "battle of the sexes" (Example 2.1), treated as a noncooperative game, the set of these vector payoffs is the shaded area of Figure 2. If the correlated strategies are not allowed (Cases a and b, above), then the range of possible agreements or outcomes may narrow. In the "battle of the sexes" it reduces to the shaded area of Figure 2. For example, the outcome $(1\frac{1}{2}, 1\frac{1}{2})$ can be reached by the following *correlated* strategy: The players agree to flip an unbiased coin. If it shows heads they agree to use their first strategies (i.e., first row and first column). If it shows tails they agree to use their second strategies. If they keep this agreement, their expected payoff is $\frac{1}{2}(2,1) + \frac{1}{2}(1,2) = (1\frac{1}{2}, 1\frac{1}{2})$. The payoff vector $(1\frac{1}{2}, 1\frac{1}{2})$ *cannot* be reached if the players are not allowed to correlate their strategies.

---

[4]The idea that "noncooperative games" should be thought of as permitting such correlated strategies was communicated to us by J. Harsanyi, who also pointed out that if the "specified strategies" in each outcome of the lottery are in equilibrium, then the entire correlated strategy can be considered an equilibrium agreement, because no player will benefit by deviating from this agreement. This idea of "correlated equilibrium" was extended by Aumann [1974] to include certain agreements that are "in equilibrium" even though they are not representable as probability combinations of mixed strategy equilibria. (*)

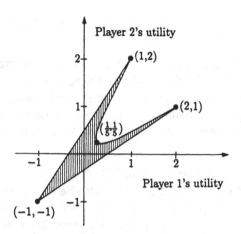

Figure 2. The set of outcomes that can be reached in the "battle of the sexes" when correlated strategies are not permitted.

If pre-play communication is allowed (Case b, above) then the players can agree on each point of the shaded area in Figure 2. If pre-play communication is not allowed (Case a), then this shaded area merely represents the set of points that the players may somehow reach.

We summarize: Except for Case c, the range of possible outcomes in a noncooperative game is, in general, smaller than the range of possible outcomes in the cooperative game based on the same payoff matrix.

If this were the only difference between the cooperative and the noncooperative games, then in the noncooperative game with pre-play communication, it would merely remain to bargain over the smaller set of possible outcomes; i.e., to reach some compromise agreement, just as in the cooperative game. However, in the noncooperative game agreements *may be violated*, so that the "compromise agreement" makes no sense. This leads us to question (ii): what agreements are likely to be kept? The answer to this question is that an agreement is likely to be kept if neither player can profit by violating it unilaterally. Such agreements will be called *equilibrium agreements* or *equilibrium pairs of strategies*, and the resulting payoff vectors will be called *equilibrium payoffs*. More precisely:[5]

DEFINITION 2.2. A pair of strategies in a noncooperative game is called an *equilibrium pair of strategies*, or *equilibrium point* for short, if no player can benefit by unilaterally switching to a different strategy. A payoff vector is called an *equilibrium payoff* if an equilibrium pair of strategies exists that leads to this payoff vector.

It is easily seen that $(2,1)$ and $(1,2)$ are equilibrium payoffs in the "battle of the sexes", and it can also be shown that $(1/5, 1/5)$ is the only other equilibrium payoff if correlated strategies are not permitted. It results from Player 1 mixing his first and second strategy with probabilities $3/5$ and $2/5$ respectively, and Player 2 mixing his first and second strategies with probabilities $2/5$ and $3/5$ respectively.

If pre-play communication is allowed, then equilibrium agreements are likely to be kept, because each player, figuring that the other player keeps the agreement, will not find it beneficial to violate the agreement.

If pre-play communication is not allowed (Case a), then agreements cannot be made and the above reasoning does not hold. The only merit that equilibrium points have in this case is of a metatheoretical nature: If for games of this type an intuitively appealing theory could ever be found that dictates a unique pair of strategies (one for each player), then this pair of strategies should be in equilibrium. Indeed, if such a theory exists then wise players should know it. If the strategies were not in equilibrium, it would pay one player, at least, to deviate from the theory; that would mean that such a theory would be self-defeating and of little value.[6]

---

[5]Definition 2.2 should be applied only to Cases a and b above. In Case c one should also consider any probability distribution over equilibrium pairs of strategies as an equilibrium agreement and any point in the convex hull of the equilibrium payoffs as an equilibrium payoff.

[6]Recently there have been several attempts to construct such theories. The leading contribution in this direction has been made by J. Harsanyi and R. Selten [1988]. (*)

If pre-play communication is allowed, one can pass now to question (iii) above and ask which of the three equilibria will be reached. Clearly, in our example, the players will reject $(\frac{1}{5}, \frac{1}{5})$, which is *inefficient* in the sense that both players prefer either of the other equilibrium payoffs to this one.[7] Thus, efficient equilibrium payoffs are analogues of core points for the cooperative game. Each of them has the property that no equilibrium payoff exists that is strictly preferred by both players.

We shall conclude our discussion of the one-shot game by the following example, known in the literature as the prisoner's dilemma.[8]

The two heavy straight line segments in Figure 3 connecting the points $(.2, .95)$ and $(.95, .2)$ to the point $(.8, .8)$ constitute the core of the game (treated as a cooperative game). The point $(.2, .2)$ is the unique equilibrium payoff of the game (treated as a noncooperative game). This example shows how different the outcomes may be even if the noncooperative game is in Case c.

EXAMPLE 2.3. (The Prisoner's Dilemma.) The payoff matrix is

.8, .8	0, 1
1, 0	.2, .2

3. Equilibrium Payoffs of an Infinitely-Repeated 2-Player Game with Complete Information

A conflict situation is seldom a one-shot affair. Usually, one conflict leads to another, whose nature may depend on the way the first conflict is resolved. Also, the new conflict may involve other participants. At present, game theory is not equipped with enough

---

[7]In Case c, the segment joining the points $(1, 2)$ and $(2, 1)$ consists of the efficient equilibrium payoffs.

[8]For the story of the prisoner's dilemma, see, e.g., Luce and Raiffa [1957].

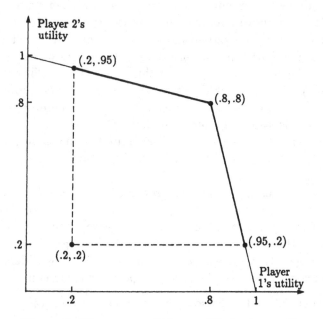

Figure 3. The core and the equilibrium payoffs
in the prisoner's dilemma.

tools to cope with the multitude of problems that arise in this connection. Nevertheless, some research has been carried out, under
severe simplifying assumptions.

One promising avenue is the study of infinitely-repeated games.
It is hoped that such research may yield insight into situations
involving a sequence of conflicts, similar in nature, where the
(present) utilities of corresponding outcomes remain, more or less,
constant over time.[9]

---

[9]This situation is not uncommon when the outcomes involved are important
for the perpetuation of mankind, safety of one's nation, or similar issues. One
can argue that such goals are basic human needs. People spend time and
effort to bring about a better future even if they know that they will not live
long enough to see the fruits. Thus, the present utility of a country being at a
certain security level in the future is, perhaps, the same, whether such future
is 100 or 500 years from now.

In this section we shall describe properties of equilibrium points of a repeated 2-player game (with complete information) that are relevant to the subsequent sections.

Our infinitely-repeated 2-player games will each consist of a specific 2-player non-zero-sum game (called the *stage game*), which is to be repeated *ad infinitum*. The stage game is most conveniently defined by a matrix, whose rows and columns represent *choices* that can be chosen by Players 1 and 2 respectively, at each stage. The stage game which we just described is played over and over again and the resulting payoffs are accumulated. At the end of each stage the players are informed of the strategies chosen in that stage. They can, therefore, calculate the proceeds for the stage.

A behavior[10] strategy for a player in the repeated game is a sequence of probability distributions over the set of his rows (or columns), which determines his actions at each stage. The probability distribution for a given stage may depend on the choices made by *both* players in the previous stages. Thus, when playing according to the specifications of a given strategy at a given stage, a player examines the double sequence of choices made in the previous stages. For this double sequence, his strategy specifies a probability distribution over the rows or columns of the stage-game matrix. He performs a lottery having this probability distribution over its set of outcomes. The result of the lottery then dictates which row or columns should be used by the player at the given stage.

Let us regard this infinite-stage game as a noncooperative game with pre-play communication, where correlated strategies are forbidden (Case b in the previous section). We would like to define its equilibrium payoffs and consider their properties. One complication that arises is that the payoffs are infinite sums, namely, the sum of the payoffs accumulated at all the stages. One way to evaluate them is to consider for each player the *average expected payoff per game* for the first n stages, and then let n tend to infinity. If the sequence of the average expected payoffs converges, the limit is regarded as the payoff to the player in the infinitely-repeated

---

[10]Since the game is of perfect recall, there is no loss of generality in limiting ourselves to behavior strategies (see H. Kuhn [1953] and R. Aumann [1964]).

game. On the basis of this evaluation one can employ a definition of an "equilibrium pair of strategies" and an "equilibrium payoff" similar[11] to those of Section 2.

It has been known for many years that *the set of equilibrium payoffs of an infinitely repeated 2-player game coincides with the individually rational points that can be achieved in a cooperative one-shot game whose payoff matrix is the stage-game matrix.*[12] In other words, every payoff that can be achieved in the cooperative one-shot game, which yields each player at least the amount that he can guarantee for himself, is an equilibrium payoff in the infinitely-repeated noncooperative game; and no other equilibrium payoffs exist.

The shaded parts in Figures 4 and 5 show the equilibrium payoffs for the infinitely-repeated "battle of the sexes" and the infinitely-repeated "prisoner's dilemma" (see Section 2).

For example, in spite of various statements in the literature to the contrary, the "cooperative payoff" (.8, .8) is an equilibrium payoff in the infinitely-repeated prisoner's dilemma.[13] The following is an equilibrium pair of strategies that yields this payoff.

Strategy for Player 1/2]: Choose at each stage your first row [column] (see the matrix in Example 2.2), as long as the other player uses his first column [row]. The moment you notice that he makes a different choice, start choosing your second row [column] in *all* subsequent stages.

Clearly, if both players abide by these strategies, their payoff for the game is $(0.8, 0.8)$. If one of them deviates unilaterally,

---

[11] Explicitly: A pair of strategies is said to be an equilibrium pair if: (i) The average expected payoff vector for the first n stages converges when n tends to infinity, (ii) Any unilateral deviation by one of the players yields a sequence of such averages whose lim sup for the deviating player is not greater than the original limit for the same player. Thus, by the second requirement, even under his best hopes (i.e., counting on the lim sup) the player cannot expect to benefit by a unilateral deviation. The first requirement imposes a restriction on the acceptable equilibrium points. In other words, the effect of not requiring (i) and modifying (ii) so that it has a meaning for non-converging sequences will only increase the set of equilibrium points.

[12] This has come to be known as the "Folk Theorem" in later literature. (*)

[13] This fact casts serious doubt on the validity of inferences from experiments in repeated prisoner's dilemma games to actual behavior of people in a single-shot game.

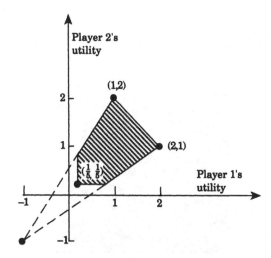

Figure 4. The equilibrium payoffs in the infinitely repeated "battle of the sexes".

his payoff reduces to .2. This shows that the above strategies are
indeed in equilibrium.

COMMENT. These strategies exhibit a feature that does not exist
in a one-shot game: They incorporate *punishments* for violations.
The punishment in this case was to switch forever to the second
row (or column) once a violation, i.e., a choice of second column
(second row) by the opponent, is observed. Of course, whatever
the gain that may be realized from the deviation at a particular
stage, it has no effect on the limit of the average payoffs.

The next example has other instructive features. It is an equilibrium pair of strategies for the repeated "battle of the sexes",
which yields $(1\frac{1}{2}, 1\frac{1}{2})$ as a payoff:

Strategy for Player 1: Choose your first row on the odd-
numbered stages and your second row on the even-numbered stages.
Do so as long as your opponent chooses his first column on the odd-
numbered stages and his second column on the even-numbered
stages. As soon as you observe a deviation, play from that stage

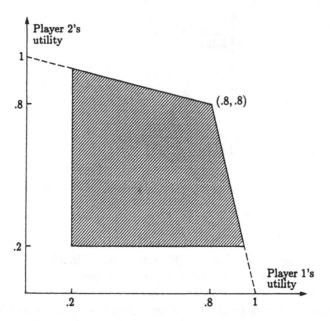

Figure 5. The equilibrium payoffs in the infinitely repeated "prisoner's dilemma".

forever a minmax strategy based on your opponent's payoff matrix.[14]

Strategy for Player 2: Same as for Player 1, except that "rows" and "columns" now read "columns" and "rows".[15]

COMMENT. Like the strategies in the previous example, these strategies, too, incorporate punishments. In addition, they specify *frequencies* for the stage choices. They describe separate agreements for the odd-numbered stages and for the even-numbered stages. This is an excellent substitute for the correlated strategies that are possible in the cooperative game—even in the one-shot

---

[14]i.e., at each stage choose the first row with probability 3/5 and the second row with probability 2/5.

[15]The minmax strategy against Player 1's payoff matrix is to choose the first and the second columns with probabilities 2/5 and 3/5, respectively.

game—but are forbidden in the noncooperative infinitely-repeated game discussed here.

The ideas expressed in these examples form the essence of the proof of the statement above, concerning the nature of the set of equilibrium payoffs of the infinitely-repeated game. We shall conclude by commenting on the implications of this statement:

1. Unlike in the one-shot game, where additional equilibrium payoffs are obtained if agreements involving correlated strategies are permitted (Case c in Section 2), no additional equilibrium payoffs are obtained in the infinitely-repeated game. Frequency strategies with a regular pattern can always be employed to avoid the need for correlated random strategies with *no* pattern; the former are perfectly permissible strategies for a noncooperative repeated game. Thus, one need not distinguish between Cases b and c of Section 2.

2. Except for payoff vectors that yield a player less than what he can guarantee for himself, there is no distinction in the infinitely-repeated game between equilibrium payoffs and payoffs that can be reached in a cooperative manner. This is so because any payoff that can be reached in a cooperative repeated game can also be reached in a one-shot cooperative game; it can consequently be obtained by a pair of frequency strategies in the repeated noncooperative game, and enforced as an equilibrium payoff by punishments.

3. It follows from the previous comment that *the efficient equilibrium payoffs* (see Section 2) *of the infinitely-repeated game coincide with the core*[16] *of the one-shot game, which in turn coincides with the core of the infinitely-repeated game.*

4. *The set of equilibrium payoffs of the infinitely repeated game can be determined from the one-shot game* (as described in 3 above).

---

[16]In a generalization of this result to more than two players, the "core" should be replaced by the "β-core" (see Aumann [1959], [1961]).

It is hard to overemphasize this last observation: Infinitely-repeated games have an infinite number of pure strategies; hence, *a priori*, it might have seemed hopeless even to attempt a computation of their equilibrium payoffs.

4. Repeated Games with Incomplete Information

Unlike the situations treated in classical game theory, a participant in a real-life conflict situation usually lacks information on the strategies that are available to him and to his opponent, on the actual outcomes and their utility to each of the participants, and on the amount of information that the other participants possess. Recently J. Harsanyi [1967–8] has laid the foundations of a chapter in game theory which deals precisely with such "games with incomplete information". It was shown in [1967–8] that the various types of incomplete information can always be reduced to one case, namely, to the case where everything is known to all players except for the utility payoffs (as functions of the chosen strategies).

In this book we deal with repeated two-player games in which one of the players (Player 2) lacks complete information on the payoffs in the stage-game matrix. We would like to find the set of equilibrium payoffs of such games and to examine whether results similar to those outlined in Section 3 hold if the information is incomplete in this sense.

We therefore assume that both players know that a certain stage game, described by an $m \times n$ matrix, is repeated infinitely. Player 1 knows the entries of the matrix, whereas Player 2 has only a subjective probability distribution on the various possible payoff matrices. At the end of each stage the players are told the choices that were made in that stage, and the payoffs are credited to the players' accounts, so that Player 2 cannot observe the payoff received. Of course, Player 1 can calculate the payoffs from the choices, since he knows the true matrix.

We assume that Player 1 knows the probability distribution that Player 2 attributes to the various possibilities, as well as the payoff matrices that 2 considers. We also assume that both players know the descriptions up to here.[17]

J. Harsanyi [1967-8] has proposed that this situation be modeled as a classical game in which a chance mechanism is involved, which can be described as follows:

First "Nature" makes a lottery with the probability distribution that Player 2 had in mind. The result of the lottery then determines the appropriate payoff matrix. Nature informs Player 1 which matrix was chosen but does not reveal this information to Player 2. The players then proceed to play an infinitely repeated game based on the chosen payoff matrix, which we call the *stage game*. At the end of each stage the players are informed of the choices made by the players in the stage, and the payoffs are accumulated in their bank accounts in sealed envelopes (see Figure 6). This representation is a regular game with complete information, because each player knows the tree and the information pattern. It involves, however, a chance mechanism delegated to "Nature", which does not exist in the original description. Harsanyi recommends that in order to play the original game, the players should agree on an equilibrium point in the above model and then play in the original game as if they were in the model and happened to reach the corresponding branch of Nature's lottery. This recommendation is justified by the fact that in doing so, no player can benefit in the original incomplete-information situation by a unilateral deviation, regardless of the true payoff matrix.

Observe that Harsanyi's model is *not* a repeated game in the sense of Section 3. This would have been the case if a new lottery were performed at the beginning of each stage. Here we have only one lottery and so to say, only part of the first stage is then repeated. It turns out that this distinction is a source of many complications, which will be described in this and the subsequent section.

If all the stage games are zero-sum, then Harsanyi's model is also a zero-sum game. In this case equilibrium pairs of strategies are exactly pairs of maximin strategies, and there is a unique equilibrium payoff, which coincides with the value of the game. This

---

[17]There is no need to assume that one of the matrices considered by Player 2 is the true matrix. If this is not the case, one simply adds the true matrix to the list considered by Player 2 and assigns to it a zero probability.

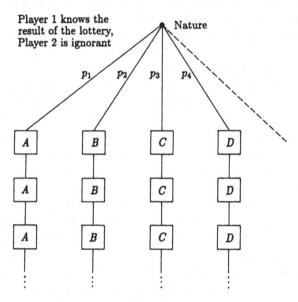

Figure 6. Harsanyi's model for a repeated two-player game with incomplete information on the part of Player 2.

case is fully treated in Chapters one and two, where it is shown that indeed a value always exists, that it can be derived from a certain one-shot game based on the stage game and, moreover, maxmin strategies can also be derived from this stage game (see also Chapter Three, where it is proved that in the case of *bilateral* incomplete information, a value need not exist).

In the following detailed example we show features of equilibrium pairs of strategies that are similar to features of equilibrium pairs in the case of repeated games with complete information. It will turn out, however, that even in this relatively simple example, a certain natural conjecture concerning the relation between the efficient equilibrium payoffs and the core does not hold. In the subsequent sections we shall show that completely new phenomena arise in the case of incomplete information. ∎

EXAMPLE 4.1.[18] (Cutting a cake with a cherry.) Each day Dick cuts a cake with a cherry into two portions and Tom chooses one of the portions for himself. The rules specify that the cake can be cut in only one of two ways: The ratio of the volumes of the portions is either 4:1 or 3:2. The smaller portion must contain the cherry. It is known that both players' utility is linear in the volume of cake received, and that Dick is totally indifferent to cherries. Dick does not know how Tom feels about the cherry, but believes that there are only two possibilities — either Tom is also indifferent to cherries, in which case we say that Tom is of type A, or he likes the cherry as much as 4/5 of the cake, in which case we say that Tom is of type B. Dick considers these alternatives equally likely and Tom knows this fact. Both players know the description up to this point.

Taking the utility of the cake to be 5 units and the utility for no cake to be 0 for each player, one obtains the following stage games:

Dick

		4 : 1	3 : 2
	ch ch	1, 4	2, 3
	ch c	1, 4	3, 2
Tom	c ch	4, 1	2, 3
	c c	4, 1	3, 2

Type A Tom (probability $= \frac{1}{2}$)

---

[18]This is a simplified version of a more general game described in Section 1 of Chapter One.

Dick

4 : 1   3 : 2

	4 : 1	3 : 2
ch ch	5, 4	6, 3
ch c	5, 4	3, 2
c ch	4, 1	6, 3
c c	4, 1	3, 2

Tom   Type *B* Tom (probability $= \frac{1}{2}$)

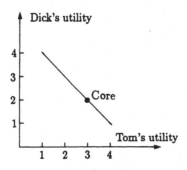

Figure 7.   Possible outcomes and core for
a type *A* Tom in the complete information case.

EXPLANATION: Dick's two ways of cutting the cake at each stage
are denoted 4:1 and 3:2. Tom has four possible strategies at each
stage, denoted by *ch ch*, *ch c*, *c ch* and *c c*. For example, *ch c*
means: "Take the small portion containing the cherry (*ch*) if he
offers the 4:1 cut, take the large portion containing only cake (*c*)
if he offers the 3:2 cut." For simplicity we assume that at the end

of each stage, both players are informed of the strategies (row and column) that were chosen, and not merely of the *actions* taken.[19]

Let us examine first the case of *complete information*, for each type of Tom separately. Figures 7 and 8 show the possible outcomes and the core (heavy dot and heavy line) if Dick knows Tom's type (see Section 3). We see that in the first case the core consists of a unique point (3,2), and in the second case it consists of a straight line segment connecting (5,4) with (6,3). Thus, for example, if Tom is of type *B* and Dick knows this, he *may* benefit during the bargaining by pressing towards an agreement near (5,4). At any rate, Dick gets at least 3, which is more than the 2 he can get in the core of the other game.

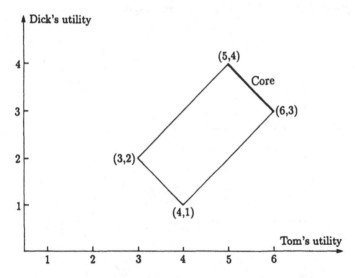

Figure 8.   Possible outcomes and core for a type *B* Tom in the complete information case.

[19]This is an extension of the rules explained previously. For example, if, upon offering the 4:1 ratio, Dick observes that Tom chose the larger piece, he can only deduce that Tom used *either* the strategy *c c or c ch*. We assume that Tom also tells Dick what he would have chosen had Dick offered him the 3:2 ratio. It turns out that the set of efficient equilibrium payoffs is unchanged by this assumption.

It would be interesting to find out whether a type B Tom can benefit if Dick does not know his identity and reach payoffs which are away from 5 and near 6. Similarly, it would be interesting to find out if a type A Tom can benefit from Dick's ignorance and reach payoffs higher than 3.

Note that both (5,4) and (6,3) are equilibrium payoffs in the one-shot stage game with a type B Tom, and (3,2) is an equilibrium payoff in the one-shot stage game with a type A Tom.

Let us first regard the incomplete-information game as cooperative and determine the core of its immediate-commitment model,[20] in the case where the rules allow for binding agreements prior to the selection by chance of Tom's true type. It turns out that the core of that model of the game consists of the straight-line segment joining (4,3) and (5,2) (see Figure 9).

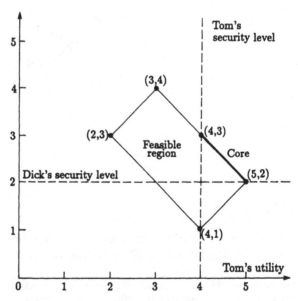

Figure 9. The Feasible Region, the Security Levels, and the Core, in Harsanyi's Cooperative Version of "Cutting a Cake with a Cherry".

---

[20] Harsanyi has discussed in [1967–8] the advantages and disadvantages of the immediate-commitment model.

PROOF: Dick can guarantee himself at least 2 in each stage by playing column 2 and Tom can hold him down to 2 at each stage by playing row 4. A type A Tom can guarantee himself 3 at each stage by playing row 4, and a type B Tom can guarantee himself 5 at each stage by playing row 1. At the end of this proof we shall show that Dick can play so that the average expected payoff will have no accumulation point higher than 3 for a type A Tom and 5 for a type B Tom. Granting this for the time being, we observe that each individually rational outcome must grant Dick at least 2 and Tom at least 4 (3 with probability $1/2$ and 5 with probability $1/2$). In order for an outcome to be group rational, it must be group rational for each type separately. Thus, each group rational outcome is the average of a point on the straight-line segment joining $(1,4)$ to $(4,1)$ with a point on the straight-line segment joining $(5,4)$ to $(6,3)$ (see Figures 7 and 8). These points constitute the straight-line segment joining $(3,4)$ to $(5,2)$ in Figure 9. The core, i.e., the set of outcomes that are both individually and group rational, is therefore the straight-line segment joining $(4,3)$ to $(5,2)$.

It remains to show that Dick can indeed hold a type A Tom to 3 and a type B Tom to 5 simultaneously. In order to show a strategy for Dick that achieves this, we consider a 4×2 repeated game with vector payoffs where the components in each entry represent Tom's payoffs for the two types.[21]

Dick

		$4:1$	$3:2$
ch	ch	$[1,5]$	$[2,6]$
ch	c	$[1,5]$	$[3,3]$
c	ch	$[4,4]$	$[2,6]$
c	c	$[4,4]$	$[3,3]$

Tom

---

[21] Dick's own payoffs are irrelevant for the present consideration.

(The vector payoffs are enclosed by square brackets in order to distinguish them from the payoff vectors in the stage games.) Figure 10 shows all possible average expected payoffs per game. In addition, the set S indicated in the figure, consisting of a portion of a right angle whose vertex is the payoff vector [3,5], is the set of all possible outcomes in which type A Tom gets no more than 3 and type B Tom gets no more than 5.

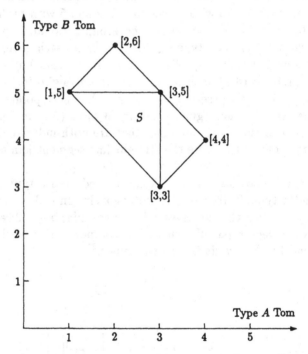

Figure 10. Blackwell's game for Tom's payoffs.

Infinitely repeated games with vector payoffs were studied by D. Blackwell [1956], where characterizations of "approachable" sets were determined. A set S of outcomes is called *approachable for Player 2*, if Player 2 has a strategy in the infinitely repeated game which, with probability 1, forces the accumulation points of the average vector payoffs into the set S, regardless of the strategy taken by Player 1.

Blackwell proves that a closed and convex set S is approachable for Player 2 if and only if it is not "excludable" by Player 1 in the one-shot game; i.e., if and only if Player 1 has no strategy for the *one-shot game* with the same payoff matrix, that yields an expected outcome outside of S regardless of the strategy taken by Player 2. Blackwell also provides an appropriate strategy for Player 2 to achieve this purpose, if S is approachable for him.

Our task will be complete if we show that the set S of Figure 10 is indeed approachable for Dick. By Blackwell's results, all we have to do is to show that this set is not excludable by Tom in the one-shot game. Let x be an arbitrary strategy for Tom in the one-shot game. If Dick chooses the first column, the expected payoff C will be a point on the straight-line segment ([1,5], [4,4])(see the payoff matrix and Figure 11). If this point is in S, then x does not exclude S. Suppose, therefore, that this point C is not in S. If Dick chooses the second column, the expected payoff D is on the line segment([2,6], [3,3]) and again, we can assume that it is not in S. But the straight-line segment connecting both expected payoffs C and D must intersect S (see Figure 11); hence by mixing his columns Dick can reach an expected payoff in S. Consequently, no such x can exclude S, so S is approachable, and Dick can simultaneously prevent a type A Tom from getting more than 3 and a type B tom from getting more than 5. ∎

COMMENT. Comparing Figure 9 with Figures 7 and 8, we see that a type A Tom has some advantage in the immediate-commitment model. For example, (5,2), which is an outcome in its core, is a combination of (4,1) to type A and (6,3) to type B; it yields 4 to a type A Tom, whereas in the complete information case he could obtain only 3. No such advantage accrues to a type B Tom.

It should be emphasized that there is an important distinction between the immediate-commitment model and the real situation. In the immediate-commitment model, agreements are made before chance selects Tom's type, whereas in the real situation the actual Tom is already of one type or the other. As far as the set of equilibrium payoffs is concerned, the model is justified, because an equilibrium pair of strategies in the immediate-commitment model induces an equilibrium pair for each type separately versus

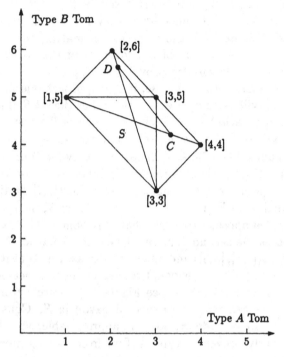

Figure 11. Checking S for approachability.

his opponent. The core is also justified because it induces individual and group rational outcomes for each type and his opponent. Problems arise, however, when bargaining starts on the choice of the particular equilibrium payoff, or of the particular core point, as the case may be. Some points are preferred by type A and others by type B, and therefore there is a danger that one's type may be revealed by one's way of bargaining. This matter requires further study.

In the rest of this section we propose to determine all the efficient equilibrium payoffs for the game of cutting the cake with a cherry. Although this determination involves several steps, we do not defer the analysis, because the arguments are relevant and highly necessary for the understanding of the subsequent sections.

STEP 1. The point $(4\frac{1}{2}, 2\frac{1}{2})$ is an equilibrium payoff.

PROOF: This point is reached by the following agreement consisting of an equilibrium pair of strategies:
For Dick: "Choose the 3:2 split at each stage".
For Tom: "Choose the $(c\ c)$-row at each stage if you are type A. Choose the $(c\ ch)$-row at each stage if you are type B".
Clearly, if Nature chooses Tom to be of type A, the expected payoff is $(3,2)$ at each stage. Otherwise it is $(6,3)$. Since each case occurs with probability $1/2$, the expected payoff is $(4\frac{1}{2}, 2\frac{1}{2})$ if both players abide by the agreement. Neither Tom nor Dick can benefit by unilaterally switching to a different strategy. ■

COMMENT. Being aware of Tom's strategy, Dick can deduce (as early as the end of the first stage) the choice of Nature by observing Tom's first-stage choice, because the strategy calls for different choices by the two types already at that stage. We say in this case that Tom's strategy is *completely revealing*.

STEP 2. Dick can play so that on the average, a type A Tom will not get more than 3 units per game, and a type B Tom will not get more than 5 units per game, regardless of Tom's strategy.[22]

This was proved during the above computation of the core.

STEP 3. The point $(4,3)$ is an equilibrium payoff.

PROOF: This point can be reached by the following agreement, which is an equilibrium pair of strategies.

Tom, type A: "Choose $(c\ c)$-row at each stage."

Tom, type B: "Choose $(ch\ ch)$-row at each stage."

Dick: "Do whatever you wish in the first stage. If Tom took the $(c\ c)$-row in the first stage take the second column from the second stage on, as long as Tom continues to use the $(c\ c)$-row. If Tom took the $(ch\ ch)$-row in the first stage take the first column from the second stage on, as long as Tom continues to use the $(ch\ ch)$-row. The moment you observe that Tom makes any move at any stage that is different from his move at the

---

[22] More precisely, with probability 1, the lim sup of the sequences of average expected payoffs will not exceed these numbers.

first stage, start the Blackwell's strategy referred to in Step 2."

If these two strategies are followed, then the outcome at each stage (except, perhaps, the first) is $(3,2)$ if Tom is of type A and $(5,4)$ if Tom is of type B. Thus, the average expected outcome is indeed $(4,3)$. From the matrix we see that Dick does not benefit by a unilateral switch to other moves. As for Tom, we must examine two kinds of deviations: (i) Deviations that are recognized by Dick; i.e., those where the move at some stage differs from the move at the first stage. Certainly such deviations would not benefit Tom, because they will be countered by a Blackwell's strategy that yields a type A Tom at most 3 and a type B Tom at most 5 (as lim sup of the average payoffs). (ii) Deviations that are not recognized by Dick: These are deviations in which one type of Tom behaves as if he were the other type, and which are not recognized because Tom's move at the first stage remains the same in all the stages. We can see that it does not pay a type A Tom to act as if he is of type B (he will get 1 instead of 3), and it does not pay a type B Tom to act as if he is of type A (he will get 3 instead of 5). Thus the above pair of strategies is in equilibrium.

∎

COMMENTS. Tom's strategy has an interesting feature. Not only is it completely revealing, but this revelation determines Dick's moves. Thus the first move is used to *signal* information on Tom's true type.

Dick's strategy also has an interesting feature: It contains a "punishment" in case Tom violates the agreement. However, unlike in Section 3, this punishment cannot be a minimax strategy based on Tom's payoff matrix, because this matrix is not known to Dick. Instead, it is a Blackwells' strategy that simultaneously punishes both types of Tom.

STEP 4. Any point on the straight-line segment connecting $(4,3)$ and $(4\frac{1}{2}, 2\frac{1}{2})$ is an equilibrium payoff.

Such a point can be achieved by a frequency strategy, as described in Section 2 (see the detailed description in Section 6). For example, in order to reach the mid-point $(4\frac{1}{4}, 2\frac{3}{4})$, the agreement is to use the strategies of Step 1 at the odd-numbered stages (regarding them as an independent infinitely repeated game by itself) and to use the strategies of Step 3 at the even-numbered stages (with the same convention). Since both strategies for Tom are completely revealing, there is no danger that, say, the moves at the odd stages will reveal too much, so that Dick could benefit in the even stages due to his knowledge about the true choice of Nature. It follows from this fact that the combined pairs of strategies are indeed in equilibrium. They also provide the desired average expected payoff.

We shall see later (Section 7) that in general, the set of equilibrium payoffs is convex, though frequency strategies are not always available. Step 4 follows from the convexity.

STEP 5. No equilibrium payoff yields Tom an average expected payoff smaller than 4.

PROOF: We have seen earlier that Tom can guarantee himself 4. He therefore always has the option of adopting a protective policy as an alternative to any proposed outcome that offers him less than 4.

STEP 6. No equilibrium payoff yields Tom an average expected payoff greater than $4\frac{1}{2}$.

OUTLINE OF THE PROOF:[23] Let (σ, τ) be an equilibrium pair of strategies. Knowing σ and observing Tom's moves enables Dick to compute, at the end of each stage n, a conditional probability p_n that chance chose Tom to be of type A.

Consider the situation after stage n. One can compute the conditional probabilities $p_n^{(1)}$, $p_n^{(2)}$, ..., $p_n^{(\alpha_n)}$ that might arise due to various possible moves of Tom under σ, and the probabilities of their occurrences $\gamma_n^{(1)}$, $\gamma_n^{(2)}$, ..., $\gamma_n^{(\alpha_n)}$. It is known that the expectation of the conditional probabilities is equal to the original probability that Tom is of type A, so

$$\gamma_n^{(1)} p_n^{(1)} + \gamma_n^{(2)} p_n^{(2)} + \cdots + \gamma_n^{(\alpha_n)} p_n^{(\alpha_n)} = \frac{1}{2}. \qquad (4.1)$$

---

[23] A detailed proof requires further elaboration that is not needed to understand the rest of the chapter.

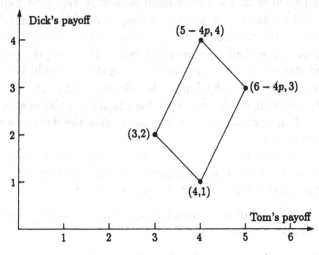

Figure 12. The stage-game for $p < \frac{1}{2}$.

When computing the expected payoff for the $(n + 1)$-th stage as a function of the moves at that stage, then setting $p_n = p$, Dick must consider the stage game

		Dick	
		$4:1$	$3:2$
ch	ch	$5 - 4p, 4$	$6 - 4p, 3$
ch	c	$5 - 4p, 4$	$3, 2$
c	ch	$4, 1$	$6 - 4p, 3$
c	c	$4, 1$	$3, 2$

Tom (label on the left of the rows)

which is a combination of the two original matrices in the proportions p and $(1 - p)$. As we shall see, this is also the game that Tom should consider at the very beginning—i.e., before he knows the choice of chance—if the initial probability of type A were p rather than $1/2$.

Figures 12 and 13 show the convex hull of these payoff vectors for the cases $p < \frac{1}{2}$ and $p \geq \frac{1}{2}$. Any agreement, when applied at a certain stage, leads to a payoff vector which is a point in the convex hull for the appropriate p.

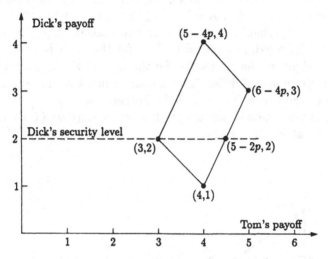

Figure 13. The stage-game for $p \geq \frac{1}{2}$.

It is known that for each pair (σ, τ) of strategies, there is a stage n_0 such that from that stage on, the changes in the conditional probabilities are negligible.[24] We shall therefore commit a negligible mistake if we assume that after stage n_0, there is *no change* in the conditional probabilities. Since a finite number of stages has no effect on the limit of the average expected payoffs, we can ignore the first n_0 stages.

For a given $p_{n_0} = p$, let us estimate the maximum limit of the average payoffs for Tom. If $p < \frac{1}{2}$, then $6 - 4p$ is an upper bound, since all the points in the convex hull in Figure 12 have a

---

[24]More precisely, given (σ, τ) and given positive numbers δ and ε, there exists a number n_0 such that the probability that a conditional probability on or after stage n_0 differs from another such conditional probability by more than δ is smaller than ε. [This says that the p_i converge in probability. It is a shallower version of the martingale convergence theorem (see Postscript a to Chapter One), according to which the p_i converge almost surely. Similar ideas are used in all the previous chapters.](*)

first coordinate not larger than this amount. If $p \geq \frac{1}{2}$, we have to look for the point with the largest first coordinate in the convex hull in Figure 13 that has a second coordinate not smaller than 2 (because Dick can defend 2 by always using the second column). That point has a first coordinate $5 - 2p$ (see Figure 13).

The heavy broken line in Figure 14 is the graph of these maxima as a function of p. A priori, p_{n_0} can take various values, each with some probability; the overall expectation of p_{n_0} is $\frac{1}{2}$ (see (4.1)). The maximum payoff to Tom for the game is the average of the heights of the broken line for the various p_{n_0}, when weighted by the same probabilities. This amount cannot be more than the value of the concavification of the broken line at $p = \frac{1}{2}$. Clearly, the concavification is the straight-line segment $[(0,6), (1,3)]$, whose ordinate at $p = \frac{1}{2}$ is $4\frac{1}{2}$. ∎

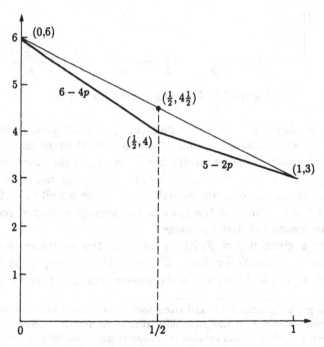

Figure 14. Tom's maximum payoff at an equilibrium payoff.

COMMENT. It follows from this proof that the only way for Tom to achieve $4\frac{1}{2}$ is to use a strategy which, with probability 1, completely reveals his type.

STEP 7. The efficient equilibrium payoffs of the game constitute the straight-line segment $[(4,3), (4\frac{1}{2},2\frac{1}{2})]$.

PROOF: By Step 4, the points on this segment are equilibrium payoffs. They are efficient because they constitute a part of the core. By Steps 5 and 6, any equilibrium point must yield Tom an amount between 4 and $4\frac{1}{2}$. Since $[(4,3), (4\frac{1}{2},2\frac{1}{2})]$ is included in the core, it follows that for any equilibrium payoff (x,y) not on this segment, the point on this segment of the form (x,η) satisfies $\eta > y$. Thus, (x,y) is not efficient except, perhaps, if $x = 4\frac{1}{2}$ and $y < 2\frac{1}{2}$. But even this last case is not an efficient equilibrium payoff, because in order that $x = 4\frac{1}{2}$, Tom's strategy must be completely revealing (Step 6) and Dick must get at least $2\frac{1}{2}$ in an efficient equilibrium payoff (see Figures 7 and 8).

We have determined all the efficient equilibrium payoffs and found that they constitute a certain proper part of the core. Thus, unlike in the case of complete information, the set of efficient equilibrium payoffs does not coincide with the core in this example of a repeated game with incomplete information.

It is interesting to note that in the noncooperative game neither a type A Tom nor a type B Tom has any advantage from Dick's not knowing the choice of chance. Indeed, Tom's strategies in the equilibria of steps 1, 3 and 4 are all completely revealing. Note also that the efficient equilibrium payoffs (Step 7) are the averages of the unique core point (3,2) in Figure 7 and a core point in Figure 8. ∎

5. The Possibility of Cheating

We have seen that it is not always advantageous, nor even harmless, for Player 1 to conceal his type. There are many cases where it is essential for Player 1 to reveal his type entirely, as we have seen in Section 4 for the equilibrium payoff $(4\frac{1}{2},2\frac{1}{2})$. (See Comment to Step 6.) We shall give a pair of examples to illustrate some of the subtleties involved.

EXAMPLE 5.1. Perhaps the simplest example in which all efficient equilibrium payoffs share this feature is the infinitely repeated game with incomplete information whose stage-game matrices are

Type A (probability $= \frac{1}{2}$)

1,1	0,0
0,0	0,0

Type B (probability $= \frac{1}{2}$)

0,0	0,0
0,0	1,1

Obviously, both players are interested in reaching the upper left corner if Player 1 is of type A, and the lower right corner if he is of type B. The outcome $(1,1)$ is the unique efficient equilibrium payoff, and it can only be achieved if Player 1's strategy is completely revealing.

One equilibrium pair of strategies yielding $(1,1)$ is as follows:

Player 1, Type A: "Play always the first row".
Player 1, Type B: "Play always the second row".
Player 2:   "Choose any move on stage 1. Choose the first column from the second stage on if Player 1 has chosen the first row in the first move; otherwise, choose the second column from the second stage on."

It is clear that the actual move of Player 1 at the first stage serves as a *signal* that yields information on his true type.[25]

---

[25]Signalling by means of the strategy choice is always possible unless Player 1 has only one strategy.

Unfortunately, it is not always possible to use signals in an equilibrium even if it is to both players' advantage.

EXAMPLE 5.2. The stage-game matrices of this example are[26]

Type A (probability $= \frac{1}{3}$)

1,1	0,0
1,1	0,0

Type B (probability $= \frac{2}{3}$)

5,0	1,1
5,0	1,1

Consider the following pair of strategies: "Player 1 signals his type by his first move. From the second stage on, both players play the upper left corner if the signal indicates type A, and the lower right corner otherwise."

We claim that this is *not* an equilibrium pair of strategies. Indeed, if Player 1 happens to be of type B he will *benefit* by signalling as if he were of type A, in which case the resulting outcome will be $(5,0)$ instead of $(1,1)$. In other words, he will benefit by *cheating* on his true type. Note that if the above pair of strategies is decided upon, Player 2 will never be able to discover whether Player 1 cheats, and therefore one cannot create an equilibrium pair of strategies by incorporating a "punishment" for such a violation.

This example has several interesting features: Type A of Player 1 loses by cheating. He likes the agreement because it gives him the maximum possible outcome and he will, therefore, tell the truth by his signal. Unfortunately, Player 2 cannot believe

---

[26]We use two identical rows instead of a single row in each matrix in order to make it possible for Player 1 to signal; alternatively, we may simply identify the strategies with the utterance of signals, since the strategies in this case have no direct influence on the payoffs.

him, realizing that type B of Player 1 would *also* signal that he
is of type A. Thus, the lack of information causes the possibility
that a signal is not credible even if its truthfulness is to the benefit of the player who makes it, and believing it would benefit the
hearer.

As a matter of fact, *no equilibrium payoff in this game is group
rational* (see Section 2).

PROOF: Any group rational outcome must result from a group
rational payoff for each game between Player 2 and a type of
Player 1. In particular, it must yield the payoff $(5, 0)$ if Player 1
is of type B, since otherwise, type B of Player 1 can benefit by
cheating. But $\frac{1}{3}(1,1) + \frac{2}{3}(5,0) = (3\frac{2}{3}, \frac{1}{3})$ is not an equilibrium
payoff, because Player 2 can guarantee $\frac{2}{3}$ for himself by always
choosing the second column. This contradiction shows that no
equilibrium payoff is group rational, and therefore no equilibrium
payoff lies in the core. ∎

6. Joint Plans

For the sake of simplicity, we shall assume in this section that
Player 1 has only two types, A and B. Generalization to more
than two types is straightforward.

In this section we shall examine some of the ideas that ap-
peared in the examples of the previous sections, and use the insight
gained to determine an important class of equilibrium payoffs.

Consider an arbitrary equilibrium pair of strategies (σ, τ) played
by the two players in the infinitely repeated game. Player 1's strategy can also be written as (σ_A, σ_B), where σ_A is the prescription
for type A, and σ_B—for type B.

If Player 2 knows σ, he can compute at the end of each stage
new conditional probabilities on 1's type, based on his observations of Player 1's moves.

We know, however, that after a certain stage[27] n_0, there is only
a negligible probability that significant changes will occur in the

---

[27]Where n_0 must in general depend on σ, on τ, and on our choice of the
parameters δ and ε that were considered in the last footnote of Section 4.

new conditional probabilities. Thus, if p_{n_0} is the conditional probability at the end of stage n_0 that 1 is of type A, then, from that
stage on, Player 1 essentially uses the same probability distribution on his moves regardless of his type, as long as Player 2 plays
according to τ. In other words, both players essentially behave as
if neither of them knew Player 1's type and both attributed the
probability p_{n_0} to the event that 1 is of type A. This infinitely
repeated game will be denoted $\Delta(p_{n_0})$. Its stage-game matrix is
a combination of the original stage-game matrices in the proportions p_{n_0} and $(1 - p_{n_0})$. It is important to observe that this[28] is
true only as long as both players *abide* by (σ, τ).

It is important to point out the following:

(1) For $n > n_0$ the true conditional may be different from
p_{n_0}, although such circumstances will occur with small
probability. This is signified by "essentially" above.

(2) n_0 is a function of (σ, τ). If Player 2, for example, decides not to abide by τ and play another strategy τ'
(and Player 1 remains at σ), then n_0 may be different.

Consider again the first n_0 stages. What is their contribution
to the equilibrium payoff? Certainly the payoff gained during the
first n_0 stages is totally unimportant for the infinitely repeated
game, because a finite number of accumulated payoffs does not
change the limit of the infinite sequence of average payoffs. The
major purpose served by the first n_0 stages is to yield information on Player 1's type in the form of a new set of conditional
probabilities. Which p_{n_0} will actually arise depends on the actual
choices of both players, but *a priori* we can compute, from (σ, τ),
the probability α for the event that at the end of stage n_0, the
conditional probability that Player 1 is of type A will be p_{n_0}. We
then have[29]

$$\alpha p_{n_0} + (1 - \alpha)(1 - p_{n_0}) = p, \qquad (6.1)$$

---

[28] Precisely, the word "essentially" in the above discussion applies only if
the players use (σ, τ). The analysis should not ignore the possibility that
Player 2, say, will defect from τ on purpose, even though such a defection has
a negligible probability under τ.(*)

[29] Formula (6.1) remains true if we substitute for p a conditional probability
p_m that was computed at a stage m earlier than n_0.

where p is the original probability that 1 is of type A.

Suppose (σ, τ) is a pair of equilibrium strategies and the players play it. Then, after many stages, the conditional probability is p_{n_0} and it is not going to change much. Can we say that they are now playing essentially $\Delta(p_{n_0})$ and from now on they can use strategies as described in Section 3? The answer is negative: Player 1 still knows chance's choice and can use it when "punishing" Player 2 if he "defects" from τ. The maxmin level for Player 1 in $\Delta(p_{n_0})$ is simply not relevant. The "punishment" implied in Player 2's strategy has to take into account that Player 1 knows chance's choice and—as we shall see, and already saw in the previous section—this can be done by adopting a Blackwell type of strategy.

The foregoing discussion suggests that it is perhaps not an easy task to characterize *all* the equilibrium payoffs of a repeated game with incomplete information. Let us therefore select *some* of the above ideas and use them to construct at least a subset of the equilibrium payoffs. In particular, we wish to find those equilibrium payoffs that can be achieved by Player 1 revealing certain information independently of Player 2's moves, and that also have the property that, after that information has been revealed, the sequence of average expected payoffs converges.

In order to achieve this modest goal, we shall develop some terminology.

A *signal*[30] is an announcement by Player 1 of either the letter "L" or the letter "R".

REMARK. A realization of a signal in the original game can be achieved if the stage game matrices have at least two rows. Then "L" and "R" can be realized, say, by selecting the first and second row, respectively, during Stage 1.[31] Signals will be used to convey information on Player 1's type.

A *pure signalling strategy* is a rule that specifies, for each type of Player 1, which signal to announce.

---

[30] For the sake of simplicity, only the case of two possible signals will be treated here. A generalization is straightforward.

[31] For more signals, one might use several stages, or one might use a more complicated "vocabulary" of signals.

A *mixed signalling strategy* is a probability distribution over the pure signalling strategies.

Given a mixed signalling strategy, if we knew what signal Player 1 had uttered, we could compute the conditional probability that he was of type A. We denote that probability by p^L if the signal was "L", and by p^R if the signal was "R". If α^L and α^R are the *a priori* probabilities of announcing "L" and "R" respectively (computed prior to the choice of chance), then we must have

$$\alpha^L p^L + \alpha^R p^R = p. \tag{6.2}$$

This formalism concerning signalling is a brief and precise way of discussing the idea of "revealing information", which is applicable when the revelation is independent of the moves of Player 2.

A *contract* is a pair of correlated stage strategies—one for each possible signal—each of which belongs to the space of correlated strategies of the one-stage game.[32]

COMMENT. We can make use of arguments similar to those of Section 3 and describe the payoffs as points in the one-shot cooperative game, $\Delta(p^L)$ if the signal was "L" and $\Delta(p^R)$ if the signal was "R". Here $\Delta(p^L)$ and $\Delta(p^R)$ are the one-stage games obtained from the original game by assuming that the probability of players being of type A are p^L and p^R, respectively, and none of the players knows this type. The contract actually yields the payoff vectors (h_L^1, h_L^2) and (h_R^1, h_R^2) in the payoff spaces of $\Delta(p^L)$ and $\Delta(p^R)$, via a procedure to be described below.

A *joint plan* is a pair consisting of a mixed signalling strategy and a contract.

A joint plan generates a payoff vector (h^1, h^2) in the following fashion: Let $(h_L^1(A), h_L^2(A))$, $(h_L^1(B), h_L^2(B))$, $(h_R^1(A), h_R^2(A))$, $(h_R^1(B), h_R^2(B))$ be the expected payoff vectors, determined by the contract for each pure signal and for each type of Player 1, in a one-stage game with the appropriate payoff matrix. Define

$$(h_L^1, h_L^2) = p^L \Big(h_L^1(A), h_L^2(A) \Big) + (1 - p^L) \Big(h_L^1(B), h_L^2(B) \Big), \tag{6.3}$$

---

[32] A contract is not an agreement for playing the repeated game, but a formal mathematical object that will enable us in the sequel to describe and characterize certain such agreements.(*)

$$(h_R^1, h_R^2) = p^R \Big(h_R^1(A), h_R^2(A) \Big) + (1 - p^R) \Big(h_R^1(B), h_R^2(B) \Big), \quad (6.4)$$

and

$$(h^1, h^2) = \alpha^L (h_L^1, h_L^2) + \alpha^R (h_R^1, h_R^2). \quad (6.5)$$

Another way of arriving at (h^1, h^2), in which conditional probabilities do not enter, is as follows: Denote the pure signalling strategies by LL, LR, RL, and RR, where the first letter in each pair denotes type A's signal and the second letter denotes type B's. Prior to the choice of Player 1's type by chance, Player 1 figures out that if he uses any of these strategies, the expected contract payoffs will be, respectively,

$$(h_{LL}^1, h_{LL}^2) = p \Big(h_L^1(A), h_L^2(A) \Big) + (1 - p) \Big(h_L^1(B), h_L^2(B) \Big), \quad (6.6)$$

$$(h_{LR}^1, h_{LR}^2) = p \Big(h_L^1(A), h_L^2(A) \Big) + (1 - p) \Big(h_R^1(B), h_R^2(B) \Big), \quad (6.7)$$

$$(h_{RL}^1, h_{RL}^2) = p \Big(h_R^1(A), h_R^2(A) \Big) + (1 - p) \Big(h_L^1(B), h_L^2(B) \Big), \quad (6.8)$$

$$(h_{RR}^1, h_{RR}^2) = p \Big(h_R^1(A), h_R^2(A) \Big) + (1 - p) \Big(h_R^1(B), h_R^2(B) \Big). \quad (6.9)$$

If the mixed signalling strategy is to play the pure signalling strategies with probabilities x_{LL}, x_{LR}, x_{RL}, x_{RR}, respectively, $x_{LL} + x_{LR} + x_{RL} + x_{RR} = 1$, then the resulting expected payoff from the contract is

$$\begin{aligned}
(h^1, h^2) = x_{LL} \left(h_{LL}^1, h_{LL}^2 \right) + x_{LR} \left(h_{LR}^1, h_{LR}^2 \right) \\
+ x_{RL} \left(h_{RL}^1, h_{RL}^2 \right) + x_{RR} \left(h_{RR}^1, h_{RR}^2 \right),
\end{aligned} \quad (6.10)$$

and it is easy to show that (6.5) and (6.10) are equivalent.

Let us pause to recapitulate. Our purpose is to find equilibrium payoffs of a given infinitely repeated game. In order to achieve this, we considered an arbitrary equilibrium pair of strategies (σ, τ), hoping to get some clues from the analysis of its features that would enable us to determine the equilibrium payoffs. We realized that two components could be identified in (σ, τ):

(1) A method of conveying information on Player 1's type in the form of a new conditional probability.

(2) Once the information has been conveyed, one is left with
an infinitely repeated game with complete information,
in which both players behave as if they are equally ignorant of Player 1's type; games of this type were analyzed
in Section 3.

At the same time we realized that, in general, the method of
conveying information *may* be much more complicated; in particular, it may depend on both players' actions. Joint plans represent
one such method, a particularly simple one. To this end we developed the concept of a joint plan and showed how a joint plan
determines a payoff vector. The question that naturally arises is:
Under what conditions is this payoff vector an equilibrium payoff?
We answer that question in the next theorem.

THEOREM 6.1. *The payoff vector* (h^1, h^2) *generated by a given
joint plan is an equilibrium payoff of the original infinitely repeated game* Γ *if the following three conditions are met:*

(i) *The mixed signalling strategy* $x = (x_{LL}, x_{LR}, x_{RL}, x_{RR})$
is such that $x_{MN} > 0$, $M, N \in \{L, R\}$, *implies*

$$h^1_{MN} \geq h^1_{PQ} \text{ for all } P \in \{R, L\}, \ Q \in \{R, L\}. \tag{6.11}$$

*In other words, every pure signalling strategy occur-
ring in* x *with positive probability yields Player 1 an
expected payoff not lower than the expected payoff obtained by any other pure signalling strategy. In particular, all the pure signalling strategies that occur in* x *with
positive probability yield Player 1 the same (maximal)
expected payoff.*

(ii) *Denote by* $w^2(q)$ *the value[33] to Player 2 of the zero-sum
infinitely repeated game* $\Gamma_2(q)$, *whose stage-game matrices for Player 2 are the same as those of* Γ, *and where
q is the probability attributed by Player 2 to the event
that Player 1 is of type A. With this notation,*

$$\text{if } \alpha^L > 0, \text{ then } h^2_L \geq w^2(p^L), \tag{6.12}$$

---

[33]See previous chapters, where values of zero-sum infinitely-repeated games
are fully determined.

$$\text{if } \alpha^R > 0, \text{ then } h_R^2 \geq w^2(p^R). \qquad (6.13)$$

In other words, for any signal with positive probability, Player 2's contract payoff is at least as large as the amount that he can guarantee by himself, taking into account the information conveyed by the signal.

(iii) Let G be an infinitely repeated 2-person game whose strategy spaces are the same as those of Γ, and whose stage-game payoffs are 2-component vectors, where the components represent the payoffs to the two types of Player 1.[34] Let

$$S^L \equiv \left\{ [u^A, u^B] : u^A \leq h_L^1(A), u^B \leq h_L^1(B) \right\}, \qquad (6.14)$$

$$S^R \equiv \left\{ [u^A, u^B] : u^A \leq h_R^1(A), u^B \leq h_R^1(B) \right\}. \qquad (6.15)$$

Then S^L and S^R are approachable sets for Player 2 in Blackwell [1956] sense. In other words, Player 2, who plays simultaneously against the two types, can, for each signal, force the outcome for each type to the payoff determined by the contract.

PROOF: We shall exhibit a pair of strategies for the original game that, if obeyed, yields the payoff vector (h^1, h^2). We shall then show that this is an equilibrium pair of strategies.

Specification for the first stage. Player 2 acts in an arbitrary manner. Player 1 realizes his mixed signalling strategy by using his first and second row for signals, as described earlier.

Specification for the remaining stages when both players concur. The move of Player 1 in the first stage corresponds to a signal L or R which, in turn, yields by the contract a specific joint correlated strategy in the strategy spaces of the one-shot game. Now, a joint correlated strategy is, by definition, a probability distribution $\{\gamma_1, \gamma_2, \ldots, \gamma_r\}$ on the r locations (i.e., boxes) of the stage matrix, where r is the product of the number of rows and the number of columns in the matrix. These probabilities depend on the

---

[34]The game shown in Figure 10 is an example of such a game G, related to the Γ of Example 4.1. Here, as in Section 4, we use square brackets to denote the vectors in G.

signal. In the original infinitely repeated game one realizes this joint correlated strategy by a *frequency strategy* in the following fashion:

Construct r infinite sequences (a_n^t), $t = 1, \ldots, r$; $n = 1, 2, \ldots$, whose elements are 0's and 1's, so that:

(1) For all $t = 1, 2, \ldots, r$, select $a_1^t = 1$.

(2) For a particular t, if a_1^t, a_2^t, $\ldots$, a_{n-1}^t were selected, compute the average $(a_1^t + a_2^t + \cdots + a_{n-1}^t)/(n-1)$. If it is larger than $\gamma_1 + \gamma_2 + \cdots + \gamma_t$, choose $a_n^t = 0$; otherwise choose $a_n^t = 1$.

These sequences have three important properties:

(a) The last sequence contains only 1's.

(b) If $a_n^t = 1$, $t \leq r - 1$, then $a_n^{t+1} = 1$. In other words, each sequence contains all the 1's of the previous sequences.

(c) $\sum_{\nu=1}^{n} a_\nu^1 / n \to \gamma_1$, $\quad \sum_{\nu=1}^{n} a_\nu^2 / n \to \gamma_1 + \gamma_2, \ldots$.

The players should now agree on the following locations in the infinitely repeated game. At each stage $n + 1$, for $n = 1, 2, 3, \ldots$, they choose a row and a column so that they land on location t, where t is is the first for which $a_n^t = 1$.

For $r = 4$, for example, if the sequences are:

	$n =$	1	2	3	4	5	6	7	8	9	10	11	12	
	1	1	0	0	1	1	1	0	0	0	0	1	0	...
	2	1	0	1	1	1	1	1	0	0	1	1	0	...
t	3	1	0	1	1	1	1	1	1	0	1	1	1	...
	4	1	1	1	1	1	1	1	1	1	1	1	1	...

then the players choose rows and columns so as to land in locations 1, 4, 2, 1, 1, 1, 2, 3, 4, 2, 1, 3, $\ldots$. By (a), the procedure is well defined. By (b) and (c), as n tends to infinity, location t will be chosen γ_t of the time, $t = 1, 2, \ldots, r$. Thus, this procedure yields average expected payoff vectors converging to the payoff vector $\left(h_L^1(A), h_L^2(A) \right)$ or $\left(h_L^1(B), h_L^2(B) \right)$ or $\left(h_R^1(A), h_R^2(A) \right)$ or $\left(h_R^1(B), h_R^2(B) \right)$, as the type and the signal may be, in accordance with the payoffs determined by the contract. Consequently, the strategies described thus far yield an outcome (h^1, h^2) in the original game.

Specifications for detected violations. The preceding description
of the pair of strategies is not complete without specifying what
each player should do when he observes that the other player does
not follow the above procedure.

If Player 2 deviates from the above procedure at a certain
stage, then Player 1 should play a Blackwell strategy from that
stage on, so that Player 2's average expected payoff will be $w^2(p^L)$
or $w^2(p^R)$, where the alternative is chosen in accordance with the
signal in stage 1, assuming that $\Gamma_2(p^L)$ or $\Gamma_2(p^R)$, respectively, is
being played (see condition (ii)).

If Player 1 deviates from the above specifications at any stage
other than the first one,[35] then, from that stage on, Player 2
should play against him a Blackwell strategy for the game G that
forces the average expected payoffs into S^L or S^R in accordance
with the signal L or R made at the first stage. By condition (iii),
this is always possible.

It is now quite clear that the above strategies form an equilibrium pair. If Player 2 deviates he will receive $w^2(p^L)$ or $w^2(p^R)$,
depending on Player 1's signal at the first stage, instead of h_L^2
or h_R^2, respectively. By condition (ii), Player 2 cannot benefit by
such a deviation (cases for which $\alpha_L = 0$ or $\alpha_R = 0$ need not be
considered.) As for Player 1, he cannot gain by a deviation at any
stage after the first; for, by such a deviation, his vector payoff to
the two types reduces to a point in S^L or S^R, as the signal may
be, whereas abiding by the contract yields him $[h_L^1(A), h_L^1(B)]$ or
$[h_R^1(A), h_R^1(B)]$, respectively. By (6.15) and (6.16), neither type
can gain.

It remains to be shown that Player 1 cannot benefit by a deviation at the first stage. Indeed, if he uses a mixed signalling strategy
$(y_{LL}, y_{LR}, y_{RL}, y_{RR})$ instead of $(x_{LL}, x_{LR}, x_{RL}, x_{RR})$, but otherwise abides by the contract, he will receive an expected payoff
of

$$y_{LL}h_{LL}^1 + y_{LR}h_{LR}^1 + y_{RL}h_{RL}^1 + y_{RR}h_{RR}^1,$$

---

[35] Except for degenerate cases, where, e.g., the mixed signalling strategy specified L regardless of type and Player 1 signals R, a violation in the first stage
will not be detected by Player 2. We do not propose any "retaliation" even
in the exceptional cases.

which by condition (i) is not greater than his payoff in (6.10). This completes the proof of the theorem. ∎

We have succeeded in determining a class of equilibrium payoffs. It is interesting to note that such payoffs can be computed from entities concerning only one-shot games. The computation, however, is extremely involved, since it requires (at the least) the determination of values of a continuum of constant-sum games, the computation of approachable sets, and concavification operations.

7. More Equilibrium Points

Although the analysis of the previous section indicates that joint plans imitate only a relatively simple class of equilibrium pairs of strategies, it does not rule out the possibility that the *payoff vectors* generated by joint plans constitute *all* the equilibrium payoffs of the game. This will be true if each equilibrium payoff generated by a pair of "complicated" strategies can also be generated by a joint plan. The next example shows that *this is not the case*; we shall exhibit an equilibrium payoff that is not the payoff vector resulting from any joint plan, which satisfies the conditions of Theorem 6.1.

This example has additional merits: it will indicate how to extend the set of equilibrium payoffs found so far, and it will lead us to a proof that the set of equilibrium payoffs is convex.

EXAMPLE 7.1. Consider the infinitely-repeated game with the following stage-game matrices:

5, 3	0, 5	0, 0	0, 0	0, 0
0, 0	0, 5	0, 0	2, 6	0, 0
0, 0	0, 5	0, 0	0, 0	0, 0
0, 0	0, 5	0, 0	0, 0	0, 0

Player 1 type A (probability $= \frac{1}{2}$)

5, 3	0, 0	0, 5	0, 0	0, 0
0, 0	0, 0	0, 5	0, 0	0, 0
0, 0	0, 0	0, 5	0, 0	2, 6
0, 0	0, 0	0, 5	0, 0	0, 0

Player 1 type B
(probability $= \frac{1}{2}$)

CLAIM 1. *The payoff vector (4,4) is an equilibrium payoff.*

PROOF: (5,3) is an equilibrium payoff. Indeed, no signal is necessary; the players simply agree to play the upper left corner at each stage, and if Player 2 ever violates the agreement, then ever afterwards, Player 1 punishes him by selecting the last row. The punishment is effective since it reduces Player 2's expectation from 3 to at most $2\frac{1}{2}$. Clearly, the agreement is an equilibrium pair of strategies.

(2,6) is also an equilibrium payoff. Indeed, the players can agree on a completely revealing signalling strategy and then contract at (2,6) for each type.

Note that $(4, 4) = \frac{2}{3}(5, 3) + \frac{1}{3}(2, 6)$. We shall exhibit an equilibrium pair of strategies leading to this expected payoff vector.

Specifications for Stage 1. Player 1 chooses one of the first three rows with equal probabilities. Player 2 chooses one of the first three columns with equal probabilities. This is indicated in the following table.

	1/3	1/3	1/3	
1/3	b	a	a	...
1/3	a	b	a	...
1/3	a	a	b	...
	...	...	...	...

Specifications for the Remaining Stages. If the players landed in stage 1 at a location marked a, they proceed with an equilibrium pair of strategies leading to the expected payoff vector (5,3). If they landed in a location marked b, they proceed with an equilibrium pair of strategies leading to the expected payoff vector (2,6).

If Player 1 chose at the first stage a row other than the first three rows ("a detected violation"), Player 2 punishes him for the remaining stages by always picking the second column. If Player 2 chose at the first stage a column other than the first three columns ("a detected violation"), Player 1 punishes him for the remaining stages by always picking the last row.

Clearly, if both players abide by the above strategies, the outcome is (4,4). It is also clear that it does not pay Player 1 to deviate unilaterally at stage 1 by picking a row other than the first three, nor does he benefit by deviating unilaterally at any other stage. Similarly, Player 2 does not benefit by unilaterally deviating at stage 1 by picking a column other than the first three, nor by deviating unilaterally at any other stage. There is still the possibility of a player deviating unilaterally at the first stage by choosing the first three rows or columns with probabilities other than (1/3, 1/3, 1/3). Such a deviation, although not detectable, could not benefit the deviating player, because if the other player stays with the above specifications, the probability of landing at a location marked a remains 2/3, and the probability of landing at a location marked b remains 1/3.

The specifications for stage 1 are such that each player controls the probability of landing at a or b regardless of any possible undetected deviation by the other player. We express such specifications briefly by saying that at stage 1 the players perform a *jointly controlled lottery* with two outcomes whose probabilities are 2/3 and 1/3.

We have just proved that the above strategies are an equilibrium pair. This shows that (4,4) is indeed an equilibrium payoff. Figure 15 is a graphical representation of the processes involved.
∎

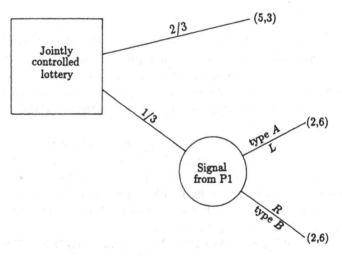

Figure 15. An equilibrium pair of strategies leading to (4,4).

CLAIM 2. *(4,4) is not an outcome of any joint plan satisfying the conditions of Theorem 6.1.*

PROOF: Suppose there is such a joint plan yielding (4,4). Denote by $L^1, L^2, \ldots, L^s$ those signals to which Player 2 attributes positive probability, and by $p^1, p^2, \ldots, p^s$ the conditional probabilities that Player 1 is of type A, given those signals.

The sum of the coordinates of $(4,4)$ is 8. This is also the highest sum of coordinates of the entries of the stage-game matrices. Consequently, for each signal L^ν, the contract must yield a payoff $(h^1_{L^\nu}, h^2_{L^\nu})$ with $h^1_{L^\nu} + h^2_{L^\nu} = 8$. Since

$$
\begin{aligned}
(h^1_{L^\nu}, h^2_{L^\nu}) \\
= p^\nu \left(h^1_{L^\nu}(A), h^2_{L^\nu}(A) \right) + (1 - p^\nu) \left(h^1_{L^\nu}(B), h^2_{L^\nu}(B) \right),
\end{aligned}
\tag{7.1}
$$

it follows that if $p^\nu \neq 0, 1$, then $both$ $h^1_{L^\nu}(A) + h^2_{L^\nu}(A) = 8$ and $h^1_{L^\nu}(B) + h^2_{L^\nu}(B) = 8$. Note, however, that a contract is a joint probability distribution on locations and that it does not distinguish between the type matrices. Consequently, if $p^\nu \neq 0, 1$, then $\left(h^1_{L^\nu}(A), h^2_{L^\nu}(A) \right) = \left(h^1_{L^\nu}(B), h^2_{L^\nu}(B) \right) = (5, 3)$, because only the upper left corner has an entry the sum of whose coordinates is 8 in both stage-game matrices. We conclude that no ν exists with $p^\nu \neq 0, 1$, since otherwise Player 1 could cheat by always signalling L^ν, thereby obtaining a payoff of 5 instead of 4. Thus, for each $\nu = 1, 2, \ldots, s$, either $p^\nu = 0$ or $p^\nu = 1$. In other words, the signalling strategy must be completely revealing. Once Player 2 knows Player 1's type, he can guarantee himself a payoff of 5 by choosing the second column against type A and the third column against type B. This, again, contradicts the assumption that the joint plan yields $(4,4)$ as a payoff vector. We conclude that $(4,4)$ is not an outcome of a joint plan satisfying the conditions of Theorem 6.1. ∎

Example 7.1 illustrates another task that can be performed during the first stage of an infinitely-repeated game. The players may perform a jointly controlled lottery.[36] In this example, the lottery had two outcomes, with probabilities $2/3$ and $1/3$. We shall now show that it is possible to construct any jointly controlled lottery on two outcomes[37] (provided, of course, that the stage-game matrices have at least two rows). Such a construction, however, may involve more than one stage. In fact, although the probability of ending the lottery in a finite number of stages is 1,

---

[36] Note that in the equilibrium pair of strategies in this example the first stage was not used to pass on any additional information on Player 1's type.
[37] The generalization to more than two outcomes is straightforward.

one cannot, in general, set an *a priori* bound on the number of strategies needed.

Construction of a jointly controlled lottery on two outcomes with probabilities α and $(1 - \alpha)$, $0 < \alpha < 1$.

Case A. Suppose $\alpha = k/2^n$, where k and n are positive integers. Arbitrarily choose k distinct sequences s^1, s^2, ..., s^k, of n elements each, whose elements are either zeros or ones. The jointly controlled lottery is performed by the following n-stage process:

At each of the n stages, both players choose independently their first and second strategies (rows or columns) with equal probabilities.

Denote by 1 the event in which either both players chose their first strategy (i.e., 1st row and 1st column were chosen), or both chose their second strategy (i.e., 2nd row and 2nd column were chosen). Denote by 0 the event in which one player chose his first strategy and the other chose his second strategy (i.e., 1st row and 2nd column, or 2nd row and 1st column, were chosen).

If both players abide by this process, the outcome is a sequence of zeros and ones of length n. If the outcome is one of previously chosen sequences s^1, s^2, ..., s^k, we say that the result of the lottery is P. If the outcome is a sequence other than s^1, s^2, ..., s^k, we say that the result of the lottery is Q.

The process has the following properties:

(i) If both players abide by it, the probability that P occurs is α and the probability that Q occurs is $1 - \alpha$. Thus this process represents a jointly performed lottery with probabilities α and $1 - \alpha$ on two outcomes.

(ii) If one player abides by the process and the other does not, then there are two possibilities: (a) The deviation is *detected*, which occurs whenever a row other than the first or second is selected or a column other than the first or second is selected. (b) The deviation is not detected. In this case the probabilities that P and Q occur are still α and $1-\alpha$, respectively. This is because if one player selects his first or second move with equal probability, then at each stage the probability that 1 results is $1/2$, regardless of the probabilities used by the other player in selecting his own first or second move.

We conclude, therefore, that this process is a jointly controlled lottery.

Case B. Suppose no n and k exist such that $\alpha = k/2^n$. In other words, suppose that the representation of α as a binary fraction is non-terminating. Choose a strictly increasing sequence of positive finite binary fractions $\alpha_1, \alpha_2, \alpha_3, \ldots$, such that

$$\lim_{n \to \infty} \alpha_n = \alpha, \tag{7.2}$$

and

$$0 < \alpha - \alpha_n \leq (1-\alpha)/2^{n+1}. \tag{7.3}$$

The process proceeds as follows:

Starting with the first stage, each player chooses at each stage his first and second row/column with equal probabilities. The selections are made independently. They continue doing so until the event "1" occurs for the first time (recall that "1" means, either both choose "first" or both choose "second".) Denote by n the stage in which this event happens. The players use the subsequent stages to perform a jointly controlled lottery, replacing α by the finite binary fraction $\beta_n = \alpha_{n-1} + (2^n - 1)(\alpha_n - \alpha_{n-1})$, where α_0 is defined as zero. They do so by the process described in Case A.

Note that

$$0 < \beta_n < \alpha_{n-1} + 2^n(\alpha - \alpha_{n-1}) < \alpha_{n-1} + (1-\alpha) < 1;$$

hence, the process is well defined.

Although one cannot specify an upper bound for n, with probability 1 the process will terminate after a finite number of stages. Let us compute the probability that the event P will occur. This probability is

$$\begin{aligned}
\mathrm{Exp}(\beta_n) &= \frac{1}{2}\beta_1 + \frac{1}{4}\beta_2 + \frac{1}{8}\beta_3 + \cdots \\
&= \frac{1}{2}\alpha_1 + \frac{1}{4}(\alpha_1 + 3(\alpha_2 - \alpha_1)) + \cdots \\
&\quad + \frac{1}{2^n}(\alpha_{n-1} + (2^n - 1)(\alpha_n - \alpha_{n-1})) + \cdots \\
&= \alpha.
\end{aligned}$$

It is easy to verify that properties (i) and (ii) of Case A hold also in this case. Note that no information on Player 1's type is revealed by the process, because both types act in the same way.[38]

We shall use the construction for performing a jointly controlled lottery in order to provide the next important results.

THEOREM 7.2. *The set of equilibrium payoffs of a 2-person infinitely repeated game with incomplete information on the part of Player 2 is convex.*

PROOF: Let (h_1^1, h_1^2) and (h_2^1, h_2^2) be two equilibrium payoffs. Let α be an arbitrary real number with $0 < \alpha < 1$. We must show that $\alpha(h_1^1, h_1^2) + (1 - \alpha)(h_2^1, h_2^2)$ is an equilibrium payoff. Denote by (σ_1, τ_1) and (σ_2, τ_2) equilibrium pairs of strategies that yield the expected payoff vectors (h_1^1, h_1^2) and (h_2^1, h_2^2), respectively. The following is an equilibrium pair of strategies that yields the desired expected payoff:

The players perform a jointly controlled lottery on two outcomes P and Q with probabilities α and $1 - \alpha$, respectively. If P results, the players proceed with (σ_1, τ_1). If Q results, they proceed with (σ_2, τ_2). We can eliminate the possibility of a detected violation of Player 1, during the lottery part, by dividing his rows into two disjoint sets, and treating a choice from the first [second] set like the first [second] row in the above construction. Similarly for Player 2.

It may be verified that all the above requirements are fulfilled.

Example 7.1 shows that Theorem 7.2 yields equilibrium payoffs that were not obtained in Section 6. Since there exist equilibrium payoffs that do not result from joint plans (as in Section 6), and since the set of equilibrium payoffs is necessarily convex, it is natural to conjecture that any equilibrium payoff can be derived from a set of joint plans by convexification.

---

[38] Here is another method of constructing a jointly controlled lottery, which generates an event P with probability α and an event Q with probability $1 - \alpha$: Let $a_1, a_2, a_3, \ldots$ be the binary expression of α. By the method of Case A, the players produce a sequence $b_1, b_2, b_3, \ldots$ of numbers 0, or 1, each independently occurring with probability $1/2$, jointly controlled by the players. The process continues until the first time $b_i \neq a_i$, for some i. If $a_i > b_i$ then P is the choice. If $a_i < b_i$ then Q is the choice. Note that the probability of ending the process at each stage is $1/2$ and therefore the process does generate the event P with probability α.(*)

In the next section we show that this conjecture is false.

8. More Equilibrium Payoffs

Suppose one studies a noncooperative game and finds a wealth of equilibrium payoffs. Why should he look for others? First, because he may miss some equilibrium payoffs that would strengthen the bargaining position of one of the players; and second, he may even miss equilibrium payoffs that *both* players prefer. We shall see in this section that we are far from exhausting all the equilibrium payoffs in repeated games with incomplete information. As a matter of fact, there may even be games for which *no* joint plan ever satisfies the conditions of theorem 6.1. For such a game (if one does exist) we have no general method of determining even one equilibrium payoff; in fact there may even exist repeated games that have no equilibrium payoff at all.[39]

EXAMPLE 8.1. Player 1 has three types, A, B and C, considered equally likely by Player 2. Their stage game matrices are

5,3	0,5	0,0	0,0	0,0	0,0
0,0	0,5	0,0	0,0	0,0	0,0
0,0	0,5	0,0	2,6	0,0	0,0
0,0	0,5	0,0	0,0	0,0	4,0
0,0	0,5	0,0	0,0	0,0	0,0

Player 1, type A

---

[39] See the notes for later developments on these issues.(*)

5, 3	0, 0	0, 5	0, 0	0, 0	0, 0
0, 0	0, 0	0, 5	0, 0	2, 6	0, 0
0, 0	0, 0	0, 5	0, 0	0, 0	0, 0
0, 0	0, 0	0, 5	0, 0	0, 0	4, 0
0, 0	0, 0	0, 5	0, 0	0, 0	0, 0

Player 1, type B

0, 0	0, 0	0, 0	0, 0	0, 0	0, 0
0, 0	0, 0	0, 0	0, 0	0, 0	0, 0
0, 0	0, 0	0, 0	0, 0	0, 0	0, 0
0, 0	0, 0	0, 0	0, 0	0, 0	0, 0
0, 0	0, 0	0, 0	0, 0	0, 0	4, 4
0, 0	0, 0	0, 0	0, 0	0, 0	0, 0

Player 1, type C

CLAIM 1. The point (4,4) is an equilibrium payoff of this infinitely repeated game.

PROOF: An equilibrium pair of strategies is represented graphically in Figure 16. Player 1 signals in stage 1 whether he is of type C (signal R) or not (signal L). If he is, both players settle on

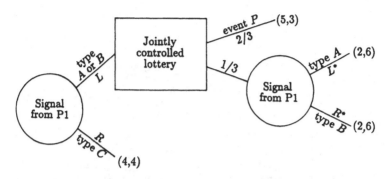

Figure 16. An equilibrium pair of strategies
yielding (4,4) in the game of Example 3.1.

the location that, for type C, yields (4,4). They play this location
for the remaining stages.

If Player 1 is not of type C, then stage 2 is used to perform a
jointly controlled lottery on two outcomes P and Q with probabilities 2/3 and 1/3, respectively, using either the general method
described in Section 6, or the specific method described in Example 7.1. A detected violation by Player 1 is punished by Player 2
choosing the second column for the remaining stages. A detected
violation by Player 2 is punished by Player 1 choosing the last
row for the remaining stages. Similar punishments are made for
detected violations in the first stage.

If P results, both players settle on the upper left corner for
the remaining stages, which yields (5,3) for both types A and B.
If Q results, Player 1 uses the third stage to signal whether he
is type A or type B. A detected violation is punished as before.
After this second signal the players settle on the location that
yields the payoff (2,6) for the appropriate type.

If both players abide by these strategies, the expected payoff
is

$$\frac{1}{3}(4,4) + \frac{2}{3}\left(\frac{2}{3}(5,3) + \frac{1}{3}(2,6)\right) = (4,4). \qquad (8.1)$$

It is a straightforward matter to verify that these strategies do
indeed form an equilibrium pair. Let us only note that if Player 1
cheats in stage 1 and signals as if he is of type C when, in fact, he
is of type A or B, he gets the same expected payoff; namely, 4. ∎

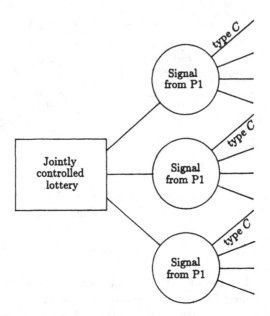

Figure 17. A hypothetical jointly controlled
lottery yielding (4,4).

CLAIM 2. The payoff vector (4,4) cannot be achieved as a lottery on equilibrium payoffs generated by joint plans satisfying the
conditions of Theorem 6.1.

PROOF: Suppose it can; then we have a jointly controlled lottery
followed by a signalling strategy and a contract for each outcome
of the lottery (Figure 17). Note that the maximum sum of the
components of the entries in the stage-game matrices is 8 and
the sum of the components of the payoff vector (4,4) is also 8.
Consequently, the joint plan associated with every outcome of the
lottery that occurs with positive probability must yield a payoff
vector the sum of whose components is 8. Consider such a joint
plan, and look at the expected payoff, for each type separately.
Again, each type should expect a payoff vector the sum of whose
components is 8. In particular, the contract should assign the
location in the second-to-last row and last column to each signal
that a type C Player 1 signals with positive probability, and should
not assign this location to any signal that a type A or B Player 1

signals with positive probability. We conclude that the mixed signalling strategy of the joint plan, together with the observed signal, completely reveals whether or not Player 1 is of type C.

Suppose Player 1 is not of type C; then the contract must assign to his signals a convex combination of $(5,3)$ and $(2,6)$. Since $(2,6)$ occurs at different locations for types A and B, a signal in which $(2,6)$ is involved with positive probability must be a completely revealing signal. This, however, is impossible, because if the contract assigns $\alpha(5,3) + (1-\alpha)(2,6)$ to a completely revealing signal, $0 \leq \alpha \leq 1$, then, in order for Player 2 not to profit by violating it, we must have

$$3\alpha + 6(1-\alpha) \geq 5; \qquad (8.2)$$

and in order for a type A or B Player 1 not to prefer to cheat and signal as if he is of type C, we must have

$$5\alpha + 2(1-\alpha) \geq 4. \qquad (8.3)$$

(8.2) implies $\alpha \leq \frac{1}{3}$ and (8.3) implies $\alpha \geq \frac{2}{3}$; these two conditions contradict each other.

We conclude that the contract must assign the payoff vector $(5,3)$ to each signal made by a type A or B Player 1 in any joint plan; and it must assign the payoff vector $(4,4)$ to any signal made by a type C Player 1 in any joint plan. (Of course we consider only joint plans and signals that occur with positive probability.) This again yields a contradiction, because it gives Player 1 an expected payoff higher than 4; consequently, the outcome $(4,4)$ cannot result from a convex combination of joint plans satisfying the conditions of Theorem 6.1. ∎

The next, somewhat more complicated example shows that the same phenomenon may occur even when Player 1 has only two types.

EXAMPLE 8.2. The stage-game matrices for the two types of Player 1 are given by

	a	b	c	d	e
1	$4\frac{1}{8},3\frac{7}{8}$	$-N,5$	$-N,0$	$-N,0$	$-N,0$
2	$-N,0$	$-N,5$	$-N,0$	$1,7$	$-N,0$
3	$-N,0$	$-N,5$	$-N,0$	$-N,0$	$-N,0$
4	$-N,0$	$4,5$	$-N,0$	$-N,0$	$-N,0$

Player 1, type A

	a	b	c	d	e
1	$4\frac{1}{8},3\frac{7}{8}$	$-N,0$	$-N,6\frac{11}{24}$	$-N,0$	$-N,0$
2	$-N,0$	$-N,0$	$-N,6\frac{11}{24}$	$-N,0$	$-N,0$
3	$-N,0$	$-N,0$	$-N,6\frac{11}{24}$	$-N,0$	$1,7$
4	$-N,0$	$-N,0$	$-N,6\frac{11}{24}$	$-N,0$	$-N,0$

Player 1, type B

Player 1's types are considered equally likely by Player 2. Here N is a very large number whose size is to be determined in the sequel.

Consider the following pair of strategies, represented graphically in Figure 18.

Type A of Player 1 signals L or R with probabilities 2/3 and 1/3, respectively. Type B of Player 1 signals L.

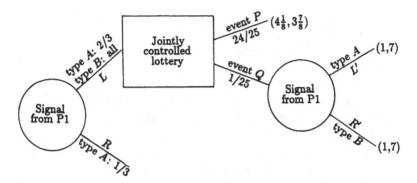

Figure 18. An equilibrium pair of strategies
yielding $(4, 4\frac{1}{6})$ in the game of Example 8.2.

On an R signal both players settle on location[40] $4b$ for the rest
of the stages; and, since R reveals that Player 1 is of type A, the
resulting payoff vector is $(4,5)$.

If the signal is L, the players perform a jointly controlled lottery on two alternatives P and Q with probabilities $24/25$ and
$1/25$, respectively. If P is the result, they settle on the location
$1a$ for the rest of the stages, yielding $(4\frac{1}{8}, 3\frac{7}{8})$ for either type. If Q
is the result, Player 1 signals again, this time completely reveal-
ing his type; the players then settle, for the rest of the stages, on
the location that yields the payoff vector $(1,7)$ to the appropriate
type. A detected deviation on the part of Player 1 is punished by
Player 2 choosing his third strategy (column c) for the rest of the
stages; a detected deviation on the part of Player 2 is punished
by Player 1 choosing row 4 for the rest of the stages.

If both players abide by these strategies, the expected payoff
vector is

$$\frac{1}{2}\left(\frac{1}{3}(4,5) + \frac{2}{3}\left(\frac{24}{25}(4\frac{1}{8}, 3\frac{7}{8}) + \frac{1}{25}(1,7)\right)\right)$$
$$+ \frac{1}{2}\left(\frac{24}{25}(4\frac{1}{8}, 3\frac{7}{8}) + \frac{1}{25}(1,7)\right) = (4, 4\frac{1}{6}).$$

(8.4)

---

[40] "Location $4b$" means that Player 1 chooses row 4, his 4th strategy, and
Player 2 chooses column b, his 2nd strategy.

To show that this is an equilibrium pair of strategies, it will be sufficient to verify that (i) Player 1 does not benefit by signalling differently at the beginning, and (ii) the information delivered by Player 1 at the first signal is not enough to enable Player 2 to benefit by deviating and gain more than $3\frac{7}{8}$ in case the signal is L and the result of the lottery is P. All other possible unilateral deviations can be checked to be unprofitable.

As for (i), Player 1's expectation if he sends signal L is $\frac{24}{25}(4\frac{1}{8})+\frac{1}{25}(1) = 4$ for each type. His expectation if he sends signal R is 4 for type A and $-N$ for type B. Thus, he does not benefit by cheating.

To verify (ii), observe that the conditional probability p^R that Player 1 is of type A, given that Player 1 signals R, is 1, so Player 2 certainly loses by deviating unilaterally. If Player 1 signals L, then the conditional probability p^L is $\frac{1}{2}\cdot\frac{2}{3}/(\frac{1}{2}\cdot\frac{2}{3}+\frac{1}{2}\cdot 1) = \frac{2}{5}$. Thus, as long as no further information is given, the stage game, as viewed by Player 2, is a combination of the two stage-game matrices in the proportions 2/5 and 3/5. Assuming that Player 1 sticks to his first row, Player 2 must consider the row

$4\frac{1}{8},3\frac{7}{8}$	$-N,2$	$-N,3\frac{7}{8}$	$-N,0$	$-N,0$

which shows that Player 2 does not benefit by shifting unilaterally from the first column.

We conclude, therefore, that $(4,4\frac{1}{6})$ is an equilibrium payoff.

We shall now show that $(4,4\frac{1}{6})$ is *not* a convex combination of equilibrium payoffs that result from joint plans satisfying the conditions of Theorem 6.1.

The idea of the proof is to show that all the joint plans satisfying the conditions of Theorem 6.1 lead to payoffs that lie on one side of a certain line l^*, whereas $(4,4\frac{1}{6})$ lies (strictly) on the other side. If this is the case, then $(4,4\frac{1}{6})$ cannot be in the convex hull of the equilibrium payoffs that result from such joint plans.

The line l^* is a line, parallel to the line l that connects the points $(2\frac{37}{48},5\frac{35}{48})$ and $(4\frac{1}{16},4\frac{1}{16})$, whose distance from l is ε, where

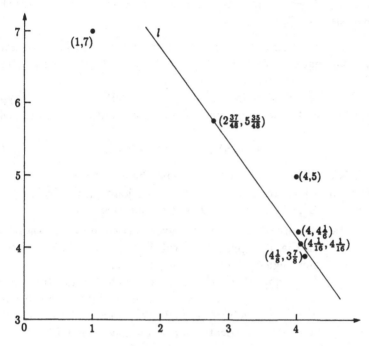

Figure 19. Looking for joint plans yielding equilibrium payoffs above l.

ε is a sufficiently small positive number, such that l^* lies above l but below the point $(4, 4\frac{1}{6})$ (see Figure 19).

STEP 1. The equation of l is

$$640x + 496y = 4615, \qquad (8.5)$$

and the point $(4, 4\frac{1}{6})$ lies above it.

STEP 2. All the entries in all the stage game matrices lie below l, with the exception of $(4, 5)$. If $(4, 4\frac{1}{6})$ lies in the convex hull of some set of equilibrium payoff vectors resulting from joint plans, then at least one of those joint plans, which we denote J, must involve $(4, 5)$ as a payoff in the contract. We therefore proceed to hunt for joint plans in which $(4, 5)$ is involved, because only those can possibly yield payoff vectors above l^*. We wish to show that if N is sufficiently large, no such joint plan J can satisfy the conditions of Theorem 6.1.

STEP 3. Let L be a signal in the joint plan J to which the contract of J associates a jointly controlled lottery involving[41] the location $4b$.

Let p^L be the conditional probability that Player 1 is of type A, given that L was announced. The contribution of location $4b$ is

$$p^L(4,5) + (1 - p^L)(-N,0). \qquad (8.6)$$

If N is very large, then, for (8.6) to be above l^* it is necessary that p^L be very near to 1. Let us replace the joint plan J by another joint plan J', obtained from J by the following changes:

  (a) Whenever type B of Player 1 is supposed to signal L in the joint plan J, he will instead signal a completely new signal L^* in the new joint plan J'.

  (b) The contract of J' should associate the location $4b$ to L (even though the contract of J might have specified a lottery involving $4b$ and other locations), and should associate the location $3e$ to the new signal L^*.

The new joint plan J' satisfies the conditions of Theorem 6.1 if J does. This follows from the fact that signals other than L and L^* reveal the same information as before and are associated with the same joint lotteries; whereas L and L^*, which are now completely revealing, are associated with equilibrium payoffs for the types A and B, respectively.

If the original joint plan J yielded a payoff vector above l^*, and if N is sufficiently large, then the new joint plan J' yields a payoff vector above a line l^{**} which runs parallel to, and midway between, l and l^*. This can be verified by noting that all the changes push the payoff towards the upper side of l^* except, perhaps, the change to the payoff $(1,7)$ associated with the new signal L^*. However, by choosing to analyze a game with a sufficiently large N, we can require that the original p^L was as near to 1 as desired, and thereby require that the probability that type B of Player 1 signals

---

[41] We assume that both this lottery outcome and the signal occur with positive probability in the joint plan.

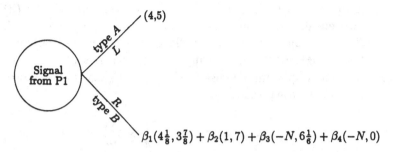

$$\beta_1(4\tfrac{1}{8},3\tfrac{7}{8}) + \beta_2(1,7) + \beta_3(-N,6\tfrac{1}{6}) + \beta_4(-N,0)$$

Figure 20. Looking for completely revealing
joint plans generating payoffs above l^{**}.

L^* is as small as we please,[42] making the influence of the change
to $(1,7)$ negligible.

STEP 4. We are looking for joint plans satisfying the conditions
of Theorem 6.1 in which the mixed signalling strategy is such
that a certain signal L, which occurs with positive probability,
completely reveals that Player 1 is of type A, while the payoff
vector associated with L is $(4,5)$; and a certain signal L^*, which
occurs with positive probability, completely reveals that Player 1
is of type B, while the payoff vector associated with L^* is $(1,7)$.
We require, moreover, that the payoff vector that results from the
joint plan lies above l^{**} (see Step 3).

There are two possibilities: Either type A of Player 1 always
signals L, or else he also signals some other signal with non-zero
probability. The first case will be treated in this step, and the
second case will be treated in Steps 5 and 6.

Assume therefore that type A of Player 1 always signals L. The
signalling strategy is then completely revealing. We can, therefore,
combine all the signals made by type B of Player 1 into a single
signal R to which the contract assigns a lottery with expectation

$$\beta_1(4\frac{1}{8},3\frac{7}{8}) + \beta_2(1,7) + \beta_3(-N,6\frac{11}{24}) + \beta_4(-N,0), \qquad (8.7)$$

where
$$\beta_1,\beta_2,\beta_3,\beta_4 \geq 0 \text{ and } \beta_1 + \beta_2 + \beta_3 + \beta_4 = 1$$

(see Figure 20).

---

[42]Because the original probability of B is $1/2$.(*)

In order for Player 2 to abide by the contract (condition (ii) of Theorem 6.1), it is necessary that for each signal made with positive probability by a type B Player 1, his expected outcome is at least $6\frac{11}{24}$, because, knowing that Player 1 is of this type, Player 2 could guarantee himself $6\frac{11}{24}$ by picking his third strategy (column c). Consequently,

$$\beta_1 \cdot 3\frac{7}{8} + \beta_2 \cdot 7 + \beta_3 \cdot 6\frac{11}{24} \geq 6\frac{11}{24}. \tag{8.8}$$

Replacing β_2 by $1 - \beta_1 - \beta_3 - \beta_4$, we obtain

$$0 \leq \beta_1 \leq \frac{13}{75}. \tag{8.9}$$

Let us now estimate the expected payoff vector (h^1, h^2) of the joint plan. We have

$$(h^1, h^2) = \frac{1}{2}(4,5) +$$
$$\frac{1}{2}\left(\beta_1(3\frac{1}{8}, -3\frac{1}{8}) + (1,7) - \beta_3(N+1, \frac{13}{24}) - \beta_4(N+1, 7)\right)$$
$$\leq \frac{1}{2}(4,5) + \frac{1}{2}\left(\beta_1(3\frac{1}{8}, -3\frac{1}{8}) + (1,7)\right). \tag{8.10}$$

The last expression yields a straight line segment, for $0 \leq \beta_1 \leq \frac{13}{75}$, whose end points are $(2\frac{1}{2}, 6)$ and $(2\frac{37}{48}, 5\frac{35}{48})$. The first end point lies below l and the second end point lies on l; therefore, the straight line segment lies below l^{**}, and consequently (h^1, h^2) lies below l^{**}.

STEP 5. Assume that L^* occurs with positive probability. Consider now the possibility that, in addition to L-signals which are used only by type A, and L^*-signals which are used only by type B, there exist S-signals that are used by both types with positive probability. The situation is represented schematically in Figure 21. Since the L-signals and the L^*-signals completely reveal that Player 1 is of type A or type B, respectively, we can replace them by single signals. Moreover, as before, we can make changes in the payoffs associated with these signals, which shift the expected payoff of the joint plan towards the upper side of l^{**}. Thus, we associate with L the payoff $(4,5)$ and with L^* the payoff[43] $\beta_1(3\frac{1}{8}, -3\frac{1}{8}) + (1,7)$, where, by the results of Step 4, $0 \leq \beta_1 \leq \frac{13}{75}$.

In order for type A of Player 1 not to benefit by cheating, his expected payoff on each signal S_ν, $\nu = 1, 2, \ldots, r$, must be 4, which is the payoff he gets when he signals L. Similarly, the expected payoff to type B of Player 1 on a signal S_ν must be $\beta_1 \cdot 3\frac{1}{8} + 1$.

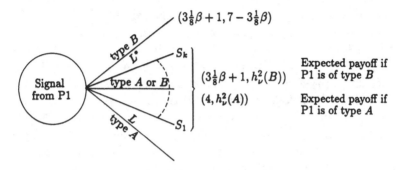

Figure 21. A situation in which all types of signals occur with positive probability.

Let us look more closely at the lottery that the contract associates with a signal S_ν, $\nu = 1, 2, \ldots, r$. We shall denote by $\left(h_\nu^1(A), h_\nu^2(A)\right)$ the expected payoffs to players 1 and 2, respectively, when Player 1 is actually of type A, the signal S_ν is given, and the associated lottery is carried out. We shall also denote by $\left(h_\nu^1(B), h_\nu^2(B)\right)$ the pair of corresponding expected payoffs when Player 1 is actually of type B. Then

$$\left(h_\nu^1(A), h_\nu^2(A)\right) = \left(4, h_\nu^2(A)\right)$$

$$= \gamma_1(4\frac{1}{8}, 3\frac{7}{8}) + \gamma_2(-N, 0) + \gamma_3(-N, 5) + \gamma_4(-N, 0) +$$

$$\gamma_5(-N, 0) + \gamma_6(1, 7) + \gamma_7(4, 5), \tag{8.11}$$

---

[43]We replace $\beta_3(-N, 6\frac{11}{24}) + \beta_4(-N, 0)$ by $(\beta_3 + \beta_4)(1, 7)$.

and

$$\left(h_\nu^1\,(B), h_\nu^2(B)\right) = \left((\beta_1 \cdot 3\frac{1}{8} + 1, h_\nu^2(B)\right)$$

$$= \gamma_1(4\frac{1}{8}, 3\frac{7}{8}) + \gamma_2(-N, 0) + \gamma_3(-N, 0) + \gamma_4(-N, 6\frac{11}{24}) +$$

$$\gamma_5(1, 7) + \gamma_6(-N, 0) + \gamma_7(-N, 0). \qquad (8.12)$$

Here, the expected payoffs are written in such a way as to summarize the essentially distinct outcomes that are possible under the contract, so that $\gamma_\mu = \gamma_\mu(S_\nu) \geq 0$, $\mu = 1, 2, \ldots, 7$, $\nu = 1, 2, \ldots, r$, and $\gamma_1 + \gamma_2 + \gamma_3 + \gamma_4 + \gamma_5 + \gamma_6 + \gamma_7 = 1$. It follows from (8.11) that $-(\gamma_2 + \gamma_3 + \gamma_4 + \gamma_5)N = 4 - \gamma_1 \cdot 4\frac{1}{8} - \gamma_6 - \gamma_7 \cdot 4$. Therefore, if N is very large, $(\gamma_2 + \gamma_3 + \gamma_4 + \gamma_5)$ must be a very small positive number. Similarly, it follows from (8.12) that $(\gamma_2 + \gamma_3 + \gamma_4 + \gamma_6 + \gamma_7)$ is very small. Consequently, by considering a game with N sufficiently large, we can ensure that such a joint plan must have $\gamma_2, \gamma_3, \gamma_4, \gamma_5, \gamma_6$, and γ_7, as small as we want. It follows that, for a given arbitrarily small positive number ε_1, we can choose N so large that

$$\left(h_\nu^1(A), h_\nu^2(A)\right) \leq (4,\ 3\frac{7}{8} + \varepsilon_1),$$

$$\left(h_\nu^1(B), h_\nu^2(B)\right) \leq (\beta \cdot 3\frac{1}{8} + 1,\ 3\frac{7}{8} + \varepsilon_1). \qquad (8.13)$$

If we increase these expected payoff vectors to $(4,5)$ and $\left(\beta_1 \cdot 3\frac{1}{8} + 1, 7 - \beta_1 \cdot 3\frac{1}{8} + \varepsilon_1\right)$, respectively, we shift the expected payoff towards the upper side of l^{**}. Even so, the expected payoff $\frac{1}{2}(4,5) + \frac{1}{2}(\beta_1(3\frac{1}{8}, -3\frac{1}{8}) + (1, 7 + \varepsilon_1))$ lies below l^{**} for $0 \leq \beta_1 \leq \frac{13}{75}$, and ε_1 sufficiently small, as we saw in Step 4. We conclude that no joint plan of the type described in this case can possibly yield an expected payoff vector above l^{**}.

STEP 6. There remains only one possibility for a joint plan J such as described in Step 3: that the mixed signalling strategy is such

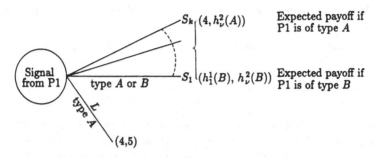

Figure 22. A situation in which signals exist
identifying Player 1 as being of type A but no
signal identifies type B completely.

that no signal completely identifies type B; i.e., L^* occurs with 0
probability. Figure 22 represents this situation schematically.

Here we can only conclude that $h^1_\nu(A) = 4$ for $\nu = 1, 2, \ldots, r$,
since no requirement is placed on $h^1_\nu(B)$. This implies that if we
had selected a game whose N was sufficiently large, we would have
required $\gamma_2 + \gamma_3 + \gamma_4 + \gamma_5$ to be as small as we wished. By (8.12),
this implies that $h^2_\nu(B) < 3\frac{7}{8} + \varepsilon_2$, where ε_2 is an arbitrarily small
positive number.

Let us denote by s^L the probability (derived from the signalling
strategy) that type A of Player 1 signals L. Also, let us denote
by s^ν the probability that a type A Player 1 signals S_ν, for $\nu =
1, \ldots, r$. The corresponding signals for type B will be denoted t^L
and t^ν, where we already know that $t^L = 0$.

The probability that Player 1 is of type B, given that a signal
S_ν was announced, is $t^\nu / (s^\nu + t^\nu)$. Therefore, Player 2 can guarantee himself $t^\nu \cdot 6\frac{11}{24} / (s^\nu + t^\nu)$, given that S_ν was announced, by
choosing his third column. Consequently, in order for the joint
plan to represent an equilibrium payoff, its contract must assign
Player 2 at least that much on a signal S_ν. Thus

$$3\frac{7}{8} + \varepsilon_2 \geq \frac{t^\nu}{s^\nu + t^\nu} \cdot 6\frac{11}{24}. \tag{8.14}$$

Simplifying (8.14), we obtain

$$s^\nu \geq t^\nu \left(\frac{2}{3} - \varepsilon_3\right), \tag{8.15}$$

where ε_3 is a positive number, which can be chosen as small as we wish.

Summing (8.15) for $\nu = 1, 2, \ldots, r$, we arrive finally at

$$s^L \leq \frac{1}{3} + \varepsilon_3. \tag{8.16}$$

Let us now aggregate all the signals S_ν, $\nu = 1, 2, \ldots, r$, into a single joint lottery S (see Figure 23), and adopt the notation of (8.11) and (8.12). The first equation of (8.12) does not hold, but we can conclude, just from equation (8.11), that $\gamma_2 + \gamma_3 + \gamma_4 + \gamma_5$ is a very small positive number if N is large; we cannot conclude that $\gamma_6 + \gamma_7$ is small, and therefore must weaken (8.13) to

$$(h_S^1(A), h_S^2(A))$$
$$\leq (4, 3\frac{7}{8} + 7\gamma_6 + 5\gamma_7 + \varepsilon_4),$$
$$(h_S^1(B), h_S^2(B))$$
$$\leq (4\frac{1}{8} - N(\gamma_6 + \gamma_7) + \varepsilon_5, 3\frac{7}{8} + \varepsilon_6), \tag{8.17}$$

where ε_4, ε_5, ε_6, are arbitrarily small positive numbers.

Finally, we can estimate the expected payoff (h^1, h^2) of the joint plan. Indeed,

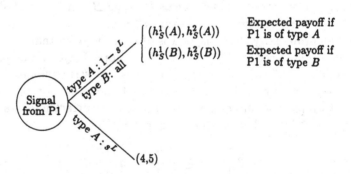

	Expected payoff if P1 is of type A
$(h_S^1(A), h_S^2(A))$	
$(h_S^1(B), h_S^2(B))$	Expected payoff if P1 is of type B

Figure 23. Aggregation of Lotteries.

(h^1, h^2)

$$= \frac{1}{2}\left(s^L(4,5) + (1-s^L)(h^1_S(A), h^2_S(A))\right) + \frac{1}{2}(h^1_S(B), h^2_S(B))$$

$$\leq \frac{1}{2}\left(4, 5s^L + (1-s^L)(3\frac{7}{8} + 7\gamma_6 + 5\gamma_7 + \varepsilon_4)\right) +$$

$$\frac{1}{2}(4\frac{1}{8} - N(\gamma_6 + \gamma_7) + \varepsilon_5, 3\frac{7}{8} + \varepsilon_6). \tag{8.18}$$

It follows from (8.5) and (8.18) that if we choose $\gamma_6 = \gamma_7 = 0$, and if N is sufficiently large, we only shift the payoff vector towards the upper side of l^{**}. Since $s^L \leq \frac{1}{3} + \varepsilon_3$, it follows that

$$\frac{1}{2}(4, \ 5s^L + (3\frac{7}{8})(1-s^L)) + \frac{1}{2}(4\frac{1}{8}, 3\frac{7}{8})$$

$$\leq \frac{1}{2}(4, \ 5 \cdot \frac{1}{3} + 3\frac{7}{8} \cdot \frac{2}{3}) + \frac{1}{2}(4\frac{1}{8}, 3\frac{7}{8}) + (0, \varepsilon_7)$$

$$\leq (4\frac{1}{16}, 4\frac{1}{16}) + (0, \varepsilon_7), \tag{8.19}$$

where ε_7 is an arbitrarily small positive number. Observe that $(4\frac{1}{16}, 4\frac{1}{16})$ lies on l. Therefore, if ε_4, ε_5, ε_6, ε_7, are chosen sufficiently small, we can identify a game (by choosing N sufficiently large), in which (h^1, h^2) cannot lie above l^{**}. For that game, no equilibrium payoff derived from a joint plan can lie above l^{**}; consequently no point in the convex hull of such equilibrium payoffs can lie above l^{**}.

But we have already shown that $(4, 4\frac{1}{6})$ is an equilibrium payoff, and it does lie above l^{**}; therefore, it is not true that any equilibrium payoff is in the convex hull of equilibrium payoffs generated by a joint plan satisfying the conditions of Theorem 6.1.

∎

POSTSCRIPTS TO CHAPTER FIVE

a. Existence of Equilibria

For games of the class treated in this chapter,[44] the question of
existence of equilibria was open for many years. The first break-
through came when Sorin [1983] showed that equilibria exist whenever $\kappa = 2$ (i.e., P1 has just two types). Matters stood there until
very recently, when Simon, Spież, and Toruńcyzk [1995] extended
Sorin's proof to arbitrary κ, in a brilliant tour de force using methods of algebraic topology. The equilibria found both by Sorin and
by Simon et al. are "enforceable joint plans"; that is, they are of
the type described in Theorem 6.1.

b. The Folk Theorem and Individual Rationality

This chapter may be seen as an examination of what happens to
the Folk Theorem (Section 3) when the condition of complete information is removed. In Theorem 6.1—the main positive result
of the chapter—Conditions ii and iii express the idea of individual
rationality for P2 and P1 respectively. Condition i, which may
be called "cheatproofness", reflects a phenomenon exclusively associated with incomplete information, which is absent from the
"classical" Folk Theorem.

c. Characterization of Equilibria: Background

Call a joint plan satisfying the conditions of Theorem 6.1 enforceable. In Section 8 there are two examples—one with $\kappa = 3$, and
a more complex one with $\kappa = 2$—in which there are equilibrium
payoffs that are not in the convex hull of the payoffs of enforceable joint plans. To achieve these equilibria, it is necessary to go
through a three-stage preliminary "communication" phase—first

---

[44]Infinitely repeated non-zero sum two-person games with one-sided incomplete information on the stage game and standard information on past play
(at each stage, each player knows the pure stage strategies previously chosen).

a signal by P1 (the informed player), then a jointly controlled lottery, then another signal by P1—before settling down to a pair of frequency strategies. This raises several questions: Can all equilibrium payoffs be achieved by such a three-step process? If not, perhaps they can be achieved with more alternations—i.e., by alternating signals from P1 with jointly controlled lotteries m times, for some $m > 3$. And if no single such m will do for all games, perhaps for each game, such an m can be found?

On the other hand, perhaps we are barking up the wrong tree altogether; perhaps no amount of alternation of signals with jointly controlled lotteries will in general do, perhaps there are equilibria of a totally different nature. After all, the alternating procedure does appear rather special.

Complete answers to these questions were found by Hart, who obtained [1985] a full characterization of all the equilibrium payoffs in all games of the class treated in this chapter. Hart's characterization yields the following answers to the above questions: Three alternations will not do; neither is there any m such that m alternations will always do; and neither can we find such an m for each game. Nevertheless, the procedure of alternating signals and lotteries *does* provide a general characterization of equilibrium payoffs; it is simply that some games require an *infinite* sequence of alternations.

Now this sounds puzzling, since the communication phase is meant to be preliminary; the actual payoff is provided by the frequency strategy eventually used, and the communication procedure is only meant to help the players decide on this strategy pair. If the preliminary communications alternate infinitely often, it would appear that the payoff will never be reached.

The answer is that though no finite number of alternations can bring the players to the equilibrium payoff precisely, they can bring them there approximately. Thus the players make the following kind of agreement: First P1 sends a signal, and in accordance with this signal, some frequency strategy is played for n_1 stages. Then a jointly controlled lottery (or *joint lottery* for short) is played, and in accordance with its outcome, some (other) frequency strategy is played for $n_2 > n_1$ stages. Then P1 sends another signal, and in accordance with this signal, some other frequency strategy is played for $n_3 > n_2$ stages. This continues ad infinitum. If the strategies are chosen so that the block averages converge, then the average payoff for all stages converges to the same limit. In a sense, this limit takes all the signals into account; thus heuristically, it is as if the frequency strategies that determine the actual payoffs are played only "after" all the communications have been sent. Needless to say, the strategies must be chosen so as to be incentive compatible, as in the body of this chapter.

Summing up, Hart has shown: (i) Each equilibrium payoff can be achieved by an agreed "program", consisting of a communication phase "followed" by payoffs. In the communication phase, signals from P1 alternate with joint lotteries, possibly infinitely often; the payoffs that follow are achievable by frequency strategies. The whole program must satisfy appropriate incentive compatibility conditions. (ii) Conversely, each such program yields an equilibrium payoff.

In the body of the chapter we had shown only (ii), and only for finite alternations.[45]

The next two notes are devoted to a precise formulation of Hart's characterization; the following one (Postscript f), to an outline of the proof.

d. Characterization of Equilibria: Geometric Preliminaries

Hart's formulation of the communication-payoff program just described is geometric in nature. The ideas are related to—though more subtle than—the idea of concavification underlying much of the rest of this book. The basic notions are those of directional martingale and directional convexity, which we now present.

Let X and Y be linear subspaces of a euclidean space[46] Z. Define a *dimartingale*[47] as a bounded martingale $\mathcal{D} := (z_0, z_1, z_2, \ldots)$

---

[45]In fact, the only case treated there completely is the "enforceable joint plan" (Section 6), where there is a signal and no joint lotteries. But in the case of an arbitrarily long finite alternation, (ii) is implicit in the discussion of the examples in Section 7.

[46]X, Y, and Z will be fixed throughout the discussion.

[47]Short for *directional martingale* with *splitting directions* X, Y. The term "direction" is here used in the sense of being parallel to a certain hyperplane, which is slightly different from the usual sense.

in Z, with $z_1 - z_0 \in X$, $z_2 - z_1 \in Y$, $z_3 - z_2 \in X$, and so on, that starts with a constant z_0. Since it is a bounded martingale, a dimartingale converges almost surely. Intuitively, one may think of a martingale as a process in which mass points split again and again; the splitting is due to some internal force, like an explosion, so the center of mass of any given set of particles never changes. (Mass corresponds to probability, and center of mass to expectation.) In these terms, a dimartingale is a process in which the splitting takes place in the directions X and Y in alternate time periods. For example, if Z is the euclidean plane, X and Y the usual x- and y-axes, then the passage from z_{n-1} to z_n represents a horizontal split when n is odd, and a vertical split when n is even.

Call a subset D of Z *diconvex* [48] if $D \cap (z+X)$ and $D \cap (z+Y)$ are[49] convex for each z in Z. Define the *diconvex hull* of a set as the smallest diconvex set including it (see Figure 24).

Define the *diconvex span* di-sp(H) of a set $H \subset Z$ as the set of all expectations[50] of dimartingales whose limit is almost surely in H. If, analogously, we define the *convex span* of H as the set of all expectations of martingales whose limit is almost surely in H, then we find that the convex span is the same as the convex hull. The "span" thus provides an alternative extension of the idea of "hull" to the diconvex case. Since the diconvex span of H is itself diconvex, and includes H, it must always include the diconvex hull. Often it coincides with the diconvex hull, but sometimes it is strictly larger (Aumann and Hart [1985]; see Figure 25).

---

[48] Short for *directionally convex* in the directions X, Y (called *convexity directions*). In words, diconvexity means that every translation of X or Y intersects D in a convex set. There could, of course, be any number of convexity directions, but the current application requires just two. The theory of diconvexity and dimartingales was developed by Aumann and Hart [1985] for the special case where X and Y are orthogonal complements; their results extend straightforwardly to the case treated here.

[49] Here $+$ denotes the algebraic sum; thus $z + X := \{z + x : x \in X\}$.

[50] All terms of a martingale have the same expectation, called the *expectation* of the martingale; in our case it is the constant z_0.

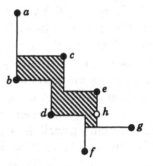

Figure 24. The diconvex hull of H when Z
is the euclidean plane, X, Y are the usual x-
and y-axes, and $H := \{a, b, c, d, e, f, g\}$. Note
that six consecutive "diconvex combinations"
are needed to construct the point h from H.
Similarly, there are H whose diconvex hulls
require arbitrarily—even unboundedly—many
convex combinations. Contrast this with ordinary convexity, where Caratheodory's theorem
guarantees that a point in the convex hull of
any planar set H is a convex combination of at
most three points in H.

e. Characterization of Equilibria: Precise Formulation

Let us return now to the game. We will consider pairs (p, h),
where p is a probability vector on the set K of P1's types, and
$h = (h^1, h^2)$ is a $(\kappa + 1)$-tuple representing the payoffs to the
two players (κ types of P1 and one type of P2). Specifically, p
represents P2's probabilities for the various types of P1; h^1 is a
K-vector[51] representing payoffs to the κ types of P1; and h^2 is
a scalar representing an expected payoff to the single type of P2,
the expectation being formed in accordance with the probabilities
p. When we wish to emphasize the role of the probability vector
p in determining P2's expected payoff, we will use the phrase
"p-payoff", rather than just "payoff", for h^2 as well as for $h :=$
(h^1, h^2).

---

[51] Vector of real numbers indexed by the types k of P1.

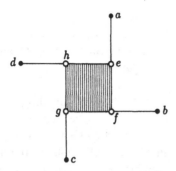

Figure 25. The diconvex span of H when Z
is the euclidean plane, X, Y are the usual x-
and y-axes, and $H := \{a, b, c, d\}$. Note that the
diconvex hull of H is simply H itself. To see
that $e \in$ di-sp(H), consider a mass of 1 con-
centrated at e. At time 1, it splits half-half
to a and f. The mass that has arrived at a
no longer splits, but at time 2, the mass at f
splits half-half to g and b. This continues indefinitely: Mass that arrives at a point in H
does not split further; the remainder—which
decreases by half at each split—rotates again
and again through e, f, g, and h. In the end,
almost all the mass is in H, with expectation
(center of mass) where it was at the beginning:
at e. Similarly f, g, and h are in di-sp(H).
Since di-sp(H) is diconvex, it follows that it
contains the depicted set. That it does not contain more requires a separation argument; see
Aumann and Hart [1985].

In the interpretation, the pairs (p, h) are associated with different situations—corresponding to different finite histories—that
may arise in the course of the repeated game (or of the corresponding communication process). The probability vector p represents
P2's conditional probability on K, given the history up to that
point; h^1 represents the conditional expected payoff of each of
P1's types, given the history; and h^2 represents P2's conditional
expected payoff, given the history.

Let a pair $(p, h) = (p, h^1, h^2)$ be given. If q is any probability vector on K, denote by $u^i(q)$ the maxmin value of i in the one-shot game $\Delta(q)$ (in which neither player is told the true k). Call h^1 *individually rational for P1* if

$$q \cdot h^1 \geq u^1(q) \text{ for all } q; \qquad (\text{N1})$$

by Lemma N4 in Postscript d to Chapter One, (N1) is equivalent to P2's being able, in Γ_∞, simultaneously to hold all of P1's types down to their components of h^1. Call h^2 *individually rational at p for P2* if

$$h^2 \geq \text{vex } u^2(p); \qquad (\text{N2})$$

since vex $u^2(p)$ is P2's maxmin in $\Gamma_\infty(p)$ (see Chapter One), (N2) is equivalent to P1's being able to hold P2 down to an expectation of h^2 in $\Gamma_\infty(p)$. Finally, call (p, h) *individually rational* if h^1 is individually rational for P1 and h^2 is individually rational at p for P2. Note that the individual rationality conditions (N1) and (N2) are essentially the same as the corresponding conditions in the body of this chapter (Theorem 6.1, Conditions iii and ii).

If p is strictly positive, call the pair (p, h) *feasible* if there is a correlated stage strategy c that yields the payoff h^1_k to each type k of P1, and yields to P2 a p-payoff[52] of h^2. When some components p_k of p vanish, the definition of feasibility is modified by allowing the corresponding coordinates h^1_k of h^1 to exceed the true payoffs.[53]

Now let Z be the $(2\kappa + 1)$-dimensional space with generic point (p, h^1, h^2). Let X be the (p, h^2)-coordinate hyperplane, Y the (h^1, h^2)-coordinate hyperplane; thus in a dimartingale where X and Y are the splitting directions, h^1 remains constant at odd stages, p remains constant at even stages, and h^2 may change at all stages.

---

[52]Thus $h^2 = \sum_{k \in K} p_k e^2_k$, where e^2_k is the payoff to P2 when P1 is of type k and the correlated stage strategy c is used by both players.
[53]The reason for modification when $p_k = 0$ is given at the end of Postscript f.

THEOREM N1 (Hart 1985). h_0 is an equilibrium payoff of $\Gamma_\infty(p_0)$ if and only if (p_0, h_0) is in the diconvex span of the set of all (p, h) that are feasible and individually rational.

Intuitively, the dimartingale embodies the program described in Postscript c, where signals alternate with joint lotteries. By sending a signal, P1 changes P2's probability vector p on P1's type. However, all possible[54] signals must lead to the same expected payoff for P1; for if not, P1 would use only those leading to the highest.[55] It follows that the expected payoff to P1 after the signal must be the same as before; thus a signal may change p but not h^1. On the other hand, a joint lottery does not convey any information about P1's type, since no single one of the players—in particular P1—can change the distribution of its outcome (that is why the lottery is called "jointly controlled"). So a joint lottery may change h^1, but not p. Thus the alternation in the dimartingale corresponds precisely to the alternation in the communication phase of the program. As for the limit of the dimartingale, this corresponds to the payoff phase of the program: Feasibility means that the payoff is achievable by agreed-on frequency strategies; and individual rationality, that it is incentive compatible. The process thus corresponds precisely to the kind of dimartingale we have been discussing.

The above provides only a very rough[56] intuition for Hart's result. An outline of the proof is given in the next note.

f. Characterization of Equilibria: Outline of Hart's Proof

What follows is far from a complete proof; many essential steps are omitted. But we hope that it will enable the reader to grasp the main ideas.

Let H be the set of all feasible and individually rational pairs (p, h). We first demonstrate the "if" part of Theorem N1. Thus let (p_0, h_0) be in the diconvex span of H; that is, there is a dimartingale $\mathcal{D} := ((p_0, h_0), (p_1, h_1), \ldots)$ whose limit—which we call (p_∞, h_∞)—almost surely exists and is in H. We will show that h_0

---

[54]Those assigned positive probability by the process.
[55]This expresses the "cheatproofness" condition mentioned in Postscript b.
[56]Indeed, not entirely correct.

is an equilibrium payoff of $\Gamma_\infty(p_0)$; i.e., will find an equilibrium point of $\Gamma_\infty(p_0)$ whose payoff is h_0.

We start with two simplifying assumptions. The first is that, at each stage, $\mathcal{D}$ undergoes at most a two-way split; i.e., that conditional on $\mathcal{D}$'s first $m-1$ stages, (p_m, h_m) has at most two values. This assumption is easily removed. The second is that almost surely, the limiting probability p_0 assigns positive probability to each type of P1. Unlike the two-way split, this is a substantive assumption. But it, too, can be removed; we will indicate how at the end of this note. Note that all components of p_m are strictly positive, since p_m is a conditional expectation of p_0.

The equilibrium is constructed by a process that interleaves communications with frequency strategies, as in Postscript c. We know that (p_1, h_1) is obtained by a two-way split from (p_0, h_0); denote the two possible values of (p_1, h_1) by (p_{0L}, h_{0L}) and (p_{0R}, h_{0R}), where $h_{0L}^1 = h_{0R}^1 = h_0^1$. Since $\mathcal{D}$ is a martingale, there are probabilities α_{0L} and $\alpha_{0R} := 1 - \alpha_{0L}$—w.l.o.g. both positive—such that $\alpha_{0L}(p_{0L}, h_{0L}) + \alpha_{0R}(p_{0R}, h_{0R}) = (p_0, h_0)$. The first communication is a random signal from P1, either "L" or "R", with a probability of $\alpha_{0L} p_{0L}^k / p_0^k$ for P1's type k to choose L. To send the signal "L" ("R"), P1 simply chooses his first (second) pure strategy at the first stage of the infinitely repeated game Γ_∞. The overall probabilities for L and R are then α_{0L} and α_{0R}, and after receiving the signal, P2's posterior probability vector is indeed p_{0L} or p_{0R}. Thus P2's posterior probability vector is a random variable with the same distribution as p_1; so, abusing our notation slightly, we denote it, too, by p_1. Similarly, we write h_1 for h_{0L} or h_{0R} according as to whether P1 signalled L or R.

This first communication is followed by a block of stages in which the players play a specified, agreed upon frequency strategy f_1 to be described below.

Next, we know that (p_2, h_2) is obtained by a two-way split from (p_1, h_1). Like before, denote the two "children" of (p_1, h_1) by (p_{1L}, h_{1L}) and (p_{1R}, h_{1R}); now $p_{1L} = p_{1R} = p_1$. Let α_{1L}, α_{1R} be complementary positive probabilities with $\alpha_{1L} h_{1L} + \alpha_{1R} h_{1R} = h_1$. The second communication is a joint lottery that chooses L and R with probabilities α_{1L} and α_{1R} respectively; these lotteries may require more than one stage[57] of Γ_∞. Also like before, we abuse our notation by writing (p_2, h_2) for (p_{1L}, h_{1L}) or (p_{1R}, h_{1R}), according as the joint lottery chose L or R.

The second communication, too, is followed by a block of stages—longer than the first—in which the players play a specified frequency strategy f_2, described below.

The process continues indefinitely. Signals from P1 alternate with joint lotteries in the communication process; the parameters defining each communication—i.e., the probabilities of the signals and lottery strategies—may depend on all previous communications (signals and joint lotteries). Between the m-th and $(m+1)$-th communication, the players play, in longer and longer blocks, the frequency strategies f_m; these, too, may depend on all previous communications. The sequence (p_m, h_m) generated by the process is a dimartingale that precisely mimics the given dimartingale $\mathcal{D}$; again abusing our notation, we will also call it $\mathcal{D}$. Note that p_m describes P2's posterior probabilities over P1's types k after the m-th communication.

We now specify[58] the frequency strategy f_m. As just noted, f_m depends on the history $\mathcal{H}_m$ of communications up to stage m. Beyond stage m, the history—and so the martingale—may continue in various ways; each such continuation will almost surely converge to a feasible, individually rational limit. The set L_m of all such limits is a (set-valued) random variable depending on $\mathcal{H}_m$. Now choose an element $(\hat{p}_m, \hat{h}_m)$ of L_m that is "fairly close[59]" to (p_m, h_m), note that it is feasible, and define f_m as a frequency strategy whose $\hat{p}_m$-payoff is $\hat{h}_m$. Using $(p_m, h_m) \rightarrow (p_\infty, h_\infty)$, it can be shown that $(\hat{p}_m, \hat{h}_m) \rightarrow (p_\infty, h_\infty)$ almost surely.

---

[57]See the body of this chapter, Section 7.

[58]It would seem easiest to use frequency strategies whose p_m-payoff is h_m. Unfortunately, this is not, in general possible. Indeed, there exists a frequency strategy with p_m-payoff h_m if and only if (p_m, h_m) is feasible. Now (p_m, h_m) is a conditional expectation of (p_∞, h_∞), all values of which are feasible; so if the set F of feasible pairs (p, h) were convex, we could conclude that (p_m, h_m) also is. But in fact, F need not be convex, because the p-payoff to a correlated strategy c is bilinear—not linear!—in p and c.

[59]One may take $(\hat{p}_m, \hat{h}_m)$ as an element of L_m whose distance from (p_m, h_m) is within $1/m$ of the infimum of all such distances.

From this it follows that the process leads, in the limit, to a p_∞-payoff of h_∞ in Γ_∞. Since $p_m \to p_\infty$ and p_m represents P2's posterior probabilities over K after the m-th communication, p_∞ represents P2's posterior probabilities over K in the limit, after all the communications. Therefore h^2 is the payoff that P2 actually expects to get in the limit; and $(h^1_\infty)_k$ is the payoff that P1's type k actually gets[60] in the limit. Since $\mathcal{D}$ is a martingale, h_m is the conditional expectation of h_∞, given the first m stages of $\mathcal{D}$; so it follows that h_m represents the expected payoffs of the players (κ types of P1 and one type of P2) from the process after the m-th communication.

In particular, it follows that the expected payoff at the beginning of Γ_∞ is h_0.

So far, we have prescribed only the "equilibrium path": the actions of the players as long as both adhere to the process. To complete the description of an equilibrium point, one must prescribe the reactions of each player to possible deviations by the other. These are as follows:

If P2 deviates from the prescribed frequency strategy during the m-th block (between the m-th and the $(m+1)$-th communication), then from then on, P1 plays so as to hold P2's long-run expected average payoff, calculated with the probabilities p_m, down to h^2_m; that he can do so follows from the individual rationality, at p_m, of h_m for P2 (see (N2)). A similar reaction is prescribed if P2 uses an inadmissible[61] pure strategy at the $(m+1)$-th communication.

If P1 deviates from the prescribed frequency strategy during the m-th block, then from then on, P2 plays so as simultaneously to hold the long-run average payoff of all of P1's types down to their components of h^1_m; that he can do so follows from the individual rationality of h_m for P1 (see (N1)). A similar reaction is prescribed if P1 uses an inadmissible strategy at the $(m+1)$-th communication.

---

[60] In the case of P1, this is not an expectation, since the frequency strategy f_m *actually* yields h^1 to P1.

[61] One other than those prescribed for use in that communication; for example, P1's third pure strategy is inadmissible when he is supposed to use his first or second to signal L or R.

If either player makes an unobserved deviation from the prescribed lottery strategy or signalling strategy (i.e., uses probabilities different from the prescribed ones), the other player does not react (as indeed he can't, since he hasn't observed the deviation).

To show that this is an equilibrium, we must show that if one player deviates while the other adheres to the prescribed strategy, then the deviating player does not gain. If either player deviates from his part of a joint lottery, the distribution of the outcome of the lottery, and so the expected outcome of the game, is not changed; in particular, there is no gain for the deviating player. Next, a deviation of P2 from the prescribed frequency strategy will not lead him to expect, at the time of the deviation, a long-run average payoff larger than that for the equilibrium strategy (because of P1's reaction, described above); and it follows that he cannot gain from it. It remains to show that a deviation of P1—other than from the prescribed lottery strategy—cannot lead to a gain for him.

Suppose, then, that P1 (and only P1) deviates, and consider the *first* time he does so. If this is a deviation from the prescribed frequency strategy, and comes during the m-th block, then P2's reaction is to hold P1 to h_m^1; so the deviation gains P1 nothing.

Otherwise, the deviation is from the prescribed signalling strategy. Let it come at the $(m + 1)$-th communication. If it consists of using an inadmissible strategy for the signal, then P2 reacts by holding P1 down to h_m^1; so again, the deviation gains P1 nothing. Otherwise it is an unobserved deviation, and there may or may not be subsequent deviations, observed or unobserved. An observed deviation at a communication stage $m' > m$ will trigger a reaction by P2 that holds P1 to $h_{m'}^1$; so again, at that point it would gain P1 nothing. We may therefore rule this out.

The only remaining possibility is that of one or more unobserved deviations by P1 from the prescribed signalling strategy. Here we make use of the dimartingale condition that $h_m^1 = h_{m-1}^1$ for odd m. Since h_m^1 is P1's expected payoff from m on, this says that the expected payoff to any type of P1 does not change as the result of sending an admissible signal. This implies that no type of P1 can gain from a *single* unobserved deviation—sending an admissible signal different from the prescribed one—since no matter what he signals, his expected payoff stays the same.

However, the possibility remains that some type of P1 could gain from a *sequence*, possibly infinite, of such deviations. Specifically, suppose P1 uses a *deviation strategy*, which prescribes for each of his types, each signalling stage m, and each history of L's or R's up to that stage, a probability mixture of signals at that stage. Assuming that P2 does not stray from his equilibrium strategy, P1's deviation strategy induces a probability distribution on the space Ω of infinite "histories" (strings ω of L's and R's); this distribution, which we call the *deviant* distribution, is different from what we get when both players follow the equilibrium path (called the *equilibrium* distribution). Consider now $\mathcal{H} := (h_0^1, h_1^1, h_2^1, \ldots)$ as a sequence of functions on Ω; here, as above, h_m^1 denotes what P2 (who is unaware of P1's deviation) thinks P1's expected vector payoff is after stage m. From the di-martingale property of $\mathcal{D}$, we know that $h_m^1 = h_{m-1}^1$ for m odd; and since $\mathcal{H}$ is derived from $\mathcal{D}$, we know that $\mathcal{H}$ is a martingale when Ω is endowed with the equilibrium distribution.

Next, we show that $\mathcal{H}$ is a martingale also when Ω is endowed with the deviant distribution. For this, we must show that $\mathrm{Exp}(h_m^1 | h_1^1, \ldots, h_{m-1}^1) = h_{m-1}^1$, where the expectation is with respect to the deviant distribution. If m is odd, this is immediate, since $h_m^1 = h_{m-1}^1$. If, on the other hand, m is even, then m is a joint lottery stage, so there is no deviation[62] there; therefore $\mathrm{Exp}(h_m^1 | h_1^1, \ldots, h_{m-1}^1) = h_{m-1}^1$, as with the equilibrium distribution.

Note that the convergence of $\mathcal{H}$ depends only on the infinite history ω; so if $\mathcal{H}$ converges, it converges to the same limit h_∞^1 to which it converges when there is no deviation.[63] This limit, moreover, is not only P2's expectation for what P1 will get, but what P1 will actually get; this is because of the use of frequency strategies as set forth above. Since $\mathcal{H}$ is a martingale w.r.t. the

---

[62]More precisely, any deviation by P1 will have no effect.

[63]That doesn't mean that in practice, deviating won't change the limit. It may well do so, because it changes the history. As a function of the history, though, $\mathcal{H}$ actually coincides with $\mathcal{D}$. The difference between the two martingales lies in the probabilities that they impute to the various histories.

deviant distribution, it converges almost surely w.r.t. that distribution; moreover, its initial term h_0^1 is the expectation, w.r.t. the deviant distribution, of its limit h_∞^1. But $\mathcal{H}$ is martingale w.r.t. the equilibrium distribution too, so h_0^1 is the expectation of h_∞^1 also w.r.t. the equilibrium distribution. Thus P1 gets exactly the same expected payoff h_0^1 whether or not he deviates, so the deviation does not pay.

This completes the proof of the "if" part of Theorem N1, subject to the assumption we made at the beginning that $p_\infty (=\lim p_m)$ almost surely assigns positive probability to each type of P1.

For the "only if" part, let (σ, τ) be an equilibrium pair of strategies in $\Gamma_\infty = \Gamma_\infty(p_0)$, whose payoff is h_0; we must construct a dimartingale starting with (p_0, h_0) whose limit (p_∞, h_∞) is almost surely feasible and individually rational. To this end, imagine that instead of having the players choose simultaneously at each stage of Γ_∞, we divide each stage into two *periods*; P1 makes his choice in the first period, and P2 in the second, but P2 is not told of P1's choice when making his. Clearly this does not change the equilibria of the game. Now consider an outside observer who starts with the same information as P2, knows that the players are playing (σ, τ), and is allowed to observe each player's move when it is made; thus at each stage of Γ_∞ the observer makes two observations, one in each period. Note that at each period, P1 knows everything that the observer does. Denote by p_m the observer's κ-dimensional vector of probabilities for P1's types, after the m-th period; similarly, denote by h_m the observer's expectation, after[64] the m-th period, for the $(\kappa+1)$-dimensional long-term payoff vector. Then we claim that $\mathcal{D} := ((p_0, h_0), (p_1, h_1), \ldots)$ is a dimartingale whose limit is almost surely feasible and individually rational.

As $\mathcal{D}$ is a sequence of probabilities and expectations conditional on more and more information, it is a martingale; so it converges almost surely. We start by assuming, as in the "if" part of the demonstration, that p_0 is almost surely strictly positive (assigns positive probability to each type of P1); later we will indicate how this assumption may be removed.

---

[64]i.e., given the m-stage history.

To show that $\mathcal{D}$ is a dimartingale, we must show that $p_m = p_{m-1}$ for m even, and $h_m^1 = h_{m-1}^1$ for m odd. When m is even, p_{m-1} and p_m are the observer's probability distributions immediately before and after a choice of P2. From a choice of P2, the observer cannot learn anything about P1's type, since he always knows as much as P2. Therefore his distribution on k after P2's choice is the same as before; so indeed, $p_m = p_{m-1}$ for m even.

Next, let m be odd; thus it is P1 who chooses at the m-th period. The question therefore is, can a choice of P1 change the expected payoff to any of his types k? The answer is no. To see this, note first that p_m assigns positive probability to k; indeed, we have assumed that p_∞ assigns positive probability to all types, and p_m is a conditional expectation of the p_∞. Thus after the m-th period, neither P2 nor the observer can rule out the possibility that P1 is of type k. Suppose now that $(h_m^1)_k \neq (h_{m-1}^1)_k$. Since the conditional expectation of $(h_m^1)_k$ given the history is $(h_{m-1}^1)_k$, it must be that some values of $(h_m^1)_k$ are larger than $(h_{m-1}^1)_k$, and some are smaller; it follows that some values of $(h_m^1)_k$ are larger than others. Each value of $(h_m^1)_k$ corresponds to some particular choice of P1 at stage m. Thus by making one choice rather than another, P1 could raise his expected payoff. But then why would he make the choice leading to the smaller payoff? The only way this could happen is if he isn't really of type k. But then P2 and the observer could also deduce that he isn't of type k, contrary[65] to our conclusion above that they cannot rule out P1's being of type k.

It remains only to prove that (p_∞, h_∞) is almost surely feasible and individually rational. The problem in proving feasibility is that different types k of P1 may have different strategies; so even if we assume that the long run averages converge, the payoffs $(h_\infty^1)_k$ to the different types k of P1, as well as the corresponding payoffs to P2, may not all be simultaneously achievable by the same single correlated strategy.

To overcome this problem, we use the martingale convergence theorem, which implies that after sufficiently many periods, p_m

---

[65] Alternatively: Since $(p_m)_k > 0$ after each choice that P1 can make at period m, it follows that at period m, type k makes each choice with positive probability, and this contradicts some values of $(h_m^1)_k$ being smaller than others.

remains "almost constant". From that point on, P1 must be playing in an "almost non-revealing" way; the reasons for this were
discussed already in Chapter One, and constitute a central theme
of this book. Therefore all his types must be playing in roughly
the same way. Ignoring ϵ's, we may suppose they are playing in
exactly the same way—i.e., the same strategy in Γ_∞; and that
p_m remains exactly constant, and so equal to p_∞. Combining
this with P2's strategy, we get a pair of strategies that induces[66]
a single limiting frequency distribution on pairs of stage strategies, one that is simultaneously valid for all types. Denoting by
c the correlated stage strategy corresponding to this limiting frequency distribution, we find that the p_∞-payoff to c is h_∞, so that
(p_∞, h_∞) is indeed feasible.

We come next to the individual rationality. If h_∞ were not
individually rational at p_∞ for P2, then there would be some m
such that with positive probability, h_m is not individually rational
at p_m for P2, since the individual rationality condition (N2) is
closed. But then P2 could guarantee a higher expected payoff by
starting to deviate at the stage after the m-th period. Similarly,
if h_∞^1 were not individually rational for P1, then there would be
some m such that with positive probability, h_m^1 is not individually
rational for P1 (see (N1)). This means that it is impossible for
P2 simultaneously to hold all types of P1 to their components of
h_m^1. In particular, P2's actual strategy τ does not hold all types
of P1 to their components of h_m^1. So there is a type k of P1 who
is not held to $(h_m^1)_k$ by τ. But then that type k of P1 could
get more than $(h_m^1)_k$ by deviating from σ starting at the m-th
period. But $(p_m)_k > 0$, since p_m is strictly positive; that implies
that there is positive probability that at the m-th period, type
k's expected payoff under (σ, τ) will be $(h_m^1)_k$. Therefore, from
the very beginning of the game, type k of P1 could increase his
expected payoff, by planning to deviate from σ if and when he
reaches the m-th period with an expected payoff of $(h_m^1)_k$. But
then (σ, τ) would not be an equilibrium, contrary to hypothesis.

This completes the demonstration of the "only if" part of
Hart's theorem, under the assumption of strict positivity of p_∞.

---

[66] We ignore here the technical problem of convergence; in the original paper,
Hart uses Banach limits to overcome this problem.

Finally, we indicate briefly how the assumption of strict positivity of p_0 may be removed, both from the "if" and the "only if" parts of the demonstration. This is not just a technical matter. There are many cases of practical interest in which P1 may prefer to reveal his true type,[67] in order to foster mutually beneficial behavior on the part of P2. Even in 0-sum games, where mutually beneficial behavior is impossible, P1 may prefer to reveal fully, as we saw already in Chapter One.

The crux of the matter is the dimartingale condition $h^1_m = h^1_{m-1}$ for odd m. At the end of Postscript e we explained the intuition behind this condition. By sending a signal at stage m—which he does alone, without P2's being involved—P1 *cannot* raise his own expected payoff; and he certainly *will not* act to lower it. This implies that there will be no change in the expected payoff to the "possible" types of P1—those with positive probability. But it does not rule out a change in the expected payoff to P1's "impossible" types—those with probability 0. Thus we seek to interpret $(h^1_m)_k = (h^1_{m-1})_k$ when $(p_m)_k = 0$.

For the analysis, the crucial stage m is that at which $(p_m)_k$ *first* vanishes; i.e., the first one at which P1's signal rules out type k. For that m, the above argument implies that whereas k's expected payoff can stay the same or go down, it cannot go up. Indeed, if k's expected payoff went up and P1 really was of type k, he would be motivated to send the signal that rules out k, thereby increasing his expected payoff. (The other side of the previous argument—that P1's type k would not willingly lower his own payoff—does not apply, as here P1 is really *not* of type k).

This is what motivates the definition of feasibility when some components of p vanish (Postscript d): (p, h) is called "feasible" if there is a payoff g that is *really* feasible (i.e., is the payoff to some correlated stage strategy) for which $h^2 = g^2$, $h^1_k = g^1_k$ when $p_k > 0$, and $h^1_k \geq g^1_k$ when $p_k = 0$. To understand this definition, think of g as the real payoff, and h as a "virtual" payoff. For "possible" types of P1 and for all types of P2, the virtual payoff equals the real payoff. For "impossible" types of P1, the virtual payoff must be *at least* as large as the real payoff. If we think

---

[67]More generally, P1 may wish to rule out some types, but not others.

of the terms h_m appearing in the dimartingale $\mathcal{D}$ as representing virtual rather than real payoffs, then the virtual payoff to all types of P1 stays the same at all signalling stages. This implies that the real payoff to each type k stays the same at each stage at which k is not yet ruled out; and at the first stage m at which k *is* ruled out, the real payoff stays the same or goes down. As indicated above, that is exactly what is required.

We content ourselves with this discussion of what happens when p is not strictly positive; while far from complete,[68] we hope it provides some intuition for the modifications that are then required.

g. An Economic Example Requiring Unboundedly Many Communications

Forges [1990] has constructed a particularly beautiful example, with a natural economic interpretation, of a game requiring unboundedly many communications (Game 1). The two rows

	job 1	job 2	layoff	job 3	job 4
Type A	6, 10	10, 9	0, 7	4, 4	3, 0
Type B	3, 0	4, 4	0, 7	10, 9	6, 10

Game 1

represent the two types of P1. Thus P1 has no strategic choice (just one strategy)[69] and all he can do is to signal his type to

---

[68] Inter alia, we have not discussed the requirement that the virtual payoffs to P1's type k remain the same at signalling periods *after* that in which k is ruled out. Also, we have not indicated in any detail how the proof must be modified to handle virtual payoffs. This is far from clear, especially for the "only if" part of the proof.

[69] Strictly speaking, each matrix should consist of two identical rows; this would enable P1 to send signals in the repeated game. With just one row, he has no technical way of sending signals.

P2, who has five strategies. This may be motivated with a "job assignment" scenario.[70] An employer (P2) must decide to assign an employee to one of four jobs, or to lay her off. The employee (P1) may be one of two types. Type A performs better in job 1, but prefers job 2 (which is more interesting); she is bad at job 3, and worse at job 4; her last choice is being laid off. Type B is similar, with the jobs reversed. P2's initial probability for each of the two types is 1/2.

There are two obvious equilibria of the repeated game. In the first, P1 reveals nothing—both her types use the same signal—and P2 does not offer the job. This, of course, is not very attractive to P1—it yields her 0 no matter what her type is—but it is an equilibrium. Another equilibrium is the fully revealing one, in which she simply signals the truth. In this case P2 will choose to offer either job 1 or job 4; in either case, P1 gets 6. Of course, one can also mix these two outcomes in any desired proportion, using a joint lottery at the beginning.

Are there any equilibria with different payoffs? In particular, is there one in which P1 gets more than 6? Can she somehow inveigle P2 into offering her job 2 or job 4 with positive probability?

The point of the example, of course, is that she wants neither to reveal fully nor to conceal fully. Suppose her type is A. What she would like to do is to hint strongly—and credibly!—that that is the case, but to leave some doubt in P2's mind. In that way, she gives P2 an incentive to assign her to one of the two jobs at which she is better; but she makes it dangerous for him to assign her to job 1, at which her type B is no good at all. If, say, P2's probability for P1's type A could be changed to $\frac{3}{4}$, then by assigning job 2, he would get $7\frac{3}{4}$ (as compared to $7\frac{1}{2}$ for job 1, and 7 for laying off). He would therefore assign job 2, which is what she wants.

This raises the possibility of P1 sending a "noisy signal", causing P2 to attribute probability $\frac{3}{4}$ to her true type and $\frac{1}{4}$ to her other type. She could do this by signalling her true type with probability $\frac{3}{4}$ and her other type with probability $\frac{1}{4}$. As a result, the employer would assign either job 2 or job 4, as the case may be. Thus P1's expected payoff would be $\frac{3}{4} \cdot 10 + \frac{1}{4} \cdot 4 = 8\frac{1}{2}$, which

---

[70] Forges's original scenario is slightly different.

is larger than the 6 she would get by revealing fully, and the 0 she would get by keeping mum. The difficulty with this is that it is not credible: If P2 abides by the plan, it becomes worthwhile for P1 to "cheat" by *always* signalling her true type; and then P2 would be better off to assign job 1 (or 4) after all.

In fact, it *is* possible for P1 to get more than 6; but only by a much more complicated communication process, which may involve arbitrarily many stages—though it does end almost surely.

Refer to Figure 26. Here, each point represents a pair $(p, h) = (p, (h^1, h^2))$, as in Postscript e. Such pairs are actually 4-dimensional: One dimension each for p, h^1_A, h^1_B, and h^2. The 2-dimensional figure is obtained by first considering only those pairs for which $h^1_A + h^1_B = 14$, and then suppressing the h^2-coordinate.[71] The heavy lines and heavy dots represent[72] the set h of all feasible and individually rational pairs (p, h). The shaded area, plus the two spikes extending to $j1$ and to $j4$, represents the diconvex span of H. (More precisely, the heavy dots and lines are the projection onto (p, h^1)-space of the intersection of H with the hyperplane $h^1_A + h^1_B = 14$, and the shaded area is the projection of the intersection of di-sp(H) with that hyperplane). The coordinates of the points of interest are listed in the table below, including the "suppressed" coordinate h^2. Here $p_A = p$ and $p_B = 1 - p$ are P2's probabilities that P1 is of type A or B respectively. When one of these probabilities vanishes, the payoff to that type does not enter the expected payoff calculations; the number appearing in parentheses is then a "virtual" payoff (see the end of Postscript f).

---

[71] That is, projecting from (p, h) to (p, h^1).

[72] The reader may verify this for himself, or refer to the end of this note, where the calculation is done explicitly.

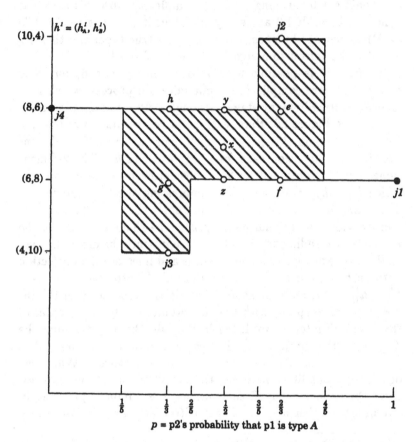

Figure 26. Forges's job example in probability-payoff space.

Point	p_A	p_B	h^1_A	h^1_B	h^2
x	$\frac{1}{2}$	$\frac{1}{2}$	7	7	$8\frac{2}{3}$
y	$\frac{1}{2}$	$\frac{1}{2}$	8	6	$8\frac{2}{3}$
z	$\frac{1}{2}$	$\frac{1}{2}$	6	8	$8\frac{2}{3}$
e	$\frac{2}{3}$	$\frac{1}{3}$	8	6	$8\frac{2}{9}$
f	$\frac{2}{3}$	$\frac{1}{3}$	6	8	$9\frac{1}{9}$
g	$\frac{1}{3}$	$\frac{2}{3}$	6	8	$8\frac{2}{9}$
h	$\frac{1}{3}$	$\frac{2}{3}$	8	6	$9\frac{1}{9}$
$j1$	1	0	6	(8)	10
$j2$	$\frac{2}{3}$	$\frac{1}{3}$	10	4	$7\frac{1}{3}$
$j3$	$\frac{1}{3}$	$\frac{2}{3}$	4	10	$7\frac{1}{3}$
$j4$	0	1	(8)	6	10

Table of probabilities and payoffs in Forges's job example

The starting point of the process is in the center of Figure 26, at the point marked x. The coordinates of x are $p = \frac{1}{2}$ and $h^1 = (7,7)$; the corresponding h^2-coordinate (which is suppressed in the figure) is $8\frac{2}{3}$. This means that at the beginning of the game, P2 assigns probability $\frac{1}{2}$ to P1's type being A, the two types of P1 each expect a payoff of 7, and P2 expects a payoff of $8\frac{2}{3}$. These expectations may be calculated from the process that we now describe.

The first communication in the process is a jointly controlled lottery, by means of which x "splits" into the two points y and z, with probability $\frac{1}{2}$ each, where $y = (\frac{1}{2},(8,6))$ and $z = (\frac{1}{2},(6,8))$. This means that after the joint lottery, either type A of P1 expects 8 and type B expects 6, or vice versa; P2's probabilities on the types remain unchanged.

The second communication is a signal from P1, as a result of which either y splits into the points e and h with $\frac{1}{2} - \frac{1}{2}$ probabilities, or (if z was reached after the first communication) z splits into f and g with $\frac{1}{2} - \frac{1}{2}$ probabilities. The expected payoff to each type of P1 remains unchanged as the result of this signal, so that the signal is credible. This brings us to one of the four points e, f, g, and h, with probability $\frac{1}{4}$ each.

Suppose first that e is reached after the second communication. Then the third communication is a joint lottery that splits e into $j2$ and f with $\frac{1}{2} - \frac{1}{2}$ probabilities. If this leads to $j2$, the communication phase is over, and job 2 is assigned for ever afterwards. If it leads to f, then at the fourth communication, P1 sends a signal splitting f into $j1$ and g with $\frac{1}{2} - \frac{1}{2}$ probabilities. If this leads to $j1$, then P2 knows for sure that P1's type is A, and so assigns her to job 1 for ever afterwards. If it leads to g, then the fifth communication is a joint lottery splitting g into $j3$ and h with $\frac{1}{2} - \frac{1}{2}$ probabilities. If this leads to $j3$, then job 3 is assigned for ever afterwards. If this leads to h, then at the sixth communication, P1 sends a signal splitting h into $j4$ and e with $\frac{1}{2} - \frac{1}{2}$ probabilities. If this leads to $j4$, the communication phase is over, and job 4 is assigned for ever afterwards. If it leads to e, then we are back where we started, and continue in the same way.

The process continues in this way indefinitely. At each communication, the probability is $\frac{1}{2}$ that one of the points $j1$, $j2$, $j3$, or $j4$ is reached. In this case the communications end, and job 1, 2, 3, or 4 is permanently assigned. Otherwise, the communications continue. Thus the process rotates through the points e, f, g, and h, with a probability that decreases by $\frac{1}{2}$ at each communication. The situation is almost exactly as in Figure 25, with $j2$, $j1$, $j3$ and $j4$ replacing a, b, c, and d respectively.

If f is reached after the second communication, then at the third communication,[73] P1 sends a signal splitting f into $j1$ and g with $\frac{1}{2} - \frac{1}{2}$ probabilities, and the process continues as above. Similarly if g or h is reached after the second communication; that is, the continuation of the process after one of the points e, f, g, or h is reached does not depend on the previous history.

---

[73]In the description of the communication process in Postscripts c through f, joint lotteries must alternate with signals, whereas here, two signals follow each other. This, however, is not essential; we could, if we wish, combine the two signals into a single one, or alternatively, insert a "degenerate" joint lottery between them. Similarly, there is no difficulty in having a joint lottery come just after another one.

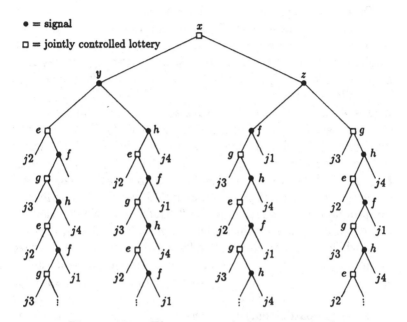

Figure 27. The communication process in Forges's job example. At each node, each alternative has probability $\frac{1}{2}$. The process ends when one of the leaves $j1$, $j2$, $j3$ or $j4$ is reached, corresponding to permanent assignment of job 1, 2, 3, or 4. At each of the intermediate nodes, labelled x, y, z, e, f, g, or h, P2's probability p and the expected payoffs h are as at the corresponding points in Figure 26.

Figure 27 represents the process in tree form. The leaves are reached with probability 1; each leaf—$j1$, $j2$, $j3$, and $j4$—corresponds to one of the job assignments. The payoffs for the leaves can therefore be read off from the payoff matrix (Game 1). The payoffs for the nodes x, y, z, e, f, g, h can then be calculated from the tree.[74] This is how the above table of probabilities and payoffs was obtained.

---

[74]In the case of x, each leaf is reached with probability 1/4 (by symmetry), so one need not sum the infinite series.

Forges's example is a good illustration of the incentive compatibility or "cheatproofness" constraints that govern signalling; in particular, of the concept of "virtual" payoff. Consider, for example, the point f, at which P1 sends one of two signals, say R or L, resulting in $j1$ or g respectively. The signal R is fully revealing: If P1 follows the agreed-on program, then he sends R only if his type is A, so type B should always signal L. But the signal L is not fully revealing; it results in P2's probability for A changing from $\frac{2}{3}$ to $\frac{1}{3}$, and so can occur in either case, whether P1's type is A or B. The expected payoff for type A is 6 whether he signals R or L, so there is no incentive for him to "cheat" (defect from the program). As for type B, his expected payoff is 8 if he follows the program, i.e., signals L. If he "cheats"—signals R—then he will be assigned job 1, which yields him 3. Since $3 < 8$, it is not worthwhile for him to cheat. The "virtual" payoff of 8 is assigned to him at $j1$ in order that his payoff at $j1$, though *actually* different from that at g, should be "virtually" the same; this is needed for the dimartingale property. As we have just seen, the result is incentive compatible only when the actual payoff does not exceed the virtual payoff.

On the other hand, consider a point like y, which splits into the points e and h depending on the signal sent by P1. At both e and h, both types have positive probability. If, say, the payoff for type A were higher at e than at h, then type A would be motivated always to send the signal A; so at h, the probability of A would vanish, which is not the case. So the payoff for type A at e is no more than at h, and similarly at h it is no more than at e. So it is the same at e and h, and similarly for type B it is the same at e and h. Thus the matter of virtual payoff for a type enters the picture only when that type has vanishing probability.

It remains to see that starting with $\frac{1}{2} - \frac{1}{2}$ probabilities on the two types, the payoff $((7,7), 8\frac{2}{3})$ cannot be attained by a bounded number of communications.[75] Indeed, we will now show that the only equilibrium programs using only boundedly many communications are, essentially,[76] the fully revealing one, the fully concealing one, or a mixture of the two by means of a joint lottery. In

---

[75] I.e., for any communication process achieving $((7,7), 8\frac{2}{3})$, and any bound b, the probability is positive that more than b communications will be needed.
[76] I.e., from the point of view of the payoff.

particular, with such a program, neither type of P1 can achieve more than 6.

The situation becomes more transparent when viewed more generally. Let H be the set of feasible individually rational pairs (p, h), and H^1 its projection onto (p, h^1)-space. Suppose that an equilibrium payoff h_0 in $\Gamma_\infty(p_0)$ is attainable with boundedly many communications. Formally, this means that there is a di-martingale of bounded length, $((p_0, h_0), (p_1, h_1), \ldots, (p_b, h_b))$, for which (p_b, h_b) is always in H. So $((p_0, h_0^1), (p_1, h_1^1), \ldots, (p_b, h_b^1))$ is a dimartingle of bounded length, whose convexity directions are the p- and h^1-hyperplanes, for which (p_b, h_b^1) is always in H^1. Now the diconvex hull of a set consists precisely of the expectations of those dimartingales with bounded[77] length that always end in that set (Aumann and Hart [1985], Remark 2.4). So it follows that (p_0, h_0^1) is in the diconvex hull[78] of H^1.

We now calculate H^1 and its diconvex hull. First, note that (p, h) is individually rational for P1 if and only if both her types get at least 0; this is because P2 can simultaneously hold both types to 0, simply by laying her off. Next, (p, h) is individually rational for P2 if and only if h^2 is at least P2's maximum expectation from any of the five possible assignments; specifically, from job 4, job 3, layoff, job 2, and job 1, when p is, respectively, in $[0, .2], [.2, .4], [.4, .6], [.6, .8]$, and $[.8, 1]$. It follows that when $0 < p < 1$,

$$
(p, h^1) \in H^1 \text{ iff } h^1 = \begin{cases} (3, 6) & \text{for} \quad 0 < p < .2 \\ (4, 10) & \text{for} \quad .2 < p < .4 \\ (0, 0) & \text{for} \quad .4 < p < .6 \\ (10, 4) & \text{for} \quad .6 < p < .8 \\ (6, 3) & \text{for} \quad .8 < p < 1. \end{cases}
$$

---

[77]I.e., with a uniform bound b on the length of its realizations.

[78]As distinguished from the diconvex span, which always includes the diconvex hull, and is sometimes much larger (Figure 25). For the record, we note that the above argument shows that in general, an equilibrium payoff h_0 in $\Gamma_\infty(p_0)$ is attainable with boundedly many communications if and only if (p_0, h_0) is in the diconvex hull of H.

When p is at an endpoint of two of the five intervals, then h^1 must be on the straight line segment connecting the points corresponding to those two intervals; for example, if $p = .2$, then h^1 must be in the segment connecting $(3, 6)$ to $(4, 10)$.

When $p = 0$, the definition of feasibility changes; we must add the "virtual" payoffs. This yields all h^1 of the form $(h_A^1, 6)$ with $h_A^1 \geq 3$. Similarly, for $p = 1$ we get all h^1 of the form $(6, h_B^1)$ with $h_B^1 \geq 3$.

The set H^1 is not itself diconvex, since it contains the points $(0, (6, 6))$ and $(1, (6, 6))$, but not the line segment connecting them. Adding this segment—i.e., all the $(p, (6, 6))$ with $0 < p < 1$—is still not enough, since then we have, say, $(1/2, (0, 0))$ and $(1/2, (6, 6))$, but not the line segment connecting them. So for each p, we must add all the convex combinations of $(p, (6, 6))$ with those points (p, h^1) that are in H^1. The reader may verify that the result of this operation is diconvex; therefore this is the diconvex hull of H^1.

What this means is that for any initial p, all equilibrium payoffs are obtained from full revelation, full concealment, or a convex combination of these two by means of an initial joint lottery. In particular, this is so for $p = \frac{1}{2}$; hence in this case, the two types of P1 get the same payoff, which must be between 0 and 6. Thus, neither type of P1 can achieve more than 6, as claimed. In particular, $(7, 7)$ is not achievable by P1 when there are only boundedly many communications.

h. Known Own Payoffs

A case of particular interest is when the uninformed player, P2, knows his own payoff—that is, when P2's stage payoff does not depend on k. This case has been studied by Koren [1988], Shalev [1994], and Israeli [1989]. For a summary of their work, see Forges [1992].

i. Communication Equilibria

A *communication device* is a device that can receive signals from the players, and/or send signals to the players, according to fixed, commonly known rules and probability distributions. The availability of a communication device may significantly enlarge the set of equilibrium payoffs in a game. When the signals can only be sent, one obtains correlated equilibria [Aumann, 1974]; when the device can also receive signals—before sending—one obtains the more general class of *communication equilibria* [Forges, 1986b]. The communication equilibria of repeated games with incomplete information have been extensively studied by F. Forges [1985, 1986a, 1986b, 1988, 1990a]; the material is surveyed in Forges [1992].

j. Perturbations

A *perturbed* game is a game of incomplete information in which, for each player, there is one type with overwhelming probability; all the other types have probability totalling less than ϵ, where ϵ is small. Perturbing a repeated game may yield rather interesting results—the set of equilibria is often significantly different from that of the unperturbed game. The pioneering work in this area is that of the "gang of four" [Kreps, Milgrom, Roberts, and Wilson, 1982]; subsequent contributions were made by Aumann and Sorin [1989], Fudenberg and Levine [1989], and others. This work is surveyed in Sorin [1992].

Bibliography*

Abreu, D., [1988], "On the theory of infinitely repeated games with discounting," *Econometrica* 56, pp. 383-396.

Aumann, R.J. [1959], "Acceptable points in general cooperative *n*-person games," in Tucker and Luce [1959], pp. 287-324.

Aumann, R.J. [1960], "Acceptable points in games of perfect information," *Pacific Journal of Mathematics* 10, pp. 381-417.

Aumann, R.J. [1961], "The core of a cooperative game without side payments," *Transactions of the American Mathematical Society* 98, pp. 539-552.

Aumann, R.J. [1964], "Mixed and behavior strategies in infinite extensive games," in Dresher, Shapley, and Tucker [1964], pp. 627-650.

Aumann, R.J. [1967], "A survey of cooperative games without side payments," in Shubik [1967], pp. 3-27.

Aumann, R.J. [1974], "Subjectivity and correlation in randomized strategies," *Journal of Mathematical Economics* 1, pp. 67-96.

Aumann, R.J. [1987], "Correlated equilibrium as an expression of Bayesian rationality," *Econometrica* 55, pp. 1-18.

Aumann, R.J. and S. Hart [1985], "Biconvexity and bimartingales," *Israel Journal of Mathematics* 54, pp. 159-180.

Aumann, R.J. and S. Hart [1992] (editors), *Handbook of Game Theory with economic applications*, Vol. 1, Elsevier Science Publishers B.V., Amsterdam: North Holland.

Aumann, R.J. and M. Maschler [1966p], "Game theoretic aspects of gradual disarmament," in *Report of the U.S. Arms Control and Disarmament Agency ST-80*, Washington, D.C., Chapter V, pp. V1-V55.

Aumann, R.J. and M. Maschler [1967p], "Repeated games with incomplete information: a survey of recent results," in *Report of the U.S. Arms Control and Disarmament Agency ST-116*, Washington, D.C., Chapter III, pp. 287-403.

---

*The letter "p" after the year of appearance signifies that the item in question is an unpublished preprint or report.

Aumann, R.J. and M. Maschler [1968p], "Repeated games of incomplete information: the zero-sum extensive case," in *Report of the U.S. Arms Control and Disarmament Agency ST-143*, Washington, D.C., Chapter III, pp. 37-116.

Aumann, R.J., M. Maschler and R.E. Stearns [1968p], "Repeated games of incomplete information: an approach to the non-zero sum case," in *Report of the U.S. Arms Control and Disarmament Agency ST-143*, Washington, D.C., Chapter IV, pp. 117-216.

Aumann, R.J. and S. Sorin [1989], "Cooperation and bounded recall," *Games and Economic Behavior* 1, pp. 5-39.

Banks, J.S. and R.L. Calvert [1992], "A battle-of-the-sexes game with incomplete information," *Games and Economic Behavior* 4, pp. 347-372.

Baños, A. [1968], "On pseudogames," *Annals of Mathematical Statistics* 9, pp. 1932-1945.

Barany, I. [1992], "Fair distribution protocols or how the players replace fortune," *Mathematics of Operations Research* 17, pp. 327-340.

Benoit, J.P. and V. Krishna [1985], "Finitely repeated games," *Econometrica* 53, pp. 905-922.

Bergin, J. [1992], "Player type distributions as state variables and information revelation in zero sum repeated games with discounting," *Mathematics of Operations Research* 17, pp. 640-656.

Bewley, T. and E. Kohlberg [1976a], "The asymptotic theory of stochastic games," *Mathematics of Operations Research* 1, pp. 104-125.

Bewley, T. and E. Kohlberg [1976b], "The asymptotic solution of a recursion equation occurring in stochastic games," *Mathematics of Operations Research* 1, pp. 321-336.

Bewley, T. and E. Kohlberg [1978], "On stochastic games with stationary optimal strategies," *Mathematics of Operations Research* 3, pp. 104-125.

Blackwell, D. [1956], "An analogue of the minimax theorem for vector payoffs," *Pacific Journal of Mathematics* 6, pp. 1-8.

Borel, E. [1938] (editor), *Traite du calcul des probabilites et de ses applications*, Vol. 4, Paris: Gauthier-Villars.

Case, J.H. [1979], *Economics and the Competitive Process*, New York: New York University Press.

Dalkey, N. [1953], "Equivalence of information patterns and essentially determinate games," in Kuhn and Tucker [1953], pp. 217–243.

De Meyer, B. [1989p], "Repeated games and multidimensional normal distributions," CORE Discussion Paper 8932, Université Catholique de Louvain, Louvain-la-Neuve.

De Meyer, B. [1992p], "Repeated games and the central limit theorem," Manuscript.

Domansky, V.C., and V.L. Kreps [1994], "'Eventually revealing' repeated games with incomplete information," *International Journal of Game Theory* 23, pp. 89–99.

Doob, J.L. [1953], *Stochastic Processes*, New York: John Wiley & Sons.

Dresher, M., L.S. Shapley, and A.W. Tucker [1964] (editors), *Advances in Game Theory*, Annals of Mathematics Study 52, Princeton: Princeton University Press.

Eatwell, J.M., M. Milgate, and P. Newman [1987], *The New Palgrave: A Dictionary of Economics*, London and Basingstoke: Macmillan.

Filar, J.A. [1976], "Estimation of strategies in a Markov game," *Naval Research Logistics Quarterly* 23, pp. 469–480.

Forges, F. [1984], "A note on Nash equilibria in infinitely repeated games with incomplete information," *International Journal of Game Theory* 13, pp. 179–187.

Forges, F. [1985], "Correlated equilibria in a class of repeated games with incomplete information," *International Journal of Game Theory* 14, pp. 129–150.

Forges, F. [1986a], "Correlated equilibria in repeated games with lack of information on one side: A model with verifiable types," *International Journal of Game Theory* 15, pp. 65–82.

Forges, F. [1986b], "An approach to communication equilibria," *Econometrica* 54, pp. 1375–1385.

Forges, F. [1988], "Communication equilibria in repeated games with incomplete information," *Mathematics of Operations Research* 13, pp. 191–231.

Forges, F. [1990a], "Universal mechanisms," *Econometrica* 58, pp. 1341–1364.

Forges, F. [1990b], "Equilibria with communication in a job market example," *Quarterly Journal of Economics* 105, pp. 375–398.

Forges, F. [1990c], "Repeated games with incomplete information," in Ichiishi, Neyman, and Tauman [1990], pp. 64–76.

Forges, F. [1992], "Repeated games of incomplete information: Non-zero-sum," in Aumann and Hart [1992], pp. 155–177.

Forges, F. [1994], "Non-zero sum repeated games and information transmission," in Megiddo [1994], pp. 65–95.

Fudenberg, D. and D. Levine [1989], "Reputation and equilibrium selection in games with a patient player," *Econometrica* 57, pp. 759–778.

Fudenberg, D. and E. Maskin [1986], "The folk theorem in repeated games with discounting and with incomplete information," *Econometrica* 54, pp. 533–554.

Gleason, A.N. [1987] (editor), *Proceedings of the International Congress of Mathematicians, Berkeley, 1986*, Providence: American Mathematical Society.

Guilbaud, G.T. [1969] (editor), "La Decision: Agrégation et dynamique des ordres de preference," Acts d'un colloque organisé a Aix-en-Provence, Juillet 1967, Paris: Edition du CNRS.

Harsanyi, J.C. [1966], "A general theory of rational behavior in game situations," *Econometrica* 34, pp. 613–634.

Harsanyi, J.C. [1967-8], "Games with incomplete information played by Bayesian players," Parts I, II, III, *Management Science* 14, pp. 159–182, 320–334, 486–502.

Harsanyi, J.C. and R. Selten [1988], *A General Theory of Equilibrium Selection in Games*, Cambridge: MIT Press.

Hart, S. [1985], "Non-zero sum two-person repeated games with incomplete information," *Mathematics of Operations Research* 10, pp. 117–153.

Heuer, M. [1991], "Optimal strategies for the uninformed player," *International Journal of Game Theory* 20, pp. 33–51.

Heuer, M. [1992], "Asymptotically optimal strategies in repeated games with incomplete information," *International Journal of Game Theory* 20, pp. 377–392.

Hildenbrand, W. [1981] (editor), *Advances in Economic Theory: Invited Papers for the Fourth World Congress of the Econometric Society, Aix-en-Provence, 1980*, Cambridge: Cambridge University Press.

Hildenbrand, W. and A. Mas-Colell [1986] (editors), *Essays in Honor of Gerard Debreu*, Amsterdam: North Holland.

Hipel, K.W., M.H. Wang and N.M. Fraser [1988], "Hypergame analysis of the Falkland Malvinas conflict," *International Studies Quarterly* 32, pp. 335–358.

Ho, Y.C. [1980], "Team decision theory and information structures," *Proceedings of the IEEE* 68, pp. 644–654.

Ho, Y.C., M.P. Kastner and E. Wong [1978], "Teams, signalling and information-theory," *IEEE Transactions on Automatic Control* 23, pp. 305–312.

Ichiishi, T., A. Neyman, and Y. Tauman [1990] (editors), *Game Theory and Applications*, San Diego: Academic Press.

Isaacs, R. [1965], *Differential Games*, New York: John Wiley.

Israeli, E. [1989], "Sowing doubt optimally in two-person repeated games," M. Sc. Thesis, Tel-Aviv University [in Hebrew].

Kadane, J.B. and P.D. Larkey [1982], "Subjective probability and the theory of games," *Management Science* 28, pp. 113–120.

Kohlberg, E. [1974], "Repeated games with absorbing states," *Annals of Statistics* 2, pp. 724–738.

Kohlberg, E. [1975a], "Optimal strategies in repeated games with incomplete information," *International Journal of Game Theory* 4, pp. 7–24.

Kohlberg, E. [1975b], "The information revealed in infinitely repeated games of incomlete information," *International Journal of Game Theory* 4, pp. 57–59.

Kohlberg, E. and S. Zamir [1974], "Repeated games of incomplete information: The symmetric case," *Annals of Statistics* 2, p. 1040.

Koren, G. [1988], "Two-person repeated games with incomplete information and observable payoffs," M. Sc. Thesis, Tel-Aviv University.

Kreps, D., P. Milgrom, J. Roberts and R. Wilson [1982], "Rational cooperation in a finitely repeated prisoner's dilemma," *Journal of Economic Theory*
27, pp. 245–252.

Kuhn, H.W. and A.W. Tucker [1953] (editors), *Contributions to the Theory of
Games II*, Annals of Mathematics Study 28, Princeton: Princeton University
Press.

Lakshmivarahan, S. and K.S. Narendra [1981], "Learning algorithms for 2-
person zero-sum stochastic games with incomplete information," *Mathematics
of Operations Research* 6, pp. 379–386.

Lakshmivarahan, S. and K.S. Narendra [1982], "Learning algorithms for 2-
person zero-sum stochastic games with incomplete information—a unified approach," *SIAM Journal on Control and Optimization* 20, pp. 541–552.

Lehrer, E. [1987], "A note on the monotonicity of v_n," *Economics Letters* 23,
pp. 341–342.

Lehrer, E. [1989], "Lower equilibrium payoffs in two-player repeated games
with non-observable actions," *International Journal of Game Theory* 18, pp.
57–89.

Lehrer, E. [1990], "Nash equilibria of n-player repeated games with semistan-
dard information," *International Journal of Game Theory* 19, pp. 191–217.

Lewis, D. [1969], *Convention*, Cambridge: Harvard University Press.

Luce, R.D. and H. Raiffa [1957], *Games and Decisions*, New York: John
Wiley & Sons.

Matthews, S.A. and A. Postlewaite [1989], "Pre-play communication in 2-
person sealed-bid double auctions," *Journal of Economic Theory* 48, pp. 238–
263.

Mayberry, J.P. [1967p], "Discounted repeated games with incomplete information," in *Report of the U.S. Arms Control and Disarmament Agency ST-116*,
Washington, D.C., Chapter V, pp. 435–461.

Maynard Smith, J. [1982], *Evolution and the Theory of Games*, Cambridge:
Cambridge University Press.

Megiddo, N. [1980], "On repeated games with incomplete information played
by non-Bayesian players," *International Journal of Game Theory* 9, pp. 157–
167.

Megiddo, N. [1994] (editor), *Essays in Game Theory in Honor of Michael Maschler*, New York: Springer-Verlag.

Melolidakis, C. [1989], "On stochastic games with lack of information on one side," *International Journal of Game Theory* 18, pp. 1–29.

Melolidakis, C. [1991], "Stochastic games with lack of information on one side and positive stop probabilities," in Raghavan, Ferguson, Parthasarathy and Vrieze [1991], pp. 113–126.

Mertens, J.F. [1972], "The value of two-person zero-sum repeated games: The extensive case," *International Journal of Game Theory* 1, pp. 217–225.

Mertens, J.F. [1981], "Repeated games: An overview of the zero-sum case," in Hildenbrand [1981], pp. 175–182.

Mertens, J.F. [1987a], "Repeated games," in Gleason [1987], pp. 1528–1577.

Mertens, J.F. [1987b], "Repeated Games," in Eatwell, Milgate, and Newman [1987], pp. 205–209.

Mertens, J.F. [1990], "Repeated games," in Ichiishi, Neyman, and Tauman [1990], pp. 77–130.

Mertens, J.F. and A. Neyman [1981], "Stochastic games," *International Journal of Game Theory* 10, pp. 53–56.

Mertens, J.F., S. Sorin, and S.Zamir [1994p], "Repeated Games," Parts A, B, C, CORE Discussion Papers 9420, 9421, 9422, Université Catholique de Louvain, Louvain-la-Neuve.

Mertens, J.F. and S. Zamir [1972], "The value of two-person zero-sum repeated games with lack of information on both sides," *International Journal of Game Theory* 1, pp. 39–64.

Mertens, J.F. and S. Zamir [1976a], "On a repeated game without a recursive structure," *International Journal of Game Theory* 5, pp. 173–182.

Mertens, J.F. and S. Zamir [1976b], "The normal distribution and repeated games," *International Journal of Game Theory* 5, pp. 187–197.

Mertens, J.F. and S. Zamir [1977], "The maximal variation of a bounded martingale," *Israel Journal of Mathematics* 27, pp. 252–276.

Mertens, J.F. and S. Zamir [1980], "Minmax and maxmin of repeated games with incomplete information," *International Journal of Game Theory* 9, pp. 201–215.

Mertens, J.F. and S. Zamir [1982], "Incomplete information games with transcendental values," *Mathematics of Operations Research* 6, pp. 313–318.

Mertens, J.F. and S. Zamir [1985], "Formulation of Bayesian analysis for games with incomplete information," *International Journal of Game Theory* 14, pp. 1–29.

Myerson, R.B. [1984], "2-person bargaining problems with incomplete information," *Econometrica* 52, pp. 461–487.

Nash, J.F. [1951], "Noncooperative games," *Annals of Mathematics* 54, pp. 289–295.

Ponssard, J.P. [1975], "Zero-sum games with almost perfect information," *Management Science Series A: Theory* 21, pp. 794–805.

Ponssard, J.P. [1979], "Strategic role of information on the demand function in an oligopolistic market," *Management Science* 25, pp. 243–250.

Ponssard, J.P. and S. Sorin [1980], "The LP formulation of finite zero-sum games with incomplete information," *International Journal of Game Theory* 9, pp. 99–105.

Ponssard, J.P. and S. Sorin [1982], "Optimal behavioral strategies in 0-sum games with almost perfect information," *Mathematics of Operations Research* 7, pp. 14–31.

Ponssard, J.P. and S. Zamir [1973], "Zero-sum sequential games with incomplete information," *International Journal of Game Theory* 2, pp. 99–107.

Radner, R. [1985], "Repeated principal-agent games with discounting," *Econometrica* 53, pp. 1173–1198.

Radner, R. [1986], "Can bounded rationality resolve the prisoner's dilemma," in Hildenbrand and Mas-Colell [1986], pp. 387–399.

Raghavan, T.E.S., T.S. Ferguson, T. Parthasarathy and O.J. Vrieze [1991] (editors), *Stochastic Games and Related Topics, Essays in Honor of Lloyd Shapley*, Amsterdam: Kluwer Academic Publishers.

Reichert, S.E. [1986], "Spider fights as a test of evolutionary game theory," *American Scientist* 74, pp. 604–610.

Reichert, S.E. and P. Hammerstein [1983], "Game theory in the ecological context," *Annual Review of Ecology and Systematics* 14, 377–409.

Rosenfeld, J.L. [1964], "Adaptive competitive decision processes," in Dresher, Shapley and Tucker [1964], pp. 69–83.

Saaty, T.L. [1969], "An application of decision theory. The development of additional tools," in Guilbaud [1969], pp. 241–250.

Sanghvi, A.P. and M.J. Sobel [1976], "Bayesian games as stochastic processes," *International Journal of Game Theory* 5, pp. 1–22.

Shalev, J. [1994], "Nonzero-sum two-person repeated games with incomplete information and known-own payoffs," *Games and Economic Behavior* 7, pp. 446–459.

Shapley, L.S. [1953], "Stochastic games," *Proceedings of the National Academy of Sciences (USA)* 39, pp. 1095–1100.

Shimkin, N. and A. Shwartz [1993], "Generated performance regions in Markovian systems with competing decision makers," *IEEE Transactions on Automatic Control* 38, pp. 84–95.

Shubik, M. [1967] (editor), *Essays in Mathematical Economics in Honor of Oskar Morgenstern*, Princeton: Princeton University Press.

Shubik, M. [1968], *On the study of disarmament and escalation*, Journal of Conflict Resolution 12, p. 83.

Simon, L.K. and M.B. Stinchcombe [1989], "Extensive form games in continuous time: Pure strategies," *Econometrica* 57, pp. 1171–1214.

Simon, R.S., S. Spież and H. Toruńczyk [1995], "The existence of equilibria in certain games, separation for families of convex functions and a theorem of Borsuk-Ulam type," *Israel Journal of Mathematics*, to appear.

Sorin, S. [1979], "A note on the value of zero-sum sequential repeated games with incomplete information," *International Journal of Game Theory* 8, pp. 217–223.

Sorin, S. [1983], "Some results on the existence of Nash equilibria for non-zero-sum games with incomplete information," *International Journal of Game Theory* 12, pp. 193–205.

Sorin, S. [1984], "'Big Match' with lack of information on one side, (Part I)," *International Journal of Game Theory* 13, pp. 201–255.

Sorin, S. [1985], "On a repeated game with state dependent signalling matrices," *International Journal of Game Theory* 14, pp. 249–272.

Sorin, S. [1989], "On repeated games without a recursive structure: Existence of lim v_n," *International Journal of Game Theory* 18, pp. 45–55.

Sorin, S. [1990], "Supergames," in Ichiishi, Neyman, and Tauman [1990], pp. 46–63.

Sorin, S. [1992], "Repeated games with complete information," in Aumann and Hart [1992], pp. 72–107.

Sorin, S. and S. Zamir [1985], "A two-person game with lack of information on $1\frac{1}{2}$ sides," *Mathematics of Operations Research* 10, pp. 17–23.

Stearns, R. [1967], "A formal information concept for games with incomplete information," in *Report of the U.S. Arms Control and Disarmament Agency ST-116*, Washington, D.C., Chapter IV, pp. 405–433.

Teneketzis, D. and D.A. Castanon [1987], "Informational aspects of a class of subjective games of incomplete information—the static case," *Journal of Optimization Theory and Applications* 54, pp. 413–422.

Tucker, A.W. and R.D. Luce [1959] (editors), *Contributions to the Theory of Games IV*, Annals of Mathematics Study 40, Princeton: Princeton University Press.

Ville, J.A. [1938], "Sur le Theorie generale des jeux ou intervient l'habilite des joueurs," in Borel [1938], pp. 105–113.

Von Neumann, J. and O. Morgenstern [1944], *Theory of Games and Economic Behavior*, Princeton: Princeton University Press.

Wallmeier, H.M. [1988], "Games with informants—an information-theoretical approach towards a game-theoretical roblem," *International Journal of Game Theory* 17, pp. 245–278.

Wang, M., N.M. Fraser and K.W. Hipel [1988], "Modeling misperceptions in games," *Behavioral Science* 33, pp. 207–223.

Waternaux, C. [1983], "Solution for a class of repeated games without recursive structure," *International Journal of Game Theory* 12, pp. 129–160.

Waternaux, C. [1983p], "Minmax and maxmin of repeated games without recursive structure," CORE Discussion Paper 8313, Université Catholique de Louvain, Louvain-la-Neuve.

Weber, R.J. [1981], "Noncooperative games," in *Proceedings of Symposia in Applied Mathematics*, Vol 24, American Mathematical Society, pp. 83–125.

Yareev, L. [1994p], "A note on repeated games with nonmonotonic value," Manuscript.

Zamir, S. [1970], *Repeated Games with Incomplete Information*, Doctoral Thesis, The Hebrew University of Jerusalem, 1970.

Zamir, S. [1972], "On the relation between finitely and infinitely repeated games with incomplete information," *International Journal of Game Theory* 1, pp. 179–198.

Zamir, S. [1973a], "On repeated games with general information function," *International Journal of Game Theory* 2, pp. 215–229.

Zamir, S. [1973b], "On the notion of value for games with infinitely many stages," *Annals of Statistics* 1, pp. 791–796.

Zamir, S. [1992], "Repeated games of incomplete information: zero-sum," in Aumann and Hart [1992], pp. 109–154.

Zermelo, E. [1913], "Über eine Anwendung der Mengenlehre auf die Theorie des Schachspiels," *Proceedings of the Fifth International Congress of Mathematicians (1912)* 2, pp. 501–504.

INDEX

Printed in the United States
By Bookmasters